WAR AND GENOCIDE

WAR AND GENOCIDE

A Concise History of the Holocaust

THIRD EDITION

DORIS L. BERGEN

ROWMAN & LITTLEFIELD
Lanham • Boulder • New York • London

Published by Rowman & Littlefield
A wholly owned subsidiary of The Rowman & Littlefield Publishing Group, Inc.
4501 Forbes Boulevard, Suite 200, Lanham, Maryland 20706
www.rowman.com

Unit A, Whitacre Mews, 26-34 Stannary Street, London SE11 4AB, United Kingdom

British Library Cataloguing in Publication Data

Library of Congress Cataloging-in-Publication Data Available
  Bergen, Doris L., author.
   War and genocide : a concise history of the holocaust / Doris L. Bergen.
   Description: Third edition. | Lanham : Rowman & Littlefield, 2016. | Includes
      bibliographical references and index.
   Identifiers: LCCN 2015043500 (print) | LCCN 2015044038 (ebook) | ISBN
      9781442242272 (cloth : alk. paper) | ISBN 9781442242289 (pbk. : alk. paper) |
      ISBN 9781442242296 (electronic)
   Subjects: LCSH: Germany—History—1933–1945. | National socialism. |
      Antisemitism—Germany—History—20th century. | Holocaust, Jewish
      (1939–1945)—Causes. | World War, 1939–1945—Causes.
   Classification: LCC DD256.5 .B3916 2016 (print) | LCC DD256.5 (ebook) | DDC
      940.53/18—dc23
   LC record available at http://lccn.loc.gov/2015043500

Printed in the United States of America

CONTENTS

Acknowledgments   vii

List of Illustrations and Photo Credits   xi

List of Maps   xix

Introduction: Holocaust, War, and Genocide: Themes and Problems   1

1   Dry Timber: Preconditions   13

2   Leadership and Will: Hitler, the National Socialist German
Workers' Party, and Nazi Ideology   45

3   From Revolution to Routine: Nazi Germany, 1933–1938   69

4   Open Aggression: In Search of War, 1938–1939   101

5   Brutal Innovations: War against Poland and the So-Called
Euthanasia Program, 1939–1940   129

6   Expansion and Systematization: Exporting War and Terror,
1940–1941   167

7   War and Genocide: Decisions and Dynamics in the Peak Years
of Killing, 1942–1943   207

8   Flashover: The Killing Centers, 1942–1944   237

9   Death Throes and Killing Frenzies, 1944–1945   275

Conclusion: Legacies of Atrocity   297

Sources and Suggestions for Further Reading   311

Index   345

About the Author   361

ACKNOWLEDGMENTS

Many people contributed to this book in countless ways. I appreciate everyone who helped with the previous editions, and in the meantime, have incurred new debts of gratitude. Students in my classes at the University of Toronto continue to educate and inspire me. I have also benefited from the undergraduate and graduate students, professors, teachers, and members of the public I encounter through the Holocaust Educational Foundation's Summer Institute on the Holocaust and Jewish Civilization at Northwestern University, the Genocide and Human Rights University Program, the Hess and Silberman seminars at the U.S. Holocaust Memorial Museum, Facing History and Ourselves, the Neuberger Holocaust Education Centre, and Toronto's Holocaust Education Week.

In Toronto some wonderful teaching assistants, many of them now professors, have deepened my understanding of the Holocaust and the challenges of teaching about it: thanks to Tatjana Lichtenstein, Tomaz Jardim, Rebecca Carter-Chand, Sophie Roberts, Ryan Masters, Vojin Majstorovic, Deborah Barton, Susan Papp, Tomasz Frydel, Maris Rowe-McCulloch, Stephanie Corazza, Nisrine Rahal, and Joanna Krongold. I am also grateful to Martina Cucchiara, Steven Schroeder, Glen Ryland, Elizabeth Strauss, Nina Paulovicova, Max Bergholz, Jon Soske, Anna Hájková, Svitlana Frunchak, Carson Phillips, Birga Meyer, Yaron Pasher, and Stacy Hushion for all I learned from reading their work.

At Toronto I have the privilege of learning from, and in some cases teaching with, remarkable colleagues: thanks to Sol Goldberg, Jeffrey Kopstein, Jacques Kornberg, Mark Meyerson, Melanie Newton, Derek Penslar, Jim

Retallack, Rebecca Wittmann, Piotr Wróbel, and Lynne Viola. Even a special thank you cannot convey how much I owe to Michael Marrus and Anna Shternshis, two incredible scholars and cherished friends.

Many people provided corrections, comments, practical assistance, and insights that helped me revise, and I hope improve, the book. I gratefully recognize the following and acknowledge others I may have forgotten to mention: Frank Bajohr, Seth Bernstein, Peter Black, Daniel Blatman, Christopher Browning, Laura Crago, Susan Crane, Alexandra Garbarini, Norman Goda, Gary Hamburg, Elizabeth Heineman, John-Paul Himka, Michaela Hoenicke-Moore, Sara Horowitz, Mark Jantzen, Uta Larkey, Andrea Löw, Semion Lyandres, Jürgen Matthäus, Geoffrey Megargee, Dan Michman, David Oliver, Mark Roseman, Na'ama Shik, Vincent Slatt, Scott Spector, Nathan Stoltzfus, Barry Trachtenberg, and John Williams. Thanks also to Rafał Witkowski and Miłosz Sosnowski, superb historians who translated my book into Polish and drew my attention to some issues that needed rethinking. Patricia Heberer-Rice deserves extra thanks for answering my questions about "euthanasia" killing sites and much more; Paul Jaskot challenged me to think harder about photographs and then generously helped me do so.

Three anonymous readers for the press provided encouragement and valuable suggestions. Thanks to the conference in Poland organized by Andrzej Kaminski, "Recovering Forgotten History: The Image of East-Central Europe in English-Language Academic Textbooks," I received incisive and extremely useful feedback from three Polish academics: Grzegorz Berendt, Paweł Skibiński, and Jakub Tyszkiewicz.

As research assistants on this project, Madeline Klimek, Jaclyn Buckley, and Ryan Masters have been absolutely brilliant, each in their own way. Thank you all, and thanks also to the Social Science and Humanities Research Council of Canada and the Chancellor Rose and Ray Wolfe Chair of Holocaust Studies for the necessary funding. And what would I do without the support and kindness of Galina Vaisman and Emily Springgay at the University of Toronto's Anne Tanenbaum Centre for Jewish Studies?

Michael J. Fisher, cartographer, went above and beyond—and then beyond that—to make the maps. Everyone at the U.S. Holocaust Memorial Museum Photo Archives was wonderful: Judith Cohen creatively and generously shared her vast knowledge, and Caroline Waddell Koehler has been enormously helpful. It is a pleasure to work with Rowman and Littlefield: Audra Figgins has efficiently and enthusiastically guided this book though the production process, and Susan McEachern, in my view, is the perfect editor—patient, persistent, flexible, firm, insightful, informed, and encouraging in all the right ways. I am deeply grateful to her.

I am very lucky to have some friends who know a lot about the subject of this book and are always willing to discuss it with me. Thank you to Daniel Mattern, Catherine Schlegel, and Linda Pardo! Thanks also to my son, Arlo Harink, for making me laugh. Finally I want to acknowledge some extraordinary people who have shared with me, and through this book with you, the readers, their profound knowledge and personal experience of the Holocaust: Sara Ginaite, Livia Prince, Gerhard Weinberg, and the late Henry Friedlander. This book owes so much to them. Its failures and shortcomings, however, are my responsibility.

LIST OF ILLUSTRATIONS
AND PHOTO CREDITS

Note: USHMM is the United States Holocaust Memorial Museum.

Cover

Jewish women herded into SS headquarters during a confiscation action in the Lodz ghetto. USHMM, courtesy of Beit Lohamei Haghetaot (Ghetto Fighters' House Museum).

Introduction

A young girl in the Loborgrad concentration camp in Croatia. USHMM, courtesy of Memorijalni Muzej Jasenovac.   10

Chapter 1

German Jewish soldiers celebrating Hanukkah in the field during World War I. USHMM, courtesy of Zydowski Instytut Historyczny Instytut Naukowo-Badawczy.   20

A group of religious Jews on a kayaking excursion. USHMM, courtesy of Marilka (Mairanz) Ben Naim, Ita (Mairanz) Mond and Tuvia Mairanz.   21

The Virovitch family gathers at the Kovno train station to bid farewell to Abrasha Virovitch who was immigrating to Palestine. USHMM, courtesy of Sara Ginaite.   23

Members of the German boxing club "Sparta" in 1929. USHMM, courtesy of Hans Firzlaff.   29

A Roma family next to their caravan. USHMM, courtesy of Kore Yoors.
Photographer: Jan Yoors.   30

Dr. Sophie Ehrhardt, Robert Ritter's collaborator at the Racial Hygiene
and Criminal Biology Institute, poses with a Romani woman.
Bundesarchiv Koblenz.   31

A scene from around 1929 in the Eldorado, a nightclub frequented by
the Berlin homosexual community. USHMM, courtesy of Schwules
Museum.   34

A 1933 poster depicting the Nazi view of Freemasonry and its purported
links to a Jewish world conspiracy. USHMM, courtesy of Hans Pauli.   36

Chapter 2

Adolf Hitler with Benito Mussolini during the German Chancellor's
official visit to Italy. USHMM, courtesy of Richard Freimark.
Photographer: Heinrich Hoffmann/Studio of Heinrich Hoffmann.   47

Illustration from a 1938 German children's book. USHMM, courtesy
of published source (Ernst Hiemer, *Der Giftpilz: Erzählungen*
[*The Poisonous Mushroom: Stories*]. *Der Stürmer*, c. 1938.)   54

Antisemitic poster for *Der Stürmer*. USHMM, courtesy of Deutsches
Historisches Museum GmbH.   55

Joseph Goebbels caught off guard. Alfred Eisenstaedt/Pix Inc./TimePix.
Photographer: Alfred Eisenstaedt.   59

Himmler speaks to an inmate at Dachau in 1936, during an SS inspection
of the camp. USHMM, courtesy of KZ Gedenkstätte Dachau.   61

Chapter 3

Photo montage by German artist John Heartfield, titled "The Gallows
Greeting." John Heartfield, 1933.   72

Watercolor by Johannes Steyer, a German Jehovah's Witness.
Hans Hesse, ed., *Persecution and Resistance of Jehovah's Witnesses during
the Nazi Regime 1933–1945*. Bremen, Germany: Edition Temmen,
2000. Used by permission.   74

A woman emerging from a Jewish-owned business in violation of the
April 1933 boycott. USHMM, courtesy of Der Stürmer Archive,
Stadtarchiv Nuremberg.   77

A filmstrip of the Reich Propaganda office titled, "The Terrible Legacy
of an Alcoholic Woman." USHMM, courtesy of Roland Klemig.   81

Members of the League of German Girls. USHMM, courtesy of
Foto-Willinger Collection, Hoover Institution Archives.   83

Germans filling an entire concert hall give the Nazi salute. A group of
girls in traditional peasant costume stand at the front of the audience.
USHMM, courtesy of James Sanders.   85

German spectators at a political rally raise their arms in the Nazi
salute in Berlin. USHMM, courtesy of the Julien Bryan Archive.
Photographer: Julien Bryan.   86

Group portrait of German girls outside their school in front of a Nazi flag.
USHMM, courtesy of Lilli Eckstein Stern.   94

Chapter 4

A Jewish woman washes clothes in the Zbaszyn refugee camp in Poland.
USHMM, courtesy of Michael Irving Ashe.   108

The synagogue in Ober Ramstadt, Hesse is destroyed by fire.
USHMM, courtesy of Trudy Isenberg. Photographer: Georg Schmidt.   109

Male Jews arrested during Kristallnacht in Baden and forced to
march under guard through the town streets. USHMM, courtesy
of Lydia Chagoll.   110

A team of Austrians pulling on a long rope or stick in an attempt to
dismantle part of the Tempelgasse synagogue after its destruction
during Kristallnacht. USHMM, courtesy of Dokumentationsarchiv
des Österreichischen Widerstandes.   111

A carnival parade in February 1939 in the south German town of
Neustadt mocks Jews. USHMM, courtesy of Stadtarchiv Neustadt.   113

Two German Jewish refugee women stand behind the counter of the
Elite Provision Store in Shanghai in 1939 or 1940. USHMM,
courtesy of Ralph Harpuder.   122

Joseph Fiszman poses with four Chinese children in a store in Shanghai.
USHMM, courtesy of Joseph Fiszman.   123

Group portrait of Jewish refugee girls who had come to England on the
Kindertransport. USHMM, courtesy of Alisa Tennenbaum.   126

Chapter 5

Rabbi David Lifszyc and another man pose in front of a cabinet full of
Torah scrolls smuggled out of the Polish city of Suwalki. USHMM,
courtesy of Chaya Lifshitz Waxman.   135

Poles seized during the "pacification" of Bydgoszcz (Bromberg) in
September 1939. USHMM, courtesy of Gertrude Adams.   138

Jews arrested in the Podgorze neighborhood of Krakow lined up with
their hands against the wall of a building. USHMM, courtesy of
Instytut Pamieci Narodowej.   139

SS personnel lead Polish women into the forest to be killed. USHMM,
courtesy of the Main Commission for the Prosecution of the Crimes
against the Polish Nation.   140

Shmuel Grossman recites the morning prayer service in his bed in the
Lodz ghetto. Beit Lohamei Haghetaot. Photographer: Mendel Grossman.   147

German soldiers watch Jewish women shop at the outdoor market of
the Lublin ghetto. USHMM, courtesy of Evan Bukey.   148

Lodz ghetto Jewish council chairman Mordechai Chaim Rumkowski
officiates at the wedding of Nachman Zonabend and Irka Kuperminc.
USHMM, courtesy of Nachman Zonabend. Photographer:
Mendel Grossman.   153

A Polish gentile woman and two Polish Jewish men forced to walk
together, probably to an execution site, 1940s. USHMM, courtesy
of the Dokumentationsarchiv des Oesterreichischen Widerstandes.   156

Copy of memorandum signed by Adolf Hitler authorizing the T4
("Euthanasia") program. USHMM, courtesy of the National Archives
and Records Administration, College Park.   161

A view of the transport of disabled men from the Bruckberg long-term
care facility in Germany. Archiv Diakonie Neuendettelsau.   162

Chapter 6

The ruins of Rotterdam after its bombing by the German air force on
May 14, 1940. USHMM, courtesy of Instytut Pamieci Narodowej.   171

Marie-Therese Delmez washing Isaac Hochberger, the Jewish child she
sheltered in her home, in a wartime picture. Yad Vashem Photo Archives.   172

French colonial troops and their German captors in an unidentified
POW camp. USHMM, courtesy of Instytut Pamieci Narodowej.   175

Prisoners gather outside their barracks in the Gurs concentration
camp in France. USHMM, courtesy of Hans Landesberg.   177

A Serbian gendarme escorts a group of Roma to their execution.
USHMM, courtesy of Muzej Revolucije Narodnosti Jugoslavije.   184

Germans pose near the bodies of recently murdered Serbian civilians in 1941. USHMM, courtesy of Mrs. John Titak III. 186

German troops at the edge of a trench used as a mass grave for the bodies of Jews and Roma. USHMM, courtesy of Dokumentationsarchiv des Oesterreichischen Widerstandes. 187

Jewish deportees under German guard march through the streets of Kamenets-Podolsk to an execution site outside of the city. USHMM, courtesy of Ivan Sved. Photographer: Gyula Spitz. 197

Jewish deportees march through the streets of Kamenets-Podolsk to an execution site outside the city. USHMM, courtesy of Ivan Sved. Photographer: Gyula Spitz. 198

A column of Soviet POWs heading toward the rear and internment. USHMM, courtesy of Archiwum Dokumentacji Mechanicznej. Photographer: Heinrich Hoffmann/Studio of Heinrich Hoffmann. 206

Chapter 7

A German soldier holding a camera directs the hanging of a Russian woman by unidentified collaborators. USHMM, courtesy of Belarusian State Archive of Documentary Film and Photography. 216

Clandestine photograph of a Polish political prisoner and medical experimentation victim in the Ravensbrück concentration camp. USHMM, courtesy of Anna Hassa Jarosky and Peter Hassa. 220

The corpse of a German Jew who committed suicide by running into the electrified barbed-wire fence in Mauthausen. USHMM, courtesy of National Archives and Records Administration, College Park. Photographer: Paul Ricken. 221

Assault units of the 62nd Soviet army battle the Germans in Stalingrad. USHMM, courtesy of the National Archives and Records Administration, College Park. Photographer: Georgy Zelma. 224

German antisemitic poster from after December 7, 1941: "Behind the Enemy Powers, the Jew." USHMM Photo Archives. 229

Antisemitic poster produced in Italy in 1942. USHMM, courtesy of Alessandra Nacamu. 230

War 1939–1945. Limburg. Stalag XII A, prisoners of war camp. Indian prisoners. V-P-HIST-01634-29A, public 1943-10. Copyright ICRC. 232

Chapter 8

Hlinka guardsmen oversee the deportation of Slovak Jews.
Copyright CTK—Photo 2015.   243

Wedding portrait of Salomon Schrijver and his bride who were
married in the Jewish quarter of Amsterdam. USHMM, courtesy
of Samuel (Schrijver) Schryver.   244

A young Jewish woman in the Lodz ghetto writes a letter before being
transported to Chelmno. USHMM, courtesy of Leopold Page
Photographic Collection. Photographer: Mendel Grossman.   246

Drawing by an unidentified artist of camp guards watching prisoners
die in a gas chamber. USHMM Photo Archives.   249

Auschwitz women inmates sort through a huge pile of shoes from
a transport of Hungarian Jews. USHMM, courtesy of Yad Vashem
(Public Domain). Photographer Bernhardt Walter/Ernst Hofmann. 254

Close-up portrait of a young man in the Bedzin ghetto. USHMM,
courtesy of Emanuel Shiber, Esq.   255

Two girls in the Kovno ghetto wearing Stars of David. USHMM,
courtesy of Henia Wisgardisky Lewin.   262

Ignac Greenbaum with two other Jewish refugees who joined the
Polish Army formed in the Soviet Union during the war. USHMM,
courtesy of Shlomo Liwer.   267

Partisans Sara Ginaite and Ida Vilenchiuk in Vilna during liberation.
Copyright Photo Soyuz Agency.   268

SS troops pass a block of burning housing during the suppression of the
Warsaw ghetto uprising. USHMM, courtesy of National Archives and
Records Administration, College Park.   270

Aerial view of German troops marching down Sienna Street after the
destruction of the Warsaw ghetto. USHMM, courtesy of Tad Brezkis.
Photographer: Tad Brezkis.   271

Chapter 9

Jewish women watch as men are rounded up in Ioannina, Greece, 1944.
USHMM, courtesy of Bundesarchiv Koblenz.   276

Jewish women and children from Subcarpathian Rus' await selection on
the ramp at Auschwitz-Birkenau. USHMM, courtesy of Yad Vashem
(Public Domain). Photographer: Bernhardt Walter/Ernst Hofmann. 284

Jewish women and children from Subcarpathian Rus' at Auschwitz-
Birkenau, near the gas chambers. USHMM, courtesy of Yad Vashem
(Public Domain). Photographer: Bernhardt Walter/Ernst Hofmann.   285

SS officers and female auxiliaries on a wooden bridge in Solahütte. One
man holds an accordion. USHMM, courtesy of Anonymous Donor.   287

Ruins of the Kovno ghetto. USHMM, courtesy of George
Kadish/Zvi Kadushin. Photographer: George Kadish/Zvi Kadushin.   289

A new family, including three survivors of the Kovno ghetto: Tanja, who
survived hidden by a gentile woman; Sara Ginaite, partisan fighter;
Misha Rubinson, partisan fighter and leader; and Anja, born after
the war. Courtesy of Sara Ginaite.   290

Prisoners passing through a village on a death march from Dachau
to Wolfratshausen. akg-images/Benno Gantner. Photographer:
Benno Gantner.   291

Polish Jews, refugees in the Soviet interior, bake matzah for Passover,
1945. USHMM, courtesy of Hynda Szczukowski Halpren.   295

Conclusion

Jewish youth liberated at Buchenwald lean out the windows of
a train, as it pulls away from the station. USHMM, courtesy
of Robert Waisman.   299

Jewish refugees who had fled to Bukhara during the war, on Victory Day,
May 9, 1945. USHMM, courtesy of Shlomo Liwer.   300

Soviet troops lead German POWs past the Majdanek crematoria and
the remains of prisoners killed there. Copyright Sovfoto/Eastfoto.   301

A Hungarian Jewish teenager identifies the body of his father, who was
shot in the woods while on a death march. USHMM, courtesy of
National Archives and Records Administration, College Park.   302

German civilians watch a film about the atrocities of Bergen-Belsen and
Buchenwald. USHMM, courtesy of Imperial War Museum.   307

German civilians exit the cinema where they were forced to see a film
showing atrocities perpetrated in Buchenwald and Bergen-Belsen.
USHMM, courtesy of Imperial War Museum.   308

David Greenfield sits in the center of a large Star of David. USHMM,
courtesy of Joseph and Rachel Greenfield.   309

LIST OF MAPS

Europe on the Eve of World War II xx

Border Changes in Central Europe, 1938–1940 105

Jewish Escape within Europe, 1933–1941 120

Jewish Refugees and Exiles from Europe, 1933–1941 120

Division of Poland, September 1939 132

Invasion of the Soviet Union and Major Killing Sites 189

Jewish Escape, Evacuation, and Exile within the Soviet Union
and East Asia 190

"Euthanasia" and Killing Centers, Major Camps and Ghettos
in Greater Germany 236

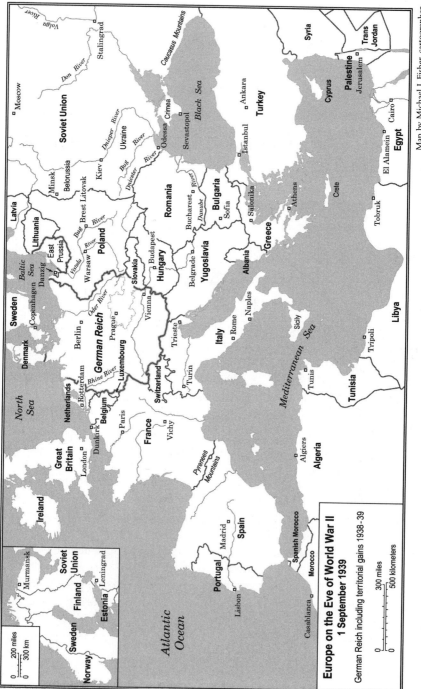

Europe on the Eve of World War II
1 September 1939

German Reich including territorial gains 1938-39

300 miles
500 kilometers

Map by Michael J. Fisher, cartographer

Introduction

HOLOCAUST, WAR, AND GENOCIDE
Themes and Problems

This book makes four major claims about the Holocaust. (1) The Holocaust was an event of global proportions with worldwide repercussions. Any effort to grasp it in its entirety must begin with recognition of that massive scope. (2) The Holocaust happened step by step. It occurred over time, as a process with no easily determined beginning or end. (3) Intertwined with World War II, the Holocaust needs to be understood in the context of that conflict. Without the war, the Holocaust would not—and could not—have happened. (4) Jews were the primary targets of Nazi German destruction, but their fates were linked with those of other victim groups: people with disabilities, Roma and Sinti, Polish elites, Soviet prisoners of war, and homosexual men.

These four points are connected by an insight so obvious it hardly needs to be stated, but it does: the Holocaust was an event in *human* history. Everyone involved—victims, witnesses, collaborators, rescuers, and perpetrators—was a human being with human feelings and needs. Recognizing that shared humanity does not excuse the killers or somehow soften the past. If anything it makes studying the Holocaust more painful.

To develop these themes, this book takes an integrated approach, drawing on personal accounts to not only illustrate but also complicate general claims. So it seems fitting to begin with one such account. Henry Friedlander was born Heinz Egon Friedländer in 1930 in Berlin. His parents were Jewish, and in late 1941 the family was among the first German Jews deported to the east, where they were forced into the ghetto in Lodz (Łódź), in German-occupied Poland. Henry's father was a doctor, and Henry remembered accompanying him to the "Gypsy section" of the ghetto, where he provided medical care to the Roma whom German police had confined there. Other recollections include a hanging in the ghetto that the authorities forced all Jews to watch. Henry's mother stood behind him and covered his eyes with her hands, to spare her son that traumatizing sight.

In 1944, with the Soviet Army nearing Lodz, the Germans closed the ghetto and sent most of its remaining inhabitants to Auschwitz. There Henry was separated from his mother, whom he never saw again. Probably she went straight to the gas chamber, though decades after the war, her son still wondered whether she might have "made it" to Bergen-Belsen and died there. Henry managed to survive Auschwitz, thanks in part to help from a non-Jewish, Communist prisoner who developed a bond with him because they came from the same part of Berlin. As the Germans retreated, they shuffled prisoners from Auschwitz westward through a series of labor and concentration camps. Henry and his father lived through that ordeal, too, until they were liberated by the British in 1945. A Jewish organization arranged for Henry to go to Canada, but his father decided to stay in Germany. So at the age of fifteen, Henry arrived in Hamilton, Ontario, alone. Initially placed in an eighth-grade class, he soon moved on to the United States. He earned a BA from Temple University in 1953 and a PhD from the University of Pennsylvania in 1968.

Henry Friedlander became a historian, an expert on the Holocaust. But he did not focus on his own experiences or even on the Nazi destruction of Jews. Instead Friedlander's most influential work examined the murder of the disabled. His book, *The Origins of Nazi Genocide: From Euthanasia to the Final Solution*, published in 1995, remains the best study of the subject, in any language. With his wife Sybil Milton, also a historian, Friedlander became a tenacious proponent of including disabled and Roma victims in scholarly and popular discussions of the Holocaust, for instance at the U.S. Holocaust Memorial Museum in Washington, DC. Something of Friedlander's personal history lives on in that museum too, because the children's exhibit, "Daniel's Story," includes elements modeled on his childhood experience.

The Holocaust took Friedlander from Germany to Poland, Canada, and the United States. Others traveled even further: Jewish refugees fled central Europe for Turkey, Palestine, India, Uganda, Cuba, and Shanghai; Soviet soldiers from Mongolia and Kazakhstan ended the war in Berlin and Vienna. The Holocaust, in other words, was a global event. Perpetrators, victims, witnesses, beneficiaries, collaborators, and rescuers came from all over Europe and else-where in the world.

Another major theme of this book involves chronology. As Friedlander's life shows, the Holocaust was not a single event or the result of one decision but a process that developed unevenly over time. This obvious point is easily forgotten in what one professor has described as her students' rush to get to the gas chambers. The Holocaust, however, began long before the first gassings at Auschwitz-Birkenau and encompassed many other methods and sites of killing. In fact Auschwitz is not mentioned until the second half of this book, and the first people killed with gas there in September 1941 were not Jews but Soviet prisoners of war and camp inmates who had become too weak to work.

This book situates the Holocaust in the context of World War II, the largest and deadliest conflict in human history, and the interconnection between these world historical events constitutes a third central theme. War and conquest delivered into Nazi German hands the Jews of eastern and southeastern Europe—Poland, Yugoslavia, Greece, Ukraine, Belorussia, Hungary, and elsewhere—as well as the smaller Jewish populations of the west, including the Netherlands, Belgium, and France. Approximately 95 percent of the Jews killed between 1939 and 1945 lived outside Germany's prewar borders.

At the same time, war—in particular the Nazi war of annihilation to Germany's east—increased the numbers and kinds of victims, as programs of persecution, expulsion, and murder demanded and created even more enemies. Mass killings of non-Jews, including thousands of black French soldiers and several million Soviet prisoners of war, were also part of the Nazi German war effort, a war launched for the related goals of race and space: so-called racial purification and territorial expansion. War provided killers with both a cover and an excuse for murder; in wartime, killing was normalized, and extreme measures could be justified with arguments about the need to defend the homeland and defeat the enemy. Yet war also ended the Holocaust. Without Allied military defeat of Nazi Germany, there would have been no Jewish survivors, including no Henry Friedlander, to tell the tale.

There is no doubt that hatred of Jews constituted the core of Nazi ideology. Hitler and his associates preached what the scholar Saul Friedländer calls "redemptive antisemitism": the belief that Jews were the root of all evil and that Germany could be saved from collapse only by total removal of Jews and Jewish influence. Jews were the main target of Nazi genocide; against the Jews Hitler's Germany mobilized all its resources: bureaucratic, military, legal, scientific, economic, and intellectual.

Nevertheless, as Henry Friedlander pointed out years ago, it was not Jews but mentally and physically disabled people who became targets of the first large-scale, systematic killings in Nazi Germany, under the euphemistically labeled "Euthanasia Program." This program, like the assault on Roma people, shared with the genocide of the Jews personnel, methods of killing, and goals of so-called racial purification. At the same time, Nazi Germany persecuted, incarcerated, massacred, worked to death, and deliberately starved millions of people in the occupied territories to the east—non-Jewish Poles, especially those in leadership positions; Soviet prisoners of war, accused partisans, and people in large cities. Back home the regime attacked German Communists, gay men, Jehovah's Witnesses, Afro-Germans, and other people deemed unwanted in Hitler's "new order." Whether or not one considers members of any or all of these groups to belong under the label "victims of the Holocaust," their fates were entwined in significant ways with that of the Jews targeted and murdered in the Nazi quest for race and space. This book seeks to identify and explore connections between and among victim groups, not in the interest of establishing some kind of hierarchy of suffering but with the hope of coming to understand how state-sponsored programs of violence and atrocity function and offering at least a glimpse into how they are experienced by those who suffer their ravages.

These are ambitious aims for a short book. Indeed, although this book is concise, it will not make dealing with the Nazi era, the war, and the Holocaust easy. That history is complex, and I have tried to present it honestly and as fully as possible in a brief survey. Nor do I promise that this small book will resolve the big questions that might be on your mind as you approach this topic: Why did such horrible things happen? If there is a God, how could such atrocities have been possible? What are human beings that they can inflict such agony on other people? Finding answers to those kinds of questions is a lifelong challenge, not something you can accomplish with one book or one class.

Nevertheless, this book will help you address some modest yet important questions regarding the history of Nazism, World War II, and the Holocaust. Who was involved and in what ways? What motivated people to behave as they did? How—through what processes—did large numbers of people, some of them "ordinary," some less so, become murderers of larger numbers of other people? How did the targets of attacks respond, and what strategies did they develop in their quest to live and keep their loved ones alive? If you care enough about the past to try to understand these matters, perhaps you will also discover some insights that help you think about brutality and suffering in our own world. What follows here is only an introduction to a subject so broad and multidimensional that you could probably read for the rest of your life and never get through all that has been written about it. I hope that you will read this book in conjunction with some of the many excellent studies that go into more depth on specific topics. A list of sources for each chapter, suggestions for further reading, and relevant movies is included at the end of the book.

A NOTE ON VOCABULARY AND SOME WORDS OF WARNING

The Holocaust originated in Nazi Germany but it by no means involved only Germans as its perpetrators, victims, enablers, or heroes. These people came from all over Europe and even farther away, drawn into a deadly force field of developments with worldwide reverberations. By the same token, many of the ideas and attitudes that fed into the Holocaust had roots and branches outside Germany, particularly elsewhere in Europe. Although much of the discussion in this book focuses on Germany, it is important to keep in mind that scholarship, opinions, and prejudices flowed freely across national borders throughout the modern era; most Germans of the 1920s and 1930s were more typical than they were atypical for Europeans in their time.

Discussing the Nazi era raises some thorny problems of vocabulary. Should we say "Nazis" or "Germans" when referring to the people of Hitler's Germany? On the one hand, using the term "Nazis" in this general way is misleading. It implies that Hitler's supporters were not themselves Germans and that the "real Germans" were somehow untouched by Nazism. On the other hand, simply saying "Germans" suggests that all Germans marched in step behind Hitler. That was not the case either. German Jews were excluded from the Nazi movement by definition—that is, they were not permitted to join the Nazi Party or its affiliates—and the same was generally true of Germans deemed disabled, Sinti and Roma, Afro-Germans, and other outsiders. Nevertheless, those people too were Germans. Moreover, some Germans also opposed the regime and tried to distance themselves from it. Edith Stein, a philosopher, convert from Judaism, and Carmelite nun, who wrote to Pope Pius XI in 1933 warning about persecution of Jews in Nazi Germany, was a German; so were two men who tried to assassinate Hitler: the carpenter Georg Elser and Colonel Claus Schenk von Stauffenberg.

Other words and phrases raise problems of their own. Does the noun "Poles" include Polish Jews? Does it encompass ethnic Germans and Ukrainians who lived within the prewar boundaries of Poland? Does it mean the same thing now, decades after the war, as it did in the 1930s and 1940s? Is there such a thing as a "baptized Jew" or a "Jewish Christian"? Or should we reject those labels, though they were widely used at the time, in favor of Nazi legal terminology—"non-Aryan Christians"—or cumbersome, detailed descriptions: "converts to Christianity from Judaism or the children and in some cases grandchildren of such converts?"

Throughout this book, I try to draw attention to the challenges of labeling and to be as precise as possible, while recognizing the unavoidability of generalization. I use the term "Roma" to refer to the Rom or Romani people, rather than "Gypsy," which has a pejorative taint, like its German equivalent *Zigeuner*.

When referring specifically to a subgroup of Rom who lived in Germany, I use "Sinti" or "Roma and Sinti." I have tried to update my own vocabulary in keeping with current usage, so that this edition refers to another group targeted under Nazism as "people with disabilities" or "the disabled" rather than "people deemed handicapped." But I have not changed the references to "homosexual men" to reflect contemporary ways of talking about sexual diversity—LGBTQ or even gays and lesbians—because doing so would create a misleading impression of the possibilities for public or even private expression of a whole range of sexual identities in Europe in the 1930s and 1940s.

It is difficult, perhaps impossible, to talk about Nazism and the Holocaust without using Nazi vocabulary. But Nazi words and phrases carry with them some nasty baggage. Referring to people as "Aryans," "non-Aryans," or "Mischlinge" reproduces categorizations and power relations based on brutal notions of superiority and the value of human lives. Calling programs of mass murder "euthanasia," "extermination," or a "final solution" implies that killing was somehow merciful to its victims, that they were vermin, or that destroying them solved some existing problem. These were the Nazis' terms of choice precisely for such reasons. The brilliant German Jewish scholar of literature and diarist Victor Klemperer observed early on how the Nazi movement developed its own way of speaking and writing German to produce a lingo Klemperer called LTI, *Lingua tertii Imperii*, the language of the Third Reich.

In this book I try to avoid euphemisms and words that echo Nazi ways of thinking and to use active rather than passive formulations. German Jews did not simply "disappear" in the 1930s and 1940s: someone excluded, expelled, arrested, robbed, and tormented them. Hundreds of thousands of Jews were not merely "deported" to Treblinka: someone rounded them up, stole their possessions, forced them onto trains and trucks, guarded them to prevent escape, pushed them into the gas chamber, and murdered them by suffocation. Millions of people did not mysteriously "perish" in the Holocaust: other people killed them, by shooting, beating, starving, or working them to death. Such direct language can be jarring, and it should be. What would it mean if studying genocide felt comfortable?

An additional word of caution: prejudices always reveal more about the people who hold them than they do about those at whom they are directed. You may not learn much about Judaism or Jews by studying antisemitism, but you can learn quite a lot about antisemites, their insecurities, and their fears. By the same token, examining the lives of Jews in Europe before World War II is important in its own right, but it will not answer the question as to why antisemites hated Jews any more than studying African American history will explain why white supremacists hate black people. Prejudices are habits of thought that produce their own justifications; they are not reasoned responses to objective realities. When you read descriptions of prejudice and persecution, keep in mind that such attitudes and actions were based on imaginings about people rather than on who those people really were.

To illustrate this point, it is useful to observe that Nazi ideology about all of the target groups followed similar patterns. Proponents of Nazi ideas focused their attacks on people who were already suspect in the eyes of many Germans before Hitler came to power. They then echoed and enlarged familiar hatreds and linked them to current concerns and anxieties. For example, in the 1920s and 1930s, many Germans were distressed by Germany's defeat in World War I. So, no matter which of their supposed enemies they described—Jews, homosexuals, Communists, Jehovah's Witnesses—Nazi propagandists accused them of causing Germany to lose the war. Similarly, many Germans in Hitler's time were worried about decadence, criminality, and supposed racial degeneration. Nazi thinkers charged every enemy group with promoting immorality, spreading crime, and polluting the bloodstream. Whether they were talking about Poles, Roma, Jews, Afro-Germans, or people with disabilities, Nazi propaganda used similar slurs. Of course there were historical specificities in each case too, but these common threads added to Nazism's contagious effect.

LOOKING AT HOLOCAUST PHOTOGRAPHS

With each edition of this book, I have included more photographs. But prompted by colleagues in the field, students, and scholarship by art historians and others trained to read images, I have also given more thought to the use of photographs here and in Holocaust Studies in general. A photograph is not a clear window onto the past any more than a written document is. Look at any image in this book. Someone took that picture for a reason. They decided what to photograph and how to frame the subject. Then someone developed the film and made prints. What happened after that? Who kept the prints or the negatives and why? Were the photographs cropped, retouched, reproduced, traded, given as a souvenir or gift, displayed, hidden, put in an album, published, damaged, defaced, restored, presented as evidence in a trial, used to identify someone, cherished by loved ones, preserved in an archive, lost, or discarded as trash?

Consider also the quality of an image, especially in terms of lighting, film stock and developing. Did a professional photographer or a well-trained amateur take the picture? Did he or she have access to a good darkroom or film stock? High-quality photographs raise questions about the role of cultural actors in the genocide. What kinds of photographers were needed or involved? Who hired them or paid them? Does a photo reveal more about the photographer and her or his context than about the subject itself? Probably not—we would still recognize a friend, even if they appeared in an SS photo—but it is important to consider how creating a picture of something or someone reflects the preoccupations and priorities of the image-maker.

Thinking about these kinds of questions when you look at a photograph reveals how complex visual images can be. Consider the picture on the cover. The caption provided by the U.S. Holocaust Memorial Museum reads as follows: "Jewish women are herded into SS headquarters during a confiscation action in the Lodz ghetto." No photographer is recorded, but it is clearly a professional-quality picture, taken by and for the perpetrators. Two of the Germans look straight at the camera, whereas the Jewish women face away. The scene is framed on the right by one man in uniform; the doorway creates a frame within the frame around two SS men. The men's heads and caps adorned with the eagle and death's head insignia dominate the image, but their weapons are visible, too. The shot seems intended to document the Germans in charge and on the job, ruling the ghetto and ensuring the collection of Jewish property, in this case, clothing.

I chose this photograph for the cover because it captures some key aspects of the book. First, it depicts what I call proximity: here we see Jews and Germans—victims and perpetrators—in the same physical space. In this case that space is the Lodz ghetto, the second largest ghetto in occupied Poland (after Warsaw), and the longest lasting. So I hoped this picture would suggest the hands-on nature of the Holocaust—it was not primarily industrial or assembly-line killing—and draw attention to the ghettos as important sites of Jewish life and death. Though seen through the eyes of the perpetrators the scene also represents a basic shared humanity: everyone has a face, everyone feels the cold. This photograph is part of the collection of the Ghetto Fighters' House Museum in Israel. Its function in that setting subverts the original Nazi purpose, and this reversal was important to me, too. Now the image serves to document German crimes and memorialize specific victims: no names are provided for the women, but someone might recognize among them their mother, sister, grandmother, or friend.

The significance of chronology is also reflected here. Photo archivists at the U.S. Holocaust Memorial Museum provide a range of dates—1940–1942, but the content allows us to fix the image somewhat more precisely. A German *Aktion*, a round-up, in September 1942 removed from the ghetto people deemed unable to work—children, the sick, and elderly—and sent them to Chelmno to be killed in gas vans. One of the women shown here, fourth from the left, appears older than the others; somewhat stooped, she is holding onto the taller woman beside her. It is unlikely she would have been alive after September 1942. The women are wearing coats, complete with fur collars, and we know that Jews in the Lodz ghetto were required to surrender their furs in December 1941. Any furs still in private hands were confiscated the following month. So this photograph likely was taken between February 1940, when the ghetto was established, and December 1941.

The photograph is visually as well as historically compelling. In the middle of the frame we see three symbols—the Star of David on the women's backs, the swastika on the SS man's armband, and the German eagle on the uniform of the man to the right. Probably these symbols were the first things that caught your eye and made the image immediately recognizable as a "Holocaust photograph." But what exactly is a Holocaust photograph? Decades later, certain symbols and scenes have become iconic, immediately associated with the Holocaust: barbed wire, the entrance at Auschwitz, Anne Frank's face. Photographs that include or evoke those images serve as a kind of shorthand to conjure up "The Holocaust" and feelings associated with it: dread, horror, and sadness. But rather than raising questions, use of such pictures can close them off by producing a sense that "of course, I already know about that, I understand." For this reason I have tried to avoid familiar images or to juxtapose them with other kinds of photographs.

Another specific image illustrates some of these points. Here is a photograph that I also considered for the cover. It is a beautiful, evocative image: the badge with the star immediately signals the Holocaust, and the girl looks like a young Anne Frank. According to the Photo Archive at the U.S. Holocaust Memorial Museum, this picture was taken in 1941 in the Loborgrad (or Lobor-Grad) concentration camp in Croatia. No photographer is named, but whoever took the picture knew what they were doing: the shot is artfully framed, with the star at the center and the line of the girl's arm following the diagonal slats on the fence. And what about the pose, in which the girl looks over her shoulder with a smile? Was the photographer drawing on knowledge of portraits like Vermeer's Girl with a Pearl Earring, or did he or she actually have more interest in the Star of David pinned to the girl's back?

Everyone to whom I showed the picture agreed it would make a striking cover. But the more I thought about it, the more problems I saw. For one thing, I just did not know enough about the photograph. Who took it and why? Who was the girl and what happened to her? Someone composed the picture with care to highlight her face and her sweet, shy smile. She appears posed yet comfortable and aware of the photographer. This image does not reproduce the perpetrators' gaze nor does it have the hasty, blurred look of a picture taken clandestinely with a concealed or improvised camera. According to the Photo Archive, "recent research" suggests the photo may have been taken in Auschwitz, although the "Ž" below the star, for Židov, the Serbo-Croatian word for "Jew," clearly links it to Yugoslavia.

A Jewish girl, probably in the Loborgrad concentration camp in Croatia, 1941. The composition of the picture, as well as the girl's calm demeanor, clean hair and clothes, may indicate that this photograph was taken as part of a rescue effort to save children interned at the camp.

These locations are linked: the Ustasha (*Ustaŝa*), Nazi Germany's partners in Croatia, held Jewish and Serbian children in the Loborgrad camp, where thousands died of torture, hunger, and disease; in 1942, Jewish children and women from the camp were sent to Auschwitz to be killed. But the girl in the picture looks healthy and clean, not like someone who has endured months in a camp and days on a transport. I learned that a humanitarian effort coordinated by Diana Budisavljević, an Austrian-born woman married to a Serbian man, rescued many children from concentration camps in Croatia. Perhaps this photograph was related to that initiative?

Even with all these unknowns, I kept returning to this picture. It captures so many aspects of the Holocaust as it is widely understood—the star, the innocence of the victims embodied in the face of a child. But precisely this familiarity gave me pause. Why do images of children, and especially of one child, tug at our heartstrings in a way that photos of adults or one elderly person do not? If you cover up the star, what if anything would make this a Holocaust photograph? What is the appeal of representations of the Holocaust that leave out the perpetrators, witnesses, collaborators, and everyone else other than the victims?

As I see it, considering these questions adds to the significance of this compelling, mysterious picture. I hope that it and the other images in the book will challenge our assumptions about the Holocaust and make us keep thinking. Whether or not you have a deep understanding of photo history, the photographs still raise questions that can be addressed with other evidence presented in other forms. In studying the Holocaust, photographs offer a powerful way to open up new questions, even if they do not always answer them.

1

DRY TIMBER

PRECONDITIONS

In order for a house to burn down, three things are required. The timber must be dry and combustible, there needs to be a spark that ignites it, and the weather has to be favorable—not too damp, perhaps some wind. Hitler's Nazi regime in Germany provided the spark that set off the destruction we now call the Holocaust, and World War II (1939–1945) created a climate conducive to brutality. But without certain preconditions—the dry timber—mass murder on such a scale would not have been possible.

Most of this book is about the fire—the Holocaust itself—from the spark to the conflagration and finally the ashes. It asks less why than *how* the Holocaust happened. Like Raul Hilberg, a political scientist and founding scholar of the field, I answer that question, "step by step." In other words, the Holocaust was not a single event or the result of one decision, but a complex process that developed over time.

This chapter tackles the deeper question: why? It considers the dry timber—the preconditions—and asks, what made the Holocaust possible? Raising this question draws attention to the problem of determining causality. Chronology provides important clues—something cannot cause something that happened prior to it—but just because one event occurred before another does not mean they are causally linked. Even when a causal relationship seems obvious, it is difficult, maybe impossible, to know which factors are most causally determinant. Another problem has to do with teleology, that is, the tendency to reason backward from specific results to their presumed causes. What in hindsight can look like a clear line of causality, even inevitability, viewed in its historical context will almost always appear full of twists and turns.

The question—how was the Holocaust possible?—can be broken down into several component parts. One sub-question is: why the Jews? To address that topic means to engage the history of antisemitism, the various forms of anti-Jewish ideas and actions that have been called the "longest hatred." The first part of this chapter explores that subject.

Antisemitism is a crucial factor but it cannot explain everything about the Holocaust. Why were non-Jews victimized? Why did the Nazis target disabled people for mass murder? And why did they kill Roma? How do we explain the participation of large numbers of professionals—doctors, lawyers, social workers, academics, police, and bureaucrats—in processes of isolating and persecuting not only Jews, but people with disabilities, Roma, homosexual men, Jehovah's Witnesses, Afro-Germans, and people deemed "asocial"?

To explore these questions requires investigation of the intertwined histories of eugenics, racism, and attitudes toward social outsiders. Pursuing those topics in turn draws attention to more recent history, from the 1700s to the twentieth century, and to the bundle of social and political changes known as "modernity"—the growth of state power and the organization of agencies and technologies that enabled states to intervene actively in the lives of all their people, and the expanding claims of science and scientific authority to be able to shape and improve humanity. The second part of this chapter examines these issues.

A third question is about time and place. Why did the Holocaust happen where and when it did? Why did it originate in Germany and wreak its most intense destruction in eastern Europe? Why did it occur in the 1930s and 1940s? To address these questions calls for a focus on political, geopolitical, and military developments, including imperialism, World War I, and the Russian Revolution. The third part of this chapter sketches some links between these events and the Holocaust. For the sake of clarity, I have separated the three lines of inquiry in this chapter, but as you will see, they are interconnected, like the long and tangled roots of a large tree.

ANTISEMITISM—WHY THE JEWS?

Antisemitism can easily be defined: it means hatred of Jews. But studying antisemitism turns out not to be so straightforward. Antisemitism can be traced back millennia but it seems to be both always the same yet ever-changing. Another challenge has to do with the relation between antisemitism and Jewish history. Persecution of Jews and Jewish suffering were never the whole story, and since the emergence of Judaism, Jews and non-Jews have coexisted. To reduce Jews to nothing but victims and the Jewish past to nothing but a chain of misery is an injustice to Jewish history. It also falsifies history in general and ignores the fact that in most societies inner-group violence—Christians against Christians, Muslims against Muslims, Jews against Jews—is more frequent than violence across group lines. *intra vs. intergroup violence*

The term "antisemitism" was coined in the 1870s by a German journalist who wanted to contrast his supposedly scientific antipathy toward Jews with religious forms of anti-Judaism. As a label, "antisemitism" is misleading, because the adjective "Semitic" describes a group of related languages, among them Hebrew, Arabic, and Phoenician, and the people who speak them. Often you will see the word written with a hyphen—"anti-Semitism"—a spelling I avoid in this book. Use of the hyphen implies that there was such a thing as "Semitism," which antisemites opposed. In fact, those who used the term in the nineteenth century (and since) have understood it to refer only to hostility toward Jews.

Antipathy toward Jews in Europe dated back much further than the 1800s—as far as the ancient world. Roman authorities worried that refusal to worship local and imperial gods would jeopardize the security of the state, which meant monotheistic Jews were liable to run into trouble. At times such unease, coupled with political conflicts, turned into open persecution and *Destruction +* attacks. In 70 CE the Romans destroyed the temple in Jerusalem, the focal *Diaspora* point of Jewish life up to that time; sixty years later they dispersed the Jews of Palestine, scattering them far from the region that had been their home.

The rise of Christianity added new fuel to anti-Jewish sentiments. Christianity grew out of Judaism—Jesus himself was a Jew, as were the apostles and important figures such as Paul of Tarsus. Nevertheless, early Christians tried to separate themselves from other Jews, both to win followers from the gentile (non-Jewish) world and to gain favor with Roman imperial authorities. Some early Christians also stressed their loyalty to the state by pointing out that the Kingdom of God was not of this earth and therefore did not compete with Rome. Such efforts paid off: in less than four hundred years, Christianity went from being a persecuted branch of Judaism to being the dominant religion of the Roman Empire.

It is significant that some early Christian accounts blamed Jews for Jesus's death even though crucifixion was a specifically Roman form of punishment commonly practiced during Jesus's time. The version of events that had Jewish mobs demanding Jesus's death while the Roman governor Pontius Pilate washed his hands allowed later Christians to emphasize their difference from Judaism and downplay the hostility that Roman authorities had shown toward

Christianity in its early stages. All of the false accusations against Jews associated with the Roman imperial period—that Jews were traitors and conspirators, that they killed Jesus—remained familiar in Europe into the twentieth century.

Yet rather than being timeless and permanent, stereotypes and negative images of Jews turn out to have changed considerably over time. For instance, the art historian Sara Lipton has shown that the association of Jews with prominent, hooked noses, a staple of Nazi and other modern antisemitic propaganda, only emerged in the 1300s. Before that Christian artists in Europe identified Jews in their paintings with words or certain kinds of hats. Those hats themselves were an artistic convention, not a representation of some kind of headgear that Jews actually wore.

In many ways the Middle Ages—from around the ninth to the sixteenth centuries—were difficult times for Jews in Europe. Often crusades against Muslims and Christians accused of heresy started off or ended up with violent attacks on Jews. Such attacks, which later came to be known as *pogroms*, a word derived from the Russian for "riot," were also common responses to outbreaks of plague or other disasters. For example, in many parts of Europe, the Black Death of 1348 sparked brutal pogroms, as Christians blamed Jews for somehow causing the epidemic of bubonic plague. Mobilized by such accusations, Christian mobs—sometimes spontaneously, sometimes urged on by state and church leaders—attacked Jewish homes and communities, plundering, destroying, raping, and killing. The scale of pogroms varied wildly, from brief local incidents to weeklong massacres that swept through entire regions. In their wake they left among Christians a habit of using Jews as scapegoats, and among Jews, a sense of vulnerability and a repertoire of defenses, such as paying protection money, sticking together, and keeping a low profile.

In addition to sporadic waves of violence, Jews faced harassment and restrictions of various kinds from governments across Europe. In some cases, regulations forced Jews to live in certain areas or ghettos; sometimes Jews were required to wear identifying badges. Jews everywhere in Europe faced limitations on where they could live, the occupations in which they could engage, and the kinds of property and titles they could hold. Certain state authorities drove Jews out of their territories altogether. In 1290, the King of England evicted Jews from his lands. Two hundred years later, Ferdinand and Isabella of Spain expelled Jews and Muslims from the Iberian Peninsula except those who converted to Christianity.

Some church leaders and secular rulers tried to convince or coerce Jews to abandon their religion and convert to Christianity. But conversion did not necessarily solve the problems of intolerance. Converts from Judaism to

Christianity in sixteenth-century Spain found that they were still viewed with suspicion and regarded as somehow tainted by supposed "Jewish blood." So even the notion of Jewishness as a "race" was not entirely original to the Nazis.

The Protestant Reformation changed but did not necessarily improve Christian treatment of European Jews. At first its leader, the German monk Martin Luther, hoped that his break with what he considered the corrupted church of Rome would inspire mass conversions of Jews to Christianity. When the anticipated wave of baptisms did not occur, Luther turned against the Jews, whom he derided as stubborn and hard necked. In 1542 he wrote a pamphlet called *Against the Jews and Their Lies.* That tract, with its vicious characterization of Jews as parasites and its calls to "set their synagogues and schools on fire," would later be widely quoted in Hitler's Germany.

Other medieval images—the association of Jews with the devil; charges that Jews used the blood of Christian children for ritual purposes—also survived into the modern era. Even those Nazi leaders who hated Christianity and mocked it for its historical ties to Judaism found it useful to invoke these powerful, old notions about Jews. In other words, Nazi antisemitism was different from previous, religious forms of anti-Judaism, but its proponents still drew on those traditional hostilities. Ancient associations of Jews with evil gave modern antisemitism a virulence that set it apart from other prejudices.

Antisemitism after the Emancipation of European Jews

In the seventeenth, eighteenth, and nineteenth centuries, European society became more secular, but bigotry toward Jews did not disappear. Instead, social, economic, and political prejudices grew alongside and sometimes in place of older religious resentments. Enlightenment thinkers in eighteenth-century Europe favored some form of religious toleration and mocked the rigidity of institutionalized Christianity. But even the self-consciously progressive French writer Voltaire labeled Jews with contempt as "vagrants, robbers, slaves, or seditious." Voltaire and others described traditional Christianity in similarly negative terms. In the nineteenth century, Napoleon and some other rulers introduced legislation to repeal old restrictions on Jews in Europe. This process is usually referred to as the emancipation of the Jews. Nevertheless, formal and informal limitations often remained in place.

Like every minority group striving to better its position while hampered by obstructions, European Jews ended up overrepresented in some occupations and underrepresented in others. Hostile non-Jews made much of the fact that in Germany by around 1900, the field of journalism included a higher percentage of Jews than did the population as a whole. However, they never mentioned the fact that German Jews were generally excluded from the highest ranks of the government bureaucracy and the military. By the late 1800s, political parties that openly championed antisemitism had sprung up in various parts of Europe. Vienna's popular antisemitic mayor Karl Lueger would make a deep impression on the young Adolf Hitler. In particular Hitler noticed how Lueger played on widespread anti-Jewish sentiments to whip up enthusiasm in the crowds he addressed and to boost his own support.

Modern antisemites claimed that their views were scientific, based on the biological "facts" of blood and race. In reality hatred of Jews was no more scientific than were European attitudes of superiority toward Africans, Asians, or indigenous peoples in the Americas. Moreover the notion of "Jewishness" as a race was invented, as were the concepts of "blackness," "whiteness," and "Orientalism" that became so central to how many Europeans and North Americans viewed the world. Still, Social Darwinist ideas about struggle between rival "races" and survival of the strongest provided fertile ground, not only for Nazi notions about Jews but for an entire, interlocking system of prejudices against people deemed inferior.

Sexual anxieties and sexualized stereotypes fed the racist mind-set in powerful, pernicious ways. Notions about Jewish and black men as sexual predators insatiable in their lust for Christian or white women coexisted with charges that Jews and men of color were feminized weaklings incapable of soldierly honor. In medieval Europe, religion had served to legitimate and justify hatreds. In the modern era science played a comparable role.

It is often pointed out that antisemitism was rife with contradictions. How could Jews be accused of both Communism and capitalism? How could they be at the same time racially inferior and on the verge of achieving world domination? Such tensions in fact are typical of many, perhaps all, enduring prejudices. They made antisemitism endlessly adaptable, able to fit the needs and anxieties of an enormous variety of people.

The Diversity of Jewish Life in Europe

Never more than a small minority in Europe—at most 1 or 2 percent of the entire population—Jews existed alongside Christians, and in some regions Muslims, for centuries. Judaism was and is a religion and a living community. Despite pogroms, massacres, and expulsions, Jews survived in Europe. They thrived as individuals and as a community in different places at different times—in Spain before the Inquisition, later in the Netherlands, over long periods in Poland and Germany. They were woven into the fabric of European society in ways that scholars in the dynamic field of Jewish studies have demonstrated over and over again.

European Jews, like European Christians, were and are a diverse group. By the early twentieth century many Jews were highly acculturated; neither their appearance, habits of daily life, or language distinguished them from their non-Jewish French, German, Italian, Polish, Greek, or other neighbors. Some attended religious services on high holidays only; others, never. Some maintained a strong sense of Jewish identity; others, very little or none at all. Jews and non-Jews got married; often Jews in intermarriages converted to Christianity, and usually they raised their children as Christians. Karl Marx, the founder of Communism, is frequently described as a Jew, but in fact his parents had converted from Judaism to Christianity. Nazi law would not recognize such conversions and instead considered converts to Christianity, as well as the children and in some cases grandchildren of converts, to be Jews.

In Europe in the early 1900s there were also more visible kinds of Jews. In some parts of eastern Europe many Jews lived in communities known as shtetls. Confined by the Russian tsars to an area in the west of the Russian empire called the Pale of Settlement, these Jews developed a lifestyle based on shared religious observance, the Yiddish language, a diet following kashrut—the Jewish dietary laws—and predominance of certain occupations. For example, many were small traders and craftspeople. Those lines of work did not require them to own land, something from which they were restricted and in some places prohibited altogether.

It is misleading to divide European Jews into the traditional east and assimilated west. By the 1920s and 1930s, many Jews in Poland, Lithuania, Hungary, and the Soviet Union lived in large cities, spoke Polish, Lithuanian, Hungarian, or Russian and participated fully in the national culture. Many also considered themselves to be fully Jewish, and they interpreted what that meant in a wide variety of ways. Meanwhile, in central and western Europe, where Jewish populations were smaller, there were acculturated Jews—high-ranking military officers in France, lawyers and judges in Germany, well-known actors and filmmakers in Hungary. But there were also Orthodox Jews in central European cities and towns and Jewish farmers in the Rhineland and in the region known as Subcarpathian Rus', which belonged at different times to Czechoslovakia, Hungary, and Ukraine.

By the twentieth century, there were many strands of European Judaism. Most of the Jews in southern and southeastern Europe came from what is called the Sephardic tradition, connected to Spain, and spoke a language called Ladino rather than the Yiddish of the Ashkenazic Jews of northern and central Europe. Some Jews were strictly Orthodox, so that their mode of dress, adherence to dietary laws, and other religious observances set them apart from the gentiles around them. Others were Reform, part of a branch of Judaism that emerged in early nineteenth-century Germany and emphasized adapting

German Jewish soldiers celebrating Hanukkah in the field during World War I. In 1916, the same year that this photograph was taken, German military authorities carried out a survey of Jewish contributions to the war effort. When results showed that Jews had served and sacrificed at least proportional to their numbers, the data were not released.

rituals and practices for modern times. Some Jews embraced the tradition of Hasidism, a movement that started in Polish lands and emphasized joyous mysticism; others were more austere. Some dressed distinctively, with the adult men wearing beards and earlocks; other Jewish men might be distinguishable only by the physical marking of circumcision. Among Jews in the Soviet Union, even circumcision became optional.

In short, there were wealthy Jews in Europe around 1930 as well as middle-class and very poor Jews. There were Jewish bankers and shopkeepers, Jewish doctors, nurses, actors, professors, soldiers, typists, peddlers, factory owners, factory workers, kindergarten teachers, conservatives, liberals, nationalists, feminists, anarchists, and Communists. Nazi propaganda would create the category of "the Jew," a composite based on myths and stereotypes. Nazi persecution then reified that generalization, as violence rendered obsolete distinctions of age, sex, class, and national origin among Jews, all of whom were slated for destruction. In reality there was no such thing as "the Jew," only Jews who often differed as much, and in many cases more, from one another than they did from the Christians around them.

A group of religious Jews on a kayaking excursion in Poland, sometime during the 1930s. Prewar Jewish life across Europe was extremely diverse, belying the stereotypes propagated by antisemites. In the middle of the rear kayak here, holding a child, is Tsvi Majranc. Mr. Majranc died of dysentery during the war in the Lodz ghetto.

Four Jewish Lives in Prewar Europe

Perhaps the best way to express the diversity of Jewish life is to look at some individuals who experienced the assault of Nazism as young people in different parts of Europe. One example comes from a memoir by Peter Gay called *My German Question*. Gay was born in Berlin in 1923 to a middle-class family named Fröhlich, which means "happy" in German. (After moving to the United States, the name would be changed to the English translation "Gay.") Peter's father bought and sold glassware; his mother worked part-time as a clerk in her sister's sewing notions store. Committed atheists, Fröhlich's parents officially left the Jewish community. They had their son circumcised but showed few other signs of Jewish identity.

Fröhlich's father fought in World War I and was wounded and decorated. An avid fan of all kinds of sports, Fröhlich Sr. had many close friends who were not Jewish. Peter was one of a handful of Jewish boys at his school; he does not remember ever being ridiculed or harassed. He and his family considered themselves thoroughly German. Gay and his parents managed to get out of Germany before World War II began in 1939. Gay eventually moved to the United States, where he became an important historian of modern Europe and a professor at Yale University. He died in 2015.

A very different Jewish life is that of Jack Pomerantz, which is recorded in his book *Run East.* A native of Radzyn, a small town near Lublin in Poland, Pomerantz was born in 1918 during a pogrom, a common occurrence in the region in the wake of World War I. His mother was hiding in a barn when she gave birth to Yankel, one of eight children. (He would later anglicize his first name to "Jack.") Yankel's father was a peddler; he wore a long beard, dark clothing, and often a prayer shawl. Although the family was poor, Yankel's mother still always tried to have a special meal for Shabbat, the best day of the week. Like all married Orthodox women she wore a wig. For the Jewish holidays most of the women in the shtetl made wonderful food, but sometimes Pomerantz's mother had nothing to cook. She would boil rags just to steam up the windows of their shack and create the impression that they too were preparing a feast.

Pomerantz spoke Yiddish at home and was very conscious of himself as a Jew. His town was about half Jews and half Christian Poles, and there was considerable tension between the two groups. Growing up Yankel heard people say they hated Jews because they "killed Christ." Once, in a fight, a Polish Catholic boy cut Yankel's cheek with a knife, right through into his mouth. At this point, it is impossible to know what that conflict was about. But looking back through the prism of the Holocaust, Pomerantz interpreted the aggression as antisemitic, one of a series of attacks and betrayals he experienced from non-Jews around him.

Like Peter Gay, Jack Pomerantz survived the war, though not with his family but alone, and not by fleeing west but eastward out of Europe, to Siberia and Central Asia. A good-looking and charming man, Pomerantz found many people, often women, who helped him along the way. In July 1944, as a truck driver for the Red Army, he was among the liberators of Majdanek, the first major concentration camp that Soviet troops encountered in Poland. A few years later he came to the United States, where he worked as a builder and contractor in New Jersey. He had not had much chance to get an education, so he wrote his memoir with the help of a professional writer. He died a few years after it was published.

Sara Ginaite's early life could hardly have been more different. Born in 1924 in Kaunas (Kovno) in Lithuania, she grew up surrounded by a large and devoted extended family. Her parents were well educated and multilingual: her father had studied engineering in France, and her mother, a graduate of a Polish high school, also spoke French fluently. Among Sara's fondest childhood memories are summer vacations with her sister and their grandparents in a beautiful resort on the Nemunas River. She loved music, theater, economics, and sports and admired her elegant and cultured parents, aunts, and uncles.

The German attack on the Soviet Union in June 1941 brought Sara Ginaite's life as she knew it to a crashing halt. In the first days of the war, Lithuanian partisans shot three of her uncles, and their mother, her grandmother, died the next day. Along with the rest of her family, Ginaite was forced to move into the ghetto established by the new German administration. They survived the major killing action a few months later, and in 1942 Ginaite succeeded in escaping from the ghetto to join the partisans fighting in the forest. She too lived through the war, but when she returned to Kaunas in the spring of 1945, she learned that almost her entire extended family had been killed. Only she, her husband Misha Rubinsonas, a member of her partisan detachment, three-year-old Tanya who was hidden with a gentile woman, Sara's sister Alice, and Alice's husband remained alive.

After the war Ginaite, a decorated hero of the resistance, earned advanced degrees in economics in the Soviet Union and became a professor at Vilnius University. Her husband, a journalist and sports commentator, died suddenly in the late 1970s, and she subsequently moved to Canada, where she still lives.

Sara Ginaite (center front, in socks) and her extended Virovichius family bid farewell to Abrasha Virovichius (next to Sara, holding a box of chocolates) as he departs from the Kovno (Kaunas) train station on his way to Palestine in 1934. Almost all of the people photographed here died in the Holocaust: murdered by their Lithuanian neighbors or German death squads; starved, burned, and worked to death in ghettos, labor camps, and on death marches.

In 1945, in the ruins of the Kovno ghetto, Ginaite found some photographs of her family's prewar life. They remain among her most precious possessions, and in 2012 she published a collection of them with other images and texts in an album called *Pro Memoria*. The picture included here was taken in 1934, when members of her mother's extended family, the Virovichius family, gathered with friends at the train station to say goodbye to her uncle, who was immigrating to Palestine. This photograph captures something of the prewar world of one Jewish family. Their stylish clothing speaks to their acculturation and success; they appear safe and comfortable in their surroundings; one uncle has his dog with him.

The picture also serves as a reminder of the terrible arbitrariness of the Holocaust. Ginaite's caption says it all: "Of all those pictured only three survived." The uncle who left for Palestine returned for a visit in 1939, to introduce his new wife to his family. When war broke out that year, they were unable to leave. He was one of the three brothers shot by Lithuanians in 1941. As an illustration in this book, the photograph of the Virovichius family at the train station has added significance. It points to the value of images not only as documents and weapons of destruction but as records of life, representations of self-assertion by people who cannot be reduced to numbers, targets, or corpses but who look out at us as if to say, "here we are."

As a young girl in Hungary, Aranka Siegal experienced yet another kind of Jewish life before the Holocaust. She describes it in her book, *Upon the Head of the Goat*. Siegal, whose name at the time was Piri Davidowitz, was an observant Jew like her parents and her four sisters. Born in 1931, she went to a public school, where her friends included Catholic, Protestant, and Russian Orthodox as well as Jewish children. Some of her fondest childhood memories are of the months she spent each summer on her grandmother's farm. It was from her grandmother that Piri learned the most about Judaism. With her grandmother she lit the Sabbath candles, recited the blessing for the new year on Rosh Hashanah, and prepared traditional foods.

Siegal's grandmother also taught her about Jewish history. Old enough to remember pogroms in Ukraine and Hungary in the 1910s and 1920s, she told her granddaughter how Christians had often used Jews as scapegoats in times of trouble. She also warned the little girl about a "madman" called Hitler, who was terrorizing Jews in Germany and Poland. Aranka Siegal's grandmother was right to be afraid. Almost everyone in the family would be killed in the Holocaust. Against all odds, Piri and one sister survived the killing center of Auschwitz. After some time in Sweden, Aranka Siegal moved to New York and later Florida. She speaks to many students every year about her experiences during and after World War II.

S͞T͞O͞P RACISM AND WIDESPREAD PREJUDICES— WHY SO MANY VICTIMS?

In their choices of target groups the Nazis reflected and built on prejudices that were familiar in many parts of Europe. Hitler and the Nazis did not invent antisemitism nor were they the first to attack Sinti and Roma or people considered disabled. Their hostilities toward Europeans of African descent, Poles, Jehovah's Witnesses, and homosexual men were not new either. The Nazis were extremists in the lengths to which they went in their assaults, but they were quite typical in whom they attacked. Nazi leaders could not simply have invented a category of enemies—for example, people between the ages of thirty-seven and forty-two—and then have expected the majority of the population to turn against them. Such a group would have been incomprehensible to most people. The identities of those targeted for destruction during World War II were no coincidence; many of these people were already victims of prejudice.

Thinking about non-Jewish and Jewish victims together reveals something important about Nazi persecution. It was not merely about "difference," as if "anyone different" was persecuted. In fact it was as much violence and persecution that created difference as the other way around. Violence turned out to be contagious, and accusations against one group easily slid over onto another. Nazi propagandists labeled all of Germany's supposed enemies as "Jews" or judaized: they depicted Jews as deformed and criminal and compared them to disabled people and Roma, whom they also described as monstrous and dangerous. Nazi ideologues linked Communists, capitalists, and liberals with a purported Jewish conspiracy; they described homosexuals, Slavs, the British, and the Americans as nothing but cover groups for alleged Jewish interests.

Eugenics and Attitudes toward People Deemed Disabled

When one considers the long history of anti-Jewish attitudes and actions in Europe, one might conclude that Jews must have been the first targets for systematic murder in Hitler's Germany. That, however, was not the case. Instead, the first category of people slated for mass killing were individuals deemed disabled. Perhaps Nazi leaders believed they would encounter less opposition to attacks on that segment of the population; perhaps they thought it would be easier to keep such a program secret. Most likely it was because disabled people, in particular those who were institutionalized, were already isolated from the rest of society. Certainly initiatives came from within the scientific and medical communities, whose members played key roles in carrying out the killings.

Attitudes toward people with disabilities in Europe developed in a manner rather different from what we have seen with regard to antisemitism. Nevertheless, here too Nazi ideology and practice built on existing prejudices in ways that were extreme but not unique.

It is hard to know exactly how the majority of the population regarded people with mental and physical disabilities in medieval and early modern Europe. Christianity, like Judaism, out of which it grew, taught compassion for the afflicted, and church as well as state law provided some protections for those who could not protect themselves. But there is also evidence, including many literary accounts, that the able-bodied often ridiculed, took advantage of, and abused those weaker than they were. Also people developed the idea that the body was the mirror of the soul, and illness or degeneracy was potentially a sign of spiritual disease.

Nevertheless it seems that in various ways society found places for those with mental and physical disabilities. The village idiot, court dwarfs, fools, beggars, and cripples were all familiar figures. They showed that, although life might not always be fair or good to those with disabilities, at least everyone recognized their existence and assumed that they, like the poor, were a permanent part of society.

By the nineteenth century the assumption that the disabled would always be present had begun to change, at least for many people in Europe and elsewhere. Scientific and medical advances together with Social Darwinist notions led to the idea that society could be engineered so that only the supposedly healthiest elements would reproduce. This way of thinking, and the sciences and professions that grew up around it, is often referred to as eugenics.

Eugenics became popular all over Europe and North America in the early twentieth century. Many places introduced programs to sterilize people considered undesirable. Even though the proponents of such plans claimed to be objective and scientific, they tended to identify people already viewed as outsiders as the least desirable "breeding stock" and to label them "feeble-minded" or "degenerate." For example, eugenics programs in some parts of the United States disproportionately targeted African Americans; elsewhere in North America native people were prime subjects. Europeans often focused on Roma and other itinerant people, and everywhere poor people came in for the closest scrutiny. In the wake of World War I, many political leaders, interested in boosting the size and health of their populations—and their armies—promoted eugenics programs. Meanwhile, perennial problems such as crime seemed solvable to people who believed that criminal tendencies were inherited and that their carriers could be identified by physical characteristics.

Even many scientists, medical experts, and social workers who considered themselves progressive reformers supported programs to attempt to "raise" the quality of the population by "selective breeding," with or without the consent of those involved. For example, in the 1910s and 1920s the British sex reformer Marie Stopes helped thousands of men and women learn about birth control and gain access to necessary technologies and supplies. One of Stopes's arguments in support of legalizing birth control was the assumed need to curb the reproduction of people considered burdens on society. When a deaf man wrote to ask Dr. Stopes a question about reproductive rights she fired back an angry letter demanding to know why someone like him would even consider having children. Of course such efforts to "improve" humanity, even at the expense of those considered inferior, were different from Nazi attempts to wipe out certain groups of people. Still, by the 1920s, as notions about building a "better race" became mainstream, they served to legitimate more extreme schemes of exclusion and domination.

A look at one influential publication illustrates the radicalization of eugenic ideas after World War I. In 1920 Karl Binding, former president of Germany's highest court, and Alfred Hoche, a German professor of psychiatry, wrote *Permission for the Destruction of Worthless Life, Its Extent and Form*. Binding and Hoche believed that the war had produced a marked increase in the number of "mental defectives." As a result, they said, Germany was weighed down with people they called "living burdens." They expressed shock at the care that was devoted to inmates of mental hospitals at a time when the country had lost so many young men in war. In their view the mentally ill were "completely worthless creatures."

Binding and Hoche did not explicitly say that people who wanted to live should be killed, but their ideas had radical implications. According to them, every human being's worth could be measured in terms of contribution to the community and the nation. Some people, they suggested, did not have any value. Although Binding and Hoche's book was controversial, the mentality it expressed was widely shared in Europe and North America in the decades before World War II. Given this background, it is no surprise that Hitler's regime would begin its program of mass murder with attacks on people deemed mentally or physically disabled. Any comprehensive study of the Holocaust must integrate this chapter, which Henry Friedlander called the "origins of Nazi genocide."

Prejudices toward Roma and Sinti

The Jews, people deemed disabled, and the Roma were the groups toward which the Nazis most consistently followed a policy of annihilation that included murdering even babies and elderly people. Anti-Roma sentiment, like antisemitism, was an old, familiar hatred in Europe, so with regard to the Roma too, Nazi Germany could draw on long-standing prejudices.

The origins of the European Roma remain somewhat contested, but many scholars agree that they moved into Europe from India during the Middle Ages. The English word "Gypsy," often applied as a pejorative term or insult, developed from the mistaken idea that the people in question originated in Egypt. The German term for Roma is *Zigeuner*, but it too has taken on negative connotations, so that many people now try to avoid using that label. Instead they prefer to speak of "Roma," "Rom people," "Romany," or "Roma and Sinti." The Sinti are a group primarily based in German-speaking Europe. It is hard to pin down whether Roma are a racial, ethnic, or social group, that is, whether they are defined by family relationships with one another, language and traditions, or lifestyle. Perhaps that difficulty itself is an apt reminder of how arbitrary such categories are. It is probably most useful to think of Roma as a group that includes elements of all those criteria.

When Roma first arrived in medieval Europe, they encountered hospitality from some European courts. Soon, however, they became targets of hostility from Europeans who were suspicious of these newcomers. Whether from habit or because of coercion, many Roma were itinerant, and their mobile lifestyle further roused the antagonism of others. The rest of European society labeled them thieves and tricksters who used their musical abilities and physical charms to lure the unsuspecting to their ruin.

A number of common attitudes toward Roma in the medieval period echoed anti-Jewish notions. Non-Jewish Europeans falsely accused Jews of stealing Christian children in order to use their blood; likewise non-Roma charged Roma with kidnapping children for evil purposes. Like Jews, Roma were easy scapegoats in times of disaster, such as plagues or earthquakes. Their opponents claimed that they poisoned the wells, practiced magic, and consorted with the devil. European folklore did not accuse Roma of killing Jesus, but because the Roma were known for their skills as metalworkers, it charged them with forging the nails that pierced his flesh.

According to European myths, Roma, like Jews, had been condemned by God to wander the earth without ever finding a homeland. One popular version of events held that while still in Egypt, the Roma had tried to prevent Joseph, Mary, and the baby Jesus from gaining refuge from King Herod, and God punished them with eternal homelessness. Probably by the twentieth century few Europeans would have accepted such myths as the literal truth. Nor would most non-Roma have realized that in some parts of southeastern Europe, Roma had been enslaved until the mid-nineteenth century. Nevertheless what remained was a widespread sense that Roma were somehow evil outsiders who did not merit the respect or protection awarded to other members of society.

Nineteenth- and twentieth-century notions about heredity and criminality also contributed to attacks on the Roma in Europe. If criminality was inherited and Roma were criminals, "experts" reasoned, then one could fight crime by preventing Roma from having children. Social scientists, medical specialists, and criminologists tended to regard Roma as if they were some kind of disease, as evident in references to the "Gypsy plague." Public authorities introduced all kinds of restrictions on where Roma could reside and what activities were permitted them, and police all over Europe were especially diligent when it came to enforcing such laws and "controlling" Roma. Years before Hitler came to power in Germany, Sinti and Roma in that country were required to carry photo identification cards and to register themselves with local police. France, Hungary, Romania, and other European countries had anti-Rom measures of their own.

Visible Victims, Invisible People

Hitler and his followers associated the Roma with criminality and degeneracy. Yet they did not place a high priority on attacking them. Instead persecution of Roma was often an add-on to other programs of assault. For

Third from the right, Johann (Rukelie) Trollmann, a Sinto from Hanover, poses with the boxing club "Sparta" following their North German championship win in 1929. Trollmann went on to win the middle-weight championship in 1933, after the title was stripped from the Jewish boxer, Erich Seelig. Soon the title was also stripped from Trollmann. He was drafted into the Wehrmacht in 1939 but discharged with other Sinti and Roma three years later. Arrested and sent to Neuengamme concentration camp, he was beaten to death by a kapo in 1944. Trollmann is memorialized by a *Stolperstein* ("stumbling block") in Berlin, near where the title fight took place.

A Roma family next to their caravan, sometime in the 1930s. Members of the family present themselves proudly, a contrast to the many photographs of Roma taken by German ethnographers around this time. The photographer here was Jan Yoors, a young, non-Roma man from Belgium, who had an adoptive Roma family. During the war, Yoors joined the British Army and helped recruit European Roma to assist with intelligence gathering and smuggling arms to the Resistance. Arrested by the Gestapo in 1943, after a year of solitary confinement and torture Yoors was released in a case of mistaken identity. Most members of his Roma family were sent to Auschwitz, and very few of them survived.

instance, Nazi officials did not create separate ghettos for Roma; they simply dumped Roma in Jewish ghettos.

The lack of documentation makes it even more difficult to make meaningful generalizations about the lives of people considered disabled and the Roma in Europe prior to World War II than it is about Jews. There is certainly much less published about members of these two outsider groups. Many disabled people were not in a position to leave written records. For that matter, many probably did not think of themselves as members of a special group whose particular experiences should be preserved. Romany tradition, it seems, may be more connected to the present than the past, more oral than written, and centuries of persecution produced a tendency to be secretive with people outside the immediate group.

Even something that seems as obvious as the numbers of people in these categories cannot be pinned down with precision. Who was considered disabled, mentally or physically, could vary enormously from place to place and

Dr. Sophie Ehrhardt of the Racial Hygiene and Criminal Biology Institute poses with a Romani woman. Ehrhardt worked with Dr. Robert Ritter in his project to produce genealogies for all Sinti and Roma in the Reich and to track their education, health, criminal histories, and social adjustment. Ehrhardt's efforts helped Nazi authorities identify Sinti and Roma, who were later rounded up and incarcerated. Here the scientist Ehrhardt is positioned as a human measuring stick that draws attention to the small stature of the woman beside her.

time to time. For their part, Roma were skilled at evading such formalities as government censuses. Experience with various bureaucracies had taught them that they had little to gain and much to lose by being counted.

The European officials who introduced restrictions on Roma and the police who enforced them were often unclear about who exactly was a Rom. Non-Roma tended to assume they could recognize "Gypsies" by their appearance: many Roma had darker hair, skin, and eyes than most people in northern, western, and eastern Europe, but by no means were there always physical markers. In some areas Roma were associated with certain trades, such as working with metal or leather. Most Europeans thought all Roma were wanderers who made a living from fortune-telling, music, dancing, and theft. In fact, not all Roma were itinerant, and many held regular jobs, for example, as civil servants. Nor were all wandering people in Europe Roma or Sinti in any sense of the word. Sometimes, however, police and other authorities treated people who were not ethnic Roma at all as if they were, because they fit the stereotype of homeless, petty thieves.

Just as Nazi ideologues invented the category of "the Jew," as if all Jews were somehow the same, they created the stereotypical, deformed "life unworthy of living" and the monolithic "Gypsy." In actuality people deemed disabled represented the full range of European society: they were Christians, Jews, Roma, women, men, children, rich, poor, beautiful, dependent, self-reliant, and anything else you might add. As for Roma, they too varied considerably from one another in terms of religion, lifestyle, language, appearance, name, and occupation. Many were Christians; some intermarried with non-Roma. Some spoke a language known as Romani, which linguists believe is linked to languages on the Indian subcontinent; others spoke the languages of the people around them. As would be the case with European Jews, the shared experience of Nazi persecution created a degree of commonality among Roma that would not have existed otherwise.

Asocials

Historians often fail to mention some of the additional groups persecuted by the Nazi regime. In some cases, such as the Jehovah's Witnesses and Afro-Germans, their relatively small numbers make them easy for people not in those groups to forget or ignore. In other cases, such as homosexual men, the persistence of prejudices against them long after collapse of the Third Reich may have blocked recognition of their suffering at Nazi hands. As for people who came under the vague label of "asocial," they have been criticized and attacked so often that their victimization is sometimes almost taken for granted. Study of the Nazi era, however, demonstrates that assaults on such people also grew out of and fed on particular ideologies.

Nazi officials created a category called "asocials" into which they put all kinds of people they considered problematic: Roma, the homeless, criminals deemed incurable, people with certain mental disorders, or those accused of sexual perversions. One did not have to be a Nazi in twentieth-century Europe to be afraid of "asocials." Explosive population growth in the nineteenth century and rapid urbanization in many parts of Europe in the twentieth century contributed to a perception among many people that the world was becoming a more dangerous place, full of bizarre and threatening people. In the decade before Hitler came to power in 1933, the Nazi Party in Germany played on such anxieties to present itself as the force that would "clean up" a society supposedly degenerating into lunacy. Propagandists and, after 1933, Nazi policymakers, used the catchall label "asocial" to stigmatize people who did not fit the national ideal. The unemployed became criminal "shirkers"; women suspected of sexual improprieties—lesbian relations, promiscuity, prostitution—became vulnerable to incarceration as "asocials." Targeting of so-called asocials reflects the contagious nature of Nazi persecution.

Attitudes toward Homosexuals

Pre–World War II prejudices against homosexuals are hard to summarize, because scholars disagree as to when the category of "homosexual" even became recognizable in Europe. It seems evident that in antiquity certain forms of intimacy between people of the same sex did not carry a stigma or preclude sexual relations with members of the opposite sex. By the modern era, however, much of this flexibility was gone, although even the supposedly prudish society of Victorian England showed considerable tolerance for at least some kinds of same-sex intimacies. For example, many people considered sexual experimentation among boys in boarding schools to be a normal part of development; loving relationships between women who often became lifelong companions were not uncommon either.

Nevertheless, by the late nineteenth century many parts of Europe had introduced laws against homosexuality. The German criminal code of 1871 explicitly forbade sexual relations between men. The state prosecuted some cases, and public interest in such "scandals" ran high. For example, it was an enormous sensation when Prince Eulenburg, a member of the inner circle of the German Kaiser Wilhelm II (1888–1918), was charged with homosexual activities and forced from public life. Somewhat paradoxically, an increased openness around the subject of human sexuality in the decades after World War I served to make homosexual men and women more visible in Europe and to increase the panic some heterosexuals felt about them.

Political changes in Germany after World War I made it possible for the first time for Berlin to develop a gay scene that included clubs, restaurants, and bathhouses frequented by homosexual men. Lesbians, it seems, tended to attract less public attention, although there were also some clubs popular with homosexual women. Laws against sex between men were still on the books in Germany's first democracy, the Weimar Republic, but enforcement was slacker than it had been before World War I, especially in the major cities. Many heterosexual Germans, however, disapproved of what they considered their overly permissive society.

Magnus Hirschfeld (1868–1935), a sex reformer and homosexual rights leader in Berlin, made an international reputation for his research in sexology, the new field of studies of sex and sexuality. Hirschfeld regarded homosexuality as the "third sex," a natural and legitimate variant between masculine and feminine. Homosexuals, he pointed out, looked and behaved normally and should be treated accordingly. For many people the work of researchers and

Patrons celebrate at the Eldorado, a nightclub in the Motzstrasse frequented by the Berlin homosexual community, around 1929. During the Weimar Republic, Berlin developed a vibrant gay scene that many conservatives and moral crusaders detested. Attacking homosexuals was one way the Nazi regime sought to curry favor with certain elements of the German population.

activists such as Hirschfeld offered new possibilities for human freedom. For others it seemed to represent the decadence of a society that had abandoned its traditional values. Hitler's Nazis capitalized on such fears as well; they forced Hirschfeld out of Germany, and his research institute was one of the first casualties of their new regime.

Attitudes toward Jehovah's Witnesses

As European outsiders, the Jehovah's Witnesses were relative newcomers. Founded in the United States in the late 1870s, the Jehovah's Witnesses, or International Bible Students, as they were initially called, were not a large group. By the early 1930s they had about twenty thousand members in Germany.

A number of beliefs and activities important to Jehovah's Witnesses made them stand out in European society. Because Jehovah's Witnesses considered themselves citizens of Jehovah's Kingdom, as a principle they did not swear allegiance to any earthly government, nor did they serve in any nation's military. The world, they believed, would soon enter a peaceful, thousand-year heavenly rule, but not until it had gone through the battle of Armageddon. In order to teach others and prepare for the end times, Jehovah's Witnesses emphasized door-to-door preaching and distribution of literature. Such efforts made them publicly visible in large German cities and even some smaller towns to an extent far out of proportion to their numbers.

Jehovah's Witnesses were not popular with mainstream European society in the early decades of the twentieth century. Members of the established Protestant and Catholic churches labeled the Jehovah's Witnesses a "sect" or a "cult" and discounted their interpretations of Christian scripture. Some critics considered the Jehovah's Witnesses' emphasis on the Old Testament suspect and intimated that they might be somehow connected with Judaism. Many people found their proselytizing efforts and handing out of tracts to win converts annoying or offensive. Public officials were suspicious because most Jehovah's Witnesses refused to serve in the military or acknowledge state authority if it clashed with their understanding of God's commands. The group's international ties and connections to the United States were also suspect to some ardent nationalists in Germany and elsewhere. Jehovah's Witnesses would be easy targets for the Nazis, who made them the first religious group to be outlawed in 1933.

Anti-Black Racism in Germany before the Nazis

Many Nazi ideas about what a race was grew out of ways of thinking about people of color that were common among white Europeans—and Americans—in the early twentieth century. An obvious illustration of some of these ideas comes from Germany in the 1920s. After World War I, the French occupied the Rhineland, an area in the western part of defeated Germany. The occupation forces included some troops drawn from France's overseas territories in Africa and Asia. Many Germans were horrified at the presence of these men of color on German soil.

Stereotypes about African men as sexual predators on white women were widespread in Europe, and German racists and nationalists played on such fears and fantasies to stir up resentments against the French occupation. Judging from the hysteria in the German press in the early 1920s, one might have thought that hordes of Africans were raping and pillaging all over Germany. In fact there were at most about five thousand black men stationed in the Rhineland at any given time between 1919 and 1923 and perhaps another twenty thousand nonwhite forces. Among these men were Senegalese and a small number of Sudanese; Frenchmen, Arabs, and Berbers from Morocco; Malagasies from Madagascar; Annamese from Indochina; and others. They seem to have gotten into no more trouble than any other French units. Nevertheless, Nazi propagandists would return to this topic in the 1930s in their own efforts to whip up German anxieties about supposed racial defilement.

Some of the French African troops in Germany in the 1920s became involved with German women, and in some cases those liaisons produced children. These few biracial individuals—who in 1924 may have numbered only seventy-eight—also attracted a great deal of attention. Fanatical German nationalists and racists of various kinds referred to these people as the "Rhineland bastards." Throughout the 1920s some Germans claimed that the existence of those biracial individuals proved there was a vast conspiracy—controlled by the French, the Jews, or simply the unnamed enemies of Germany—to befoul German blood and weaken the German nation. It is no surprise that once in power, Hitler and his Nazi regime would take steps against Germans of African background, too.

A 1933 poster depicting the Nazi view of Freemasonry and its purported links to a Jewish world conspiracy. The temple, apron, square, and compass are all Masonic symbols. The text reads: "Jews—Freemasonry. World Politics—World Revolution. Freemasonry is an international organization beholden to Jewry with the political goal of establishing Jewish domination through worldwide revolution."

Attitudes toward Freemasons

For reasons connected to their paranoia about international conspiracies, Nazi authorities were also hostile to members of the Freemasons, a European association dating back to the eighteenth century and devoted to the ideals of the Enlightenment: progress, freedom, and tolerance. Many well-known Europeans in the age of the French Revolution and afterward belonged to the Freemasons. Mozart was an enthusiast, for example, and he incorporated some of the ideas and rituals of the Masons into his opera *The Magic Flute.*

Over the years the Freemasons had developed some secret rites, and the air of secrecy that surrounded the group made it seem all the more threatening in the eyes of its critics. Especially in central and eastern Europe, conservatives and nationalists regarded the Freemasons with suspicion, accusing them of spreading atheism, liberalism, and disobedience to authority. People fearful of Freemasonry associated it with the "decadent" West, especially France, and with French traditions of secularism and anticlericalism. There were rumors of bizarre sexual rituals, too. Not surprisingly, opponents of the Freemasons also often hinted that the organization was run by Jews as part of some supposed international Jewish conspiracy. When they attacked the Freemasons too, the Nazis chose a familiar target.

In fact, the number of Freemasons in twentieth-century Germany was always very small, and the organization neither wielded any significant power nor posed a threat to the state. Nevertheless, after 1933, under Nazi rule, men who belonged to the association would face a range of discriminatory measures. Some lost their jobs; others ended up in prisons and concentration camps.

WAR AND GEOPOLITICS

Long-standing hatreds alone did not cause the Holocaust. Sadly, the world is full of old prejudices; fortunately, only rarely do they erupt in genocide. Leadership, political will, and manipulation of popular sentiments were needed to fan hostility into organized killing. By the early twentieth century, many Europeans had direct experience with mass violence and genocide in the territories they claimed for their empires.

Imperialism

European imperialism, especially its nineteenth-century forms, was a precondition to the Holocaust, although scholars disagree over how directly it can and should be linked. Through the experience of ruling over subject peoples in their overseas colonies and other conquered territories, Europeans gained habits of behavior and thought that lent themselves to developing hierarchies among peoples within Europe. From their experiences in Africa, Asia, and elsewhere, Europeans learned methods and technologies for oppressing and enslaving large groups of people. Ways of thinking about subject peoples whom Europeans considered inferior to themselves were also transferred onto targets of abuse within Europe, such as Jews. The notion that humanity was divided into races that struggled with one another for survival and dominance was in large part a product of the colonial experience.

Over the course of the nineteenth century, Europeans divided almost the entire continent of Africa among themselves. The British and French had large colonial holdings in Africa, as did the Portuguese, Belgians, Italians, and Germans. These and other European powers already dominated vast territories around the world. In Asia, the British controlled India, for example, and the Russians, Central Asia. The Dutch held Indonesia, and various European powers had colonies in the Pacific, the Caribbean, and the Americas.

The rule of law and protections of citizens' rights that had been introduced in many European jurisdictions by the late 1800s usually did not apply in the colonies, so missionaries, entrepreneurs, administrators, and military men often had very few limits on their behavior once they were overseas. They could and did use flogging, torture, and even death for offenses committed by native peoples that could not have been punished so severely at home. In the Belgian Congo, for example, European rubber magnates sometimes ordered that the hands be cut off of Africans whose production did not meet certain quotas.

Europeans' technological and military advantage enabled them to carry out such acts more or less with impunity. A massacre known as the Battle of Omdurman provides a graphic illustration. In 1898, a small group of British military on an expedition south of Egypt encountered resistance from local Sudanese tribesmen. The British, armed with machine guns, opened fire. The Sudanese, mounted on horseback and equipped with swords and other weapons for hand-to-hand combat, rode wave after wave into the barrage. The British killed an estimated eleven thousand Sudanese and lost only twenty-eight of their own men. Such events must have contributed to a sense among many Europeans that human life—at least the lives of people they considered inferior—was extremely cheap. Notions of superiority—racial, religious, cultural—were by no means unique to Germany. In the Belgian Congo, millions of Africans were killed by the Belgians and their agents. The Russians for their part proved to be brutal conquerors in the Caucasus.

Germans engaged in their own atrocities during the imperial era. Since 1883, Germany had a protectorate over Southwest Africa, today the country of

Namibia. By 1904 white pressure on native lands led to a revolt of the largest tribe in the area, the cattle-herding Herero. A smaller group called the Nama joined the rebellion. It took some fourteen thousand German soldiers three years to crush these uprisings. By 1907, fifteen hundred German men had died in the Southwest African conflict, half of them from illness.

But the Herero and Nama suffered far more. In what developed into genocide, the Germans slaughtered more than fifty thousand Herero and ten thousand Nama. They shot many, especially adult men; hunted women, children, and old people into the desert, where they died of thirst and starvation; and forced others into concentration camps, where inadequate food, horrendous conditions, and disease took a terrible toll. In the end, between 75 and 80 percent of all Hereros died; among the Nama the death rate was over 45 percent. This carnage was not ordered by German authorities in Berlin but evolved out of specific military goals: a demand for "total victory" and a drive to annihilate the enemy in order to prevent any possibility of resurgence. German accusations that the Africans were irregular combatants who shot from concealed positions, used women and children as warriors, and mutilated the bodies of their victims served to legitimate ruthless acts of "retaliation" that treated soldiers and civilians with equal viciousness. Such practices left a brutal legacy that would be evident in both World War I and World War II.

Anti-Slavic Attitudes

Looking back on European history, it seems evident that certain widespread German attitudes toward eastern Europeans, especially some Slavic peoples—Poles, Russians, Ukrainians, Czechs, Serbs, and others—also played into the atrocities of World War II. In earlier editions I followed convention and spoke of anti-Slavic attitudes, but it is not so simple. Slavic refers to a language group. Some Slavs were allied with Nazi Germany—Slovaks, Croats, Bulgarians—some were deemed enemies: Czechs, Serbs, Poles, Russians. Others, notably Ukrainians, found themselves in both categories at various times.

The extent and origins of negative ideas about eastern Europeans are hard to identify. Certainly nineteenth-century German nationalists commonly contrasted what they considered their culture's unique achievements with the supposed primitivism and barbarism of their neighbors to the east. Even the German language included slurs against Poles. For example, a common German expression for a chaotic situation was a "Polish economy." Many twentieth-century Germans claimed Polish people were backward, uneducated, slovenly, brutish, and childlike. The fact that eastern European industrialization lagged behind that of the west seemed to confirm those stereotypes for many Germans who conveniently ignored the artistic, cultural, and scientific achievements of their eastern neighbors. German projects of domination and Germanization of Polish lands during the nineteenth century in turn justified these ways of thinking.

It is often noticeable how recent "ancient hatreds" turn out to be when you look into them. Violence itself serves to create hatreds and hardens categories. Developments in the early twentieth century added new dimensions to German notions of superiority. After World War I, for the first time since the late 1700s, an independent Polish state was established. Until the war, territories in which many Polish people lived had been ruled by the German, Austro-Hungarian, and Russian empires. With the defeat of Germany, the collapse of tsarist Russia and the old Habsburg empire in Austria-Hungary in 1918, the way was cleared for creation of an independent Polish state. Many Germans resented this new neighbor and the loss of territories formerly under German control to Polish rule.

Instead of disbanding at the end of World War I, some German soldiers reformed themselves into units called the Freikorps (Free Corps) to fight Communists and others they considered Germany's enemies. Freikorps activities included attacks on Poles both inside Germany and across the border in Poland. During the decades before Hitler came to power, Germans inside Germany also encouraged the ethnic Germans who lived in Poland to provoke clashes with Polish authorities.

A similar situation existed with the German minority who lived in Czechoslovakia, a newly created state after World War I. Politically and economically weak, it was no match for its powerful German neighbor. Some members of Czechoslovakia's German-speaking population were happy enough to live in a country where they were far fewer in number than Czechs and Slovaks, but others resented their minority status. Here too Nazi agitators in the 1930s would find fertile ground for their notions of German superiority and their plans to rearrange the borders of Europe in Germany's favor.

Russian Revolution

Developments in Russia also added a new dimension to German suspicions. Germany won some of its most dramatic victories during World War I against Russia. In fact, the Russian military effort collapsed in 1917, and as soon as Lenin and the Bolsheviks had claimed control of the country, they sued for peace with Germany. It was all the more humiliating for the Germans a few months later in 1918, when, still flushed with their successes in the east, they had to concede defeat in the west and abandon all claims to the territories they had won from Russia.

The Russian Revolution of 1917 and the civil war that followed were dramatic and violent events. Accounts of the bloodshed reached Germany and, at least for some, seemed to add more reasons to fear and hate Russians. After World War I, many Germans believed they were surrounded by enemies who conspired for Germany's destruction. The fact that Communist ideology called for world revolution and the existence of a very visible Communist party in Germany itself after 1918 seemed proof that such a conspiracy was indeed under way.

Antisemitic Germans often linked their fear of the Soviet Union with their hatred of Jews. They pointed to some prominent Communists who were Jews or had Jewish names as evidence that Jews were somehow responsible for the Russian Revolution. Of course there were Jewish Communists, but there were also many non-Jewish Communists as well as many anti-Communist Jews. Sometimes antisemites imagined or invented Jewish identities for powerful individuals, such as Lenin, who was often described as Jewish but in fact came from a Russian Orthodox family. This tangled web of prejudices toward Poles, Russians, Communists, and Jews would emerge in a more massive and violent but still recognizable form in Hitler's Germany.

World War I and the Cheapening of Human Life

It is important to address the influence of World War I (1914–1918). This cataclysmic event had a profound impact on Europe and on the world as a whole. In significant ways it too formed part of the preconditions that set the stage for the Nazi era, World War II, and the Holocaust.

The connections between World War I and the horrors of the Nazi era are rather different than is often claimed. You may have read that the victorious French and their allies imposed such a humiliating peace on the defeated Germans after 1918 that the Germans had no choice but to seek the restoration of national honor at any price. You may also have read that the victors in World War I, in particular the French, forced the Germans to pay crushing reparations, thereby sparking hyperinflation in the 1920s and destroying the German economy. According to this line of argument, the desperate Germans turned to Hitler to rescue them and turned on the Jews as a scapegoat for their suffering.

Both of these common sets of assumptions are deeply flawed. The Germans did lose the war—in fact, it was their military leaders Generals Paul von Hindenburg and Erich Ludendorff in October 1918 who convinced the civilian government that it was necessary to sue for peace. And the Germans did have to accept the terms of the Treaty of Versailles in 1919, without having been part of the negotiations that drew up that accord. Still, the treaty was not exceptionally harsh. In fact, if you compare it to the Treaty of Brest Litovsk, which the Germans had imposed on the defeated Soviet Russia just a year earlier, you might almost call it generous.

In March 1918 the Germans had demanded that the Russians cede about 30 percent of their territory, including much of their agricultural, industrial, and mineral wealth. Under the terms of the Treaty of Versailles the Germans lost about 10 percent of their territory, much of it fairly recently acquired: Alsace and Lorraine, for example, taken in 1870 from France. Contrary to what is often said, the Treaty of Versailles did not blame the Germans for the war itself. Article 231, often referred to as the "war guilt clause," was not a moral judgment but a general, legal statement stipulating that Germany was responsible for paying for damages in the places outside Germany where most of the fighting had occurred. A similar clause appeared in the treaties with Germany's former allies Austria, Hungary, and Turkey.

As for reparations, the Germans paid only a very small amount of the bill originally presented to them, which was repeatedly adjusted downward. The victorious nations, above all the British and the French, had neither the ability to make Germany pay nor the will to risk another war after all the suffering and loss they had experienced between 1914 and 1918. Certainly the payments that were made imposed hardships on the Germans, and especially in the aftermath of a devastating war, the notion of reparations itself was psychologically harsh. All of Europe, however, faced terrible economic problems after what had been an extremely costly war, and the Germans were by no means alone in their difficulties, although admittedly the knowledge of widespread hardship probably provided little comfort to anyone.

World War I did not cause Nazism or World War II in such direct ways. Its impact was both less obvious and more insidious. Although the Germans ended World War I in better shape economically than many of the actual victors, they cultivated a politics of resentment that promoted a bitter sense of humiliation and poisoned the chances for the new German democracy formed in 1918. Refusal to accept the reality of defeat led many Germans to search for people to blame for what they perceived as a betrayal. That climate of scapegoating, in turn, created a kind of open season on many familiar outsiders. For example, old accusations that Jews had crucified Jesus dovetailed with the popular stab-in-the-back myth that blamed treacherous Jews for Germany's loss of the war. Communists, homosexuals, and hostile neighbors were blamed too, especially by German military leaders who falsely claimed that their forces had been undefeated in the field. Even the disabled came under attack, from legal and medical experts like Binding and Hoche, who resented them for receiving care that could have been devoted to men at the front.

World War I brought tremendous bloodshed and disastrous implications that extended far beyond Germany. An estimated 20 million Europeans died in the war and the epidemics and deprivations that followed in its wake; the war wiped out almost an entire generation of young men. Those who made it home again included many wounded, crippled, and shell-shocked. In addition to combat, blockades, food shortages, and disease took their tolls. From the Russian steppes to Belgium, from England to Serbia, by 1918 there would be scarcely a European family without casualties.

Entire nations based their postwar legitimacy on resentments about the war and the peace. Italians spoke of the "mangled peace." Hungarians felt cheated out of territory that went to Romania and Czechoslovakia. Romanians faced the challenge of incorporating vast new lands whose populations did not necessarily fit ideas of who was a reliable Romanian.

In many cases, soldiers, their families, and their political leaders emerged from four years of carnage with a deep fear of ever risking another war. In other cases, however, they took away different, and more dangerous, lessons: the notion that only in warfare could a man prove himself a real man; the conviction that the sense of camaraderie between fighting men was the most perfect form of human communion possible; the belief that sheer force was in the end stronger than anything in the world. Sometimes they and their families felt the sacrifice had been so high that losses must be avenged and gains defended at any cost.

Perhaps most importantly, the Great War, as it was called at the time, seemed to many Europeans to prove that human life was cheap and expendable. It brought home the extreme violence that had been practiced in the colonies with devastating results. It sparked a cult of violence that flourished in the brutality of the revolution and civil war in Russia, in the paramilitary groups that sprang up around Europe in its wake, and in the nihilistic pessimism of so many Europeans in the 1920s and 1930s. World War I did not lead inevitably to the rise of Nazism, the outbreak of World War II, or the Holocaust. However, the massive legacy of death and suffering it left behind did constitute one of the preconditions that made possible an unprecedented explosion of violence just two decades later.

2

LEADERSHIP AND WILL

HITLER, THE NATIONAL SOCIALIST GERMAN WORKERS' PARTY, AND NAZI IDEOLOGY

The previous chapter described some starting points and preconditions for the Nazi era: antisemitism, eugenics, racism, colonial violence, negative German attitudes toward Poland and Poles, and the brutalization of total war. If historical prejudices and tensions made the timber of European and German society combustible, Hitler lit the match that set the house on fire. This chapter examines the leadership provided by Adolf Hitler and the National Socialist German Workers' Party, better known as the Nazi Party. Who was Hitler, and what was his view of the world? How did he come to power in Germany? How was he transformed from an unremarkable individual into the leader of a massive enterprise of destruction?

ADOLF HITLER

Any discussion of Adolf Hitler (1889–1945) raises both general and specific questions about the role of the individual in making history. Do personalities shape events? Would the Nazi era, or World War II, or the Holocaust have occurred without Hitler? Certainly common wisdom assumes that Hitler was central to the shaping of those sets of events. There is no denying that Hitler has caught the popular imagination like no other tyrant—the evidence is ubiquitous. Fascination with Hitler seems to cut across all kinds of lines: nationality, age, gender, level of education.

Is so much interest in Hitler justified? Scholars in fact disagree about just how crucial Hitler was. One group, often referred to as intentionalists because they emphasize Hitler's intentions and consider the Holocaust the result of long-term planning, describes Hitler as the mastermind of mass murder. These scholars point to the consistency of Hitler's views from the early 1920s right down to his final testament in 1945. They emphasize the direct, hands-on way he made the major decisions in Nazi Germany.

Others, sometimes called functionalists because they describe the Holocaust as a function of other developments, especially during the war—something that evolved over time in an improvised way—downplay the role of Hitler. Some functionalists argue that Hitler was actually a weak dictator, more a pawn swept along by forces outside his control than the orchestrator of colossal events.

Scholars influenced by Marxism have also tended to pay little attention to Hitler. In their interpretations, Nazism was an extreme form of capitalism that had much more to do with broad, economic structures than with the ideas or actions of any one individual.

These debates about Hitler have moral as well as historical implications. Some people criticize the intentionalist stance because they think it focuses too much on Hitler and lets everyone else off the hook. Others attack the functionalist and Marxist positions for depersonalizing the past. They say that functionalists, who describe the Holocaust and other crimes of Nazism as the result of developments or events, draw attention away from the people who in fact made the decisions and took the actions that produced genocide. Still other people reject both the intentionalist and the functionalist positions and argue that we should pay less attention to the perpetrators altogether and concentrate instead on the victims of Nazi crimes.

In this book I proceed on the assumption that in order to understand the causes of Nazi crimes we need to study those who initiated and carried them out. With regard to Hitler I take what might be called a modified intentionalist position. Hitler was an essential factor in Nazism and the genocide it ignited. He did not have absolute control—even dictators depend on popular support—and a program as massive as the crimes of Nazism required many accomplices. Keenly aware of the need to appear powerful, Hitler paid scrupulous attention to his image: where and how he was photographed, the staging and design of public spectacles. But he was neither a mad megalomaniac who sought power for its own sake nor a mere opportunist; he operated from a consistent view of the world. Hitler could be flexible, pragmatic, and responsive to the situation "on the ground," but he set the agenda: he took the initiative and provided much of the drive and the will that put Germany on the path to war and genocide. Without Hitler, Nazism, World War II, and the Holocaust would have taken very different forms, if they had occurred at all.

Hitler and Mussolini during the German chancellor's visit to Italy in 1934. Heinrich Hoffmann, Hitler's favorite photographer, took this picture. It reveals the photographer's privileged position—notice how close he could get to the leaders—and reflects the public relations priorities and challenges of "the Führer." Framed to highlight Hitler's taller stature, the image contrasts Hitler, in the suit and tie of the statesman, with Mussolini, in Fascist military garb. Hitler was a great admirer of the Duce, and in 1934 Mussolini was the senior partner, although this relationship would change dramatically. Here even the expert photographer could not conceal the distance between the two men, Mussolini's disinterest, and Hitler's discomfort.

A Brief Biography

Adolf Hitler was born in 1889 in the small Austrian border town of Braunau am Inn. Not much is known with certainty about Hitler's childhood, because the most detailed source—his autobiographical book *Mein Kampf* ("My Struggle")—was a work of propaganda intended to depict him as someone who had been marked from his earliest days for greatness. In fact,

Hitler's early life seems to have been fairly typical for a middle-class boy in late nineteenth-century central Europe.

Adolf was the fourth child of an Austrian customs official and his third wife, but the first to live past infancy. The family was comfortable although not wealthy and did well enough to afford a cook and a maid. Adolf's father, Alois, was a strict, authoritarian man with a bad temper, who seems to have taken little interest in his family. For reasons now unknown, Alois changed his last name from Schicklgruber to Hitler, more than a decade before the birth of the son who would make the new name notorious. Alois Hitler died in 1903, when Adolf was still an adolescent.

Adolf's mother, Klara, was much younger than her husband, whom she met when she worked as a maid in his household. According to the account of her doctor, Klara Hitler was a gentle, pious woman devoted to her children, especially her one surviving son. Adolf returned the affection and later wrote in *Mein Kampf*, "I had honored my father, but loved my mother." Other than his mother, Hitler does not seem to have been close to anyone in his family.

Even decades after his death the rumor persists that Hitler had "Jewish blood." That claim is false. It is true that Hitler did not know the identity of his paternal grandfather, because his father, Alois, was born to an unmarried woman. Alois was baptized into the Roman Catholic Church, as his son Adolf would be, too. In the 1920s and later, rumors circulated that Adolf Hitler's grandmother had been a maid in a Jewish household and had become pregnant by one of her employers' sons. Those allegations were unfounded. In fact there were no Jews in the town where Hitler's grandmother lived, because Jews were prohibited from living in that part of Austria at the time.

What is the significance of this rumor? First of all it shows the extent to which people in Hitler's time became obsessed with issues of blood and race. In Nazi Germany, accusations of so-called Jewish blood were a sure way to discredit someone. It is no surprise that similar rumors circulated about many top Nazis and about other people, too.

The persistence of such a rumor may also tell us something about our own society. What would it actually explain even if the rumor of Hitler's "Jewish blood" were true? Obviously nothing, just as it would explain nothing if there were any truth to the claims that Hitler was secretly homosexual or that he had only one testicle. (Both of those common allegations, to the best of anyone's knowledge, are false as well.) Such claims reflect a desire to find easy explanations for historical processes that in fact have many complicated causes. Rumors of that kind also reflect a widespread tendency to blame the victims for their misfortunes, as if someone who was "part Jewish," or "secretly gay," or in some way disabled might somehow be expected to initiate programs to murder Jews, persecute gay men, or kill people with disabilities. An honest understanding of history requires a critical—and self-critical—response to such simplistic notions.

As a child Hitler was a mediocre student. Later, in *Mein Kampf*, he would claim that he led his class in geography and history. That was not the case, although he did better in those subjects than in some others, where he received failing grades. When he was sixteen he dropped out of school. Young Hitler spent the next two and a half years in the Austrian city of Linz, idling, dreaming, drawing, and redesigning the city on paper. He always had a penchant for grandiose plans.

In 1907 Hitler relocated to Vienna, where he planned to study art. He failed to get into art school, however, a fact he concealed from members of his family and even close friends for as long as possible. Hitler's many drawings, paintings, and architectural sketches showed some technical ability but little creativity. It is not surprising that years after his death an ambitious forger would have no trouble cranking out many convincing fakes. Hitler later made much of his dire poverty during his years in Vienna, and he did face some hard times when he could not afford lodgings and had to live in a men's shelter. His means of support included selling cards on which he painted local scenes. During most of his young adult years in Vienna, however, Hitler received funds from his family that enabled him to live quite comfortably without ever being employed. For example, he could afford to see Richard Wagner's opera *Lohengrin* and other favorites over and over again.

While in Vienna Hitler picked up on many ideas and currents around him. He was interested in Pan-Germanism—the conviction that Germans should be unified in one state instead of dispersed throughout central and eastern Europe—as well as in ultranationalism and antisemitism. He admired Karl Lueger, mayor of Vienna from 1895 to 1910 and a member of the antisemitic Christian Social Party. Lueger's use of propaganda particularly impressed Hitler.

In Vienna Hitler began to fuse his ideas into a worldview and to get acquainted with political extremists of various kinds. He became enthusiastic about Social Darwinist theories that described life as a struggle between so-called races. His reading consisted mostly of popular tracts about mythology, biology, and even the occult. Hitler preferred to read summaries and pamphlets rather than the actual writings of people such as the philosopher Friedrich Nietzsche. Enthusiasm for the operas of Wagner encouraged Hitler's tendencies toward a grandiose style. If you have seen or heard any of Wagner's operas you know something about their huge casts, imposing music, exaggerated passions, and powerful depictions of Germanic myth; all of those elements inspired Hitler as he developed his own vision of politics and power.

In 1913 Hitler left Vienna for Munich. He crossed the border from Austria to Germany in violation of Austrian law, which required him as an able-bodied young man to perform military service for his homeland. Hitler's motivations for moving are not known for certain, but he had never made a secret of his contempt for the Austrian government and his conviction that the future lay with Germany.

In Munich Hitler's self-education was interrupted by the outbreak of war in 1914. He volunteered for the German army, where he reached the rank of corporal. Hitler served as a runner who relayed messages from the rear to the front. The job had its dangers, and he was wounded in action and awarded an Iron Cross for bravery. But it was not the combat role he would later imply he had played, and it is now evident that much of what Hitler claimed about his wartime past was exaggerated or invented. Once he became a celebrity, he made sure to block people who had served with him from publicizing their versions of events. The last thing he needed was a report by a superior commenting that he lacked leadership qualities or an admission by a member of his unit that he had no recollection of the gawky runner, usually shown in photographs off to the side and disengaged from the other men.

It is not completely clear when and how Hitler developed his fanatical antisemitism. In Vienna he certainly came into frequent contact with antisemites, although he also had acquaintances, associates, and even what might be called friends there who were Jewish. In any case, Hitler's experience of Germany's defeat in World War I deepened and hardened his hatred of Jews, and he would later claim that his conversion to antisemitism came in 1918. To his mind, the Jews were somehow to blame. That reaction was completely unfounded; German and Austro-Hungarian Jews had fought and died loyally alongside fellow citizens in their countries' armies. But as he would do with every disappointment he faced throughout his life, whether it was failing to get into art school or losing a war, Hitler considered the Jews at fault. In this respect he was not different from many other people of his time or of Western civilization in general, which for centuries had made a habit of blaming Jews for everything from the Black Death to the French Revolution.

In 1919, a year after the war ended, Hitler got involved in a political organization called the German Workers' Party. It would soon change its name to the National Socialist German Workers' Party. The German acronym was NSDAP. English speakers commonly use the abbreviation "Nazi," taken from the first two syllables of the German pronunciation of "National." Within a year Hitler had become a full-time agitator and extremely popular speaker for the group.

On November 9, 1923, Hitler and a group of co-conspirators that included the war hero Erich Ludendorff launched what became known as the Beer Hall Putsch in Munich. They intended to overthrow the government of Bavaria in order to install a regime that would be the beginning of a national revival in Germany. Poorly planned and disorganized, the Putsch failed; Hitler was captured and sentenced to five years in prison for high treason. He served only thirteen months in Landsberg Prison, where he was treated like a celebrity by most of the staff and many of his fellow inmates. So many admirers flocked to visit him that he eventually stopped receiving them in order to have time to write the book he had begun. By the time Hitler was released in 1925, he had written and published *Mein Kampf*, a combination of memoir and propaganda tract. The book did not become a best seller until Hitler became chancellor of Germany in 1933.

In this earlier phase of his career, Hitler was still relatively obscure, part of the fringe elements that proliferated in German society after World War I. Most Germans outside Bavaria knew little about him and did not take him seriously. His modest background, his relatively unremarkable military career, and his lack of education and experience with the wider world all made him seem almost laughable to some of the people he encountered. For example, one German aristocrat, a Bavarian baron called Fritz Percy Reck-Malleczewen, described his early impressions of Hitler with contempt. He once saw Hitler in a deserted restaurant in the early 1930s, Reck-Malleczewen recorded in his journal, later published as *Diary of a Man in Despair*. Reck-Malleczewen had a pistol in his pocket and could easily have killed the future dictator. "But I mistook him for a cartoon character," the baron wrote, looking back on the event, "and I did not shoot."

Because of the tremendous fascination with Hitler, the person, we know quite a bit about some details of his daily life. He was a vegetarian who loved animals and hated cigarette smoke. He liked to watch movies, especially comedies, and enjoyed reading Westerns, like those by the popular German writer Karl May. May, like Hitler, never set foot in the Americas. Hitler's most intense emotional attachment after the death of his mother seems to have been his relationship with his niece Geli Raubal, the daughter of his half-sister Angela. Hitler had invited Angela to live with him to supervise his household in Munich.

Evidence points toward some kind of affair between Hitler and his much younger niece. Proud of the vivacious young woman and possessive of her time and attention, Hitler was often seen with her in public. Geli seems to have chafed under the control of her domineering uncle, and some observers later claimed she was trying to get away from him. In 1931 Geli died under suspicious circumstances. The official verdict was suicide, but rumors of foul play persisted for years. The young woman was found in her uncle's Munich apartment, shot with his pistol. Stories circulated—Geli was pregnant, people whispered; she had a Jewish lover, some hinted; her jealous uncle had her killed, people speculated. Given the few documents and witnesses available and the years that have since passed, it is unlikely that we will ever get to the bottom of events surrounding Geli Raubal. Scandalous and intriguing as the whole affair is, it does not seem to have played a major role in shaping Hitler or his view of the world.

Indeed, none of the details of Hitler's life that can be found have managed to provide the clue needed to explain the strengths of his obsessions or his ability to realize his convictions. The magnitude of the crimes he initiated remains oddly out of proportion to the banality of his person and his life.

Hitler's Worldview

It is impossible to talk about Nazi ideas without borrowing Nazi terminology, most of which, even translated into English, is offensive, nonsensical, or both. Words like "Aryan," "race," and "blood" had particular meanings within the Nazi system of thought, but those terms do not describe objective realities. However, once Nazi ideology became enshrined in laws and regulations and implemented in practice, such labels took on very real implications of life and death.

The main elements of Hitler's ideology developed during his years in Vienna, his time in Munich, and his years with the German army during and immediately after World War I. Those ideas remained remarkably constant from the beginning of his political career in the early 1920s to his death in 1945.

Hitler's core ideas can be summed up in the phrase "race and space." Hitler was obsessed with two notions: that humanity was engaged in a gigantic struggle between "races," or communities of "blood"; and that "pure Germans," members of the so-called Aryan race, needed space to expand, living space that Hitler called by the German term *Lebensraum*. For Hitler, these two notions of race and space were intertwined. Any race that was not expanding, he believed, was doomed to disappear. Without living space—land to produce food and raise new generations of soldiers and mothers—a race could not grow. Hitler saw the potential living space for German "Aryans" to Germany's east, in the territories of Poland and the Soviet Union. The "races" that he considered prime threats to the survival and dominance of his "Aryans" were the Poles, Russians, and others who occupied that land and the Jews, who, in his theory, sought to infiltrate, weaken, and destroy German strength.

What was an "Aryan"? Like all races the category "Aryan" was an invention, a social construction rather than a physical fact. Hitler did not coin the term "Aryan" but borrowed it from eighteenth- and nineteenth-century European racial theorists who used various labels for the categories into which they divided humanity. The word "Aryan" originally referred to a group of people in ancient India. Hitler drew on vague theories that these people, supposedly taller and lighter skinned than their neighbors, were a superior group who somehow ended up in Europe, where they continued to be the bearers of all cultural creativity. Hitler and other Nazi writers tended to be rather vague when it came to the details of their theories, and they were not troubled by internal contradictions. Thus Hitler considered the ancient Greeks to have been Aryans; so, at least in his mind, were the best elements in ancient Rome as well as the Germanic tribes that finally destroyed Roman power.

Using the term "Aryan" to describe his supposed master race gave Hitler a degree of flexibility that proved very useful. Had he simply preached the "German" master race he would have had to find some way to exclude German Jews, many of whom were certainly as German as their fellow citizens in terms of language and ethnicity. Emphasis on "German" rather than "Aryan" superiority would also have made it difficult to find allies for the wars ahead.

Had Hitler drawn exclusively on terms like "Nordic," which tended to describe physical appearance rather than less visible qualities of blood and character, he might have had some explaining to do with regard to the inclusion of many loyal Nazis in the privileged category. As it was, jokes circulated during the Nazi years about the less-than-perfect specimens who led the supposed master race: "What does the ideal Aryan look like? As tall as Goebbels, as slim as Göring, as handsome as Himmler, and as blond as Hitler." In fact, propaganda minister Joseph Goebbels was short and had a clubfoot. Hermann Göring, commander of the German air force, was a fat man, Heinrich Himmler, head of the SS, was notoriously homely, and Hitler had dark hair.

In general the label "Aryan" combined the ring of scientific authority with the vague, elastic quality of a new invention. It could be and was redefined as needed to fit the imperatives of race and space. The only reliable constant was the claim that "Aryan" was the opposite of "Jew."

By the early 1920s, hatred of Jews was a fixed point in Hitler's ideology. No mere opportunist, he maintained until his death a fanatical antipathy to anything he considered Jewish. Hitler's antisemitism incorporated all of the strands of previous generations. It had metaphysical dimensions: he regularly spoke of Jews as evil enemies of virtue and honor. It was political, too: his theory of a Jewish conspiracy extended in every direction. At various times Hitler described Communism, capitalism, liberalism, anarchism, atheism, Christianity, Britain, the United States, and France as parts of some international Jewish plot. There were cultural elements to Hitler's antisemitism: he considered jazz, abstract art, and many other forms of modernism somehow degenerate and "Jewish," because, in his view, they distorted reality and lured people away from racial purity.

Of course, Hitler's hostility included familiar social and economic resentments. He shared all the stereotypes of Jews as greedy bankers, legalistic pedants, lecherous males, and seductive, destructive females. "Jewish" to him meant everything he considered negative, the antithesis of the supposedly perfect

Aryan. Hitler regarded Jewishness as a race, a biological fact that could not be altered by any change of religion, name, or habits. The sheer multidimensionality of Hitler's antisemitism gave it a kind of mass appeal. Many Germans could find something in it they shared, even if they did not buy the whole package.

Hitler drew on old forms of antisemitism, but he combined them in ways that produced something new. The historian Saul Friedländer has labeled Hitler's particular strain of hatred "redemptive antisemitism." By this phrase Friedländer means that Hitler combined a murderous rage with an idealistic goal. Hitler, and the hard-core Nazis who accepted his views, had a religious fervor, a fanatical conviction that attacks on Jews were necessary to save the

„Wenn ihr ein Kreuz seht, dann denkt an den grauenhaften Mord der Juden auf Golgatha…“

An illustration from a 1938 German children's book. Nazi antisemitic propaganda borrowed images and accusations from Christian anti-Jewish traditions. The text at the bottom reads, "When you see a cross, think of the horrible murder committed by the Jews on Golgotha." Here the reference is to the old lie that Jews crucified Jesus; Golgotha is a hill outside Jerusalem.

world for Aryan Germany. Hitler stated his faith at the end of the second chapter of *Mein Kampf:* "Today I believe that I am acting in accordance with the will of the Almighty Creator: by defending myself against the Jew, I am fighting for the work of the Lord."

Hitler's view of "the Jew" was full of internal contradictions. He called Jewish men effeminate and weak yet also characterized them as sexual predators. He denounced Jews as inferior idiots yet believed they had a cunning intelligence, which made them a diabolical threat to the supposedly superior

A poster produced for *Der Stürmer* announces publication of a newspaper that will reveal the identity of the murderer in a case in the Saar-Palatinate, a region in western Germany. The words RITUAL MURDER and the Star of David made it clear that the answer given would be "the Jew," represented here as a menace to the safety and purity of "Aryan" womanhood. *Der Stürmer* was posted in public places all over Germany. Here we see the power of juxtaposition in a visual image: merely by putting the face of the woman with her hair pulled back next to the star, the poster links Jewish men with rape.

"Aryans." Certain images enabled him to reconcile these contradictory accusations, at least rhetorically. One of his favorites was that of the germ. A germ or a parasite, Hitler was fond of pointing out, was very small, even invisible, and yet it had an incredible, superhuman ability to kill. He claimed that Jews were similar: they might seem few and weak, but according to Hitler's paranoid view, they had enormous powers of destruction.

Another important feature of Hitler's ideology was its sense of urgency. According to Hitler, time was running out: it was five to midnight for the Aryan race, he warned, and the clock was ticking. The race was already dangerously polluted, he insisted; if it were not saved immediately it would perish. That notion of impending doom added an apocalyptic dimension to Hitler's thought. His belief in the necessity—and desirability—of war gave that mythical struggle concrete form. Only war would redeem the Aryan race, Hitler maintained: war in the name of racial purity and in the quest for living space.

Other traits of Hitler's worldview were also connected to his key notions of race and space. Hitler became a vociferous anti-Communist, although for a brief period right after World War I he served the revolutionary Socialists in Bavaria, and even in power he proved willing to make at least temporary concessions toward Communism in favor of his more central goals. By the late 1920s he regularly linked Communism and Bolshevism with Jews, and he accused Jews of creating Communism as part of a plot to destroy Germany. The popular notion that Jews and Communists caused Germany to lose the war in 1918—the so-called stab in the back myth—fit neatly into this mind-set. During World War II, Hitler would return repeatedly to the idea of some diabolical Jewish-Communist plot in order to rally Germany against the Soviet Union. One of Hitler's typical terms of derision was "Bolshevik Jewish internationalists."

Hitler's ideas about women and men also fit into his worldview. He claimed that he would restore women to what he called their rightful place in the home. He regarded women's bodies as important to the state, because they produced new generations of soldiers and breeders. But women's bodies in Hitler's view could also be the floodgates to racial impurity, the means through which supposed pollutants entered the Aryan bloodstream. Some German women found such theories appealing, because they seemed to offer women a powerful position as mothers and guardians of the master race. Others recognized the misogyny inherent in Nazi ideas.

Hitler's sexism and antisemitism were mutually reinforcing. He used anti-woman images and vocabulary to belittle Jews and other so-called enemies. At the same time, he equated feminists with Jews and derided Jewish men as defilers of Aryan womanhood and champions of homosexuality and other supposed perversions. Such sexual images caught the attention of Hitler's audiences and played on many of their own anxieties.

Hitler endorsed a position that he and other National Socialists referred to as the "Führer principle." The German term *der Führer* means "the leader" in English. Hitler would later take that title for himself. The Führer principle meant commitment to uncontested leadership. When individuals in the Nazi organization grew powerful enough to pose a potential threat to Hitler's position, he found ways to clip their wings, even if it meant temporarily weakening the Nazi Party's base of support. Hitler believed power had to be focused in order to be effective; the crucial focal point, in his view, was himself.

As Führer, Hitler demanded total loyalty from his followers. One of his most devoted associates turned out to be Joseph Goebbels, later minister of propaganda, who wrote in his diary: "I love you, AH." Hitler rewarded faithful subordinates with privileges, powers, and, in special cases, access to him and his inner circle. Admittedly, spending time with the Führer had disadvantages even for the most dedicated Nazis: his impromptu speeches, lectures, and dinner diatribes could last for hours and often put his listeners to sleep. Nevertheless, the Nazi focus on Hitler as leader gave the movement and subsequently the entire system a powerful dynamic that the historian Ian Kershaw calls "working toward the Führer." Once his position and power were assured, Hitler did not need to issue specific orders in most cases. It was enough to let his wishes be known in general terms and his underlings would rush to fulfill and even anticipate them, in the hope of winning his favor and advancing their own careers. In the words of one Nazi functionary: "It is the duty of every single person to attempt, in the spirit of the Führer, to work towards him."

The Führer principle was also linked to the goals of race and space. Hitler was convinced that he needed unquestioned power to complete his historic mission. Democracy, he claimed, was a product of Jewish-Bolshevik liberal internationalism; in his opinion, democratic institutions obstructed the work of "great individuals." Hitler's Führer principle was both a means to achieve his policies of race and space and an end in itself.

Adolf Hitler was not a brilliant, original thinker. There was nothing really new about his ideas. His ideology was a mix of nineteenth-century racial theories, Social Darwinism, post–World War I resentments, antisemitism, and sexism dressed up in familiar symbols drawn from nationalism, mythology, and even Christianity, although Hitler and many of his closest associates simultaneously professed and detested Christianity, which they considered a religion for the weak. What was different was the intensity with which he held his views and his ability to captivate large audiences in such a way that many who heard him speak felt he gave voice to their own feelings and beliefs. Above all, what differentiated Hitler from the many other demagogues and ideologues in Europe between the wars was the tremendous power he achieved after he became chancellor of Germany in 1933. From that position he was able to harness an entire government—its military, diplomacy, and bureaucracy—behind implementation of his notions of race and space.

Old Fighters and "True Believers"—The Inner Circle

Hitler neither developed his ideas in a vacuum nor rose to power alone. A rather motley crew of men formed his inner circle. Its membership changed many times, as people fell in and out of favor. Three individuals who stuck with Hitler throughout his political career and gained international profiles were Hermann Göring, Joseph Goebbels, and Heinrich Himmler. All of them would play key roles in the Nazi regime, each amassing enormous power even as they fought among themselves for dominance and for Hitler's favor.

Hermann Göring (1893–1946) was a hero of World War I who rose through the air force to become commander of the famous Richthofen Squadron. Somewhat at a loss after the war ended with Germany's defeat and massive demilitarization, he joined the Nazi Party in 1922. One of Hitler's oldest associates, Göring had the distinction of having been wounded at the Beer Hall Putsch in 1923. Nazi lingo reserved the label "old fighters" for those of the faithful who had been members before the failed Putsch.

Hitler often presented Göring as one of Nazism's more respectable figures. Göring's father had been a judge and consular official, and he had ties with conservative and nationalist circles. Göring senior had even served as resident minister plenipotentiary in German Southwest Africa, site of the German genocide of the Herero and Nama people in 1907. In fact there was a major street named after him in Windhoek, the capital of Namibia (now Daniel Munamava Street).

Throughout the 1930s Hitler showered appointments on Hermann Göring. When the Nazi Party became the largest party in the German parliament, Göring became president of the Reichstag (as the German parliament was called). Göring established the Gestapo, a political police force, and was named commander in chief of the Luftwaffe (air force). In 1936 Hitler chose Göring to head the Four-Year Plan to prepare Germany for war. A swaggering, flamboyant individual who relished luxury and excess, Göring was also an ambitious schemer and a vicious infighter.

Joseph Goebbels (1897–1945) was a rather different kind of Nazi. A journalist and writer, he had a PhD and wrote a novel called *Michael*, although it remained unpublished until the Nazi Party press picked it up in 1929. Goebbels first came into contact with members of the Nazi Party in 1924; by 1926 he was Gauleiter (Party leader) of Berlin, and two years later Hitler made him head of propaganda. In 1933 Goebbels became minister for popular enlightenment and propaganda. He kept that post throughout the entire Third Reich, although his ambitious, energetic nature meant that he was always trying to find ways to play even bigger roles.

Goebbels was a master propagandist who excelled in stirring up hatred and orchestrating gigantic extravaganzas, such as the annual Nazi Party rallies. He was the only one of Hitler's early associates who stayed with him right to the end. When Hitler committed suicide in 1945, Goebbels did so, too: he and his wife, Magda, had their children poisoned before he had her and himself shot. Goebbels's extensive diaries, large parts of which have been published, reveal him to have been a "true believer," committed to Hitler as a person and to realization of his ideas. To many observers Goebbels was the sinister face

Joseph Goebbels caught off guard by renowned photographer Alfred Eisenstaedt at a League of Nations conference in Geneva in 1933. Here, in a moment not stage-managed by the Nazis, something of the propaganda minister's sinister character is revealed. Of this image Eisenstaedt said, "This picture could be titled 'From Goebbels with Love.'"

of Nazism, an image captured by photographer Alfred Eisenstaedt in a 1933 picture taken at the League of Nations conference in Geneva. Eisenstaedt, who was Jewish, left Germany in the 1930s for the United States, where he became one of LIFE magazine's most celebrated photographers.

It was not Goebbels but his rival Heinrich Himmler (1900–1945) who would become, next to Hitler, the most powerful man in the Third Reich. Head of the elite Nazi guard known as the Schutzstaffel (SS) from 1929 to 1945, by 1936 Himmler had also become chief of all German police. In these positions he presided over a vast network of offices and agencies that implemented terror and mass murder all over German-occupied Europe.

Himmler was neither flashy like Göring nor educated like Goebbels. Mousy and awkward as a young man, he read voraciously and had developed his own conspiratorial view of the world even before he met Hitler in 1926. Like Hitler, Himmler feared and hated Jews and believed in the superiority of the so-called Aryan race. Himmler too was convinced that Germany had to expand to the east. Dogged and capable of meticulous attention to detail, Himmler involved himself directly in projects that targeted homosexual men and Roma as well as Poles and Jews. With justification the historians Richard Breitman and Peter Longerich consider Himmler the "architect" of Nazi genocide.

Himmler was not personally charismatic, but his enormous power and access to Hitler caused ambitious men to flock to him. He had a knack for identifying highly capable, driven individuals who would prove ruthless in pursuit of their goals. Some, like Reinhard Heydrich (1904–1942), whom Himmler personally recruited for the SS and named chief of its Security Service, became almost as famous as their boss. Others, with Himmler's help, made tremendously successful careers, particularly during the war, but are no longer household names. For example, Odilo Globocnik, Friedrich Jeckeln, and Erich von dem Bach-Zelewski, three of Himmler's trusted associates, achieved positions of almost unbounded power in the occupied east. Together they were responsible for the murder of literally millions of people.

There were no women in Hitler's inner circle, nor did any women wield direct political power. The closest was Gertrud Scholtz-Klink (1902–1999), national women's leader from 1934 until 1945. A true believer in Hitler's worldview, Scholtz-Klink described herself as fighting for Hitler's cause with the weapons of a woman. According to Scholtz-Klink, the crowning achievement of a Nazi woman was motherhood. Her own three marriages produced eleven children. Hitler referred to Scholtz-Klink and her Nazi women's organizations when it suited him to do so, but he did not consult her or for that matter seem to take her seriously. Like many women in the Third Reich, Scholtz-Klink played the role of the enthusiastic supporter and beneficiary of Nazism.

Heinrich Himmler speaks to an inmate at Dachau in 1936, during an SS inspection of the camp. Opened with much fanfare in March 1933, Dachau was the first official concentration camp in Nazi Germany. This photograph, clearly taken to showcase Himmler, displays the spectacle of SS power, with the horde of uniformed men pressing in on one inmate.

THE NAZI RISE TO POWER

How did Hitler come to power in Germany? It is important first to outline some of the common—and mistaken—answers to this question. Hitler's rise to power was not inevitable. It was neither an automatic product of Germany's defeat in World War I nor the unavoidable result of the Great Depression. Hitler was not swept to power by a stampede of German voters hypnotized by his oratorical skills, nor did he seize power in an illegal coup d'état. The road that brought Adolf Hitler into the chancellor's seat by 1933 was both less direct and more mundane than these standard interpretations suggest. Briefly put, it was a combination of difficult circumstances, political maneuvering, luck, treachery, and miscalculation on the part of many people that catapulted Hitler into power.

The Weimar Republic

What was the situation in Germany prior to Hitler's rule? In the wake of military defeat in 1918, Germans introduced a form of government new to them: a republic based on a democratic constitution. It has become known as the Weimar Republic, after the city of Weimar, which served as its temporary capital until the situation in Berlin was stable enough for the government to set up shop there.

In hindsight it is easy to dismiss the Weimar Republic as a failed experiment in German democracy, nothing more than a chaotic prelude to Nazism. In fact, although novel in many ways, the Weimar Republic built on long-standing political parties, legal and bureaucratic structures, and even electoral practices in Germany. Moreover, it lasted two years longer than the Nazi regime Hitler and his followers promised would be a "Thousand-Year Reich." The Weimar Republic persisted in some form for fourteen years, from its proclamation in November 1918 to Adolf Hitler's appointment as chancellor in January 1933.

The Weimar Republic witnessed considerable achievements in the political and cultural spheres as well as in foreign policy and the economy. Antidemocratic Germans often complained that the victorious powers of World War I had forced democracy on a defeated Germany. The Weimar Republic, however, was able to build on liberal and democratic tendencies within Germany that predated the war. Under the Weimar Constitution of 1919, Germany became the first major European power after Russia to give women the vote. Weimar Germany produced the most modern, innovative film industry in the world at the time, and it returned Germany to international respectability with the country's incorporation into the League of Nations in 1926. In short, the existence of the Weimar Republic by no means made Hitler's rise inevitable.

It may come as a surprise that Weimar Germany had the strongest economy in continental Europe for most if not all of its history. Its postwar recovery was eased by the fact that very little of the fighting in World War I had taken place on German soil. As a result Germany's infrastructure and industry remained mostly intact. In contrast, Germany's neighbors to the west—France and Belgium—had been demolished by the war. They sought reparations, but the Germans managed to avoid paying most of the sums charged, by negotiating the amounts downward, by falling behind on payments, and eventually by ceasing payments altogether. To the east, the territories of Poland and the Soviet Union had been on the whole less industrialized than Germany already before 1914. The enormous costs and devastation of years of war put their struggling economies even further behind the Germans.

Of course Weimar Germany faced very real economic problems itself, the most dramatic of which was inflation. In 1923, inflationary tendencies spiraled into a hyperinflation that saw the value of the German Mark plummet to impossible levels. The situation got so bad that people needed enormous quantities of bills merely to buy a loaf of bread or a glass of beer. Images of desperate

Germans demanding their pay hourly before it could become worthless and moving their petty cash in wheelbarrows have become standard features in histories of the Weimar years.

The hyperinflation of 1923, however, was not simply the result of crushing reparations payments, as is often assumed. Instead it was irresponsible fiscal policies on the part of the German government during the war and an attempt to thwart French and Belgian efforts to seize reparations directly from Germany afterward that destroyed the value of the German currency. Moreover, all of Europe experienced inflation after the war, although the months of massive inflation in Germany in 1923 were especially dramatic.

As in any inflation, some Germans lost a great deal. Those on fixed incomes, such as pensioners, and people who had loaned out money were particularly hard hit. Yet there were also big winners in 1923, as is true of every inflationary situation: people with property in forms other than money, speculators, and above all debtors who could pay back what they owed in currency worth a fraction of its value when they borrowed it. Currency reform in 1923 halted the hyperinflation and began a period of economic stabilization in Germany that lasted until the end of the decade. By the time Hitler came to power, the hyperinflation of 1923 was ten years in the past.

Weimar Germany's situation in terms of national security was also much stronger than is often recognized. The venerable Habsburg Empire, once Germany's rival for power in central Europe, disappeared completely in the war, leaving a small, weak Austria as Germany's neighbor to the south. Before World War I, the Habsburg Empire had ruled large parts of central and eastern Europe, including territories that now lie in Austria, Poland, Hungary, the Czech Republic, Slovakia, Croatia, and other countries. After the war, those lands were organized as much smaller, independent countries that often had reasons to focus their animosities on one another rather than competing with or challenging German power in Europe.

After World War I, Germany's former rival to the east, the once formidable Russian Empire, was gone too, replaced by Lenin's new Soviet Union. Racked by civil war until the early 1920s, the Soviet Union was in no position to threaten German interests. In any case, the postwar settlement in Europe meant that Germany no longer shared a border with Russia, because the creation of an independent Poland created a buffer between the two larger nations. After 1918, Germany's immediate neighbors included Poland in the east and Czechoslovakia in the southeast. Poland had a long national history but was newly reestablished as a state, for which its people had paid a high price: in addition to losses in the World War, the Poles had also stopped a Soviet offensive in 1920. Czechoslovakia was a tenuous, new nation engaged in its own struggles for stability.

In short, all of Europe faced enormous economic, political, and social challenges in the 1920s. Even Great Britain, with its massive empire, was weakened after years of war. The British retained wartime rationing of bread longer after hostilities ended in November 1918 than did the Germans. The Weimar Republic had as good a chance to survive as did most of its European counterparts. Being surrounded by neighbors poorer and weaker than itself gave it some significant advantages.

World War I and the Myth of a Stab in the Back

But what about the shame of defeat? Many people assume that Germans who wished to return their nation to greatness naturally turned to Hitler to lead them out of humiliation. This view is oversimplified. Military defeat need not usher in tyranny and destruction. In fact it can generate reassessment and reform, as was the case after 1806, when Prussia's defeat at Napoleon's hands led Prussian reformers to introduce remarkable changes to their country's military, bureaucracy, and system of education. Likewise, it was Russian defeat in the Crimean War of 1853–1856 that prompted the tsar to free the serfs. In Germany after 1918, however, such positive change was blocked by a widespread refusal to accept the reality of defeat.

In the fall of 1918 Germany's military leadership—Generals Paul von Hindenburg and Erich Ludendorff—had insisted on suing for peace. Germany simply did not have the resources to fight on, its top generals realized. Even before the armistice was concluded, however, they began to spin their account of events to save their own reputations. They claimed it was not the military but German civilians who had lost their nerve. It was the disloyal, revolutionary home front, they accused, that had stabbed the fighting men in the back and betrayed them to their enemies.

The myth of a stab in the back spread quickly. Many Germans needed an explanation for defeat in a war that their military leadership had never let on it was losing. The fact that the war ended with almost no foreign troops on German soil lent credence to the idea of betrayal from within Germany. And the notion of an undefeated military fit with comforting myths about national greatness. In the eyes of many Germans, their new, democratic government symbolized the civilian weaklings who had supposedly betrayed Germany's fighting heroes. This perception in turn undercut the authority of the Weimar Republic.

Hitler would later capitalize on the stab-in-the-back myth. He was able to do so because, by the time he appeared on the national scene, the idea had been propagated within Germany for more than a decade: by military leaders who refused to take responsibility for defeat; by nationalist professors, schoolteachers, and clergy; and by antidemocratic politicians and publicists who found it easier to live in a glorified past than to face the challenges of the present. Defeat in World War I did not make Hitler's rise to power inevitable, but the way that many Germans chose to respond to the challenges of defeat weakened the base of support of their own government and prepared the way for even more extreme manipulation of public opinion.

The National Socialist German Workers' Party in the 1920s

From its beginnings, the Weimar Republic faced a crisis of legitimacy. Its critics on the left wanted a revolutionary, Communist regime instead of a liberal, democratic republic. Conservatives and those further to the right considered the whole idea of democracy to be weak, ineffective, and non-German. Beset by extremists of all kinds, Weimar authorities tended to crack down hard on the left but treat the right with leniency.

The new government in 1918 had not purged the judiciary or the civil service, so the republic's judges, lawyers, and bureaucrats were the same people who had served the German kaiser before World War I. Many of them were less than enthusiastic about the democratic constitution they supposedly upheld. When faced with illegal actions or revolutionary efforts by Communists, they dealt out long prison terms and imposed death sentences. Right-wing extremists charged with criminal acts or caught in plots to overthrow the government received much lighter penalties. Critics of the Weimar system often fault its liberal constitution for tolerating antidemocratic movements such as the National Socialists. But there were laws that might have curbed the growth of Nazism; they were simply not enforced.

Hitler's early career is a case in point. In 1923 he was arrested for his role in the Beer Hall Putsch and charged with high treason. Instead of being a setback, the trial gave Hitler a chance to gain national publicity. He was sentenced to five years—a rather light term for someone caught in the act of trying to overthrow the government—and served a total of only thirteen months. Communists in the Weimar Republic charged with similar offenses regularly received much harsher treatment: life terms and death sentences were not uncommon for them.

Hitler spent the decade after the failed Putsch building his party. He presided over a two-pronged approach. On the one hand was the paramilitary, street-fighting wing of the movement: the SA (Sturmabteilung), or Stormtroopers. On the other hand was the legal, political party, the National Socialist German Workers' Party (NSDAP). The brown-shirted Stormtroopers, modeled after Benito Mussolini's Fascist Black Shirts in Italy, brawled with Communists and Social Democrats, harassed and attacked Jews and others, and generally used terror tactics to intimidate the public. At the same time, the existence of the Nazi Party allowed for legal actions: collecting funds, organizing local support, putting forward candidates for election, and hosting rallies and other events.

Until 1929 the NSDAP was just one of many splinter political groups vying for the attention of voters. That year brought electoral breakthroughs in local and state elections, most notably in Thuringia, and a dramatic increase in party membership. Evidence of national popularity preceded the Great Depression; it was not simply economic hardship that brought some Germans to support the NSDAP, although hard times certainly brought some new voters and activists. Indeed a general climate of political polarization meant that all parties at the extremes—Nazis and ultranationalists on the right, Communists on the left—gained at the expense of the moderate middle. Over the course of the 1920s, the NSDAP became a genuine mass party with voters in all social classes: workers, members of the lower middle class, students, academics, clergy, the wealthy, women as well as men.

The 1930s and the End of Democracy in Germany

The U.S. stock market crash of 1929 was felt all over the world, not just in Germany. It is with good reason that the depression associated with that event has been called a world depression. Germany faced growing unemployment as did much of the industrialized world. German farmers, like their counterparts elsewhere, faced falling commodity prices and shrinking markets. Economic hardship did not make the rise of a Nazi dictator inevitable, but it did add to the challenges of the Weimar Republic.

By early 1930 economic difficulties had brought Germany into a political crisis. High taxes, increased tariffs, cuts in government spending, and deflationary policies did nothing to ease the situation. In the midst of that misery and strife, few people even noticed the evacuation of the last French troops from German soil in June 1930.

The chancellor, Heinrich Brüning, was unable to get the backing of the Reichstag for his measures. So he convinced the German president, the old war hero Paul von Hindenburg, to invoke Article 48 of the constitution. Article 48 allowed the president to govern by decree in a state of emergency. Brüning had no problem convincing Hindenburg. Never a fan of democracy, Hindenburg had long believed that parliamentary government was too chaotic. By 1930 he was an old man—some say he was senile. A joke made the rounds: one aide to another, "Don't put that paper your sandwich is wrapped in in front of the president. He might sign it!"

From 1930 until the end of 1932, Hindenburg and his various chancellors ruled by decree rather than relying on the democratically elected Reichstag.

Democracy was essentially dead in Germany, but there were still alternatives to Hitler: some people awaited a military coup; others expected some kind of conservative, authoritarian rule.

In that climate Hitler and the Nazi Party ran in a number of important elections. In one, the presidential election of 1932, Hitler lost his bid for the presidency to the aged Hindenburg. In another, in July 1932, the Nazi Party won 37 percent of the votes cast, its highest return in a free election ever.

Although some Germans later would claim that no one could resist the magnetic force of Hitler's oratory, more than 60 percent of German voters had no trouble doing so in 1932. Some of them are on record as having found his style braying, annoying, low class, and offensive. Nevertheless, the July election brought the Nazis more seats than any other party in the Reichstag.

In the third election, in November 1932, support for the Nazis dropped, and the party lost two million votes. With 196 seats, it was still the strongest party in the Reichstag, but the Communists, with one hundred seats, were not far behind. Some observers thought the Nazis had peaked. In his disappointment Hitler wondered whether he had missed his opportunity and contemplated suicide.

Hitler was saved, not by his own ingenuity but by the miscalculation of his rivals. Former chancellor Franz von Papen, a conservative and nationalist, convinced Hindenburg to name Hitler chancellor. Papen reckoned that giving Hitler the post would buy popular support for his own cause—he planned to make sure it did so by getting himself named Hitler's vice chancellor. From that position, he told Hindenburg, he and others loyal to the president would be able to control the Nazi upstart.

Other conservatives and some industrialists backed Hitler as well. They hoped to defuse discontent among workers and prevent any increase of Communist strength. Hitler could not do much harm, they told President Hindenburg, as long as he was surrounded with members of the cabinet who were not Nazis. Hitler for his part said he would accept the chancellorship only if he could name two of the Nazi Party members of the Reichstag as government ministers. Hindenburg agreed, and on January 30, 1933, Hitler became chancellor of Germany. Like all the members of his cabinet he swore an oath to the constitution. A photograph widely distributed in the German press showed him shaking hands with President Hindenburg. The Bavarian aristocrat Reck-Malleczewen described the look on Hitler's face as that of "a headwaiter as he closes his hand around the tip." Hitler did not need to seize power. It was handed to him.

3

FROM REVOLUTION TO ROUTINE

Nazi Germany, 1933–1938

Looking back it is easy to forget that half of the Nazi era occurred before World War II began. Those first six years proved crucial. Between 1933, when Hitler became chancellor, and 1939, when German forces invaded Poland, Nazi rule revolutionized Germany. During those same years, the "Third Reich" or third empire, as Hitler and his followers called their new Germany, became routine for many Germans. This chapter examines those two phases of Hitler's rule: first, the Nazi revolution, and second, the routinization of Nazism that followed. How did Hitler begin to implement his ideas of race and space during the peacetime years of Nazi rule? How did the German public respond, and what was life like for Germans under the Nazi system?

The previous chapter outlined Hitler's worldview and described how he came to be chancellor of Germany. Throughout that discussion you might have noticed an imbalance between the ordinary aspects of Hitler's life and the extraordinary impact he had. There was nothing so unusual in Hitler's background, nor were his ideas original. Even the factors that brought him to power—misfortune, opportunism, miscalculation—were unsensational. And yet the destructive role that Hitler would play was far from ordinary. Even today, when asked to name one individual who has dominated the past millennium, many people say "Adolf Hitler."

That same dichotomy or gap between the extraordinary and the ordinary is evident throughout the entire Nazi period. On the one hand, Hitler revolutionized Germany, but on the other hand, the ways in which he did so seemed undramatic to many participants and observers at the time. Between 1933 and 1938, Nazism became everyday routine and ordinary for many Germans, but that routine normalized terror and legalized extraordinary persecution.

PHASE I: THE NAZI REVOLUTION, 1933–1934

Hitler's appointment as chancellor in January 1933 was in itself unspectacular. Since 1918, Germany had seen many chancellors from a range of political parties, and many of their governments had been short-lived. Yet that seemingly unremarkable event on January 30, 1933, marked the beginning of a revolution that would transform German politics and society. The new chancellor lost no time in attacking the elements of the population he despised, but he did so in ways that expanded his own power even as he isolated his enemies.

Political Revolution

Hitler's political position in early 1933 was not that strong. His party's support had dropped from its July 1932 peak, and even then it had received only 37 percent of the votes cast. The Nazi Party faithful themselves were divided into factions with very different visions for Germany's future. Some emphasized the "Socialist" part of the name National Socialist and favored a social revolution that would redistribute wealth and property in radically egalitarian ways; others wanted to bolster traditional elites. Meanwhile, Hitler's cabinet included only two members of the Nazi Party besides himself: Hermann Göring and another longtime associate, Wilhelm Frick, as minister of the interior. The rest of the cabinet posts were assigned to conservatives and nationalists, members of the Catholic Center Party, and military men who thought they could control their inexperienced new chancellor. Instead he proved to be skilled at manipulating them.

Hitler made his first major move in early 1933 against the Communists, a target he chose with care. Communism could have posed a real threat to Nazi power. Like the Nazi Party, the Communist Party had local cells throughout Germany. It was well represented both in the Reichstag and in the streets, where its men had fought the Nazi Stormtroopers for more than a decade. The Communists, however, were an ideal first target for another reason as well: Hitler was guaranteed to have allies against them. Precisely those elements in German society that had helped Hitler into the chancellor's seat—conservatives, nationalists, industrialists, and military men—hated and feared

Communism. They were unlikely to protest any anti-Communist measures, no matter how unconstitutional or harsh.

On February 27, 1933, the Reichstag—the German parliament build-ing—burned down. The Reichstag fire gave Hitler the opportunity he wanted. His spokespeople insisted that Communists had torched the building, and the German press, relying on information from Nazi sources and reluctant to speak against the new regime, echoed those accusations. At the time some non-Nazi Germans assumed that Hitler's own people had started the fire, but they could do little except grumble in private, unless they were willing to risk being accused of sympathizing with the Communists. For a long time, research seemed to indicate that the blaze was the work of a lone, Dutch arsonist named Marinus van der Lubbe, who was linked to neither the Communist nor the Nazi party. Subsequent work, however, points back to the Nazis as the instigators.

Hitler ordered massive reprisals against the German Communists in response to the fire. He had thousands arrested, beaten, and tortured; hundreds were "shot while trying to escape." That phrase was a euphemism or indirect way of saying that police or soldiers had shot them in the back. Thousands more fled into exile. Shortly after the Reichstag fire, in March 1933, German newspapers announced the opening of the first official concentration camp—at Dachau, near Munich. Among the first prisoners sent there were many Communist men.

With the actions of late February 1933, Hitler crippled Communist power in Germany. That assault was only the beginning: by the end of the Nazi regime, about one hundred and fifty thousand German Communists would be arrested, and many of them would be killed by 1945. The crackdown also gave Nazis an opportunity to attack leaders of Germany's trade unions. It is not surprising that Communists produced some of the most influential anti-Nazi texts and images in the early years of Hitler's rule. John Heartfield, a German who anglicized his name from Helmut Herzfeld during World War I to protest rampant anti-British sentiment, created some of those images, including a pho-tomontage in response to the Reichstag fire. Heartfield's indictment of Göring as a human gallows appeared in a popular Czech weekly, the *Arbeiter Illustrierte Zeitung* (workers' illustrated newspaper).

The Reichstag fire gave Hitler a pretext to dismantle what was left of Germany's democratic institutions. Pointing to the supposed risk of disorder and to his now-proven ability to act decisively, he convinced the members of the Reichstag to pass the Enabling Law of March 23, 1933. The Enabling Law allowed Hitler to put through any measure without approval from the Reichstag. He no longer even needed to have the president declare a state of emergency or sign a decree. Social Democratic representatives opposed the Enabling Law, but they were the only mainstream party to do so. In effect the

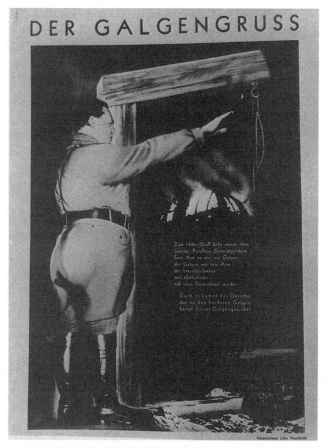

The German Communist artist John Heartfield created this photomontage in response to the Reichstag fire in 1933. Titled "The Gallows Greeting," the text reads: "He raises his arm for the 'Heil Hitler,' Göring, Prussia's General Policeman. His arm is like a gallows, the gallows like his arm, which blackened by fire and flecked with blood, stretches itself across Germany. But the judgment is coming that will hang this gallows-face on the highest gallows." Given the prevalence of Nazi propaganda and the fascination with it long after the fact, it is easy to forget there was also a powerful tradition of anti-Nazi visual propaganda.

Reichstag was now defunct; its own members had voted it out of existence. Their reasons for doing so varied: quite a few welcomed the new regime they thought would replace the cumbersome parliamentary system they hated with authoritarian order; others felt intimidated by Nazi attacks on Communists and Social Democrats; some hoped to curry favor with Hitler and his people by proving how willing they were to cooperate.

By the end of the summer of 1933, Hitler had used his authority to dissolve or outlaw all political parties except the Nazi Party. Even the facade of

German democracy was gone. Hitler's political revolution was not without violence, but he established his dictatorship through means that were, at least in a narrow sense of the word, legal.

Social Revolution—Testing the Waters

The Nazi revolution had immediate effects on those groups Hitler had described as enemies for years. It was not only political opponents like the Communists who felt early blows; homosexuals, Jehovah's Witnesses, German Jews, people considered physically or mentally disabled, and Afro-Germans all experienced attacks within the first year of Nazi rule.

Hitler and his associates in the new German leadership struck in dramatic, decisive ways, but they always tested the public response to each move before proceeding further. This mixture of boldness and caution would be typical of Nazi tactics throughout the Third Reich, from its inception in 1933 to its collapse in 1945. Public opinion was very important to Hitler. A firm believer in the stab-in-the-back myth, he was convinced that a disgruntled German public had caused Germany to lose World War I. He was determined to avoid a repeat of that situation under his rule, during the wars he intended to wage.

In *Mein Kampf* Hitler had made it clear that he planned to "deal with" the Jews. He started his social revolution, however, with attacks on a group that was even less likely to receive public support: homosexual men. In the 1920s and early 1930s, Berlin and other major German cities had become centers of a small but vibrant gay culture. Even before the Nazis came to power, police had sometimes harassed men known or suspected to be homosexual; many Germans regarded homosexuality as deviant and decadent and urged their government to crack down by imposing what they considered moral and sexual order.

Since 1871, Paragraph 175 of the German criminal code had outlawed sexual relations between men: "A male who indulges in criminally indecent activities with another male or who allows himself to participate in such activities will be punished with jail." The prohibition did not mention sexual acts between women. Hitler built on this law in early 1933 to ban homosexual rights organizations in Germany. According to National Socialist teachings, homosexuals were an abomination because they opted out of the reproduction of the so-called Aryan master race. Moreover, according to Himmler and others, homosexual men in public positions of any kind were dangerous because they were always vulnerable to blackmail.

It was also politically expedient for Hitler's new government to lash out against gay culture, because opponents of Nazism charged the movement, in particular the Stormtroopers and SS, with fostering and glamorizing intimate relations between men. Communist and Socialist enemies of Nazism had been known to mock those obsessively male organizations as stomping grounds for deviants, and some conservative and Christian critics leveled the same accusations.

Antagonistic Nazis focused on gay men; they seemed for the most part not to see lesbians or bisexual women as posing a particular threat, because women did not exercise public power by serving in the military or at high ranks of the bureaucracy. In any case women, some Nazi activists presumed, could always be forced to bear children for the German Volk, regardless of their own sexual orientation. Nevertheless, in individual cases lesbians were persecuted as so-called asocial elements.

Leadership from above prompted initiatives by people acting out their own hostilities. In 1933, Nazi Stormtroopers and other thugs raided gay bars and clubs in German cities and forced many of them to close. A few managed to remain open longer—some intermittently until the end of World War II—but under constant threat of raids and violence. In May 1933, a group of Nazi students stormed and destroyed the Institute for Sexual Research in Berlin. Its director was the gay rights activist Magnus Hirschfeld, whom his opponents also vilified because he was Jewish. For the most part the German public was indifferent or cheered such offensives.

Johannes Steyer, a German Jehovah's Witness, spent ten years in Nazi concentration camps, prisons, and forced labor units. During the 1970s he painted a series of watercolors depicting his persecution under the Third Reich. In this scene, Steyer, preaching under surveillance, is told: "We do not want Jehovah God's Kingdom! We have our church and our Führer!" Steyer's painting draws attention to the role of so-called ordinary Germans in the isolation of people targeted by the Nazi regime.

There was likewise no protest within Germany in the spring of 1933, when Nazi regulations banned the Jehovah's Witnesses. In fact, some mainstream Protestants and Catholics churches encouraged state measures against a religious group they considered a dangerous cult. Most Germans were just as unlikely to complain when the new regime used existing laws and conventions to bear down hard on Sinti and Roma. Stereotyped as shiftless wanderers, Roma and Sinti had suffered police harassment and public prejudice for decades, even before Hitler came to power. Nazi persecution in its early stages hardly seemed new.

Germans of African descent were easy targets as well. They were few in number—probably only hundreds in the early 1930s—and vulnerable in their visibility; those with dark complexions stood out in a nation of white people. Some had come from Germany's former colonies in Africa—territories in what are now Cameroon, Namibia, Burundi, and Tanzania—or were children of colonials. Some were the offspring of African soldiers or other men of color stationed in the Rhine area after 1918 as part of the French occupation forces. Many Germans had responded with panic to the appearance of black troops in their midst, and the children some of them left behind seemed to many racist Germans to be living examples of Germany's humiliation. Even before he came to power Hitler had spoken of his desire to see all Germans of African descent—people he, like others, called the "Rhineland bastards"—sterilized. The early months of Nazi rule brought attacks, official as well as spontaneous, on these people as well. Compulsory registration of all Germans deemed "half-breeds" revealed 385 such individuals, 370 of whose fathers had been part of the French occupation. In 1937 most of those 385 people were sterilized.

One woman named Doris Reiprich recalls how her landlord evicted her and her African father, white German mother, and sister from their apartment after Hitler came to power. Officials tried to convince the girls' mother to divorce their father, but she refused. Doris lost her job, and her sister, Erika, was tormented by her classmates at school. Teachers were no better; they forced Erika to take part in a course on "race" and listen to such statements as, "God made all whites and blacks; half-breeds come from the Devil." Erika recalled a field trip to see an exhibit about supposed racial degeneration. On display were pictures of black and biracial people, some of whom Erika recognized as her parents' friends. The photographs had been retouched to make them appear ugly and threatening.

Both Afro-German sisters would make it through the war by acting in movies. They recount their experiences in the book *Showing Our Colors: Afro-German Women Speak Out*. German filmmakers needed a few people of color to make movies that promoted German colonialism in Africa. Throughout the Nazi years most Afro-Germans had no such protective positions. Like Doris

Reiprich and her sister, they suffered a whole range of indignities and abuses, and many of them experienced even harsher treatment—sterilization, incarceration, and death.

The Nazi Revolution and the Jews

Of course the Nazi revolution also meant assault on German Jews. In 1933 Germany's Jewish population was small: about half a million people, less than 1 percent of the total population. New regulations in April banned Jews from the German civil service. That same month the Nazi Party organized a boycott of Jewish businesses throughout Germany, although the boycott did not succeed in the way its planners had anticipated.

Hitler's Nazis used a combination of intimidation and legislation to create a mood of hostility toward Germany's Jews, a kind of open season for abuse. During the boycott Stormtroopers stood outside Jewish businesses to frighten potential customers. Nazi activists staged public humiliations of Jews and friends of Jews, and Jewish children experienced vicious harassment in school from teachers as well as fellow students. Especially singled out for attack were German Jews and non-Jews who were involved in intimate relationships. In one case, for example, Stormtroopers forced a gentile woman and her Jewish boyfriend to stand in the street wearing sandwich boards. Hers read, "I am the biggest pig in the place and go around only with Jews." His said, "As a Jewish boy I only take German girls to my room."

In this climate of persecution print and visual propaganda served to disseminate stereotypes, normalize stigmatization, and further isolate Jews and other targets of abuse. All over Germany insulting reports accompanied by photographs and lewd cartoons from the antisemitic newspaper, *Der Stürmer*, appeared in public display cases. The headlines named names: they charged Jewish doctors with abusing "Aryan" girls, accused Jewish community leaders of extracting blood from Christian children, and denounced Protestant pastors for abetting Jewish perfidy by baptizing converts to Christianity. Nazi activists hid near businesses owned by Jews and photographed customers who violated the boycott. Such pictures too were published and displayed, as was the snapshot reproduced on the next page.

The civil service ban and the boycott created terrible situations for Jews in Germany. At the same time, for Nazi planners they revealed complications in implementing anti-Jewish measures. For one thing, there was no concrete definition of who exactly counted as a Jew, so it was not always clear to whom the ban on employment applied. Given Hitler's sensitivity to public opinion, officials did not want to antagonize potential "Aryan" supporters by mistaking them for Jews. Moreover, by April 1933, German Jews had not yet been

This snapshot shows a woman, taken by surprise, emerging from a Jewish-owned business in violation of the April 1933 boycott. Such photographs, circulated and displayed, were used to denounce individuals and intimidate members of the German public into compliance with anti-Jewish measures.

isolated from the rest of population. The Nazi government did not dare impose formal measures against Jewish veterans of World War I, for example, or against Christian spouses of Jews. There was also uncertainty around how to regard people who had converted from Judaism to Christianity. Outraged German Jews who did not yet know how far the regime would go in attacks on them deluged authorities with petitions and requests for exceptions, and sometimes non-Jews supported their efforts.

But there were also non-Jews who went even further than the civil service law to introduce anti-Jewish measures on their own. Some gentile spouses divorced "undesirable" Jewish mates, and many people cut contact with friends and former coworkers. University administrators fired scholars who were not in fact targeted by the law, for example, Christian men with Jewish wives or people whose parents had converted from Judaism to Christianity. Removing such individuals made their supervisors look especially eager to cooperate with the new government. Students and the other professors were not too likely to complain, because they hoped to benefit from the situation. After all, professorial positions were in high demand in German society, with its many educated people, high level of unemployment, and great respect for academics.

In the Protestant church, pro-Nazi clergy who belonged to a group called the German Christian Movement tried to expel from the pulpits any pastors who had converted from Judaism to Christianity or who were the children or grandchildren of such converts. Only a handful of clergy actually fell into those categories. Uneasy as to how Protestant church people inside Germany and abroad would respond, Nazi government authorities decided in 1933 not to back that scheme. Public opinion was still more important to Hitler than complete thoroughness. There would be time to widen the net later. Meanwhile, individuals and organizations were free to develop anti-Jewish initiatives that suited their own purposes. German municipal governments, strapped for cash, found it expedient to drop Jewish recipients of public support from their welfare lists, before authorities in Berlin had even thought of the idea.

As for the anti-Jewish boycott of April 1933, it did not really catch on. Some German gentiles complained that the ban on Jewish businesses disrupted their lives and created public disorder. Many continued to frequent Jewish shops out of habit or convenience. Outside Germany there was considerable negative publicity around the anti-Jewish measures. In the United States, Britain, and elsewhere, Jews and people who generally opposed abuses of human rights threatened to organize a counter-boycott of German goods to pressure the German government into curbing antisemitic behavior.

There were other, less obvious issues, too. What constituted a Jewish business? If the issue was Jewish ownership, what about "Aryan" employees? What about enterprises owned jointly by Jews and non-Jews? In a complex, modern economy that included large, incorporated firms with thousands of employees and stockholders, it was by no means clear who would be hurt by the boycott. Even in very small businesses, Jewish and non-Jewish interests were intertwined. For instance, Susanne Weilbach's father was a Jewish dairy farmer in the Rhine valley. Boycotting him would also destroy the livelihood of his non-Jewish hired hand and impoverish that man's family.

Aware that the anti-Jewish boycott was damaging his public image at home and abroad, Hitler called it off ahead of schedule. Still Nazi leaders learned some lessons from these early anti-Jewish experiments. First, they realized that it was easiest to attack people who were already marginalized. Second, they learned that members of the general public were more likely to participate in or at least tolerate attacks on minorities if they stood to gain rather than to lose from such initiatives. In any case, leading Nazis found out that unanimous approval was not required. Indifference of the majority was all that was needed to carry out many plans.

In another sense, for the regime the boycott was not a failure at all. By revealing how tightly Jews were woven into the fabric of German economic life it proved the need to isolate Jews before mounting a direct, all-out attack.

Meanwhile it gave hard-core antisemites an opportunity to act out their hatred. A useful trial balloon, the boycott typified what became a common pattern for Hitler: push, wait to test public response, and then push again in the direction of least resistance. In this way Nazi authorities learned what the German people would accept and gained valuable experience for implementing subsequent measures. Moreover, by pulling back from an extreme position, they appeared flexible and concealed the radical nature of their goals.

German Jewish Responses

How did German Jews respond to Nazi attacks? Like Communists and homosexuals, some left the country. Departure, however, was not a simple proposition, especially for people with families and deep roots in Germany. There had been Jews in German territory for some sixteen hundred years; many Jews were at home in German society in ways that made leaving almost unfathomable. Moreover, some of the people who antisemites considered Jews did not regard themselves as Jewish at all. Over the centuries Jewish Germans had intermarried with Christians and some had converted to Christianity, but because Nazi ideology was based on the notion of blood, its adherents suspected such people of still being Jews.

Unlike Communists, who could (in many cases, mistakenly) expect a haven in the Soviet Union, there was no obvious place for Jews to go. No State of Israel existed in the 1930s, and the traditional countries of immigrants—the United States, Canada, Australia—all had very restrictive immigration policies. Economic problems linked to the Great Depression and a climate of nativism made governments and public alike hostile to immigrants, especially those who were not Christian or did not come from western Europe. Still, during the first year of Hitler's rule, some thirty-seven thousand Jews fled Germany. Many did not go far: they chose destinations where they had relatives, business connections, or other prospects. For 73 percent of them that meant elsewhere in Europe; 19 percent went to Palestine, and only 8 percent overseas. Anne Frank's family from Frankfurt am Main moved to the Netherlands. George Mosse, later an influential historian, left with his family for Switzerland, though only after his father, who owned a large publishing conglomerate, had been forced at gunpoint to sign over his assets to a fake organization for war veterans.

Many German Jews tried to find new ways to pull together within Germany. They organized self-help efforts and sought to combat social isolation by providing educational and cultural opportunities for themselves. To these ends, in September 1933 a group of Jewish leaders created the Reich Representation of the German Jews to unify attempts to preserve Jewish religious life and offer practical assistance to Jews from all over Germany. The group's president, Berlin Rabbi Leo Baeck (1873–1956), would steadfastly refuse to leave even when he had opportunities to do so. As long as any Jews remained in Germany, Rabbi Baeck believed, he belonged with them.

Once German officials began transporting German Jews to ghettos and sites of killing in the east in late 1941, the Reich Representation of the German Jews lost its always limited ability to do anything to help its members. Its leaders too were sent to be killed. In 1943 German police sent Rabbi Baeck to the ghetto and transit camp at Theresienstadt, also known as Terezin, near Prague. Rabbi Baeck survived the war and moved to London.

In 1933 some German Jews joined Zionist associations. The Zionist movement had emerged in the late nineteenth century. Its members believed that Jews were not only a religious group but a distinct people who deserved a country of their own. Zionists took their name from the biblical name "Zion," the hill in Jerusalem on which the Jewish temple had stood. They worked to establish a Jewish national homeland, and some moved to Palestine. Before the 1930s Zionism had been rather unpopular among German Jews, but Nazi measures convinced many Jews in Germany it was their only alternative. After Hitler came to power, some German Zionist leaders who promoted immigration to Palestine found ways to work out arrangements with Nazi authorities who wanted Jews out of Germany. Others continued to wait and hope that somehow the storm would pass.

The Nazi Revolution and the Disabled

The Nazi revolution advanced on all fronts in its drive for so-called racial purity. In May 1933 Hitler introduced a law to legalize eugenic sterilization, that is, sterilization to prevent reproduction by people deemed unworthy on the basis of mental or physical conditions. More radical legislation followed just two months later.

In July 1933 Hitler proclaimed the Law for Prevention of Hereditarily Diseased Offspring. It ordered sterilization of people with certain physical and psychiatric conditions. The list included people characterized as severe alcoholics, epileptics, schizophrenics, and a number of other loosely defined categories such as the "feebleminded." Roma and Sinti were targeted too, though indirectly, as "asocials." Nazi minister of the interior Wilhelm Frick went so far as to suggest that 20 percent of the population should be sterilized. Ultimately the number of Germans sterilized under this law would come to less than 0.5 percent of the German population, but that still meant destroying the reproductive capabilities of some four hundred thousand people without their consent and in many cases against their wills.

There was criticism of the sterilization law, especially from Catholic clergy. Proponents of the measure countered by finding a few Catholic theologians who were willing to endorse it. Meanwhile enforcement required the participation of many people: lawyers who drafted the legislation; medical and social workers who reported people to be sterilized to the authorities; bureaucrats who handled the paperwork; doctors, nurses, and aides who performed the procedures. As the Nazi regime established and reinforced its power, it involved ever larger numbers of people, who in turn developed a stake in its continuation. Through this dynamic, Nazi ideas gained acceptance, even among people who might earlier have opposed them.

Like programs of forced sterilization elsewhere, the Nazi variant also played on common prejudices and fears. Some of these are displayed in a propaganda image titled "The Terrible Legacy of an Alcoholic Woman." The precise numbers give the appearance of scientific rigor, but how could anyone know how many "asocials"—beggars, criminals, murderers—had descended from one individual and how much money they had cost the state? Who

This image comes from a filmstrip of the Reich Propaganda office titled, "The Terrible Legacy of an Alcoholic Woman." It claims that within eighty-three years, one such woman produced 894 descendants, 50 percent of whom were "asocial," including 40 paupers, 67 habitual criminals, 7 murderers, 181 prostitutes, and 142 beggars. Taken together, these "deviants" allegedly cost the state 5 million Reich Marks. The use of precise numbers (even if invented) was meant to give scientific legitimacy to fear mongering.

would define who counted as a "pauper" or a "whore"? The combination of scare tactics and an appeal to self-interested practicality was typical of Nazi eugenic and racial propaganda.

The Policy of Coordination

The Nazi revolution brought rewards for those who cooperated as well as attacks on those deemed undesirable. Many Germans of all ages enjoyed participating in an exciting, dynamic movement that welcomed them as long as they were "the right kinds of people."

In 1933 Hitler and his accomplices introduced a process called Gleichschaltung, which means "coordination," literally "shifting into the same gear." In the name of national unity, new Nazi organizations swallowed up other, independent groups and clubs. For example, the Nazi-run German Labor Front replaced the old trade unions. Nazi organizations of farmers, women, boys, girls, writers, and artists absorbed associations of people in those categories. These new groups had monopolies over their clienteles and did not tolerate competing organizations.

Local cooperation and leadership were essential to the success of "coordination." So was a bombardment of propaganda from party-controlled newspapers and publicists enthusiastic about the "national awakening." For at least some Germans the surge of group activities provided an exciting sense of belonging. Melitta Maschmann, a teenager in 1933, later described how she loved being part of the BDM, the Nazi League of German Girls (Bund Deutscher Mädel). It gave her a chance to assert independence from her parents, she said, and to feel like someone important, part of dramatic new developments. Testimonials collected from Nazi Party members in the 1930s by the American social scientist Theodore Abel echoed those sentiments: joining the Nazi movement empowered many Germans.

Hitler's government introduced all kinds of programs to win favor with the majority of the population. Enormous publicity was devoted to job creation and massive public works programs. Many people still claim that Hitler "saved" Germany from the Depression, and indeed, Nazi policies did accelerate the process of economic recovery. At the same time, many of Hitler's schemes continued what his predecessors had begun, and in any case, by 1933, the slump seemed to have bottomed out in Germany. Of course Hitler took credit for all improvements, and the Nazis even set up an agency called Strength Through Joy (*Kraft durch Freude*) to organize workers' leisure activities and plan holiday trips. Strength Through Joy set up package tours, such as cruises to the Mediterranean or Scandinavia or short trips within Germany. It also sponsored mass production of the "people's cars"—Volkswagens—and set up savings plans

Members of the League of German Girls (Bund Deutscher Mädel, or BDM) take children from large families for an airing in the park while the mothers of the infants are busy elsewhere. Activities of the BDM, the female complement to the Hitler Youth, aimed to prepare young "Aryans" ideologically, socially, and physically to serve the Reich as mothers. Positive images like this one depicting the benefits of inclusion in the "people's community" were the flipside of the propaganda of exclusion.

so that workers could arrange to buy them. Even fun was to appear to be a gift of the Führer.

Terror and Pageantry

The Nazi revolution claimed to restore order, but from the beginning it was enforced with terror. In March 1933, not even two months after Hitler became chancellor, Nazi authorities opened the first official concentration camp. Located at Dachau, just outside Munich, its initial prisoners were political—Communists arrested in the wake of the Reichstag fire—but it also held men charged with homosexuality and common criminals. Dachau Concentration Camp was no secret. To the contrary, the Nazi press covered its opening in detail, on the theory that merely knowing it existed would serve as a public deterrent.

Dachau and the network of similar camps that followed were under the control of Heinrich Himmler, one of Hitler's longtime associates, and the head of the SS, Nazism's elite force. By July 1933 German concentration camps held an estimated twenty-seven thousand people in what was euphemistically called "protective custody."

Violence itself served the Nazi regime as a form of propaganda. In May 1933, Hitler's minister of propaganda, Joseph Goebbels, organized public book burnings, which presented intimidating spectacles of Nazi force. Thousands of pro-Nazi students proved especially eager to participate. They and other Nazi supporters made huge bonfires of books by Jewish authors such as Albert Einstein and the satirist Kurt Tucholsky. They also burned works by Communists and others associated with left-wing positions—for example, the playwright Bertolt Brecht and the writer Heinrich Mann; liberals such as Thomas Mann; and foreigners, including the American Jack London, author of *Call of the Wild*, an adventure story about a sled dog in the Klondike. Photographs of heaps of books and crowds massed around the flames showed up on the pages of newspapers in Germany and all over the world, a warning and a threat to critics of Nazism.

Pageantry was the flip side of Nazi terror, another show of strength. The first months of Hitler's rule featured endless torchlight parades with columns of marching men. Observers after the fact often interpret footage of those events as evidence of the unanimity of Germans behind Hitler. It would be probably more accurate to see those demonstrations as efforts on the part of the new regime to create an image of unanimity that itself worked to deter opposition. It must have been a lonely and terrifying experience to be on the outside of a torchlight march looking in. What chance would one feel one had against that monolith of power?

The columns of Nazis often sang as they marched. Supporters adapted old songs and wrote reams of new ones, everything from sentimental folk songs to outright vicious fighting songs, with lyrics about "Jewish blood" spurting from German knives. The most famous Nazi song was the "Horst Wessel Lied." It was named after its lyricist, a Nazi Stormtrooper who had been killed in a brawl with a Communist in 1930. Set to a familiar folk tune, Horst Wessel's lyrics extolled the Nazi flag, called for unity against the foe, and praised the comrade-heroes who had died for the cause. During the Third Reich the Horst Wessel song became part of Germany's official national anthem. It was always sung with the right arm outstretched in the "Hitler salute."

Newspapers, magazines, and newsreels propagated images of cheering crowds, their arms raised in unison. A 1933 photograph from Pößneck, a small town in Thuringia, is typical: up front are the dignitaries in SS and Stormtrooper uniforms, more uniformed men fill the balcony, and foregrounded are women and girls in traditional dirndls. The photographer is not identified,

Filling an entire concert hall, an enthusiastic audience gives the Nazi salute during a ceremony or festival. Young women in traditional peasant costume stand near the front. Undivided, exuberant support for the regime was a prevalent feature of Nazi gatherings from the early days of Hitler's rule to the dying days of World War II. Photography was an important tool in propagating an image of unanimity.

but clearly he or she took this picture with official permission, from the stage. Viewing this photo together with another crowd scene highlights the role of the photographer and his or her perspective in shaping the view.

Julien Bryan, an itinerant American, photographed a political rally in Berlin in 1937, standing not in front but in the middle of the crowd. Instead of a sea of glowing faces and outstretched arms, he captured a range of actions: another photographer composes a shot, a woman looks disapprovingly at someone or something outside the frame (perhaps at Bryan), and a man appears to hesitate as he raises or lowers his arm. Bryan took many other photographs while in Germany—of Nazi Party rallies, daily life, and anti-Jewish propaganda. Back in the United States, those images, shown in numerous film and slide lectures that he gave, incorporated into documentary movies, and reportedly even screened at the White House, helped create an informed view of Nazi Germany and the dangers it posed.

A Revolution in Foreign Policy

As he had at home, Hitler used a combination of boldness and caution to bring about a revolution in foreign policy. He was a master of making his aims

German spectators at a rally in Berlin in 1937. Julien Bryan, the American who took this picture, was an untrained photographer who traveled around Germany taking hundreds of shots of Nazi leaders, political rallies, and everyday life. His photographs and films of Nazi Germany toured extensively in the United States. In this photograph one can glimpse the reality behind the image of unanimity that the Nazis projected in Party rallies and through propaganda.

look safely conventional, even while his intentions were dangerously radical. Hitler railed against the Treaty of Versailles, but so had almost all German politicians since the war. He talked about restoring German boundaries to their "rightful" location; so had many German nationalists. Hitler's plans, however, were far more ambitious, and he wanted nothing short of world domination. Nevertheless, in the first stage of his rule he used diplomacy to work toward achieving his goals.

In this regard too, Hitler chose his priorities carefully. His first major foreign policy success came in July 1933, shortly before announcement of the new sterilization law. That month Hitler's representatives signed an agreement called the Concordat with the Vatican in Rome. Hitler promised to respect the rights of Catholics and the Catholic Church in Germany. Pope Pius XI, for his part, hoped to protect Catholic interests within Germany and to use Hitler's Nazi regime as a defense against Communism all over Europe. For Hitler the Concordat turned out to be an effective way to gain legitimacy both at home and abroad.

Germany's population in 1933 was almost 40 percent Roman Catholic, and Hitler himself was raised in the Catholic Church. Nevertheless many

German Catholic clergy were initially suspicious of Nazism. They saw Nazi ideas as anti-Christian, especially the emphasis on race and blood and the obvious disrespect for human life. Before the Concordat, some priests in Germany had refused to administer the sacrament of communion to church members in Stormtrooper or SS uniforms.

The Concordat undermined potential Catholic opposition in Germany. How could parish priests criticize a chancellor who had been recognized by their pope? What possibility remained for a united Catholic front against the sterilization program? Meanwhile, abroad the Concordat added to the prestige of Hitler's new regime. Even if the pope no longer wielded much political power, he still had moral authority with Catholics all over the world.

Other foreign policy successes followed. By January 1934 Hitler's diplomats had negotiated a Non-Aggression Pact with Poland that was supposed to last for ten years. Hitler had no intention of keeping that promise, but such deals bought valuable time. Meanwhile, Germany withdrew from all its multilateral arrangements; most notably, in October 1933, it left the League of Nations.

Under Hitler Germany actively began to rearm. Because the Treaty of Versailles restricted German military power, rearmament at first had to be secret. In 1933 Hitler's government set up a phony initiative called the Agricultural Tractor Program, which was a cover for a project that in fact built tanks. By 1934 Germany was producing explosives, ships, and aircraft in quantity. In 1935 Hitler dropped even the pretense of secrecy. Germany had become a military power once again, with an air force, a navy, and an army based on conscription.

The Nazi revolution was difficult to oppose because it occurred with a mixture of subtlety and force. The regime did not snap into place in January 1933 as a full-blown totalitarian prison. There was still room for Germans—at least those who were not considered disabled, Jewish, or otherwise unwanted—to maneuver, even to criticize. Precisely those mainstream members of society, however, were the least likely to recognize the revolutionary nature of the new regime. Many of them stood to gain from the measures it introduced, and others were apathetic. What did any of it have to do with them? It was those in the most vulnerable positions—Nazism's targets—who were the first to recognize what was at stake. They, however, had little power to do much about it, other than to warn people like them, who often preferred to hope for the best instead of heeding alarmists, or to try to convince a busy and often hostile world of their impending doom.

A Telling Incident

An incident recounted by a German waiter and recorded in Bernd Engelmann's book *Inside Hitler's Germany* captures the dynamics of the early months of Nazi rule. In early 1933, the man worked at a restaurant in a small town. One day a group of Nazi enthusiasts came in. The editor of the town's Nazi newspaper was there, so were the chief Stormtrooper and the local Party leader. At another table all alone sat an elderly lawyer who had lived in the town all his life.

The group of Nazi functionaries got louder and drunker. Suddenly they summoned the waiter, a young man at the time, to their table and told him to deliver a note to the lawyer. Afraid to refuse, the waiter complied, but as he put the note down on the table he saw that it said something like: "Get out, you Jewish swine."

The lawyer read the note and began trembling with rage and shame. He stood up at his table and addressed the three men. How dare you, he challenged them: "I am a veteran of the World War. I risked my life for this country." The restaurant became deathly still. No one at any of the other tables spoke or even seemed to breathe. The waiter remembered being able to hear the sound of pots and pans in the kitchen.

The three Nazis broke the silence. They taunted the lawyer again and turned back to their beers. The lawyer summoned the waiter and, still shaking, handed him money to cover his meal, and left the restaurant.

Later the waiter realized that the man had given him far too much money. He went to the lawyer's home to return the extra. There he found the man dressed in his hat and coat with a suitcase in his hand. He was leaving, he told the waiter, because there was no future for him in Germany.

What would have happened to any of the other Germans at that restaurant if they had spoken in defense of their Jewish neighbor? At that point, in early 1933, probably not much. The aggressors were drunken bullies new to their roles. The observers likely knew them personally, as they did the lawyer. So why did they say nothing? Perhaps they did not want to risk an unpleasant scene. Maybe they would have taken the chance for someone else, a woman, say, or a Christian clergyman. In any case, they were silent, and their silence emboldened the ruffians. All over Germany the silence of others like them sent a message back up to Hitler: it was safe to keep pushing.

The Night of Long Knives and the End of the Revolutionary Phase

The end of Nazism's revolutionary phase can be marked with reference to a specific event—the so-called Night of Long Knives, also known as the Röhm Putsch, of June 30, 1934. Ernst Röhm (1887–1934) had been Hitler's associate since the early 1920s, when he had been instrumental in building up the Stormtrooper organization. By 1934 Röhm was head of 2.5 million Stormtroopers. A veteran of World War I, Röhm and his Stormtroopers had played a powerful role in destabilizing the Weimar Republic and consolidating Hitler's new regime. After some professional setbacks and personal scandals, Röhm immigrated to Bolivia in 1928, but Hitler brought him back to Germany in 1930 to reorganize the Stormtroopers.

After Hitler became chancellor, he began to view the Stormtroopers as a liability. Restless for action and disgruntled with what seemed a slow pace of change, many of them thought Hitler had sold out their movement's ideals for the sake of respectability. The SS, or Schutzstaffel (protective staff), Nazism's elite guard headed by Himmler, had grown more powerful and wanted the upper hand over its rival organization, the Stormtroopers. Meanwhile the army and Hitler's new conservative friends considered the Stormtroopers disreputable thugs who disrupted the public order; some also castigated them as a group dominated by homosexuals.

Hitler had to choose. Would he cast his lot with the SS and the army or be loyal to his old brown-shirted Stormtrooper allies? He decided to move against the Stormtroopers. On the night of June 30, 1934, on Hitler's orders, the SS struck.

It is often said that a revolution devours its own children. Hitler's revolution was no exception. In a bloody rampage, SS men fanned out to kill Röhm, other old allies of the Führer such as the Nazi ideologue Gregor Strasser, and Hitler's rivals, including former chancellor General Kurt von Schleicher and, for some reason, Schleicher's wife. In general, Hitler and SS leader Himmler used the purge to get rid of people they found problematic. The list of dead even included a priest who had helped write *Mein Kampf* when Hitler was in prison. Perhaps that man was a victim of mistaken identity, or Hitler may have thought he knew too much to be trusted.

The total number of people killed is unknown. Some place it as low as 150; others estimate it in the thousands. At least eighty high-ranking Stormtroopers were shot. The numbers of more lowly individuals killed on local initiatives, that is, not on direct orders from Hitler or Himmler, may have been much higher. Hitler did not dismantle the Stormtroopers after the purge, but he clipped the organization's wings and subordinated it directly to his authority.

Hitler dressed the bloodbath in the guise of conventional morality. Ernst Röhm was openly and actively homosexual. Hitler had known about Röhm's sexual preference for years and never seemed to have considered it a problem. Now, however, in his bid for legitimacy, Hitler publicly reviled Röhm. The killings, Nazi press reports contended in lurid detail, were part of a cleanup of the movement, a necessary measure against decadence and perversion.

How did the German public react? You might expect shock or horror. In fact there was little of either expressed in Germany, at least in public. President Hindenburg sent Hitler a telegram of congratulation for restoring order, and

German military leaders likewise praised what they considered appropriate measures in the interest of public safety. Members of Hitler's cabinet declared the purge retroactively legal. Many observers believed that now the Nazi regime had become an ordinary government, its dangerous, extremist days behind it.

Victor Klemperer, a German professor of Jewish background in Dresden, had a different opinion. After such blatant criminality, he was certain that the rule of brutes had to fall. Surely the old German elite would come to its senses and throw out the upstarts, he hoped, but Klemperer was wrong. The Night of Long Knives left Hitler stronger than ever.

PHASE II: ROUTINIZATION, 1934–1937

June 1934 marked a turning point in the Nazi regime. By no means did it signify the end of brutality, but it did usher in a new phase of routinization. Instead of uncontrolled, revolutionary shows of force, Nazi authorities concentrated on systematizing violence and normalizing coercion. They did so by centralizing power in the hands of a few and passing laws to make their measures at least look respectable. Inventing rituals and convincing people to police their own behavior in keeping with Nazi regulations were also parts of the process.

Centralization of Power

One component of routinization was centralization, which took many forms. One of the most significant was the centralization of police power under Himmler and the SS. The Night of Long Knives brought the Stormtroopers under Himmler's control. In 1934, Himmler, along with Heydrich, who ran the intelligence office known as the Security Service, took over all political police, known in Germany as the Gestapo. By 1936 Himmler had pulled the criminal police into his orbit as well, so that the head of the SS and the concentration camps was now in charge of all police forces in Germany.

Himmler and his tens of thousands of SS men were crucial to the Third Reich. Unlike the German military, the SS was officially linked to the Nazi Party organization, not to the government of Germany. Throughout the Third Reich, the Nazi Party retained its own separate hierarchy with headquarters in the Brown House in Munich. Its status gave the SS an unprecedented degree of independence from any kind of authority that predated Hitler's rise to power. The SS was an ideologically dynamic organization that combined the functions of a conventional, repressive political police force with a drive to implement the "Führer's idea." Himmler saw his goal as defending "purity of the blood" and persecuting those who he believed threatened it: Communists, Freemasons, Jehovah's Witnesses, homosexuals, Jews, Roma, and others.

In August 1934 President Hindenburg, the man who had appointed Hitler chancellor of Germany, died. In another act of centralization, Hitler united the offices of president and chancellor in his own person. That change did not substantially alter Hitler's duties, nor did the president's death remove a major obstacle to the expansion of Hitler's power. Hindenburg had done little to check Hitler's activities in the first year and a half of Nazi rule. Nevertheless, for some Germans the death of the old man Hindenburg meant the end of any hope that Hitler and Nazism would be stopped.

There were also practical repercussions to the uniting of the offices of chancellor and president in the person of the Führer. According to the German constitution, still officially in force, the president was the supreme commander of the German armed forces. Hitler now claimed that position for himself and used it to require members of the military to swear an oath of personal allegiance to him.

Legalization

A second component of routinization involved legalizing Nazi measures. The goals of Hitler and the Nazi "true believers" were twofold: "racial purity" and spatial expansion. In this phase of development after the Nazi revolution of 1933–1934, pursuing those goals meant revamping German law. Members of all professions—teachers, journalists, doctors—served the Nazi cause, but lawyers and judges played an especially important role in giving the regime and its measures a veneer of legitimacy that was important to international observers and to many Germans. As he consolidated and expanded his power, Hitler had to operate within the prevailing view of Germany as a state governed by law.

The first minister of justice under Hitler, Franz Gürtner, was not a Nazi, although he supported authoritarian rule. Gürtner was prepared to sanction the blatant illegalities of the revolutionary phase, including attacks on Communists and the Röhm Putsch massacre. Justice Minister Gürtner also presided over laying the legal foundations for what would become mass murder of people considered disabled and of Jews.

The key pieces of legislation when it came to attacks on Jews were the Nuremberg Laws, passed in the fall of 1935. The laws had two parts. First was the Law for Protection of German Blood and Honor, which forbade marriage or sexual relations between Jews and "Aryan" Germans. Jews could not fly the German flag nor employ German gentile women under age forty-five in their households. Such measures were intended to isolate German Jews from the rest of the population and stigmatize them as disloyal, destructive outsiders.

The second component was the Reich Citizenship Law of November 1935. This legislation defined, for the first time in detail, who was to count as a "Jew" in Nazi Germany. According to Nazi ideology, Jewishness was a racial trait, but in fact there was no way to measure distinctions of blood, because they did not actually exist. In other words, there were no reliable markers of appearance, blood type, or any other physical traits that Nazi "experts" could use to separate Jews from "Aryans." Instead the Nuremberg Laws fell back on religion as the only way to define Jews. Under the law it was not one's own religion but that of one's grandparents that mattered. People with three or more grandparents of the Jewish faith counted as Jews. Most Germans defined as "Jews" under the law lost the rights associated with German citizenship.

The Nuremberg Laws considered people who had two grandparents of the Jewish faith to be *Mischlinge*, or "mixed bloods," a category that would remain in dispute throughout the entire Third Reich. Mischlinge who were Jewish by religion or who married people categorized as Jews also counted as Jews. Some Mischlinge who had no contact with Judaism or Jews likewise ended up being treated as Jews, perhaps because they looked stereotypically Jewish or had especially hostile neighbors or coworkers. There were, however, people categorized as Mischlinge who managed to continue living in German society throughout the Nazi period, and a few even served in the German military in World War II. The law did not address people with one Jewish grandparent, but in practice some of them would also face disadvantage and discrimination of various kinds.

The Reich Citizenship Law offered no definition of "Aryan" other than the implied opposite of "non-Aryan" or "Jew." Thus, by default, Germans with four grandparents who were baptized into a Christian church were assumed to be "Aryans."

The Nuremberg Laws contributed to what can be called the social death of Jews in Germany. "Social death," a term coined by the sociologist Orlando Patterson to describe the marginalization, dishonoring, and power-lessness of enslaved people, is used by the historian Marion Kaplan as a way to analyze how official discrimination and persecution systematically cut Jews in Germany off from the majority non-Jewish population. Formal and informal measures combined to isolate Jews in ways that were both brutally public and intensely personal.

The prohibition against sexual relations between people defined as Jews and those classified as Aryans reveals how the process worked. Denunciation was central for enforcement of the law: who would know who had sex with whom unless someone contacted the police? Investigations of charges of *Rassenschande*—"racial shame" or race defilement, the Nazi name for the supposed crime—were public affairs that often involved sensational press coverage and open trials. No details were too intimate to be exposed by police detectives and prosecutors eager to demonstrate their dedication to the Nazi cause. Even people who were acquitted found their lives destroyed. Small wonder that many Jewish and non-Jewish Germans broke off relationships and friendships, whether out of fear or a desire to protect the feelings and reputations of others. Meanwhile, cases of Rassenschande served to educate the general public as to the costs of associating with Jews.

In the wake of the Nuremberg Laws the regime introduced an endless stream of prohibitions that heaped indignities and hardships one on top of the other and further separated Jewish Germans from their neighbors. Jews were forbidden from using public swimming pools; owning radios, telephones, and typewriters; attending school; practicing medicine; wearing dirndls and leder-hosen; buying chocolate; shopping other than at specified times; and giving the "German greeting": "Heil Hitler!" Hundreds of such restrictions tormented and stigmatized Jews by translating antisemitic ideas into everyday routines that required no effort whatsoever from most non-Jewish Germans: they only needed to obey the law and follow their self-interest.

Jewish children were especially hard hit, because they had daily contact with non-Jews at school and on the way there and back. Many memoirs looking back on childhood in Nazi Germany include accounts of harassment, beatings, and other forms of violence. Georg Iggers, who was about ten at the time, remembers being threatened with knives and shoved down some stairs by members of the Hitler Youth in Hamburg. Susanne Weilbach recalls school-yard bullies and mean, antisemitic, or simply ambitious teachers who could do whatever they wanted to Jewish children, knowing they were backed by official policy. When her teacher banished Jewish and Romany children to a bench at the back of the room, it is not surprising that her classmates taunted her and threw stones.

Nazism was not simply about "difference," as if "anyone different" were persecuted. In fact persecution itself served to create and enforce difference along officially designated lines.

Consider this group portrait of German girls posing outside their school in Heldenbergen, near Mainz, in 1935. The photographer has arranged them in front of the flag, with the swastika centered and rising like a sun behind them. The girls are dressed in white, wreaths of flowers in their hair, traditional garb for a Corpus Christi procession. One of the girls shown is Lilli Eckstein (later Stern), who was expelled from the school six months later for being Jewish. But which one is she? The tiny girl in the center of the front row? The dark-eyed girl next to the teacher? The girl in the back, whose polka dot dress is not quite concealed by the classmates in front of her? Or maybe she is the unsmiling girl on the far left in the middle row, the only one who appears not

German girls from Heldenbergen pose outside their school in front of the Nazi flag in 1935. To Nazi leaders, children and adolescents represented the future of the Third Reich, and there were intense pressures put on them to conform to Nazi ideals by teachers, administrators, and fellow students, as well as by the Hitler Youth and League of German Girls.

to be holding anyone's hand. The archive's description of the photo does not tell us, and the faces, hair, body types, and expressions of the girls are as different from one another as they are similar. But Nazi law and everyday practices of exclusion transformed Lilli from a member of the group to an outsider and a refugee. By the end of 1938, she and her family had left Germany and were living in Swaziland.

Most non-Jewish Germans gave little thought to the Nuremberg Laws and other anti-Jewish regulations. They seemed to be just more bureaucratic measures that would have little direct impact on their lives. Nor did the international community regard the laws as especially significant. After all, every nation reserved for itself the right to determine who counted as its citizens, on what basis, and what rights they received. Their mundane appearance notwithstanding, the Nuremberg Laws proved to be a crucial step toward the destruction of Germany's Jews. All kinds of attacks on Jews were now directly sanctioned, even mandated, by law. Moreover, once Jews were defined, it would be much easier to isolate, rob, deport, and eventually kill them.

Although focused on Jews, the Nuremberg Laws had repercussions for other target groups as well. Regulations that followed meant that under certain conditions, Sinti and Roma, as "alien to the Aryan species," could also lose the rights of German citizens. They too faced prohibitions on marrying so-called Aryan Germans. Eager German racists applied measures described in the Nuremberg Laws to Afro-Germans as well. One woman remembers how as a small girl she was sent home by a teacher who forbade her, as a "non-Aryan," to march behind the German flag.

The phase of routinization also brought increased measures against homosexuals and men charged with homosexual acts. In June 1935, Paragraph 175 of the German criminal code was revised to expand the definition of "criminally indecent activities between men." Now sexual relations did not have to be established; any physical intimacy assumed to lead to sexual arousal could be grounds for prosecution. It became easy for denouncers to lay charges of homosexuality, and the courts used their power to impose a crackdown that brought thousands of men accused of homosexual behavior into prisons and concentration camps.

Meanwhile, Nazi sterilization developed its own routines, and new regulations extended the assault on those considered disabled. For example, a 1935 law required any pregnant woman who should have been sterilized under the 1933 law but had not been to have an abortion. The laws and regulations already introduced against people with disabilities routinized worsening conditions in institutions and hospitals around Germany. What kind of treatment would you expect health-care workers to mete out toward people whose government labeled them "useless eaters" and "unworthy lives"?

Ritualization

In addition to centralization and legalization, a third component of Nazi routinization was ritualization. After the first year, Nazi pageantry developed a ritualized rhythm. The largest event was the annual Party Rally, held each year in the southern German city of Nuremberg. It was an enormous spectacle, choreographed by propaganda experts to the smallest details. As with the early torchlight marches, these imposing shows of strength were supposed to create a sense of unanimity and invincibility so that any opponents of the system would feel isolated and helpless. In 1934 the German director Leni Riefenstahl filmed the rally and released it under the title *Triumph of the Will*. It has become one of the most famous propaganda movies of all time.

Later some Germans would describe their participation in these Nazi extravaganzas as among the high points of their lives. In particular children seemed impressed. Alfons Heck, a member of the Hitler Youth (Hitler Jugend) from a small town near the French border, described his trip to the Nuremberg Party Rally in 1935 in his book *A Child of Hitler*, which he wrote many years later. Heck was awed by the pageantry, the uniforms, and the scale of the whole affair. No doubt those sensations contributed to his devotion to the Nazi cause and his desire to share in such amazing power.

Of course, for others inside Germany Nazi spectacles brought other kinds of routines—predictable harassment and the drudgery of confinement. In preparation for the 1936 Olympics in Berlin, an event that Nazi organizers used to showcase the "new Germany," police forced about six hundred Sinti out of Berlin into detention in a camp near a sewage dump and the cemetery in the nearby suburb of Marzahn. Guarded by police and their dogs, the camp had only three water pumps and two toilets. Under those conditions, contagious diseases ran rampant. Otto Rosenberg, a Sinto from Berlin, had just turned nine when police shipped him, his grandmother, a teenaged aunt, and a brother and sister to Marzahn. The smell of sewage was terrible, he recalled, and people lived in huts knocked together from sheet iron they scrounged for themselves. The glories of the Third Reich looked rather different from the vantage point of what amounted to an overcrowded, filthy, open-air prison.

Self-Coordination

A fourth important aspect of routinization might be called self-coordination. In the years between 1934 and the beginning of the war, Nazism lost much of its momentum. Some people became disillusioned or bored with the new system, but most of the population, even those who were not overly enthusiastic, fell into the habit of going along with the regime. They grumbled in private, perhaps, or expressed their criticism in ineffective forms, such as jokes. In either case they posed no real threat to Nazi control.

One popular joke that poked fun both at Hitler's pretensions and at public gullibility went as follows. Hitler and Goebbels were driving through the German countryside when their car struck a dog. Hitler, who loved animals, was devastated. "Go and find the masters of that loyal German dog," he ordered his minister of propaganda. "Apologize to them in the name of the Führer." Sometime later Goebbels returned, beaming and bearing all kinds of gifts: bread, sausage, and beer. "What happened?" Hitler demanded. "Were they unhappy?" "Not at all, mein Führer," Goebbels answered. "All I said was 'Heil Hitler! Der Hund ist tot' [The dog is dead], and they started to celebrate."

Self-coordination also involved self-policing. Since 1933 a law called the Malicious Practices Act had banned remarks that offended or subverted Nazi authority. Such prohibitions can only be effective if people report one another, and they did so in Nazi Germany. Throughout the 1930s denunciations poured into the offices of the Gestapo, the political police in charge of crimes against the state. Some people denounced others in order to demonstrate their own loyalty to the Nazi cause. Others sought to better their positions, attack outsiders, or just carry out old grudges. The prevalence of denunciations and police raids inspired German wits to invent two new national "saints," Maria D'enunciata and Marie Haussuchung—that is, Holy Mary the Denouncer and Mary of the House Searches.

Fear of denunciation led people to develop what became known as the "German glance"—the quick look over the shoulder before one spoke to see who might overhear. The SD or Security Service employed an elaborate network of infiltrators and informers whose job it was to report in detail on the public mood across Germany. Nazi routinization depended on consensus and co-option as well as coercion.

Nevertheless Nazi Germany cannot simply be characterized as a "police state." Indeed, as the historian Robert Gellately has shown, there were in fact relatively few police per capita in Germany in the 1930s. A high level of cooperation from the general public, not an unusual number of men in uniform, made Nazi control possible. Smooth functioning of the system did not require all Germans—or even most—to share every tenet of Nazi ideology. Enough enthusiasts could always be found to stage enormous public shows of support, such as the annual Nuremberg Party rallies. On a day-to-day basis, the Nazi regime only needed most people to obey the law, try to stay out of trouble, and promote their own interests as best they could under the current circumstances.

Preparations for War

Even during the period of routinization Hitler did not lose sight of his goals of race and space. In various ways he presided over Germany's preparation for war. After two years of secret rearmament, in 1935 Hitler's government went public. It reintroduced conscription and revealed its new military machine to the world.

No one had altered the Treaty of Versailles, but German contravention of its terms had become routine under the Nazis. The victors of World War I were not in a position to risk a new conflict in order to check German violations. Impoverished by the war and the difficult years that followed and faced with their own problems at home, the British and the French had no desire to play the role of international police. The United States had retreated into isolationism, and most of its people opposed its government involving them again in the turmoil of European affairs.

In 1936 Hitler took his biggest foreign policy gamble so far. Under the Treaty of Versailles, the westernmost part of Germany along the Rhine River had been demilitarized to provide a buffer zone for France. A year after reintroduction of conscription, rumors began to circulate that Hitler intended to reoccupy the Rhineland with Germany's new military. For some months he seemed to waver, waiting until the Winter Olympics in Berlin had ended and collecting the views of his inner circle, Germany's diplomats, and military leaders. By the beginning of March, he had made his decision and prepared to act.

Hitler made the announcement in a speech on March 7 to the Reichstag and, by radio, to the people of Germany. It was a lengthy and in places emotional speech, which denounced Versailles and railed against Communism. Hitler saved the punch line for the end. "In the interest of the primitive rights of a people to the security of its borders and safeguarding of its defense capability," he proclaimed, "the German Reich government has therefore from today restored the full and unrestricted sovereignty of the Reich in the demilitarized zone of the Rhineland." The six hundred deputies in the Reichstag, all in Nazi uniform, went wild, stretching out their arms in the Nazi salute and screaming "Heil!"

Meanwhile, German troops were approaching the Hohenzollern Bridge across the Rhine River in the city of Cologne. Propaganda minister Goebbels had arranged for planeloads of journalists to be on hand to record the event, and thousands of Germans crowded into nearby streets to cheer the soldiers as they crossed into the demilitarized zone. Even in this moment of national euphoria, Hitler and his advisers retained some caution. They made sure that the forward troops were instructed to withdraw and fight if they met military resistance from the French. As Hitler had expected, the French did not respond by sending in troops. Instead the gamble paid off by giving Hitler's prestige at home its most enormous boost yet.

Even as he publicly pledged his commitment to European peace, Hitler announced to his inner circle in 1936 that Germany must be ready for war within four years. To that end he named his old associate Göring head of a "Four-Year Plan" to prepare the German economy and military for war. Göring took over economic planning, and a year later the Minister of Economics, the banker and old-guard figure Hjalmar Schacht (1877–1970), resigned.

In the winter of 1937–1938, Hitler completed the routinization and consolidation of his rule by dumping the old elites who had been so instrumental in bringing him to power. Those old-fashioned conservatives had been useful throughout the phases of Nazi revolution and routinization. They had lent respectability to the regime when it needed it and had provided expertise and continuity as it consolidated its power. Now, as Hitler prepared to move to a more aggressive phase, they had become a burden.

In November 1937 Hitler met with leaders of the German army, navy, and air force. It had been two years since Germany had announced its rearmament. Since 1936 German forces had been involved in the Spanish Civil War on the side of General Francisco Franco and the enemies of the Spanish Republic. Hitler had pushed German intervention even though many

Germans opposed it. Because the Soviet Union backed the Republic in Spain, support of Franco gave Hitler a way to attack Communism. Moreover, Mussolini was actively behind Franco as well. So Spain offered a chance for Germany and Italy to practice cooperation in the spirit of their leaders' mutual admiration. For the Germans the Spanish Civil War was also an opportunity to try out new military equipment. In particular they broke in their new air force by bombing Spanish towns and cities. Now Hitler was ready to risk more.

Hitler gave those gathered at the November meeting a lengthy harangue on Germany's need for more space. They were skeptical. How could Germany be ready for war? Hitler's response to their misgivings was typical. In early 1938 he launched a purge of the military leadership, replacing old conservatives with men more amenable to Nazi plans. He retired fourteen senior generals, replaced or pensioned approximately sixty others, and assumed command of the armed forces as minister of war.

Hitler made a clean sweep of all positions directly related to his plans for war. He replaced the conservative foreign minister Constantin von Neurath with the loyal Nazi Joachim von Ribbentrop. The Nazi general Walter von Brauchitsch became head of the army in place of Werner von Fritsch. There were new Nazi ambassadors to Rome, Tokyo, and Vienna.

Hitler's methods in early 1938 were quite different from those he had used to purge the Stormtroopers less than four years earlier. This time he employed less violent means, in keeping with the stature of the individuals involved and the spirit of routinization rather than revolution. But the tactics were no less vicious for all their bloodlessness. For example, Hitler disposed of the war minister Werner von Blomberg by stirring up a scandal around his new wife. She was a former prostitute, the Nazi press claimed; how could a man thus compromised hold a position of such responsibility? The fact that both Hitler and Göring had served as witnesses at the wedding was conveniently omitted, and Blomberg went abroad in disgrace.

Two years earlier, rumors of homosexual activities on the part of Fritsch, the head of the army, had been ignored. Now Fritsch had to go, and the old charges provided the perfect means to force him out. He, like the others, had served his purpose; he had supported Hitler's regime in its early stages and helped provide it with a veneer of legitimacy by linking the new system to familiar, experienced military leaders. After four full years in power Hitler had consolidated his position, and preparations for war were under way. Fritsch and Blomberg had outlived their usefulness to Hitler, and it was no problem to find replacements eager for their positions. Meanwhile those members of the military elite who kept their jobs fell into line with barely a murmur. It would become much more difficult to challenge Nazi rule now that not only the police but the military was firmly in hand.

Contrary to the image presented by Nazi propaganda—Germans marching in massive columns, their arms raised as one in the salute to Hitler—not all Germans fell into line. Friedrich Thimme, a trained historian and fervent German patriot who had headed the Foreign Office's division on the so-called War Guilt Question in the 1920s, railed in his private and not-so-private correspondence against Hitler and his henchmen and refused to break ties to his Jewish friends. Thimme's daughter Annelise, a teenaged schoolgirl in Berlin in the early years of the Third Reich, announced to her classmates that obviously the Nazis had lit the Reichstag fire themselves, and she scoffed at Nazified teachers who preached the party line in the classroom. With a group of high-spirited schoolmates, Annelise once played a trick on one of the worst offenders. One at a time the girls rode by the teacher, who was on her own bicycle, calling out "Heil Hitler" so that the woman repeatedly had to raise her right arm in salute until she lost her balance and fell. In a small way, that youthful prank reveals the continued presence in Hitler's Germany of people who for all kinds of reasons—family ties, personal loyalties, religious and moral principles, political allegiances—remained skeptical and even critical of their government and its actions.

In early 1938, however, most Germans were not thinking about challenging Nazi rule. Looking back on his youth in Germany, Alfons Heck can see some of the factors that made him an enthusiastic Nazi. There was the indoctrination in school and in the Hitler Youth, for example, and the unrelenting propaganda. But there were also concrete ways that Nazism benefited him. It promised action, rewards for his ambition, power, a chance to be an insider, and a role in something enormously successful. Heck, like many of Hitler's German supporters, was no brainwashed automaton. He was just one of millions of "ordinary people" who, for all kinds of ordinary reasons, endorsed and accepted a brutal system.

4

OPEN AGGRESSION

In Search of War, 1938–1939

By early 1938, Nazi rule had become a familiar routine for most Germans. For some, like the eager Hitler Youth member Alfons Heck, it was a comfortable yet exciting existence. Ambitious and enthusiastic, Heck could expect to realize his goal of becoming an airplane pilot. To him it seemed Germany was becoming richer and stronger. Its new air force beckoned him from its triumphs in Spain; his teachers and the books and newspapers he read assured him the future was his. Born in 1927, Heck could hardly remember the Nazi revolution. The normalization of Nazi power coincided with his development of political and social awareness. It was really the only world he knew.

Born the same year as Alfons Heck, the Sinto boy Otto Rosenberg also grew up with the Nazi system. By 1938 he knew all the miseries of the Marzahn "lot" and had mastered some ways around them. Often hungry, he pulled weeds for nearby farmers in exchange for pennies and food: Belgian buns with icing, coffee with milk. He became used to seeing the riot squad beat people and haul them off to what was known in local parlance as the "concert-camp." In 1938, he watched police round up the young men of Marzahn and load them into trucks that took them to Sachsenhausen. Still, when his mother, who had arrived in Marzahn after him, was ordered to report to police in Berlin, Rosenberg expected her to return. Instead she was sent straight to the women's concentration camp at Ravensbrück.

For others, such as Victor Klemperer, professor of French literature in Dresden, the routinization of Nazi rule meant an ever-tightening trap. The university dismissed Klemperer in 1935, even though he was both a convert from Judaism to Christianity and a veteran of World War I. One insult and deprivation followed another. Klemperer was forbidden to publish. He lost borrowing privileges at the library, and eventually library staff refused even to let him use the reading room. Over the years Nazi regulations robbed Klemperer of his car, his house, his driver's license, even his pets. If the years from 1933 to 1938 seemed to fly on magical wings for the Nazi boy Heck, for his counterpart Rosenberg, they were a blur of close calls and hard knocks. For the middle-aged "non-Aryan" Klemperer, time crawled by, an endless drudgery of discouragement and abuse. The years ahead would be even worse.

Beginning in early 1938, Hitler's Germany entered a third stage of its development. After the euphoric phase of revolution and the consolidating phase of routinization, Hitler and his inner circle took off the gloves and began actively seeking war. For Hitler war was more than military conflict; it was to be a decisive step toward realizing his ideas. By 1938 he had already prepared the ground by rearming, isolating target groups, and appointing loyal support-ers in key positions. Now, open aggression would characterize developments in Nazi Germany even before the invasion of Poland in September 1939.

This chapter outlines some key events of that turbulent period in 1938 and 1939: annexation of Austria in March 1938, the Czech crisis later that year, the so-called *Kristallnacht* pogrom in November 1938, the Hitler-Stalin Pact, Jewish efforts to escape Nazi Germany, and the beginnings of a program to kill Germans deemed disabled. In dramatic ways, Hitler began to realize his goals of purging the "race" and expanding its territory even before he got the war he wanted.

SKEPTICISM AND SUCCESS

Contrary to the stereotype, most Germans were not foaming at the mouth, eager for war, in 1938 and 1939. In fact, the German public as a whole, includ-ing many people who welcomed aspects of the Nazi domestic program, was skeptical about some moves that Hitler and his Nazi elite made in this phase of open aggression. It was one thing to assert German strength and revolution-ize conditions at home, but it was quite another to risk war when, for many Germans, memories of the previous war remained painfully fresh. Such uneasi-ness, however, was not enough to derail Hitler's plans. Instead he was able to use 1938 and 1939 to construct a unified front for the cause of race and space. He did so by resorting to such old loyalties as nationalism, patriotism, and solidarity against common enemies. Even more important, he built support through success.

It is often said that nothing succeeds like success. Certainly Nazi Germany seems to confirm that saying. Every time Hitler took a risk and won, he decreased the anxiety among the German people and convinced more of them to trust him. Many feared war because they dreaded bloodshed, personal and financial loss, and defeat. The wounds of world war and especially its bitter outcome in 1918 were still raw for most adults, but what they perceived to be Hitler's foreign policy triumphs in 1938–1939 did a great deal to relieve their concerns.

Events in 1938–1939 demonstrate how domestic and foreign policies were intertwined in Hitler's Germany. Foreign policy successes helped ease concerns and buy support at home. Meanwhile Hitler's regime pursued its goals on both fronts: abroad it attacked Germany's supposed enemies and took steps toward a military offensive; at home it enforced "racial purity" and trained its people for war.

THE ANSCHLUSS—GERMAN ANNEXATION OF AUSTRIA

The first of Hitler's string of foreign policy successes in 1938 and 1939 was the Anschluss, the German annexation of Austria in March 1938. The Treaty of Versailles had forbidden Austria and Germany from uniting. In 1936, in order to placate Mussolini's Italy, Hitler had issued assurances that Germany would not violate Austrian independence. Mussolini and some other Italians were worried about German designs on Austria and on territories long disputed between Austria and Italy: South Tyrol and Trieste. Like all of Hitler's promises, that pledge to respect Austrian independence was made to be broken.

In early March 1938, the Austrian chancellor Kurt von Schuschnigg announced a plebiscite to show Austria's determination to resist Nazi power. The next day, Hitler called together his military leaders to address the possibility of German occupation. It took only hours to prepare a plan; Hitler ordered German forces to cross into Austria on March 12.

Wehrmacht units streamed across the border, unopposed by Austrian or international forces and greeted by euphoric crowds. Although ill prepared—German tanks reportedly had to stop en route to refuel at commercial gas stations, and rumors were that one commander relied on Baedeker's guide, a popular handbook for tourists, to plot his route—the Anschluss was a tremendous success for the Nazi regime.

Jews bore the full brunt of German aggression. In Austria, measures introduced over the course of five years in Germany were swept in overnight with the eager help and often on the initiative of local gentiles. Vienna, 10 percent of whose residents were Jewish, erupted in pogroms. Mobs robbed, plundered, and assaulted Jews and their property and staged public humiliations. Thugs forced Jews to clean public toilets with their hands, scrub streets with toothbrushes, sing and dance as onlookers jeered. In some cases the targets were prominent people—public figures, employers, professors, and neighbors of those who abused them—but Jews of all kinds got hit. In a city plagued by housing shortages, Jews' homes were often the first thing stolen from them.

The other European and international powers did not try to stop the German annexation of Austria. Many foreign observers saw the event simply as Germans taking control of their own backyard. Meanwhile German authorities together with local supporters moved quickly to implement the Nazi revolution in Austria. Measures against Jews, Roma and Sinti, the disabled, Communists, and others that had been implemented over five years in Germany were rushed through in the new Nazi lands within months. Members of target groups in Austria had even fewer options to help themselves than did their counterparts within the pre-1938 German borders.

Initially there were some popular misgivings about the Anschluss within Germany itself. Many Germans worried that this blatant defiance of the Versailles settlement could mean war. When the response instead was accolades within Austria and assent around Europe, they too welcomed this destruction of an independent nation as a legitimate expression of German strength. Once again Hitler had followed his familiar pattern, push forward hard and wait to see if anyone pushes back. If not, keep pushing.

Memoirs by Austrian Jews provide moving accounts of the impact of the Anschluss. In her book, *Still Alive*, Ruth Kluger, a young girl in Vienna in 1938, recalls the events of that year. She remembers lying in her bed hearing bands of men march by outside singing the song about "Jewish blood" spurting from German knives. One day her mother sent her to see the Disney movie *Snow White and the Seven Dwarfs*. The girl was afraid to go; she knew Jews were not allowed in the cinema. Ridiculous, her mother insisted; no one would bother a child. They did bother, young Ruth learned. She ended up sitting next to the teenaged leader of the neighborhood Nazi girls' club, who threatened and shamed her. Sometimes children grasped more quickly than adults how things had changed.

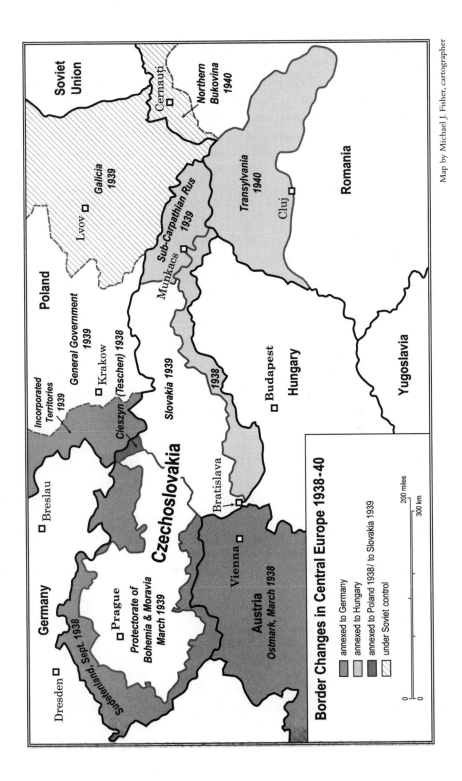

Map by Michael J. Fisher, cartographer

Border Changes in Central Europe 1938-40

Legend:
- annexed to Germany
- annexed to Hungary
- annexed to Poland 1938/ to Slovakia 1939
- under Soviet control

Scale:
0 — 200 miles
0 — 300 km

Labels on map:

Soviet Union

Galicia 1939

Lvov

Poland

General Government 1939

Incorporated Territories 1939

Krakow

Cieszyn (Teschen) 1938

Breslau

Dresden

Sudetenland, Sept. 1938

Germany

Prague

Protectorate of Bohemia & Moravia March 1939

Czechoslovakia

Slovakia 1939

1938

Bratislava

Vienna

Austria Ostmark, March 1938

Budapest

Hungary

Yugoslavia

Sub-Carpathian Rus 1939

Munkacs

Cernauti

Northern Bukovina 1940

Transylvania 1940

Cluj

Romania

THE SUDETENLAND CRISIS

Emboldened by success in Austria, Hitler made his next move against Czecho-slovakia, a country he had already identified as the first target of his planned expansion. At a 1937 meeting with military and foreign policy leaders, recorded in the Hossbach Memorandum, Hitler called for overthrow of Czechoslovakia in order to increase German security and provide food and other resources. He was willing to risk war; in fact he sought it and was disappointed in 1938 when it did not happen. With regard to Czechoslovakia the issue used to generate a crisis was the ethnic German minority in the Sudetenland, near the border with Germany.

In the summer of 1938, members of the ethnic German minority became increasingly vocal with complaints of mistreatment at the hands of the Czech government. Nazi agents from Germany encouraged and provoked their dis-content. In response to reports that Hitler planned military action to rescue the ethnic Germans of the Sudetenland, the Czechs began to mobilize their own forces. They also appealed to the French and the British for help.

Alarmed by the prospect of war, representatives of the European powers agreed to meet with Czech and German negotiators to seek a resolution. At the Munich Conference in September 1938, French, British, and Italian delegates decided Czechoslovakia should cede the Sudetenland to Germany. The area had a substantial ethnic German population, they reasoned, and if they made this concession to Hitler's demands, he and his supporters would be satisfied.

Decades after the Munich Conference, it and its most famous spokes-man, British Prime Minister Neville Chamberlain, are still synonymous with the term "appeasement." The term is almost always invoked with contempt, and Chamberlain is mocked for his triumphant announcement that he and his colleagues had achieved peace in their time. Some critics even suggest that the appeasers were somehow responsible for World War II, as if a harder line from them in 1938 would have melted Nazi aggression.

Chamberlain and the others may have shown weakness but they wanted peace, whereas Hitler was set on war. Instead of rejoicing at his successful maneuver, Hitler felt cheated when he returned to Berlin with a negoti-ated settlement giving Germany control of territories that had belonged to Czechoslovakia. Hitler worried that the optimum moment for war might have passed him by, because Germany's enemies would now have time to prepare for confrontation. A show of force at Munich from the British and the French would not have prevented war. It would only have moved it to a timetable that Hitler himself, at least in hindsight, considered preferable.

This time too there were misgivings at home. At the peak of the war scare, Protestant church leaders sponsored prayers for peace that landed a number of pastors in prison for their implied criticism of Hitler's actions. Within the army, some of the top brass worried about what seemed a slide toward a war they thought Germany could not win. There were even some tentative plans for a coup against Hitler in case it came to hostilities. All came to nothing. Instead Hitler's successful bid for the Sudetenland—although he regarded it as a failure—gave his prestige within Germany another substantial boost.

In March 1939, just months after the Munich Conference granted Sudetenland to Germany, German troops entered the rest of Czechoslovakia. With the world distracted by Franco's recent victory in Spain, Hitler ordered the Czechoslovak state dismantled. Some territory was incorporated into the German Reich, and the old Czech lands of Bohemia and Moravia were organized as the Protectorate, a kind of colony. Slovakia became a client state under the government of the Roman Catholic priest Josef Tiso.

The destruction of Czechoslovakia added to the number of would-be Jewish refugees and increased the pressure on possible destinations. These changes did not, however, cause doors for Jews to open. Less than 10 percent of Jews from the Protectorate—some twenty-six thousand people—managed to escape the Nazi trap through emigration.

Those who blame the supposed harshness of the Treaty of Versailles for the rise and expansion of Nazism should take note of the considerable territories the Germans had gained even before war began in 1939. By the end of 1938 Germany had already recouped most of its World War I losses. With the destruction of Czechoslovakia in 1939, Germany acquired lands it had never controlled before, but Hitler was not satisfied. His ambitions went far beyond merely revising the terms of Versailles.

THE KRISTALLNACHT POGROM

The year 1938 also signaled a heightened wave of aggression in anti-Jewish policies. Its most dramatic expression was the attack on Jews in Germany, including annexed Austria and the Sudetenland, on the night of November 9–10, 1938. Nazi leaders, following Goebbels, called the pogrom the *Kristallnacht* (in English, the "night of broken glass"). That label, like many Nazi terms, is misleading, as if only shop windows were shattered in the wave of rioting, and as if all Jews were wealthy owners of luxury stores. In fact it was the synagogues, sites of Jewish religious and communal life and visible manifestations of Jewish presence, that were the first targets of attack.

In October 1938, the German government expelled fourteen thousand Jews who resided in Germany but were citizens of Poland. The order followed a Polish decree requiring citizens living outside the country to revalidate their passports or lose the right to return. Worried they would be stuck with these people, German authorities struck first, brutally rounding up Jews of Polish citizenship and dumping them at the border. But Polish authorities refused many of them entry. Only after weeks in limbo, when Jews inside Poland promised them shelter, were they allowed into the country.

Among those thrown out of Germany were the parents and sister of Herschel Grynszpan, a seventeen-year-old student in Paris. Grynszpan read about the situation in French newspapers and learned details in a postcard from

A Jewish woman, expelled from Germany, washes clothes in the Zbaszyn refugee camp in Poland. In October 1938, German authorities expelled some fourteen thousand Jews living in Germany who held Polish citizenship or were stateless. Polish officials refused to allow many of them to enter Poland, and they remained in limbo for weeks. Finally, they were moved to a refugee camp organized by relief workers inside Poland, which operated until summer 1939. This photo was probably taken to try to raise international awareness and funds from Jews abroad for the refugees.

his sister. Days later, he went to the German embassy and shot an official. His motive, he told French police, was outrage at the treatment of his family and all Jews. Rumors of a homosexual liaison between Grynszpan and the German official subsequently surfaced, perhaps invented by Grynszpan to undermine the show trial the Germans planned for him after they invaded France. It has also been suggested that Grynszpan was trying to blackmail the official in order to get papers he needed to stay in France. In any case, for the Nazi leadership, this incident provided the excuse for a violent assault against Jews. Hitler, Goebbels, and other believers in the stab-in-the-back notion considered forcing Jews out of Germany to be a necessary step in preparing a successful war.

Nazi propaganda described the pogrom that followed the announcement of Grynszpan's shooting of the German diplomat as a spontaneous expression of hatred of Jews by the majority German population. In fact the event was

On the morning after the Kristallnacht pogrom, local residents watch as the synagogue in Ober Ramstadt, Hesse is destroyed by fire. The fire department prevented the blaze from spreading to a nearby home but did not try to limit damage to the synagogue. Georg Schmidt, a young man from an anti-Nazi family, took this photograph of the burning synagogue. Police confiscated the film, developed it, and kept the prints and negatives in city hall, where they were found after the war.

the carefully prepared culmination of a period of increasing pressure on Jews in Germany. Even the date was chosen with care: November 9, the date of Hitler's attempted Putsch in 1923, was a holy day in the Nazi calendar.

Permission—and instructions—from national and local Nazi leaders unleashed the hatred of Stormtroopers, members of the Hitler Youth, and other activists. All over Germany they torched synagogues and destroyed ritual objects associated with Judaism, such as Torah scrolls. Others joined in the attack, some driven by antisemitic fervor, others lured by the possibility of loot, still others just eager for action. Crowds smashed the windows of businesses owned by Jews; they vandalized and stole Jewish property. The attackers did not spare Jewish homes. They forced their way in, robbing, beating, raping, and demolishing. Memoirs describe the clouds of feathers that surrounded Jewish residences as the aggressors slashed bedding in their quest for valuables and their lust for destruction. They burned scores of synagogues all over Germany and Austria and killed about a hundred Jews. Nazi authorities rounded up some thirty thousand Jewish men and sent them to concentration camps. Those men seized in the Kristallnacht pogrom were the first Jews in Germany arrested en masse simply for being Jewish.

Jewish men arrested during Kristallnacht are marched through the streets of Baden-Baden to the synagogue as curious onlookers watch. The men were later forced to listen as a Jewish professor read sections from Hitler's *Mein Kampf* and then made to memorize the "Horst Wessel" song. Many of the men were eventually imprisoned in Dachau. On the right-hand side of the picture, on the raised ground, a spectator can be seen taking a photograph.

Responses to the violence varied widely. Alfons Heck recounts how he and another boy eagerly joined a crowd singing as it stormed a synagogue. For them the pogrom was a chance to throw rocks and "smash some stuff." An outraged uncle caught them and dragged them away by the ears. Foreign journalists watched the event with horror. Their accounts differ considerably in the degree of popular participation they describe. Some observed how onlookers joined the rampage and plunder, whereas others sensed disapproval from ordinary citizens. (You can read some of those reports for yourself on the front pages of such well-known newspapers as the *New York Times* and in smaller papers, including the *South Bend Tribune* and *Winnipeg Free Press*.)

Certainly the German public as a whole was less enthusiastic about Kristallnacht than the pogrom's instigators had hoped. In this case it seemed that misgivings had less to do with fear of war or support of Jews than with a dislike of disorder. There was grumbling about the mess, the disruption, and the general impropriety of such open violence. Still such uneasiness did not produce a general outcry. At most it took the form of private aid to acquaintances. Peter Gay, a young boy in Berlin in 1938, recalls how a non-Jewish friend of the family hid his father from the police for weeks during and after the pogrom. More commonly, misgivings prompted non-Jews to turn their backs on the violence.

Austrian men pull on a rope as they dismantle the Tempelgasse synagogue in Vienna during Kristallnacht. Here, one can see men in street clothes working with police officers to tear down the building, a glimpse of the public participation that marked the destruction of Jewish life in Austria after the Anschluss. Anti-Jewish measures that took years to implement in Germany proper were enacted practically overnight.

Photographs taken during the Kristallnacht reveal how public the violence and destruction were. Notice the participatory nature of all three of the scenes included here. Men, women, and children mill around in front of the burning synagogue in the small town of Ober Ramstadt; crowds line the street in Baden, their bicycles propped up behind them, to gawk at the column of Jewish men being marched through the city by police. Most dramatic, in the photograph from Vienna, a group of men tug on a long rope or pole to help tear down a vandalized synagogue. It is easy to conclude that the onlookers and participants shown in these pictures all hated Jews and took pleasure in the attacks on them.

A closer look and consideration of other sources complicate such generalizations. The Ober Ramstadt photo was taken by Georg Schmidt, a young man from an anti-Nazi family. Police confiscated his camera and the film in it so that he could not use the images for negative publicity. Only decades later were the prints found, in Schmidt's police file. Those photos are at the same time a record of public involvement in the Kristallnacht and evidence of Schmidt's opposition. Susanne Weilbach, in 1938 a little girl in a village in the Rhineland, describes how her teacher made everyone go to the window to watch as a group of "Aryans" taunted and humiliated local Jewish men. Among those victims was Weilbach's father.

In Vienna, Nazi thugs tormenting Jews in the street almost caught Herta Leng, a young science teacher. She was with her boyfriend, another Jewish teacher, who was trained in psychology. He took her hand and told her, "Keep walking until we near them. Then laugh." The pair stopped and laughed long and heartily before strolling by. A photograph of the scene would have shown a happy couple enjoying the sight of persecuted Jews. It would not have revealed their fear, their desperate performance, or the shame that the man's daughter, Carol Ascher, remembers lingered around the story when her father recounted it years later.

Nazi authorities, always alert to public opinion, noticed even low levels of disapproval. It is no coincidence that Kristallnacht marked the last open pogrom they sponsored in Germany. In the future they would avoid having reluctant "Aryans" witness wide-scale violence at home. It would prove easy enough to move blatant attacks further from the "Aryan" public eye.

As in the cases of the Anschluss and the Sudetenland crisis, success made Kristallnacht more palatable for nervous Germans. Many Jews, shaken by the open attack and acutely aware of their vulnerability, became frantic to leave Germany. Non-Jewish Germans benefited as they scooped up Jewish property at bargain-basement prices. No doubt many who had shaken their heads at the unruly mobs on November 9 nevertheless were willing to share in the spoils. Once they had the goods those people had a stake in the continuation of Nazi anti-Jewish policies.

Afterward the German government added insult to injury by requiring the Jewish community to pay for the material damage of Kristallnacht. It extorted an estimated $400 million from Jews for the death of the German diplomat and another $100 million for damages to property. These measures placated insurance companies and prevented a rise in rates for non-Jewish Germans. No doubt that cynical approach also furthered the false notion that Jews were a bottomless source of wealth they did not deserve.

As for Jews themselves, how did they react? Between 1933 and the outbreak of war in September 1939, approximately half of the Jews in Germany—some three hundred thousand people—left the country. Much of this exodus took place in the wake of Kristallnacht, from what had been Austria and the Sudetenland as well as from all over Germany. For most European Jews it took enormous perseverance and ingenuity to get out, to find somewhere to go, and to figure out ways to start new lives.

Successful relocation also took luck. Many Austrian, Czech, and German Jews saw the threat of Nazism and tried to move beyond its reach. Some had

A carnival parade in February 1939 in the south German town of Neustadt mocks Jews. The float features a burning synagogue; the man in front represents Moses with the Ten Commandments. Note the false noses on some of the men. Images like this one reveal the public nature of anti-Jewish persecution in Germany during and after the Kristallnacht pogrom.

the resources, connections, or relatives necessary to get to Palestine, Britain, or the United States. Others, often blocked from those most desirable destinations, sought refuge in Asia, Africa, or Latin America. Many found their way to neighboring European countries: France, the Netherlands, and Poland. How could they know that within years, in some cases months, they would end up in Nazi hands once again?

EXPANSION OF THE CONCENTRATION CAMP SYSTEM

Open aggression in 1938 and 1939 meant expanding the network of concentration camps begun in 1933 with the creation of Dachau. The history of the camps provides a kind of microcosm of the development of Nazi persecutions.

The German word for concentration camp is *Konzentrationslager,* often abbreviated as "KZ," "KL," or "Lager." Throughout the 1930s the SS set up new camps so as to provide regional coverage. For example, Buchenwald, built in 1937, was located near Weimar; Sachsenhausen was not far from Berlin. Many of the Jewish men arrested in November 1938 were sent to those places. Ravensbrück, a camp for women inmates, started up as well. After 1935 many German municipalities set up detention sites into which police forced thousands of the country's thirty-five thousand Sinti and Roma, ostensibly in order to prevent crime. Those places became sites of anthropological research and compulsory sterilization as well as sources of forced labor. The anthropologists Dr. Robert Ritter and Eva Justin found human subjects in Marzahn for their studies of Roma and Sinti. One of them was Otto Rosenberg, who, as part of the project, slept overnight at Justin's home in Berlin and was served kohlrabi by her mother.

Concentration camps echoed the regime's ideological goals. Originally their founders described their purpose as reeducation. In the camps, political opponents—Communists, Social Democrats, liberals, Roman Catholic priests—and so-called antisocial elements—vagrants, Roma, men accused of homosexuality, Jehovah's Witnesses, and others—were to be turned into useful citizens. Authorities also spoke of the camps as a place to put troublemakers into "protective custody for the restoration of law and order." Under that guise, the Nazi government gave itself the legal right to imprison suspects without a trial. From their start the camps were brutal places with terrible conditions for inmates. Torture, beatings, and deprivation were the order of the day.

As we have seen elsewhere, the move from Nazism's revolutionary phase to the consolidation of power did not mitigate the suffering of its targets. Instead that transition gave violence new forms backed by the full weight of the state and its institutions. The camps were an example. Between 1933 and 1939 the number of inmates skyrocketed, as attacks on target groups proliferated and increased in intensity. To the majority population, the expansion of camps and prisons likely seemed normal, the maintenance of law and order. To those on the receiving end of the violence, it was a brutal assault and a warning of worse to come.

The Nazi revolution of 1933 and 1934 brought large numbers of Communists into the camps. Homosexuals and Jehovah's Witnesses followed. The Sterilization Law of July 1933 brought a wave of arrests of supposed degenerates. Despite the Concordat with the Vatican, Nazi suspicion of the Christian churches also brought people into the camps. In violation of the agreement reached with the pope, Nazi authorities placed restrictions on Catholic priests, in particular regarding youth work. Some German priests refused to comply, and more than one hundred served terms in the camps as a result.

The period of routinization also enlarged the camps. When German courts and police tightened the enforcement of antihomosexual laws, they caused a jump in camp populations. At the same time the authorities became more proactive, arresting men and then pressuring them to reveal the names of their sexual partners, so that they could be charged as well. The Nuremberg Laws created a whole new category of crime, *Rassenschande,* or crimes against the blood. The 1936 Berlin Olympics meant a "cleanup" of vagrants, sex workers, pickpockets, and Roma. The result: more people dumped into camps.

In some cases police created new camps, such as Marzahn, outside of Berlin, which was set up especially for Sinti and Roma. Otto Rosenberg, who spent several years there as a boy, remembers it not as a camp in the formal sense of having guards and barracks, but as an empty lot or field. The people confined had to fend for themselves and cobble together shelters using scavenged materials. Meanwhile existing camps, among them Dachau, continued to expand.

Persecution of Jehovah's Witnesses

German Jehovah's Witnesses added to the population of the concentration camps as well. Arrests of group members peaked in 1937 and 1938. German authorities cooked up many reasons to be suspicious of them. Their organization had international connections, in particular to the United States, although the same was true of the Seventh Day Adventists and the Church of Jesus Christ of Latter-Day Saints, whose members were not generally persecuted. Because Jehovah's Witnesses emphasized the Old Testament and believed Jews had to return to the "Holy Land" before the world would end, their critics accused them of being pro-Jewish and Zionist. Perhaps most significant at a time when Germany was preparing for war, many Jehovah's Witnesses refused to serve in the military. Nor would most participate in political rallies or give the Hitler salute. Few in number and generally law abiding, Jehovah's Witnesses never posed a real threat to the stability of the Nazi German state. Evidence suggests that at least some of their leaders tried in 1933 to win the favor of Hitler's government by insisting that Witnesses were loyal Germans who did not look kindly on Jews. Nevertheless their insistence that their loyalty belonged to Jehovah alone and their refusal to abandon public proselytizing made them dangerous in the eyes of the regime.

Nazi authorities used their usual weapon—force—against the Jehovah's Witnesses, but with less success than they expected. Only about twenty thousand Jehovah's Witnesses lived in Germany in the 1930s; approximately ten thousand of them were arrested over the years and sent to prisons and concentration camps, where they were beaten and tormented like their fellow inmates. Some were executed for refusing military service. Some had their children taken from them; many lost their jobs, their pensions, and their civil rights. Officials dragged them before special courts for refusing to enlist, to undertake air raid watches, or to stop preaching.

The Jehovah's Witnesses proved remarkably resilient. Camp authorities gave many of them the option of release if they signed a statement repudiating their religion. Few did so. Instead they concentrated on building a strong network within the camps. They sang hymns, preached to the guards, and continued to meet as best they could. They interpreted ridicule and persecution as a fulfillment of prophecy, proof that they were correct in their faith. Those who remained outside tried to keep the faith as well. When police arrested one local leader, another took his or her place. They persisted in distributing their literature, even to Nazi Party headquarters. In all, between twenty-five hundred and five thousand Jehovah's Witnesses were killed in German camps and prisons between 1933 and 1945.

One such victim was Wolfgang Kusserow. In 1942, Kusserow, a twenty-year-old Witness, was executed for refusing to perform military service. One of eleven children in his family, he assured his parents, brothers, and sisters in a farewell letter, "Our faith will be victorious." Helene Gotthold also paid for her faith with her life. The mother of two children, Gotthold was arrested many times for continuing her Jehovah's Witness activities despite the government's ban. Condemned to death, she was beheaded in Berlin in 1944.

German authorities viewed the Jehovah's Witnesses more as an annoyance than a major threat. Nevertheless members of the group suffered badly during the Third Reich. Their resolve earned them a kind of grudging respect, even from some top Nazis. Himmler, for example, considered using them to resettle parts of the territories to be conquered by Germany. They were docile, obedient, and productive, he said, perfect qualities for pioneers. Inside the camps Jehovah's Witnesses sometimes functioned as personal servants to the SS. Who else could be trusted as barbers wielding razors? In general it seems Jehovah's Witnesses retained the respect of their fellow inmates and tried to do what they could to alleviate the sufferings of those even worse off than they were.

The third phase of Nazi development—open aggression in 1938 and 1939—added to the camp network in other ways too. The annexation of Austria meant building camps there; Mauthausen is the best known. The crisis around the Sudetenland brought some German Protestant clergy into the camps, mostly for short sentences. In November 1938 arrests of Jews during the Kristallnacht pogrom added about thirty thousand male inmates. Hundreds died in the camps, many from being beaten; others were released in exchange for huge payments and often agreement to leave the country.

DIPLOMATIC INITIATIVES

Throughout this third phase of Nazi development—preparation for war— Hitler's approach to foreign policy was to talk peace and plan for war. His diplomats had been active during the 1930s making pacts that, like the Concordat with the Vatican and the Non-Aggression agreement with Poland, were intended to be broken. In 1935, for example, Hitler signed the Anglo-German Naval Agreement with Britain, which he then began spending enormous amounts of money to contravene. The agreement was supposed to prevent a naval arms race by limiting the German fleet to a certain percentage of the British navy. Instead it got the British to approve a German violation of the Treaty of Versailles. Meanwhile Hitler ordered construction of as many new super-battleships and aircraft carriers as he pleased, all designed to be used against Britain and the United States, on the assumption that the British would not discover the violations until it was too late. Although only two of the planned ships could be completed before the war was over, German intentions were nevertheless clearly the exact opposite of the peaceful arrangement promised by the agreement.

In May 1939 Germany signed the Pact of Steel with Italy, promising friendship and mutual aid. This arrangement would lay the foundation for what would develop into the wartime alliance called the Rome-Berlin Axis. The summer of 1939 also brought nonaggression treaties with Estonia, Latvia, and Denmark. The crowning achievement of this phase of preparation for war, however, came in August 1939 with the German-Soviet Nonaggression Pact, sometimes referred to as the Hitler–Stalin Pact or the Molotov–Ribbentrop Pact, after the two foreign ministers involved.

The deal had two parts. The first included public proclamations of friendship and nonaggression between the two rival powers. To a world that had seen six years of Nazi attacks on Communists and the proliferation of German anti-Soviet propaganda, this part of the pact was shocking enough, but the second part went much further. In a secret arrangement, Hitler's and Stalin's negotiators agreed to divide eastern Europe into German and Soviet spheres of interest. They settled on a line through the middle of Poland as their secret boundary. Initially, the Baltic states were also divided, with Estonia and Latvia going to the Soviets and Lithuania to Germany, but the Germans later traded most of Lithuania for more of Poland.

For Hitler the pact with the Soviet Union required some fairly dramatic reversals. In a sudden about-face he dropped his public anti-Communist stance to proclaim friendship with Stalin. Given Hitler's goals, the gains were well worth the inconvenience. By cutting such a deal Hitler secured the eastern border of Poland in case of war. Instead of worrying that the Soviet Union might attack invading Germans, he could rest assured that the Soviets would be busy securing their own designated sphere of interest. Germany would have a free hand in Poland, at least in the half that the secret pact reserved for German control. Even more important, given Hitler's plans, he could wage war with the West with impunity. War with the Soviet Union, which Hitler believed was ultimately necessary to accomplish his mission, could wait.

In the meantime, Hitler and his henchmen spent the spring and summer of 1939 preparing for war. They conducted a massive propaganda campaign against Poland, accusing the Polish government and people of violating the rights of the ethnic German minority.

Already on January 30, 1939, Hitler had proclaimed his vision of the war to come to the German representatives in the Reichstag. As his speech made clear, it would be a war for race and space. "Europe cannot find peace until the Jewish question has been solved," Hitler told his audience. By the end of his remarks he had become more explicit:

> In the course of my life I have very often been a prophet, and have usually been ridiculed for it. During the time of my struggle for power it was in the first instance only the Jewish race that received my prophecies with laughter when I said that I would one day take over the leadership of the State, and with it that of the whole nation, and that I would then among other things settle the Jewish problem. Their laughter was uproarious, but I think that for some time now they have been laughing on the other side of their face. Today I will once more be a prophet: if the international Jewish financiers in and outside Europe should succeed in plunging the nations once more into a world war, then the result will not be the Bolshevizing of the earth, and thus the victory of Jewry, but the annihilation of the Jewish race in Europe! (Noakes and Pridham 3:1049)

FLIGHT FROM NAZI GERMANY

Not everyone was deaf to Hitler's boastful warnings. Ever since 1933, large numbers of Germans had been leaving the country, fearful for their own safety. Finding a place of refuge could prove very difficult for all kinds of reasons. Thousands of German Communists fled to the Soviet Union after Hitler came to power. There some of them ran into troubles of their own with Stalin's paranoid and repressive regime. The purges of the 1930s did not spare these newcomers; Stalin and his associates had some evicted from the Communist Party, forced into labor camps in Siberia, imprisoned, and even killed. Still, to an important extent, German Communism would survive the Nazi era in the Soviet Union. Many Jews from Germany and later Poland, the Baltic states, and the western parts of the Soviet Union also found an unlikely refuge later during the war behind the lines in Soviet Central Asia, the Caucasus, and Siberia.

Among the German Communists who escaped to the Soviet Union in the early 1930s was a young Jewish physician and writer named Friedrich Wolf. Convinced that theater should expose injustice, Wolf wrote a play in 1933 called *Professor Mamlock*. It told the story of a German Jewish surgeon who struggled to preserve his livelihood, his dignity, and his life under Nazi assault. The play was performed in Yiddish in a Warsaw theater where Herbert Rappaport, an Austrian-Soviet screenwriter, happened to see it. Rappaport decided to make it into a movie, which he filmed in Leningrad and released to enthusiastic acclaim in 1938.

Millions of Soviet citizens saw *Professor Mamlock* and understood its central message: that Nazi Germany was a brutally antisemitic state bent on war against Jews, Communists, workers, and decent, peace-loving people inside and outside its borders. *Professor Mamlock* also attracted huge audiences in the United States, where it opened two days before Kristallnacht. Many people valued its warning of the clear and present danger posed by Nazism, but others dismissed it as anti-German propaganda. In August 1939 Soviet censors banned the movie, after the Molotov-Ribbentrop Pact transformed Hitler from Stalin's enemy to his friend. It fell out of favor in the West, too, where some critics deemed it too pro-Communist, others worried that it depicted Jews as Communists, and still others found it too willing to distinguish between the German people (good) and the Nazis (bad).

Other Germans also tried to get out or found themselves refused reentry by the Nazi government when they returned from trips abroad. Jews, liberals, pacifists, openly gay and lesbian activists, outspoken critics of National Socialism—all kinds of people went into exile. International feminist activists and longtime companions Lida Gustava-Heymann and Anita Augspurg stayed in

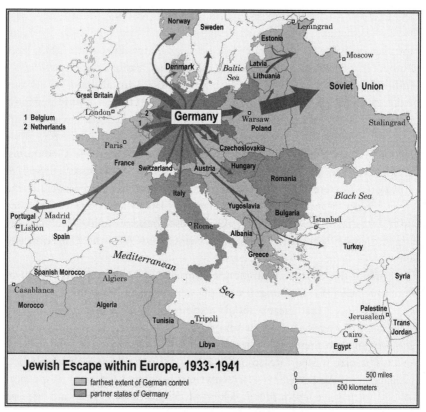

Jewish Escape within Europe, 1933-1941

- farthest extent of German control
- partner states of Germany

0 _____ 500 miles

0 _____ 500 kilometers

Map by Michael J. Fisher, cartographer

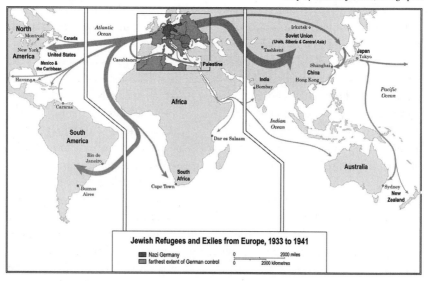

Jewish Refugees and Exiles from Europe, 1933 to 1941

- Nazi Germany
- farthest extent of German control

0 _____ 2000 miles

0 _____ 2000 kilometres

Map by Michael J. Fisher, cartographer

Switzerland after a trip rather than risk imprisonment back home. The writer Thomas Mann ended up in the United States as did the physicist Albert Einstein, the playwright Bertolt Brecht, and the filmmaker Fritz Lang. The actress Marlene Dietrich left Germany for personal reasons, but she ended up being an important anti-Nazi voice in America. Expatriates and exiles from Nazi Germany, some but not all of them Jewish, played an important role in building the Hollywood film industry in the 1930s and 1940s.

In 1939, American immigration authorities decided to allow only about twenty thousand Germans and Austrians to immigrate to the United States. There was no separate quota for Jews. Of course a large proportion of the Europeans who applied for entry into the United States were Jewish. Only those who had relatives in the United States willing to sponsor them would be admitted. Sponsors had to demonstrate that they had enough money to support their relatives once they arrived, if necessary. They also had to make their way through a mountain of red tape. Many Jews in Europe spent years trying to get visas to the United States, and most of them failed. It was even more difficult to get into Canada or Australia. In a time of economic depression most people in those countries worried that immigrants would cost money and take away jobs. Between 1933 and 1939, at most two thousand Jews from Germany succeeded in getting permission to enter Canada and then making their way there.

Far-Flung Destinations: Safety and Isolation

Even for those who recognized the dangers of Nazi Germany it was very hard to escape. Money and occupational skills such as medical training helped but did not guarantee success. For some people, distant destinations in India, China, Africa, and the Caribbean proved the only possibility, and conditions upon arrival could be difficult. In the summer of 1939 some seventeen thousand Jews from Germany, including annexed Austria and the Czech lands, made their way to Shanghai. Unable to get visas permitting them to enter places more culturally familiar to them, they seized the chance to get out of Europe even though it meant leaving behind almost everything they knew. Most of them would survive the war, including the Japanese occupation of China.

One family that left Germany for Shanghai in 1939 included seven-year-old Karin Zacharias. The Zachariases lived in a town in East Prussia not far from Königsberg (later the Russian city of Kaliningrad). Karin's father saw the writing on the wall early on with Hitler's government in Germany. Since the mid-1930s he wanted to get the family out of Europe, but his wife was not willing to go without her aging parents, who refused to leave their home.

Only in 1937, after the two older people both died, could the Zacha-riases begin to tackle the enormous project of getting out of Germany and finding a new home. Karin's father, educated as a lawyer, needed to learn a trade in order to get exit papers, so he became a welder. The family had to jump through endless bureaucratic hoops. To facilitate the process they relo-cated to Berlin.

Finally, in 1939 they left for China, where they would remain until 1948, when they were allowed to enter the United States. Karin, daughter of an assimilated German Jewish family, spent much of her childhood and her early teenage years in Shanghai. Karin Pardo, as she was later called, moved to Chicago, where she had many close friends who also grew up in China. Her experience is a reminder that the Holocaust was truly a worldwide event.

Geographic distance could mean safety but it did not prevent the shock of grief. Anka Voticky, a Czech Jew, also survived the war in Shanghai. Her recollections of the immediate aftermath emphasized neither the adventure of escape nor triumph—she had managed to bring her children and her par-ents with her—but unmitigated loss. In September 1945 she and her husband Arnold received a letter from a cousin describing the fate of their extended family. Arnold's parents and many other close relatives had been murdered in Treblinka; altogether sixty-five members of their family had been killed. For two days after reading the letter, Voticky recalls, her husband sat in a chair: "not

Cousins Gerda Harpuder and Kate Benjamin behind the counter of the Elite Provision Store in Shanghai in 1939. The Harpuders fled Berlin earlier that year, sold their belongings, and opened a delicatessen in Shanghai. Jewish refugees who could not obtain visas for traditional countries of European immigration, such as the United States and Canada, often undertook complicated and arduous trips to less familiar places, including Shanghai, India, and South America.

Joseph Fiszman poses with four Chinese children in a store in Shanghai in the early 1940s. A Yiddish writer from Poland, in December 1939, Fiszman fled Warsaw with his father, first to Vilna and eventually, with the help of the Japanese diplomat Sugihara, to Japan. Father and son would survive the war in Shanghai; Fiszman's mother and sister were imprisoned in the Warsaw ghetto and eventually killed in Trawniki.

moving, not speaking, not eating, not drinking, not sleeping." When he finally spoke it was to express utter isolation:

> Tomorrow is Yom Kippur. You can do whatever you want, but I am not fasting. In all my life I never saw my mother in her underwear. The thought that in Treblinka she had to undress in front of everybody and, naked, my parents had to dig their own grave. . . . I no longer believe that there can possibly be a God. (Voticky, 74–75)

Other survivors' accounts underscore how distance could bring safety but also paralyzing loneliness. In early November 1938, Gerhard Maass, a young

German Jew, arrived in Canada. Rather than relief he recalls feeling so frightened by the news from home that he could neither work nor think. His father in Hamburg was arrested during Kristallnacht and sent to a concentration camp, and although Maass's brother and cousins wrote to him, he could do nothing. In the fall of 1939, shortly after Canada declared war on Germany, he almost lost his foot in an accident at work. A Royal Canadian Mounted Police officer visited him in Montreal's Jewish General Hospital, but it was no social call. If he tried to send another letter to Germany, the police warned him, he would be deported. Years later, Maass struggled to describe his state of mind at the time: "How to explain? To be a man without a country in a strange country . . . I was on my own. I was frantic" (quoted in Klein, 34).

Scholarship on the Holocaust has barely begun to take seriously its global reach. In 1938, under pressure to address the looming refugee crisis, American officials called an international conference at Evian in France. The Evian Conference is often depicted as a turning point when the world, in particular traditional countries of immigration, refused to admit Jewish refugees. To highlight this failure it is often pointed out that at Evian, only the Dominican Republic agreed to open its doors, offering to take one hundred thousand Jewish refugees. But there is a back story.

In October 1937, under orders from President Rafael Trujillo, Dominican soldiers massacred an estimated twenty thousand Haitians inside the Dominican Republic. Although the motives for the killings and for the subsequent invitation to Jewish refugees continue to be debated, it seems evident that these developments were connected. Perhaps both were part of an effort to "whiten" the population, or the generous refugee policy may have been a form of damage control, in the wake of an international investigation whose outcome remained under negotiation. In any case, for some eight hundred Jews, being able to enter the Dominican Republic made the difference between life and death. Still, viewing that haven in its context of extreme violence is essential to comprehend the complex, interconnected, and brutal world in which the Holocaust took place.

The Voyage of the St. Louis

In early 1939, the government of Cuba agreed to grant visas to a number of Jews desperate to get out of Europe. Some enterprising individuals also produced fraudulent visas, which they sold in Germany. Armed with papers of various kinds, between eight hundred and nine hundred people, almost all of them Jewish, set sail from Hamburg to Havana on board the steamship *St. Louis.* Before the ship came in, Cuban authorities changed their minds about the refugees, and when the *St. Louis* arrived, they refused to allow the passengers to disembark. For days the ship remained offshore while representatives of the passengers tried to negotiate with the Cubans or find some alternative destination. Finally, the *St. Louis* left Havana. Sailing slowly up the coast of Florida, its captain radioed to officials all along the way in the United States and Canada, but no one would permit the ship to dock.

The crew had no choice but to return to Europe. Negotiations by Jewish organizations managed to get refuge for many of the passengers in Britain, France, and the Netherlands. In the years ahead some of those people, like most of those forced to return to Germany, would end up dead at Nazi hands, but some also found ways to stay alive. Careful research at the U.S. Holocaust Memorial Museum has traced all but a handful of the passengers of the *St. Louis.* Their stories show that foresight alone could not save a Jew from the Nazi trap. Connections, money, and determination were all factors, but so, above all, was luck, or whatever one might call chance at a time when no Jews could be counted lucky.

The Kindertransport

In 1939, a special program organized by private citizens, known as the Kindertransport—transport of children—brought some ten thousand Jewish refugee children from Germany, Austria, Czechoslovakia, and Poland to Great Britain. Forced to leave their families behind on the continent, most of them never saw their parents again.

Two veterans of the Kindertransports were Ilona and Kurt Penner, children of a Polish Jewish father and a Hungarian Jewish mother. Born in Berlin in 1928, the twins were sent to England in March 1939, where they were placed separately. Their parents, owners of a dry goods store, managed to leave Germany in 1940, although they initially only got as far as France. Fortunately, in 1941 they were able to secure passage to the United States. Kurt joined them there that year; Ilona, two years later.

Under the pressures of the Nazi system, persecution, escape, rescue, and separation connected and coexisted in complicated ways. It is no coincidence that the Kindertransport took off after Kristallnacht. In hindsight, the biggest hurdle appears to have been persuading British authorities to admit refugee children, but of course Jewish parents had to be willing to send their children off into the unknown.

Anecdotal evidence and timing suggest that fathers who suffered Nazi incarceration were instrumental in making the wrenching decision to send their children off alone. Hundreds of the German Jewish men arrested in November 1938 died in the camps, and many of those who emerged were unrecognizable to their families, physically debilitated and emotionally crushed. Camp authorities made them swear upon release never to speak of what they had

Jewish girls pose for a photograph in Tynemouth, Great Britain, after arriving on a Kindertransport. In the wake of Kristallnacht, the British government loosened immigration restrictions for specific categories of refugees, and an unspecified number of children under the age of seventeen were allowed to enter from Germany and the annexed territories of Austria and Czechoslovakia. This photograph was taken on September 1, 1939, the day Germany invaded Poland. Escape routes for Jewish refugees would disappear as the Third Reich expanded its reach. Facial expressions on photographs are always open to interpretation, but it is difficult not to read concern on the faces of many of these girls, especially the older ones.

suffered. Although silenced, men acted on the terrible lessons they had learned as prisoners. Many who had previously been reluctant to leave Germany were now frantic to get out.

After Max S., a tailor in Berlin, was released from Dachau, he and his wife Golda arranged to put their two oldest sons, thirteen-year-old Heinz and nine-year-old Benno, on a train to Holland, with nothing but tickets, a suitcase, and ten marks each. They hoped the boys would make contact with Jewish refugee aid organizations. Indeed, the two boys escaped into Holland and from there joined a Kindertransport to England. Their parents and younger brother who remained in Berlin were murdered in Auschwitz.

THE PROGRAM TO KILL DISABLED CHILDREN

Like Jews in Germany, people with disabilities also experienced the open Nazi aggression of 1938–1939. Hitler and other proponents of so-called racial purification would have to wait for the cover provided by war to implement murder on a mass scale, but by 1939 they felt confident enough to take steps in that direction. They began with the most defenseless segment of an already vulnerable group: the children.

In the winter of 1938–1939, a man named Knauer wrote to Hitler. He and his wife had a deformed baby. They wanted to have "this creature," as he called the child, killed. Hitler seized on the request as a way to begin having children who were considered "unworthy of living" killed. He assigned his personal physician, Dr. Karl Brandt, and the head of his personal staff in the Nazi Party, Philipp Bouhler, to deal with the Knauer case. Hitler instructed Brandt and Bouhler to inform the doctors involved that they could kill the child. Brandt and Bouhler were to tell the doctors that if any legal action were taken against them, the case would be thrown out of court.

Hitler authorized Brandt and Bouhler to deal with similar cases in the same way. They recruited a group of officials and doctors who were positively disposed toward such ideas. The group's official title was the Reich Committee for the Scientific Registration of Serious Hereditary and Congenitally Based Illnesses. By August 1939 the Reich Committee required all midwives and doctors to report the existence of any children with deformities. It then passed the forms received on to three pediatricians. They marked each form with a plus or a minus sign to indicate whether the particular child was to die or be allowed to live. Those doctors never saw the children whose fates they decided.

Brandt, Bouhler, and their committee were not confident that most of the German people would support the killing of children with disabilities, so they shrouded the process in secrecy. Still they had no trouble finding enough personnel to participate in these early stages of the program. The program to kill disabled children served Nazi planners as a kind of trial balloon, sent up to test reactions. The responses they perceived and the cooperation they received from the relevant professions indicated that it was possible to go even further in attacks on people considered disabled.

5

BRUTAL INNOVATIONS

War against Poland and the So-called
Euthanasia Program, 1939–1940

In 1939 Hitler got his war, not against Czechoslovakia but against Poland. Still Poland was not a surprising target; along with many of Germany's leading military men, Hitler considered existence of an independent Polish state to be anathema, and for Germany, Poland was the gateway to the east, where Hitler intended to find *Lebensraum*—living space—for his superior "Aryan race."

With the German invasion and conquest in 1939, Poland would become a site of innovation in expanding Nazi rule and implementing Nazi ideology. There the Germans seized control of large numbers of Jews and Poles, people Nazi teachings described as inferior. In conquered Polish territories, German planners began to implement schemes to recast the face of Europe. They forced millions of people to move, resettled those they deemed desirable, and robbed, evicted, enslaved, and eventually killed those they did not want. For two years, even before establishment of the first killing centers for Jews in 1941, the German occupiers of Poland tried out various solutions to what they considered their population problems, above all their self-made "Jewish problem."

This first stage of the war also brought experiments of another kind—in the murder of people deemed disabled. In 1939 and 1940 the so-called Euthanasia Program got into full swing within Germany. The word "euthanasia" comes from the Greek for "good death" or "good dying." In the Nazi case, that label was a lie because it suggested the decision to kill had something to do with the patients' wishes or their well-being. It did not. The initiators of this program of murder did not care what the people they targeted wanted or whether they were suffering. They asked only whether they could contribute to the productivity and supremacy of the "Aryan race." For this reason, the label "euthanasia" appears in this book with quotation marks or qualified as so-called euthanasia.

As in conquered Poland, planners and functionaries in the "euthanasia" program tested methods and developed techniques to implement the teachings of race and space. The results involved learning how most easily to kill large numbers of people and then dispose of their bodies. In the years ahead the lessons of this early initiative against disabled people would be applied against other targets, too.

This chapter traces Nazi German innovations in mass brutality in 1939 and 1940. From the outset we can identify two principles that characterized German practices, both in occupied Poland and with regard to people with disabilities. First, Nazi leaders encouraged experimentation and rivalry among the people who carried out their plans. Rather than easing the situation of those targeted for persecution, the chaotic conditions that resulted often increased the victims' vulnerability. Second, German decision-makers endorsed the notion of divide and conquer. Whenever possible they stirred up dissension among those over whom they ruled in order to advance their cause. That kind of manipulation by Nazi overlords of their subject peoples added to the wartime misery, too, first in Poland and later throughout Europe.

THE GERMANS IN POLAND

Blitzkrieg

On September 1, 1939, German forces invaded Poland. German planners tried to disguise this act of aggression as a defensive measure. They staged a mock attack on a German radio station near the border and then fabricated "proof" that Poles were to blame. Their evidence was a dead man dressed as a Polish saboteur, but in fact the Gestapo had arrested that man and killed him themselves. For the purposes of Nazi propaganda, this incident served to justify military action.

Hitler and his inner circle were not confident that the German public was ready for war. They had already spent the summer of 1939 rousing anti-Polish sentiment in Germany, using the newspapers to publicize wild accusations of Polish crimes against the ethnic German minority in Poland. Still, within Germany the initial reaction to war was cautious. When Hitler appeared on his balcony in Berlin following announcements of the attack on Poland, he expected to be greeted by throngs of zealous supporters. Instead the crowd was so small that he went back inside to avoid embarrassment.

The assault of September 1, 1939, did not take the Poles completely by surprise, because they had had plenty of opportunities to observe German saber-rattling in the preceding months. They were, however, stunned by the rapidity of the German advance. The Germans' technological advantage enabled them to wage a blitzkrieg—a war at lightning speed. First they attacked from the sky. It was an awesome show of power: Jack Pomerantz, at the time a young man in the Polish town of Radzyn, recalls that he had never seen an airplane until the German attack on September 1, 1939. That day the sky was black with them.

But the Polish air force exacted a high price: in the first week of the war, the Germans lost eighty planes, and several hundred more in the weeks that followed. Still the Luftwaffe was able to gain air superiority. Nazi propaganda spread the myth that the Polish air force had been destroyed on the ground, and decades later, that misconception persists.

Then tanks rolled in to crush resistance and clear the way for occupying troops. With eleven cavalry brigades, a single tank division, and seven hundred and fifty armored vehicles, the Poles could not stop the Germans, who smashed into Poland with fifteen tank divisions and thousands of armored vehicles.

Renya Kulkielko, a teenager in Jędrzejów, about 50 miles from Krakow, felt the panic that spread with the German attack. People streamed from the cities to the countryside and ran from one town to another, hoping to find safety. Wounded people and cattle lay on the roads; low-flying planes sprayed bullets. She described the heart-rending cries of babies whose mothers had been killed, the stench of dead bodies, and entire villages in flames. German tanks appeared, then German soldiers, who entered houses and took whatever they fancied. In Kulkielko's town they surrounded the Jewish street, locked a group of Jews in the synagogue, and lit it on fire. Similar scenes occurred all over western and central Poland.

Decisions made and actions taken in those tumultuous days had enormous and unforeseeable consequences. France and Britain declared war on Germany, although for the time being they remained outside the fray. The Hitler-Stalin Pact of August 1939 assured the Germans of nonaggression from the Soviet Union. And, as the secret arrangements had anticipated, the German offensive was followed, beginning on September 17, by a Soviet advance into Polish territory from the east, up to the line previously agreed upon. By early October, the Poles were forced to surrender. Eastern Poland would remain under Soviet control until mid-1941.

The Germans and Soviets killed sixty-six thousand Poles in the 1939 attacks. German losses were lower but still considerable, some seventeen thousand men; and the Soviets lost about seven thousand. At least one million Poles,

Map by Michael J. Fisher, cartographer

including many Jews, were taken prisoner—many by the Germans but also a substantial number by the Soviets. Anti-Polish prejudices and a military culture that called for absolute destruction of the enemy fueled German brutality. The assumption that Poles were dangerous bandits, irregular combatants who attacked from concealed positions, served the Germans as justification for a massive assault on soldiers and civilians, Christians and Jews, alike.

By late September Warsaw surrendered, and the Polish leadership fled to France and later on to London to establish a government-in-exile. Members of the Polish army buried caches of arms rather than relinquish them to the Germans. Those weapons would provide the nucleus for the underground armies in the half decade of struggle that still lay ahead for the Poles. Meanwhile, members of the Polish army would fight on, in Norway, Britain, France, North Africa, Italy, and on the western front in 1944–1945.

In hindsight, the first days and even years of the war are overshadowed by the massive scale of atrocities that followed. But eyewitness accounts reveal the trauma of events in Poland. On September 1, 1939, Adina Blady Szwajger was a 22-year-old medical student and newly-wed in Warsaw. For a few days classes continued, under heavy air raids, but soon the university was closed. Szwajger and two friends made the rounds of hospitals, trying to find a way to help the growing number of wounded. Whether because they were Jewish or in the chaos of the blitzkrieg, no one took them on, so together with a neighbor, a nurse, Szwajger organized a small first-aid station on her block. There she delivered her first baby and had a teenaged boy, a neighbor's son, die in her arms, hit by shrapnel during the bombing of the Jewish district on Yom Kippur. Szwajger heard the mayor, Stefan Starzynski, give his final speech as the city surrendered. She remembers standing in a silent crowd, everyone pale and weeping as they watched the Germans march in.

Szwajger and her husband, a law student, went to the Soviet zone, where she hoped to be able to complete her medical studies. Both filled out a questionnaire asking whether they intended to return to Poland after the war or stay in the Soviet Union. Like almost everyone, they answered they would go back home. Most people who gave that response ended up in one of the deadly Soviet labor camps known as Gulags. However, a colleague warned Szwajger, and she managed to evade deportation and return illegally to Warsaw. There she worked as a pediatrician in the ghetto, served as a courier for the Jewish underground, and survived the war.

Division and Dual Occupation

From the outset, "divide and conquer" was the German byword in occupied Poland. The arrangement with the Soviet Union contributed to this approach as did the German decision to divide its own part of conquered Poland into two parts. The western areas, known as the incorporated territories, were annexed by the Greater German Reich. This area included such important cities as Danzig—now called Gdańsk—and Lodz (Łódź), which the Germans would rename Litzmannstadt. The incorporated territories were home to 10 million people, around 80 percent of them ethnic Poles. Also living there were ethnic Germans, Jews, and smaller numbers of Czechs, Ukrainians, Roma, and others.

The Germans called the remaining part of their Polish territory the General Government and administered it like a colony. Warsaw, Krakow, and Lublin were its major cities. Under the leadership of Governor General Dr. Hans Frank, a longtime associate of Hitler, the General Government became a key site of Nazi brutality. Much of the mass killing of Jews after 1941 would be done there; plans to reduce Poles to slaves of Germany also found early implementation in the General Government.

Like the Germans, the Soviets sought to secure their conquest through terror, and they too regarded Poles as enemies. In fact, Poles inside the Soviet Union topped the list of ethnic groups victimized under Stalin. During the Great Purge of 1937–1938, Soviet security forces had arrested tens of thousands of ethnic Poles on accusations of espionage, executed at least eighty-five thousand of them, and sent the rest to the Gulags.

Soviet leaders shared Hitler's aversion to the existence of an independent Polish state. So when Soviet forces took over eastern Poland in 1939, they sent many prominent Poles to forced labor in Siberia. Moreover, in the decades since the Bolshevik Revolution, the Soviet Union had developed a reputation for attacking Christianity and the churches. No wonder many Poles, especially the wealthy, staunchly nationalist, and devoutly Catholic, considered Soviet rule the worst tragedy that could befall them. As a result, when the Soviets arrived in September 1939, some Poles ran toward the Germans.

In contrast to their Christian neighbors, Polish Jews tended to regard Soviet rule as a lesser evil than Nazi German domination. At least in theory, antisemitism did not exist under Communism. Even in practice, Jews had possibilities to make lives for themselves in the Soviet Union, including as officers in the military. Nazi Germany offered no such option, as news from the west and waves of refugees had made clear since 1933. So while some Polish Christians fled west, many Polish Jews, like Jack Pomerantz, took their chances by running east.

We tend to assume that shared hardships draw people together. Often, however, the opposite occurs. The tribulations faced by all Poles in the early stages of World War II tended to drive wedges between Christians and Jews. Those Poles who were already suspicious of Jews interpreted it as a betrayal

Having fled to Lithuania, Rabbi David Lifszyc (left) and another man pose in front of Torah scrolls smuggled out of Suwalki, Poland. This photograph was taken in 1940. Rabbi Lifszyc (later Lifshitz) and other community leaders hid the town's Torah scrolls fearing confiscation or destruction after the German occupation in September 1939. Lifszyc eventually managed to obtain the necessary visas and tickets to travel across the USSR and, in May 1941, he set sail from Japan to San Francisco.

when some Polish Jews cast their lot with the Soviets. Those who had long accused Jews of being Communists could now claim to have found proof. Conversely, Jews who already regarded ethnic Poles as vicious antisemites could point to some Poles' preference for Nazi Germany as evidence that they had been right. Possibly neither Hitler nor Stalin foresaw these outcomes when the pact was signed in August 1939, but both stood to gain from anything that helped divide and rule the Poles.

Poles faced hard times on either side of the German-Soviet divide. Policies of resettlement and Germanization meant that hundreds of thousands of ethnic Poles were expelled from the incorporated territories. In the General Government the Germans targeted Poles for impoverishment and forced labor.

Anyone who welcomed the Soviets in 1939 would be disappointed, too. Their new rulers had no intention of respecting Poles or protecting Jews. Instead they shut down Jewish community institutions, banned organized activities, and confiscated private assets from Jews as well as non-Jews. They deported large numbers of Poles—Jews and non-Jews—to Siberia and Central Asia as prisoners and laborers. All young men in the areas under Soviet control had to enlist in the Red Army. Some Poles—Jewish and gentile—complied. Others went west rather than risk being stranded in the Soviet Union and separated from their homeland and families forever. In 1939 they could not know that, within two years, for a Jew to be trapped anywhere in Poland would amount to a death sentence. At least in the Soviet Union a person could keep moving east. From German-occupied Poland there was no place to go.

Imposing German Rule

Germans, in particular Nazi Germans, are often described as hyperorganized. German rule in the territories of occupied Poland, however, contradicts that stereotype. Rather than orderly, it was characterized by overlapping jurisdictions and competing authorities. The German military was involved as was the SS under Himmler. Hans Frank and his administration in the General Government played an important role; so did Göring, Hitler's deputy and head of the Four-Year Plan for the German economy. Local Nazis took initiatives, especially in the incorporated territories, as did German police and representatives of the interior ministry.

Almost every ambitious German Nazi activist, military man, and bureaucrat wanted a piece of the action. So did many German women—social workers, teachers, nurses, journalists, and others—who sought adventure and new career opportunities. Those who wanted to get ahead in defeated Poland found it expedient to further Nazi goals. Whether in the incorporated territories or in the General Government, they tried to distinguish themselves from their colleagues and rivals by being more effective—that is, harsher—and more ambitious—that is, more brutal—in their treatment of the local populations.

Hitler and his inner circle had grandiose plans for Polish territories. Initially they intended to force the ethnic Poles farther east, confine Jews to some desolate reservation, and establish an area of "Aryan"/German settlement. Although details remained vague, implementation began immediately.

On September 7, 1939, Heydrich issued an order to the special units of police and SS under his jurisdiction. It would be necessary, he instructed, to destroy the leadership class in Poland and expel all Jews from areas in German hands. In short, as he told a subordinate, the "nobility, clergy, and Jews must be killed."

Heydrich's position was in line with the views of his bosses Hitler and Himmler. They wanted to reduce the Poles to a people of slaves, to destroy their intellectual and religious leaders and their sense of tradition—anything that might give them a way to organize against Germany. Accordingly, they encouraged German forces to target Catholic priests and the Polish intelligentsia. In the opening months of the war, Germans shot fifteen hundred priests and imprisoned countless others. They also humiliated, arrested, and murdered many other prominent Poles, including journalists, professors, and artists. Under the code name "AB-Aktion" the effort to eliminate the Polish intellectual and spiritual leadership continued in 1940, with thousands of victims. The destruction of the Polish elites would have a devastating effect on society in the years of occupation ahead.

German authorities prohibited activities that advanced the education of Poles, fostered communal ties, or promoted national feelings. They imposed curfews and seized Polish businesses. They shut down Polish newspapers, closed cultural institutions, and used forced labor and public hangings to make examples of people who defied them. Members of the SS, police, and regular military, along with local collaborators, also terrorized Poles, Jews and non-Jews, in less organized ways that included theft, beating, castration, and rape.

Even photography could be a form of oppression. German soldiers and civilians took pictures that added to the humiliation of their victims by turning them into trophies to be flaunted. The three photographs here were all taken between September and December 1939. They depict the violence of the German invasion and early occupation of Poland. Yet they also suggest ways that atrocity photographs play multiple, even contradictory roles.

The first image shows Poles seized during the "pacification" of Bydgoszcz (Bromberg). Men of the German 6th Motorized Police Battalion prepare to shoot five people lined up against a fence as they already have done or will do next to the people lying on the ground. Clearly someone trusted by the Germans, perhaps one of the police, took this picture. Its amateur look contrasts the professional quality of the second photograph, taken in Krakow a few months later.

Here it is a group of Jews up against a wall, their vertical forms both accentuated and diminished by the lines and angles of the pavement, the building blocks, and the windows. This scene looks like an expressionist movie where everything is ominous and skewed. No photographer is recorded, but again, the picture was obviously the work of someone close to the German authorities, someone able to get near the action and take time to compose the shot.

A note on the back of the photo indicates that this image changed hands and dramatically changed its function, from a trophy of the perpetrators to evidence of their crimes. Someone wrote, in Polish, as follows: "I have found (stolen) the originals of these photos at the commission shop 'Furniture Antiquities and Pictures' at the outlet of Grodzka Street and main Market Square in Krakow in the first days of November 1942." Presumably that act was motivated by a desire to call the Germans to account for atrocities against Poland and Polish Jews. The timing is significant, too: by November 1942, the Allies were hammering the Germans and their Axis partners in North Africa

A group of Poles in Bydgoszcz (Bromberg) about to be shot by men of the German 6th Motorized Police Battalion. On September 3, 1939, two days after the German invasion of Poland, armed groups of ethnic Germans staged an uprising against the local Polish garrison. It was put down the next day, just before Wehrmacht units arrived in the city. During the following week, German troops, assisted by military field police and Einsatzgruppe IV, executed at least five hundred Polish civilians, including members of the local intelligentsia and Catholic priests, and arrested over one thousand more, in accordance with instructions from Himmler and Heydrich for the "political housecleaning" of Poland.

and at Stalingrad. Whoever found/stole the photograph could look ahead to something inconceivable in late 1939: German defeat.

The third photograph shows SS men leading Polish women from the Pawiak and Mokotow prisons in Warsaw into the forest to be killed. Once again, only someone trusted by the killers could have come close enough to take this picture. But someone, perhaps the photographer, the person who developed the film, or someone else, managed to get this photo into the hands of members of the Polish underground. They sent it to the Polish government-in-exile in London, where it was used to illustrate German terror.

The war in 1939 brought massive expansion of the network of concentration and labor camps. Some Poles were forced to build roads and dams under perilous conditions. Others were sent to Germany. The existing camps in Germany could not hold all of the possible inmates, so German authorities repurposed former Polish prisons and set up provisional camps in their newly

Jews arrested in the Podgorze neighborhood of Krakow are lined up against a wall, December 1, 1939. The proximity and positioning of the photographer so close to the Germans, as well as the striking lines and framing, suggest that this photograph may have been taken by a professional with ties to the Germans rather than an amateur passerby

acquired territories. Within a few months they had detained more than one hundred thousand Poles.

The Germans showed additional, often improvised brutality toward their numerous, new Jewish subjects. In the 1930s far more Jews lived in Poland than in Germany. Germany's half million Jews in 1933 made up less than 1 percent of the population; Poland's more than 3 million Jews in 1939 represented approximately 10 percent.

The first phase of the war became a kind of open season against Polish Jews for Stormtroopers, SS, Nazi Party members, and unruly soldiers. Undisciplined and often drunk, they roamed around occupied Polish territories

In late 1939, SS personnel lead Polish women from the Pawiak and Mokotow prisons in nearby Warsaw into the forest to be killed. Members of the Polish underground sent this photograph to the Polish government-in-exile in London to illustrate German terror in occupied Poland.

burning, looting, and raping. The distinctive appearance of Orthodox Jewish men made them favorite targets for ridicule and violence. Rowdy Germans pulled out their beards and forced them to crawl in the street. Thugs attacked synagogues, where they desecrated ritual objects and abused the observant. Hostage takings and demands for ransom were common. In October 1939, for example, Germans murdered one hundred Jews in a café in Lodz and forced others to pay for their lives.

Ethnic Germans and Resettlement Schemes

Nazi racial policy had two sides: attack on people deemed undesirable and advancement of those considered "Aryan." In 1939 and 1940 the second part of that scheme included locating ethnic Germans, known as *Volksdeutschen*, people living outside Germany who identified themselves culturally as Germans (but not as Jews). In 1939 German experts estimated there to be about seven hundred thousand Volksdeutschen in Poland alone.

German forces used the ethnic Germans to increase the terror of the early months of the war. Some ethnic Germans were killed by their Polish neighbors for helping the invading Germans. The numbers are unclear; respectable estimates range from two to five thousand such casualties, but official German reports claimed that vengeful Poles had slaughtered fifty-eight thousand ethnic Germans in early September 1939. That charge served to whip up hatred against Poles within Germany and also helped the SS form ethnic Germans into vigilante groups that attacked Poles and stole their property.

Many German officials who flocked into the newly conquered Polish territories busied themselves drawing up lists of people who should count as ethnic Germans. They organized programs to relocate such people to the most desirable areas and evict the Poles who had been living there.

Officials also introduced a whole range of measures intended to differentiate Poles and Germans, two groups that in fact were not always easy to separate in a part of Europe that had long been ethnically mixed. Poles were not permitted to say, "Heil Hitler," nor could they serve Germans in shops. Laws forbade friendships between Germans and Poles and criminalized sexual relationships. Nevertheless, sexual assault of Polish women by German men was common. Later in the war German military authorities forced some Polish women into brothels to serve German men and non-Germans who fought for the Reich.

Plans for resettlement of ethnic Germans took on massive proportions. In October and November 1939 German diplomats worked out deals with Estonia, Latvia, and the Soviet Union so that Volksdeutschen in those parts of Europe would also be brought "home into the Reich." The idea was to move ethnic Germans out of the Baltic states and eastern Poland into the newly incorporated territories. Of course, bringing ethnic Germans in required throwing other people out.

By 1940 some two hundred thousand ethnic Germans who had signed up for resettlement needed homes. That year German police forced hundreds of thousands of Poles to leave the incorporated territories for the General Government. Often they were given only hours to get out, with instructions to leave their houses swept and the keys in the cupboard for the new inhabitants. Meanwhile, in the General Government nothing awaited the deportees but misery.

At the same time, in late 1939 and throughout 1940, German police evicted hundreds of thousands of Polish Jews from their homes and squeezed them into ghettos. The most desirable residences and businesses went to ethnic Germans or Germans from the Reich. Poor properties were allotted to Polish gentiles. The resettlement scheme, like all the German plans for Poland, bred conflict. Privileging ethnic Germans turned them against Poles and Jews and encouraged them to betray their neighbors. Dangling promises of Jewish property in front of gentile Poles gave them a stake in attacks on Jews.

SS leader Himmler encouraged his men to do all they could to turn ethnic groups within Poland against one another. It was a good idea to recruit local policemen and mayors from minority groups, he maintained. That way the majority's anger would be diverted from the German occupiers onto those petty officials. Accordingly Germans in the General Government often used Volksdeutschen, Ukrainians, and Belorussians against ethnic Poles and Jews. In many cases German authorities relied on local Polish gentiles to point out who was Jewish.

In 1940, Richard S., a twelve-year-old boy in Wadowice in southwestern Poland, experienced German divide-and-conquer tactics firsthand. Along with other Jewish youths from the region, he was assigned to a forced labor squad. One day German police took his group to do some of the grunt work of throwing Poles out of their homes in preparation for the arrival of ethnic Germans being resettled in the incorporated territories. "They brought us into the houses and made us take out the belongings," Mr. S. recalled in an interview. "One image is imprinted in my brain," he continued:

> The Poles in our town were very religious. They had a lot of pictures of Mary, Jesus, and saints in their houses, crucifixes, things like that. One SS man pointed to a crucifix hanging on the wall and then shouted at us: "Take that Jew down!"

Looking back, Richard S. grasped the horrible irony and the disastrous repercussions of the Germans' methods. "There are probably Poles walking around today who remember that," he observed, "or maybe they have told their children and grandchildren that when the Germans threw us out of our homes, Jews were there too, helping them" (quoted in Bergen 2012). In this situation, the German conquerors manipulated Jewish slave laborers to help expel disempowered Poles. In other circumstances they used Volksdeutschen against Jews and Poles, Poles against Jews and Roma, even Roma against Jews. Such incidents in turn deepened old rifts and generated new grounds for resentment and suspicion.

Individual Initiatives—The Example of Eichmann

Some German officials took their own initiatives against people whom Nazi ideology deemed inferior. By doing so they hoped to catch the attention of their bosses and advance their careers. For example, in the fall of 1939, Adolf Eichmann (1906–1962), an ambitious bureaucrat in Heydrich's Reich Security Main Office, began to organize transports of Jews to the General Government—from Vienna, from Silesia in the incorporated territories, and from parts of former Czechoslovakia.

After the war, when he was tried in Israel for his role in the Holocaust, Eichmann would insist that he had never been an antisemite. It does seem that for Eichmann, careerism was at least as strong a motivation as antisemitism, although in the context, those factors were mutually reinforcing. In any case Eichmann played a central role organizing the forced emigration of Austrian Jews in 1938 and of Czech Jews a year later. Throughout 1942 and 1943 he would be instrumental in arranging transportation of Jews from all over Europe to killing centers. He also coordinated transport of Hungarian Jews to Auschwitz in 1944. In 1962 Eichmann was hanged in Israel.

Eichmann, trained as an expert in Jewish affairs, had no formal authorization for his 1939 project. Nor had he made arrangements for the Jews when they arrived in the General Government. Instead his men simply dumped their prisoners off at a place called Nisko, near the city of Lublin, and told them to get lost. Most of the Jews fled into the woods, and the Germans shot those who returned.

As the Nisko incident illustrates, competition among German authorities often made the situation of the people they targeted worse. Sometimes the resulting disorganization undermined the Germans' ability to achieve their goals. By early 1941, top Nazis had to stop sending Poles to the General Government, because the situation had become too unstable. Hans Frank announced he could not take any more Poles in his area, and Göring agreed that it was economically unwise to keep up the transports. Certainly neither of them was motivated by humanitarianism, and both sought above all to expand their own power. In 1941 both would be instrumental in moving German policy from the confused resettlements and expulsions of 1939 and 1940 to the so-called Final Solution of the Jewish Question: annihilation.

Protests against German Brutality

Some people spoke out against German atrocities in Poland. Shocked by the slaughter of Polish Catholic priests, Roman Catholic leaders in Poland and even some Germans appealed to the Vatican. Perhaps Hitler would listen to the pope, they reasoned.

Many people begged the pope to take action, but Pius XII did not respond. His reasons are unclear. He may have believed that a strict policy of neutrality was the most powerful position the Vatican could take. Perhaps he feared reprisals against Catholics within Germany, or against the Vatican itself. A staunch opponent of Communism, he may have thought that Nazi Germany—even given its excesses—was still preferable to Soviet domination of Europe. The anti-Communist argument, however, rings hollow for 1939, when Nazi Germany and the Soviet Union worked in tandem to dismember Poland, and both powers singled out Polish Catholic clergy for abuse. In any case, the pope's inaction in the fall of 1939—when the victims of German aggression were priests in his own church—would make it hard for him to speak out later in the face of crimes against Jews.

Some members of the German army also protested the brutality around them. The best-known case involved General Johannes Blaskowitz, commander of a German military region in occupied Poland. In early 1940, Blaskowitz sent a long memorandum directly to Hitler that provided specific examples of German crimes. For example, Blaskowitz described how a drunk German policeman beat a Polish man to death and forced a woman who may have been his wife to bury the body while scores of Germans and Poles looked on. Blaskowitz also told about some German soldiers who raped a teenaged Jewish girl in a cemetery. His account included many other cases of viciousness on the part of German police and SS men.

Such behavior was counterproductive, Blaskowitz warned. It would lead to a breakdown in discipline among the German forces, stir up bad press abroad, and alienate those elements of the population that might otherwise have been sympathetic to the Germans. According to Blaskowitz, German abuses would drive Polish Jews and gentiles together. Polish gentiles, he reported, feared that anything done to Jews would eventually be done to them too.

Hitler dismissed Blaskowitz's memorandum as childish and naive. One could not "win a war with Salvation Army tactics," he allegedly responded. You might expect that Blaskowitz was shot or imprisoned for daring to send his report, but he was not. Instead he was merely transferred. Others were happy to take over his powerful position in occupied Poland.

Over time such protests ceased. Other military men who may have felt as Blaskowitz did in the fall of 1939 got used to conditions or forgot their misgivings in the face of Germany's triumphs. Meanwhile, those who showed they were willing or even eager to fight a war of atrocity found themselves favored for promotions. By consistently rewarding behavior that furthered the goals of race and space, the Nazi leadership made sure it always had a supply of ambitious, loyal individuals at every level of the hierarchy.

As the case of Blaskowitz indicates, Nazi Germany did not need unanimity in order to function. The Third Reich was not merely the work of "true believers"—fanatics who blindly endorsed every detail of Hitler's ideology. It also built on the efforts of critical Nazis and even opponents of Nazism, people who grumbled about some of its excesses while they applied their energies and abilities to ensuring its stability. Not mass brainwashing but the participation of ordinary people of all kinds enabled the Nazi system to operate as it did.

The Polish Underground Army

War did not end in Poland with the German defeat of the Polish army in 1939. Instead many Poles fought on in underground armies. There were several variants of the Polish underground army: most important were the national army, which fought for an independent Poland, and the Communist underground.

The Polish national army, known as the Home Army, or AK, maintained links to the Polish government-in-exile. Many of its leaders were prewar Polish officers, and it was very well organized though less well equipped. The Home Army's record with regard to Polish Jews was mixed. Some of its officers were themselves antisemitic, but others tried to assist Jews in various ways. In some cases members of the Home Army participated in killing Jews in the forests. Nevertheless, the Home Army did devote considerable attention to learning about what was happening to the Jews in Poland. Its intelligence assumed that any methods applied to Jews would later be used against Polish gentiles.

The much smaller Communist underground army also had a complicated relationship with Jews. Some units were open to Polish Jews who wished to join their ranks but others were hostile. In most areas the Communist underground was rather weak and disorganized. Its leaders had little time for people ill equipped to take part in fighting: children, elderly people, and the unarmed.

Later in the war some Jews would form their own underground fighting organizations. At least one of those, the Bielski partisans in western Belorussia, did accept older people, women, and children. Led by the dynamic Tuvia Bielski, that forest community combined fighting and rescue activities. By 1944 it included more than twelve hundred Jews. Nechama Tec describes its efforts in her aptly titled book *Defiance*.

GHETTOIZATION OF POLISH JEWS

At first German decision-makers were not sure what to do with the many Jews who fell into their hands in 1939. Not until 1941 would they come to adopt total mass murder as the "solution" to the "Jewish problem." From the outset, however, they tried to separate Polish Jews from the rest of the population. They targeted Jews in ways that made them vulnerable and contemptible and pushed non-Jews to lose sympathy for them.

Ghettoization, the measure that German authorities developed in late 1939 and early 1940, was a logical extension of the approach of divide and conquer. All over Polish territories German officials forced Jews out of their homes, in villages, small towns, and cities, into designated urban areas called ghettos. There Jews were to be concentrated and isolated. Meanwhile German authorities seized Jewish property to dispose of as they saw fit. In some cases eager non-Jewish neighbors rushed in before them to pick up the spoils. Often ethnic Germans were the first in line.

German planners may have considered ghettoization a temporary measure, a sort of holding pattern until subsequent steps could be taken. But what were those steps to be? In 1939 and 1940 some Nazi decision-makers were still talking about a Jewish reservation in the east, near Lublin. Officials in the

German Foreign Office would propose another scheme, the Madagascar Plan, to ship all of Europe's Jews to an island off the coast of Africa. Others floated different ideas such as using the Jews in the ghettos as slave labor or leaving them to die of starvation and disease. The Nazi leadership encouraged every plan as long as it aimed to destroy Jewish life.

Between 1939 and 1941, during this phase of experimentation with regard to German policy toward Jews, over half a million Polish Jews died in ghettos and labor camps. Many starved to death; many also died of diseases brought on by the crowding and terrible sanitary conditions. Police, guards, and overseers shot and beat others to death—for trying to escape, for smuggling, failing to work to the level demanded, or simply for sport. The ghettos were not yet a formal program of annihilation, but they proved deadly for hundreds of thousands of Polish Jews of all ages.

There were more than one thousand ghettos, all of them sites of death yet also of Jewish life. In ghettos people of all ages and genders lived together, often as families. Ghettos both undermined ties between people and intensified them. People with little or nothing in common before the war were crammed into close quarters: old and young; urban, secular, Polish-speaking Jews with Orthodox, Yiddish speakers; Hasidic Jews with Zionists, Communists, and Bundists (Jewish socialists).

Still, people found ways to continue Jewish life—to educate children, observe religious traditions, and organize social services. Large ghettos had hospitals, nursing homes, orphanages, and theaters, and all ghettos were sites of individual creativity. Emanuel Ringelblum, a historian in Warsaw, observed that in the ghetto, everyone wrote. People kept diaries, wrote poetry, plays, stories, songs, reports, philosophical and theological treatises, letters, and jokes. Many of those writings were destroyed or lost, but some survived, hidden, buried, mailed to people on the outside, or committed to memory.

One of the scribes of the Warsaw ghetto was Shimon Huberband, a young rabbi. His wife and child had been killed in the early days of September 1939, when German planes destroyed the town in which they had sought refuge. He wrote down all kinds of things—jokes, legends, and messianic signs—that might provide sources to study Jewish life and death in the ghetto. Hitler was the subject of many of the jokes: "A teacher asks his pupil, 'Tell me, Moyshe, what would you like to be if you were Hitler's son?' 'An orphan,' the pupil answers." Another played on the color brown, symbol of Nazism: "Where does Hitler feel best? In the toilet. There, all the brown masses are behind him" (quoted in Roskies, 399, 403).

Hunger and misery undermined the possibilities for Jewish solidarity, but people did what they could to preserve dignity and bonds of affection. Josef Zelkowicz, a talented journalist from a Hasidic family, wrote a series of reports on housing in the Lodz ghetto. In one apartment he found seventeen people crowded together. When the ghetto was sealed, 77-year-old Devorah Hannah had welcomed all of them into her home. With only three beds, not everyone had a place to sleep. Mrs. Hannah shared a nest of blankets in a corner with her youngest grandchild—the orphaned, 18-month-old Leibeleh. Food was scarce and strictly rationed. Young children whimpered, and family members bickered. But, in Devorah Hannah's estimation, "the main thing is that they are all together, thank God."

The German government-run leisure organization "Strength through Joy" organized bus tours to the ghettos so that members of the supposed master race could see the degeneracy of their alleged inferiors. No matter that the Germans themselves had created the filth and desperation evident there. That squalor was offered as proof that Nazi theories of race and space held true.

Photographs from the ghettos provide a study in contrasting perspectives. Mendel Grossman's photo of his father reciting the morning prayers in his bed in the Lodz ghetto is a portrait of love, devotion, agony, and piety. How

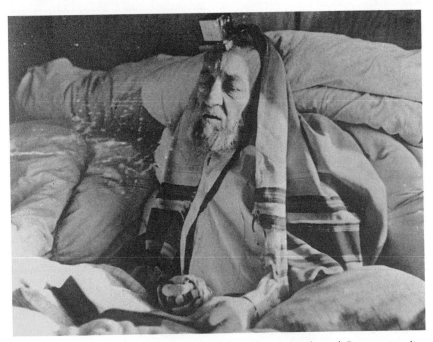

Wearing his tallis and tefillin (prayer shawl and phylacteries), Shmuel Grossman recites the morning prayer service in his bed in the Lodz ghetto. Grossman died in the ghetto at the age of sixty. His son, the photographer Mendel Grossman, took this picture in 1941 or 1942. The elderly were a particularly vulnerable segment of the ghetto population.

German soldiers watch Jewish women at the outdoor market of the Lublin ghetto, sometime in 1941 or 1942. Following the ghettoization of Polish Jews, many German soldiers and Nazi functionaries toured the ghettos to marvel at and mock what the Nazis claimed were the inherent destitution and filthiness of Jewish life—conditions caused by the Nazis themselves. Photographs like this one were sometimes made into postcards and sent to girlfriends, wives, and other family members back in Germany.

different from the voyeuristic gaze of the German soldiers laughing and ogling Jewish women in the market in the Lublin ghetto.

The Example of Lodz

One of the largest ghettos was established in Lodz in the incorporated territory in the winter of 1939. By April 1940 it had been sealed off completely from the rest of the city. The Lodz ghetto lasted in some form until August 1944, when almost all the Jews remaining there were sent to Auschwitz to be killed. Although every ghetto was different, Lodz illustrates some general conditions.

In Lodz, as elsewhere, German authorities had varying opinions about the nature of the ghetto. Was it primarily for forced labor? Was it to be self-supporting? If so, how, when it was allocated no resources? To what extent was it to be self-administered? All of this uncertainty added to the misery of those imprisoned within the poorest parts of the city.

The ghetto was disastrously overcrowded. In Lodz, an average of seven people occupied a single room—that is, in 1940 an estimated two hundred and twenty-three thousand people were crammed into some thirty thousand apartments, most of them one room only. Only about 725 of those lodgings had running water. Many had electricity, but it did little good; police forbade those in the ghetto from using their lights most of the time.

Lodz was one of the most isolated of all of the ghettos. Before the war, Lodz was known for its textile industry, and ghetto leaders built on that capacity in their strategy of "survival through work." Workshops and factories were set up inside the ghetto to make uniforms, mattresses, and other things useful for the war effort or profitable for certain powerful Germans. Without the regular movement of people in and out, it was almost impossible to smuggle food or weapons, convey news, or get people out of the ghetto. The city of Lodz itself was slated to be "Germanized"—that is, German planners intended to remove ethnic Poles, Jews, and others from the area and replace them with Germans from the Reich and ethnic Germans from elsewhere in Europe. As a result, previous friendships and contacts in the city were of little help to Jews in the ghetto.

Food was woefully scarce—potato peels became a prized item. Lice and rats thrived; typhus, tuberculosis, and other diseases ran rampant. Nevertheless, hard work was required of everyone who wanted a chance to stay alive. By 1943 ghetto workshops were churning out uniforms, boots, underwear, and bed linen for the German military; ghetto workers produced goods of metal, wood, leather, fur, down, and paper, and even electrical and telecommunication devices. Children as young as eight slaved away for pathetically small rations of food.

Under these conditions it is no surprise that people died in terrible numbers. In 1940, some six thousand Jews died in the Lodz ghetto. By the following year the number had almost doubled, to eleven thousand. In 1942 there would be eighteen thousand dead. By the end of 1941, the primary cause of Jewish death would no longer be starvation and illness in the ghettos but death by gassing in the nearby killing center at Chelmno.

SS race and resettlement experts came to think of the ghettos as repositories for people they considered human trash. Beginning in 1941 they dumped Jews from all over Europe—Luxembourg, Germany, Austria, Czechoslovakia—in Lodz. German officials also shipped some five thousand European Roma to the Lodz ghetto, where they inhabited a specially designated area and, like the Jews, suffered beatings, starvation, and disease. In December 1941 and January 1942 those Roma still in Lodz were gassed at Chelmno. It is said that no Roma survived the Lodz ghetto. Nazi authorities also sent Roma to Jewish ghettos in other cities, for example, Warsaw, Lublin, and Bialystok.

The Jewish Councils

German officials saved themselves work by setting up Jewish councils (in German, *Judenräte*) to enforce Nazi orders and administer the daily affairs of the ghettos. They appointed members in various ways, sometimes seeking recognized community leaders, sometimes making Jews decide among themselves. Inside the ghettos, the Jewish councils distributed scarce resources, organized social life, set up charities, and tried to find ways to maintain some kind of human community.

There were precedents for such bodies. Historically Jewish communities had councils (*kehillot*) who negotiated with secular authorities and collected taxes. European colonizers commonly ruled through indigenous elites or appointed intermediaries to do their bidding. In both contexts the middlemen were lightning rods for resentment. In the ghettos, Jewish councils found themselves forced to make terrible choices. When the Germans in charge decided to purge a ghetto of those deemed unfit to work, they demanded that the Jewish council turn over a certain number of people. If not, the entire ghetto would be destroyed. But who would be in that group?

Faced with such dilemmas Jewish councils responded in different ways. Some refused to cooperate and were killed by the Germans and replaced with more compliant men. Some committed suicide. Others tried to bribe the Germans or negotiate, in the hope that sacrificing some Jews would save others. Many tried first to protect their own family, friends, and the people who worked for them, especially the Jewish police. In the end most members of the Jewish councils were killed, like other people in the ghettos.

The Jewish councils have often been criticized. Some people even suggest that the Jewish leadership formed part of the machinery of destruction. Hannah Arendt, a political philosopher and refugee from Nazi Germany, has been accused of taking that stance in her study *Eichmann in Jerusalem*. Arendt drew attention to what she considered the failure of Jewish leadership, and publication of her book in the early 1960s sparked a heated controversy.

Two observations help navigate this difficult terrain. One is that many Jews at the time were bitterly critical of the Jewish councils. In diaries, letters, and private conversations, inmates of the ghettos excoriated Jewish leaders who assigned privileges to themselves, members of their families, and their friends. The scarcer resources became—whether work permits, food, shelter, access to medicine or medical care—the more people resented those who appeared to have more, and often did. The pressures of life in the ghetto also exacerbated preexisting tensions, and when one political faction or group dominated the Jewish council, rivals and opponents found even more reason to complain.

In the Warsaw ghetto, Chaim Kaplan, a Hebrew instructor, watched his wife dying of typhus. Angry and destitute, he confided to his diary that he expected no help from the Jewish council or its welfare institutions. Those, he wrote, were available only to "bootlickers," to "lackeys" of the leadership. Words like Kaplan's can be found in many personal accounts, especially those written at the time or immediately after the war. Probably they say more about the helplessness and grief of people surrounded by death and dying than they do about the actions or intentions of Jewish leaders in the ghettos. If Kaplan had survived to edit his diary or write a memoir with the wisdom of hindsight, he might have excised such passages.

The second observation is that the autonomy of the Jewish councils was more apparent than real. Unable to escape German goals and priorities, Jewish leaders were caught between conflicting demands. Above them loomed German orders; below them spread the ever more desperate needs of their communities. Jewish councils had to respond to German orders for funds, goods, information, and workers. If they refused or failed, the Germans would come and take whatever they wanted anyway. At the same time, Jewish councils tried to help their people, to maintain order, preserve lives, and feed, clothe, and heal the Jews in the ghettos.

It was impossible to reconcile these sets of goals in a situation where the German priority was destruction of the Jews. But in the conditions that the victorious Germans created in occupied Poland, the two tasks of the Jewish councils could not be separated either. A Jewish council might try to convince Germans to keep Jews alive by increasing the productivity of the ghetto. Increasing productivity, however, meant abandoning those unable to work—children, the sick, and the elderly. Once again we can see the dynamic of divide and conquer at work.

Jewish Police in the Ghettos

Compared to prisons and concentration camps, German presence in the ghettos was limited. The Germans typically used local police, who worked under German supervision, to guard the ghetto from the outside. For instance Polish police were posted around the Warsaw ghetto, and Lithuanian police guarded the Kovno ghetto. Internal matters were left to Jewish police, who officially worked under the supervision of the Jewish council but were subordinate to the non-Jewish police and often subjected to direct German pressure.

Beginning in late 1941, in response to German demands, Jewish councils prepared lists for transports out of the ghettos—to killing centers. Often they used the Jewish police to round up those slated for destruction. Not surprisingly, these police, sometimes referred to as the Jewish Order Police or Jewish militia, were reviled and feared. But the situation of the Jewish police was complicated, and the roles they played varied from ghetto to ghetto, as illustrated by some examples.

By 1940 the Jewish council in Lublin was dealing not only with the ghetto in that city but with about fifty work camps. Under the wretched conditions, food, medicine, and doctors were all woefully inadequate. Overwhelmed, the council resorted in some cases to bringing in auxiliary police recruited from local ethnic Germans to keep order. Known for their viciousness toward Jews, those police contributed to the hatred that many Jews felt for the Jewish council. Eventually, the Lublin council formed its own Jewish Order Police. Inhabitants of the ghetto detested those enforcers, whether Jewish or not, as the most visible representatives of German power.

In Warsaw the head of the Jewish police, Jozef Szerynski, was a convert to Christianity who had been trained in the Polish police force. He was indifferent and even hostile to Jewish traditions. Most of the population of the ghetto regarded him and his seventeen hundred policemen as tyrannical. The requirement to pay a special police tax roused particular bitterness. By contrast, in Riga the Jewish police were recruited from among the Zionist youth. They included some of the best of Jewish society and were widely respected and viewed as helpers in the ghetto.

In Kovno the Jewish police cooperated in significant ways with the resistance. They helped smuggle children out of the ghetto and get food and weapons in. They were crucial in enabling Jewish fighters to leave the ghetto and join partisan groups in the forest. In 1944, when the Germans rounded up many police for interrogation, the men vowed to divulge nothing. Even in the face of brutal torture, they remained silent. The Germans then shot thirty-three policemen, including the entire leadership of the force. Meanwhile armed Germans and Ukrainians, accompanied by dogs, raided the ghetto, looking for children and elderly people. Within one day they seized one thousand victims, whom they sent to Auschwitz to be killed. Members of the Kovno Jewish ghetto police, aware of the complex role they played and the resentment with which many members of their community viewed them, kept a secret chronicle, which was published in English in 2014.

Contested Reputations

Critics of the Jewish councils note that some Jewish leaders relished the power that their positions in the ghetto gave them. There were cases of Jewish leaders who suffered from delusions of grandeur. Moishe Merin, the thirty-year-old head of the Central Council of Elders for Eastern Upper Silesia, fancied himself a kind of dictator of the European Jews. Chaim Rumkowski, head of the Jewish council in Lodz, was even more blatant. He had money and stamps printed bearing his image; he encouraged a kind of cult of personality around himself. Still, both men tried to save the Jews in "their ghettos," not merely to expand their own power.

Jewish leaders came to recognize their powerlessness, too. In 1943 Merin would address those still alive in his jurisdiction with the following words:

"I stand in a cage before a hungry and angry tiger. I stuff his mouth with meat, the flesh of my brothers and sisters, to keep him in his cage lest he break loose and tear us all to bits" (quoted in Hilberg, 197).

For most Jewish leaders, their position was not a reward but a burden. Some, like Adam Czerniaków in Warsaw, saw no way out but suicide. Few withstood the temptation to try to save themselves and those close to them. Nevertheless, in the end their thankless task guaranteed nothing. Jacob Gens

Lodz ghetto Jewish council chairman Mordechai Chaim Rumkowski officiates at the wedding of Nachman Zonabend and Irka Kuperminc in January 1944. This photograph was taken by Mendel Grossman, one of the photographers who worked for the Jewish council taking pictures at official ceremonies and other public events, as well as for identity cards and to document ghetto productivity. Grossman also took thousands of other photographs of Jewish life in the ghetto, including executions and transports. Note the painting of Rumkowski watching over the ceremony and the newlyweds. Was Grossman honoring Rumkowski or subtly mocking him?

spent years as head of the ghetto police and then the Jewish council in Vilna, doing all he could to increase the ghetto's productivity. The Germans shot him anyway, when they liquidated the ghetto in 1943. Rumkowski, for all his pomp, ended up in a transport from the Lodz ghetto to Auschwitz. He too died with his people; rumor has it they killed him themselves.

Critics often add another accusation: the Jewish councils should have warned their people. Could and should the Jewish councils have done more to alert Jews in the ghettos of German intentions or to rouse resistance? The case of the ghetto in Lublin illustrates the complexity of this issue. In 1939 there were thirty-eight thousand Jews in Lublin, more than 20 percent of the city's population. It was one of the oldest Jewish communities in Poland. After the German invasion in September, Jewish refugees flooded into the area. The Germans set up a ghetto and a Jewish council, whose vice chairman was a lawyer named Mark Alten.

Alten believed that the terror of late 1939 was a temporary, local aberration. Things would get better once German power was centralized and control established, he assumed. He worked hard to cultivate contacts with Germans and used his influence to plead for exceptions, to urge a stop to arbitrary violence. More than once he was arrested for his efforts. But in the end everything Alten did was futile. In 1942 almost all the Jews of Lublin were murdered, just like their counterparts all over occupied Poland.

Hell, according to the French philosopher Jean-Paul Sartre, is a self-service cafeteria—the worst suffering, in other words, is that which you inflict on yourself. Nazi planners seem to have understood that concept instinctively. By forcing Jewish leaders to involve themselves in decisions about the fate of people in the ghettos they both lightened their own sense of responsibility and increased the suffering within the Jewish community. Powerless as they were, the Jewish councils had painfully few options. In a lose-lose situation where the options were destruction or destruction—death or death—there could be few, if any, right decisions. It should not be surprising that Jewish leaders based their strategies on the only two hopes available to them: that the Germans would be defeated sooner rather than later, and that somehow at least some Jews could be kept alive until that day.

Jewish-Christian Relations in Poland

Poland occupies a particular place in the history of the Holocaust. Half of the Jews murdered during the Nazi era were Polish, and major killing centers were located in conquered Polish territory. There were also sites of mass slaughter elsewhere—for example, the killing fields in Transnistria, where many Romanian Jews were killed, and the shooting pits in Lithuania and Ukraine—

and there is evidence that German planners intended to build a killing center near Minsk in Belorussia but decided against it. In the case of Auschwitz, moreover, the camp was in the part of former Poland that was incorporated into the German Reich and most of the Polish locals were forcibly removed from the surrounding area. Nevertheless, the significance of Poland in the Holocaust calls for a special look at the relationship between Polish Christians and Jews.

The topic remains emotional. Some common interpretations can be categorized into three main groups. One idea might be called the "Poles as arch-antisemites" theory. According to this view, Polish gentiles were even more hostile to Jews than were Nazi Germans, and Polish antisemitism was an essential factor in the Holocaust. This interpretation, however, oversimplifies the past and neglects the difficult situation of all Poles under German rule. It also ignores the fact that the percentage of Jews killed was almost as high in the Netherlands—where antisemitism was traditionally weak—as in Poland.

At the other end of the scale is a position one might label "all Poles were victims." Proponents of this view maintain that Polish gentiles did all they could for their Jewish neighbors under circumstances in which they too were victims. Studies written from this perspective have done important work to draw attention to the suffering of non-Jewish Poles during World War II, but they sometimes do so by downplaying Jewish victimization.

A third alternative can be called the "unequal victims" theory. According to this view, Nazi Germany attacked Polish gentiles and Polish Jews, but in different ways and to different extents. For some time it was assumed that approximately equal numbers of Polish Christians and Jews were killed during the war. In the case of non-Jewish Poles, the estimate of 3 million included many people killed by the Soviets as well as by the Germans. That number computes to over 10 percent of Polish gentiles, and, even if one accepts the lower estimate of 1.5 million, it is a terrible toll. The same number—3 million—amounts to close to 90 percent of Polish Jews, a total catastrophe. The "unequal victims" approach has validity, but as the label itself suggests, it all too easily disintegrates into a competition in suffering or a numbers game in which human agony is quantified in ways that do not make moral sense.

Debates intensified with the publication in 2000 of *Neighbors*, a book by Jan Gross. In graphic detail, Gross recounts how on one day in July 1941, half of the residents of the eastern Polish town of Jedwabne murdered most of the other half. In Jedwabne, according to Gross's account, Poles, not Germans, initiated and carried out the slaughter of hundreds of local Jews. Gross's study is not simply one more accusation of some kind of intrinsic, uniquely Polish antisemitism. Instead he shows the complex interplay of forces in a region first terrorized by Soviet rule between 1939 and 1941, then overrun by the Germans. Poles accused Jews of collaborating with the Soviet oppressors, but in fact it was often precisely those individuals most deeply implicated in Soviet crimes who were quickest to take the lead in attacks on Jews—attacks that would serve both to deflect the anger of their neighbors and to curry favor with the new German occupiers.

Gross's analysis and the controversy it has sparked caution against generalizing and emphasize instead the wide range of actions and experiences on the part of Poles during World War II. Some collaborated with the Soviets, some with the Germans; some helped their Jewish compatriots, often at great risk to themselves. The fates of Polish Christians and Polish Jews under German occupation were linked and entangled in ways we cannot understand unless we study these groups of people together.

A Polish gentile woman and two Polish Jewish men are forced to walk together, probably to an execution site, sometime in the 1940s. The sign around the woman's neck reads, "For selling merchandise to Jews." German policies deliberately tried to prevent and break down ties of solidarity between Christian and Jewish Poles.

Particular Features of the Polish Situation

Several key factors shaped the Polish situation in the Holocaust. One important point involves chronology. Poland came under German domination very early—in 1939—and remained, at least in part, in German hands until early 1945. Unlike the Italians, who began to contend with German occupation only in 1943, the Poles were broken down by years of abuse and persecution.

A second factor was ideological. Nazi racial theory described Poles as *Untermenschen,* inferior people. Polish gentiles occupied a higher position on the ladder of Nazi racial theory than did Jews, but they nevertheless counted in German eyes as lesser, worthy at most to serve their "Aryan" masters as slaves. Hitler's Germans considered the northern Europeans over whom they would come to rule—the Danes, Norwegians, and Dutch—to be more closely related racially and culturally. Accordingly they tried to preserve what they considered their valuable "Nordic blood" and to co-opt them into their system of world domination, but they rarely showed such regard for the Poles.

Demography—ethnic division within Poland—was a third factor that shaped the Polish situation. Many of the inhabitants of Poland in 1939 were not ethnic Poles. The area seized by the Soviets in 1939 and held until 1941 was particularly mixed. Its 12 million inhabitants included only about 4.7 million ethnic Poles. The rest were Ukrainians, Belorussians, Russians, Jews, and others. Relationships among these groups were often tense, and as we have seen, the invaders proved adept at pitting ethnic groups against one another to further their own ends.

The poverty of many people in eastern Europe also played into German hands. In hindsight one is struck by the small stakes that induced some gentiles to betray Jews to the Germans or kill them themselves. Life was indeed worth very little. For instance, in one town during the war Germans promised a kilogram (2.2 pounds) of salt to anyone who brought in the head of a Jew. Local Ukrainians fanned out through the nearby forests and returned clasping severed heads. In other cases, bags of sugar served as a reward. Sometimes just the promise of whatever possessions the Jews carried with them sufficed.

Discussion of the roles that greed and need played in the Holocaust draws our attention to the "banality of evil." Hannah Arendt first used that phrase in her book *Eichmann in Jerusalem.* Most of the people involved in mass killing—as perpetrators, onlookers, and beneficiaries—were not crazed maniacs but ordinary people with familiar motivations. There were Polish peasants who deplored German brutality but willingly took the property of Jews forced into ghettos. There were ethnic German families who moved into homes from which the Polish owners had been evicted and eagerly accepted the booty for themselves. Such people did not necessarily initiate destruction, but they profited from it and developed a stake in its continuation.

Nevertheless, one can also find many accounts that show Poles who risked their lives and the lives of their families for others, including Jews. Yad Vashem, the Holocaust memorial and archive in Israel, honors non-Jews who helped Jews during the Holocaust as "the righteous among nations." One of the criteria for being recognized as one of the righteous is that the person did not profit monetarily from what she or he did. Of all the countries of Europe, Poland has the greatest number of gentiles recognized for saving Jews—as well as the largest number of Jews killed in the Holocaust.

An important effort to organize Polish rescue efforts was Zegota, the council for aid to Jews. Its network of operatives provided aid, food, and medication to Jews all over Poland. Zegota also produced scores of forged documents. Its work is credited with saving the lives of tens of thousands of Jews.

The Complexity of Polish-Jewish Issues: An Illustration

In his book *Anton the Dove Fancier,* Bernard Gotfryd recounts a story that shows how the lives of Polish Jews and gentiles were intertwined. When the war began Bernard was a young Jewish boy living in the Polish city of Radom. His neighbor Anton was a Polish Christian who raised and trained pigeons.

Anton was a rough man. He drank, threatened to cook his beloved birds, and neglected and scolded his wife. One day German officials requisitioned Anton's pigeons for the Reich. Instead of turning them over to the enemy, Anton killed every one of them. He was arrested for disobedience and sent to a camp.

Later during the war Bernard himself ended up in the concentration camp of Majdanek. There he saw Anton, now wearing the uniform of a kapo. A kapo was a prisoner whom the Germans had elevated to a position of authority over other prisoners. Many kapos were known for their brutality.

Anton recognized Bernard and gave him some warm clothes and extra bread. Later he provided Bernard with water, cigarettes to barter, and advice. Somehow Bernard Gotfryd lived through the war. While he was still in a camp he learned that Anton had been killed by his fellow prisoners in revenge for his cruelty.

Gotfryd returned to Radom, where he saw Anton's wife. She told him that she too had been born Jewish. As a child she had been orphaned and taken in by Anton's mother. Anton had never known about her origins. Now she planned to leave for Palestine.

This case shows the danger of assuming clear-cut categories when studying a situation as complicated as that in occupied Poland. As Anton demonstrated, the same person could be a resistance figure, a perpetrator of brutality, a hero, and a victim of German aggression. As his wife's experience suggests, even the line between "Christian" and "Jew" could be blurred. There is little that is simple about Polish-Jewish relations during the Nazi era.

MURDER OF THE DISABLED

Hitler's Germany first crossed the line from persecution to mass murder not with Jews but with people considered disabled. The year 1939 would see initiation of a program to murder people defined as "lives unworthy of living." Here, too, experimentation would characterize the early stages of implementation, and the outbreak of war provided both cover and justification for the killers.

The idea of "purging" the population of elements considered undesirable predated Nazi rule and was not exclusive to Germany. Such notions, however, got a big boost with Nazi ideology and its idea that the "collective good"—at least the well-being of those judged superior—overrode the good of the individual. Nazi planners measured the value of a human life by its contribution to the national community, not by some inherent worth.

The T-4 Program

Even before the war began in 1939 Hitler had authorized Dr. Karl Brandt and Philipp Bouhler to organize a children's "euthanasia" program. Under this scheme children selected for killing were sent to certain clinics where medical personnel starved them to death or gave them lethal injections. One such site was Eglfing-Haar, an institution in Bavaria where 332 children were killed in a special children's ward. Doctors and research scientists also used some children for experiments that they hoped would advance their own careers.

In the summer of 1939, Hitler instructed another physician, Dr. Leonardo Conti, to organize a similar program for adults. Conti, the Reich Doctors' leader and state secretary in the interior ministry responsible for health matters, set up a huge administrative machinery that involved doctors, professors, social workers, nurses, and other health-care professionals. Their main target would be institutionalized adults with mental illnesses and other disabilities. Code-named "T-4" for the address of its headquarters in Berlin, Tiergartenstrasse 4, the program was operating by October 1939.

Conti's committee prepared forms to be sent to all psychiatric institutions. The form was short and asked such questions as whether the patient received regular visitors or had any "non-Aryan" blood. Obviously the criteria for selection had little to do with the actual health of the person in question. Teams of medical evaluators examined the forms. They marked with a red plus sign those people to be killed; they used a blue minus sign to specify who was to be left alive. Rarely did they examine or even see the patients themselves. Some doctors refused to participate. For example, the director of one asylum declined with the explanation that he was "too gentle" for such work. He and others like him did not suffer major consequences. It was no problem to find enough ambitious professionals to keep the program running smoothly.

The T-4 experts experimented with various methods of killing. They used injections and poison in the early months but soon sought quicker means. By January 1940 they had conducted the first successful gassings, at Brandenburg, not far from Berlin. Other early gassings were carried out in Württemberg, at Grafeneck, a former palace that had been made into a hospital for physically disabled people. State authorities moved the patients out and took over the building, which they revamped as a killing center.

An employee at the killing center of Hadamar, in Hesse, described viewing a gassing there. He "looked through the peephole in the side wall," he remembered:

> Through it I saw 40–45 men who were pressed together in the next room and were now slowly dying. Some lay on the ground, others had slumped down, many had their mouths open as if they could not get any more air. The form of death was so painful that one cannot talk of a humane killing, especially since many of the dead men may have had moments of clarity. I watched the process for about 2–3 minutes and then left because I could no longer bear to look and felt sick. (Noakes and Pridham 3:1027)

Meanwhile, other initiatives began against institutionalized people in Poland. Already in late September 1939, Germans began shooting patients in Polish asylums and mental hospitals in the district of Bromberg/Bydgoszcz. By November 1 they had murdered almost four thousand people this way. Elsewhere in territories conquered from Poland, SS execution squads carried out similar murders. One SS special commando used a van labeled "Kaiser's Coffee" as a mobile killing unit. Carbon monoxide gas was fed from a container in the cab into the back of the van to asphyxiate the passengers. During December 1939 and January 1940 the SS special commando murdered hundreds of patients from Polish asylums in that van.

Such killings were not motivated by a drive for racial purity—Nazi Germans had made it clear they had no interest in strengthening the "Polish race"—but by practical considerations. The occupiers needed large buildings and pleasant grounds for their own purposes, for SS and police headquarters, military officers' quarters, even as prizes for loyal agents. Sometimes the killings were a direct response to requests from bureaucrats in the resettlement offices who needed beds for ethnic Germans being brought into an area. These massacres reveal the contagion of extreme violence. Empowered by their superiors and confident of their impunity, for members of special SS squads and other Germans who had become professional killers in 1939, killing had become one of the obvious solutions for all kinds of problems.

Hitler's Backdated Authorization and Efforts to Maintain Secrecy

Worried about possible repercussions for their activity, the organizers of the T-4 program approached Hitler for formal authorization that would serve

Copy of an original memo signed by Hitler authorizing the T4 ("euthanasia") program. Because of the sensitivity of the murder of "Aryan" men, women, and children, and the possibility of criminal prosecution, those placed in charge of "euthanasia" sought Hitler's personal authorization in writing. Perhaps Hitler later regretted issuing such a statement; there is no evidence of a similar written order regarding the murder of Jews.

to cover them should objections be raised. Sometime in October 1939, T-4 officials persuaded Hitler to sign a short statement. He had it typed on his personal notepaper rather than issued as an official document. The statement read: "Reich leader Bouhler and Dr. Brandt are charged with responsibility to extend the powers of specific doctors in such a way that, after the most careful assessment of their condition, those suffering from illnesses deemed to be incurable may be granted a mercy death" (Noakes and Pridham, 3:1021).

It is significant that Hitler backdated this note to September 1, 1939, the day of the German invasion of Poland. Presumably he did so in order to link the decision to begin killing disabled people with the demands of war. In fact the murders were not a response to the exigencies of war; they were an initiative in population management. The upheaval of wartime, however, provided the opportunity to carry out such plans with reduced public scrutiny.

The program's organizers tried to keep the killings secret, but total concealment was impossible. There were simply too many people involved and too many ways for information to leak out. Staff at hospitals and asylums saw patients taken away for killing. Family members received letters that

View of a transport of disabled men from the Bruckberg care facility in 1941. Their destination was probably the "euthanasia" facility in Ansbach, because the bus is marked "Reisedienst Ansbach" (travel agency Ansbach). In early 1941, there were three large transports of patients from Bruckberg to Ansbach for killing. Note the photographer's perspective, looking down on the courtyard from inside the complex, a reminder that some staff and patients understood what was happening.

announced the deaths of their loved ones. In some cases officials made errors; for example, they wrote that someone had died of appendicitis when the person's appendix had been removed years earlier; they listed another cause of death as spinal disease, but the relatives had just seen the man and he had been in perfect health. The patients themselves in some cases figured out what was going on and pleaded for their lives.

News also circulated in the German communities near the killing centers and beyond. Employees of such places sometimes frequented local bars, where they spouted off about what they had seen. The stench of bodies burning in crematoria drifted beyond fences and walls that enclosed the sites of killing. Even small children playing teased one another about being taken away in the buses with the darkened windows if they acted crazy.

Protest against the Killings

News of the killings of disabled people upset many Germans. Relatives of some of those murdered launched protests of various kinds. Some wrote directly to Hitler to express their disapproval. Some shared details with their pastors or priests. Probably the ease with which the program got started had convinced Hitler that the public would be indifferent. Perhaps most people were, but those opposed made their views known.

Leaders in both the Catholic and the Protestant churches in Germany learned about the killings in direct ways, because many asylums were run by the churches. Many of those institutions and their personnel cooperated with the program, although there were exceptions. Nevertheless, it was from church circles that the most concerted protests to the killings would emerge.

Catholic priests and bishops and some local Protestant clergy made public calls to respect the sanctity of human life. In December 1940, Pope Pius XII issued a statement that denounced "killing of an innocent person because of mental or physical defects." The most pointed protest did not come until the summer of 1941. By then between seventy and eighty thousand people had been killed in the program in Germany alone. The number of Polish disabled people murdered is unknown, but in all it is estimated that by 1945 the Germans murdered some two hundred and seventy-five thousand people they deemed disabled from all over Europe.

In August 1941 the Catholic bishop of Münster, Cardinal August Count von Galen, decided to take a stand against the killings. He preached a sermon in which he made it clear that he knew exactly what was going on and considered it a crime against God and humanity. Galen quoted the German Penal Code's prohibition against murder and warned the government that its policies would backfire. He told of a German soldier whose father had been institutionalized for some mental disturbance. As the younger man went off to defend his nation, his father in Germany was being killed by his German national comrades. Whose life would be safe in such a society, Galen asked his parishioners?

Galen's sermon was duplicated and circulated all over Germany and even abroad by sympathetic elements within the Christian churches. Nazi leaders were furious, but they dared not take action against Galen. He was too well known and too popular. In wartime the government could not risk alienating its own population, so Galen kept his post.

Late in August 1941 Hitler gave an order to halt the "euthanasia" program. That order was little more than a ploy, though it did signal a change in the program. The murders did not stop—nor did Hitler intend them to. The major gassing operations were ended, however, and the killing decentralized into hospitals and other smaller sites. So the end of the first phase—gassings at Brandenburg, Grafeneck, Hadamar, Hartheim, Bernburg, and Sonnenstein in 1940 and 1941—gave way to phase two of killing by other means, at some of those same places and at least one hundred other sites.

At Hadamar, killing continued in the second phase, from 1942 to 1945, but using starvation and lethal injections. One of the new adult "euthanasia" sites was Meseritz-Obrawalde, in the Prussian province of Pomerania (today Miedzyrzecz in Poland). At least seven thousand people were put to death there by lethal overdoses of medication. Among them was Emmi G., a sixteen-year-old housemaid diagnosed as "schizophrenic" and killed with an overdose of tranquilizers in December 1942. Eichberg, near Frankfurt, was a smaller, local killing site whose hundreds of victims included children and adults. Its director, Dr. Friedrich Mennecke, was also one of the T-4 evaluators. Sentenced to death at the Eichberg trial in 1946, the second of the "euthanasia" trials under the jurisdiction of German courts, he died before the sentence could be carried out.

During the second phase, under a new codename, 14f13, new groups of people were targeted, above all inmates of concentration camps and prisons who had become unable to work. At Hartheim, prisoners from Dachau and other camps were gassed; Bernburg and Sonnenstein also operated as 14f13 killing sites.

It is not clear to what extent Hitler's order to halt was a response to Bishop von Galen's sermon. Certainly decentralization and stepped-up efforts at concealment were intended to placate the German public. Nazi authorities also had an eye to morale in the military. During wartime the last thing soldiers needed was the worry that they would be killed by their own government if they were injured. Meanwhile, the invasion of the Soviet Union in June 1941 and the accompanying massacres of Jews made it clear that the priorities of the German leadership had shifted to eastern Europe. Nevertheless, the killing of disabled people continued until the end of the war and even after. The last victim of the Nazi "euthanasia" program was a four-year-old boy murdered in a Bavarian hospital on May 29, 1945, three weeks after Germany's unconditional surrender.

6

EXPANSION AND SYSTEMATIZATION

Exporting War and Terror, 1940–1941

The previous chapter described the first year of the war as a period of
Nazi German breakthroughs in conquest, persecution, and mass killing.
Just as the Nazi revolution in 1933 had been followed by routinization, the innovations of 1939 gave way to what might be labeled a time of expansion and
systematization. During 1940 and 1941 the size of Hitler's empire increased
tremendously as German forces overwhelmed more and more of Europe. After
Poland, the Germans first turned their military attentions to the north and
west, attacking Denmark, Norway, the Netherlands, Belgium, Luxembourg,
France, and Britain in the spring and summer of 1940. Able to conquer all
but the British, they moved south and east—against Yugoslavia and Greece in
spring 1941, and then in June 1941 against the Soviet Union.

Terror and suffering grew along with Hitler's empire as programs of
killing became both much larger and more efficient. By the end of 1941
German mobile killing units would have murdered hundreds of thousands of
Jews in eastern Europe—men, women, and children—many of them shot into
mass graves. Preparation of killing centers to massacre even more staggering
numbers of people would be under way, and over two million Soviet prisoners
of war would be dead or dying in German captivity.

This chapter surveys the campaigns of 1940 and 1941 that brought most
of Europe under Nazi German control. It explores the repercussions as Hitler's

Germans took their projects of territorial expansion and supposed racial purification ever farther from home.

WAR IN THE NORTH AND WEST

Within days of the invasion of Poland on September 1, 1939, both Britain and France were at war with Germany. Bound by agreements to Poland, the British and French declared war on Germany on September 3 but initially remained inactive. This early phase was known in Britain as the "phony war." The French referred to it as a *drôle de guerre*, a "funny war," and the Germans spoke of a *Sitzkrieg*, an immobile "war of sitting," in contrast to the rapid Blitzkrieg, "lightning war," in Poland.

There were a few skirmishes on the border between France and Germany in 1939 but otherwise nothing on land. Siegfried Knappe, a young German artillery officer, describes in his memoir *Soldat* how he spent much of the fall and winter of 1939–1940 in western Germany, mere miles from the border with Luxembourg. Days and then weeks passed as the Germans prepared for an attack from the French that never came. Rather than the dangers and strains of combat, Knappe and his men faced the challenge of readying their horses and themselves for action, tasks that left plenty of time to celebrate German victories in Poland by drinking beer and dancing with the locals. From Knappe's vantage point, it must have been easy to view Hitler's early triumphs as confirmation of German superiority.

At sea there was more action as the Germans began their attack on Allied shipping. In return the British navy organized a convoy system and began actively breaking German codes. The work of Polish mathematicians before the war and cooperation between Polish, British, and French intelligence were crucial components of this success.

By mid-1940 this phase of the "phony war" in the west would come to an abrupt halt. In the spring, after a winter spent consolidating their hold on Poland and continuing preparations for further offensives, the Germans moved north and west. Hitler and his generals knew that their ambitious plans remained impossible unless they crushed and subordinated France and Britain, the dominant countries in Europe and, through their empires, major world powers. That goal could only be achieved through war.

For Hitler war in the west was a prerequisite for grabbing land in the east and establishing German dominance in Europe and beyond. It had been part of the plans put forward in Hitler's "second book," written in 1928 (though not published), and in the 1937 meeting summarized in the Hossbach Memorandum. The western conflict, however, did not take quite the form Hitler had foreseen. Already in 1938 Hitler believed Germany could be ready for war against France and Britain, and he had thought that war might even precede hostilities with Poland. The German air force—the Luftwaffe—had been built up under Hermann Göring with an eye to campaigns in the west. It was in the west that Hitler anticipated the most difficult fighting for the Germans, as had been the case in the previous world war. And in Nazi eyes, eastern Europe was populated by inferior people, including many Jews, surely easy opponents for members of a "master race."

German warfare in the west would generally be less brutal than in the east. Nazi ideology regarded western and northern Europeans, at least those who were not Jewish, as "racially valuable" people, suitable partners for German "Aryans." But ideology was not the only factor, nor did patterns of violence follow a neat east/west divide. German conquest and occupation tended to be harsher in areas where the Wehrmacht encountered more opposition. Poles, Czechs, and Slovaks were all Slavic peoples, but the Germans were ruthless against the Poles, milder toward the Czechs, and allied with the Slovaks. With the exception of Britain, the western countries once attacked either surrendered quickly or agreed to cooperate with Germany. Also relevant was the size of the Jewish population. In regions with significant numbers of Jews—Poland, for instance—the German invaders tended to be more violent, against Jews and non-Jews.

Still the Germans proved ready to deploy extreme violence in the west when it suited their purposes. Certainly they stole and plundered in western Europe as they did in Poland. For leaders who believed that Germany had lost the previous war because of public discontent—the stab in the back from the home front—nothing was more important than placating the people back home. What easier way to do so than to let them enrich themselves at the expense of others?

Invasions of Denmark, Norway, and the Low Countries

In April 1940 German forces entered Denmark, and that small nation surrendered without a struggle. The Germans moved on to Norway, where they had to fight their way in, but by June 1940 they had defeated the Norwegians too. The British and French tried to help Norway, but without adequate air support and thorough coordination their landings failed.

The Norwegian government fled to London, where it established itself as a government-in-exile. Norwegian merchant ships also escaped to Britain, where they could be used in the war effort against Germany. A local fascist leader, Vidkun Quisling, took power—or more accurately, became the German's instrument—at home. His name, "quisling," has become a synonym for "cowardly collaborator." The Norwegians would execute Quisling as a traitor in 1945.

What did German military planners want with Denmark and Norway? A look at a map gives some explanation. The Germans needed to secure the supply route of Swedish iron ore for their war machine. They also sought to broaden their base for a sea war with Britain and eventually the United States. Scandinavia would provide naval bases from which to attack the British with submarines and access to routes around Britain.

In May 1940, just a month after the offensive against Denmark and Norway began, German forces invaded and conquered the neutral nations of the Netherlands, Belgium, and Luxembourg, often referred to as the Low Countries. Here too victory was swift. For instance, in the Netherlands, German armored forces penetrated the borders, while airborne units took strategic airfields and bridges. The Dutch soon surrendered. First, however, there were some significant developments. The queen and her government left Holland for Britain, where they too formed a government-in-exile on the side of the Allies. The Dutch were important to the Allied cause because they controlled a large colonial empire and a substantial merchant fleet, both of which would prove valuable in the war effort.

On May 14 the Luftwaffe bombed the Dutch city of Rotterdam in an attempt to terrorize the Dutch into surrender. The Germans clearly aimed at civilian targets to intimidate and demoralize their opponents. They destroyed the center of the city and killed hundreds of people. At the time, the panicked British press reported the inflated figure of thirty thousand Dutch casualties. For the Allies, the bombing of Rotterdam provided an early manifestation of German ruthlessness and demonstrated a new kind of warfare: unlimited war from the air. Within a few years the Germans would reap what they had sown with the destruction from the air of their own cities.

One of the eyewitnesses to the German conquest of the Netherlands was Anne Frank, a young girl living in Amsterdam. Her parents were German Jews who had left Frankfurt for Holland after Hitler came to power. As it turned out, they had not fled far enough. Unable to get out of Europe in 1940, their only option would be to try to disappear within the city of Amsterdam.

Anne's father began to use his business contacts to prepare a hiding place for his family and some acquaintances. It was in their "secret annex" between July 1942 and August 1944 that Anne would write a diary, now one of the most famous documents of the Holocaust. Betrayed by an anonymous tip-off to police, the Franks and the people in hiding with them were sent first to the Dutch transit camp of Westerbork and then on to Auschwitz. A group of them were later moved to the Bergen-Belsen concentration camp in Germany,

The ruins of Rotterdam after bombing by the German air force in May 1940. The attack destroyed the old city core and killed hundreds of civilians. It was not the first time the Germans had targeted civilians, but Rotterdam caught international attention in a way the destruction of Polish towns and cities in 1939 had not. Frank Capra's famous *Why We Fight* films, made under U.S. government supervision, had a lengthy segment on the bombing of Rotterdam that incorporated German newsreel footage.

where Anne died in early 1945. Of the eight residents of the hiding place, only Anne Frank's father, Otto, survived the war.

There were about seventy thousand Jews living in Belgium when the Germans invaded in 1940. The vast majority of those—perhaps 95 percent—were not Belgian citizens. Among them were recent refugees from Nazi Germany and Austria and also people who had left Poland and Romania in the 1920s. Antwerp had the largest number of Jews, many of them working in the diamond trade. Because of its location, Belgium was also where many Jews trying to get out of Europe got stranded by the outbreak of war in 1939 and the German invasion less than a year later.

Some of the Jews trapped in Belgium were children, whose parents had managed to get them that far but no further. One such child was Isaac Hochberger. His mother, Regina Hochberger, had brought him as a toddler from Poland to Les Petites Abeilles ("the little bees"), a Red Cross children's home in Brussels. She also placed one of his sisters in a Red Cross institution and sent another daughter to Palestine, but she and her husband were stuck in Poland. When Marie-Thérèse Delmez, a nurse who cared for Isaac, heard that the Germans planned to shut down Les Petites Abeilles; she took the little boy home with her to her parents' village. There, renamed Yves Berger, he lived through the war in safety. A few years later, thanks to Delmez, he was reunited with his parents, who had been sent by the Soviets to Siberia, where they survived the war. Between them the five members of this family experienced the Holocaust and its repercussions in central, western, and eastern Europe as well as the Middle East and Asia.

This wartime photograph, showing a woman kindly yet firmly washing a somewhat unhappy looking child, is in itself unremarkable. As with most

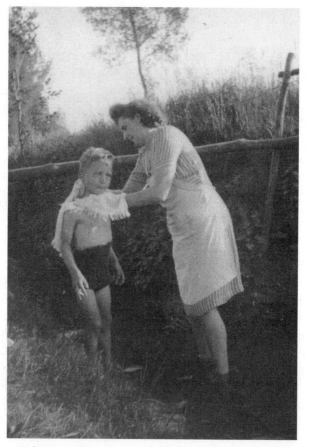

Marie-Thérèse Delmez washing Isaac Hochberger, the Jewish child she sheltered in a village in Belgium. Delmez worked in a Red Cross institute in Brussels, where she cared for Hochberger. His mother had managed to get him to Belgium, but she and her husband were stuck in Poland. They survived the war in the Soviet interior and were reunited with their son in 1947. Photographs of rescuers in action are understandably rare and more likely to capture the everyday rather than the dramatic aspects of rescue.

family photos, there is no record of who took the picture, when, or exactly where. But the significance of this image is enormous. For the Hochbergers, who did not see their son for eight years and no doubt feared the worst, it must have been a priceless record of a childhood they missed. It was also one of few pieces of evidence that linked the adolescent, French-speaking Yves with the little Polish Jewish boy, Isi. After he left the only life and family he had known, perhaps this photo helped Isaac Hochberger connect the parts of himself. And it supported the case for recognizing Delmez as one of the Righteous among the Nations, a gentile who risked her life to save a Jew. This simple, familiar scene illustrates the impossibility of capturing on film the drama and intensity of "rescue" in the Holocaust: instead we see the everyday realities involved.

German Attack on France

In May 1940 German troops entered France. They came through Belgium from two directions, the north and the south. The French had concentrated their best forces in the north and were unprepared for a German attack through the Forest of Ardennes in southern Belgium. By May 12, German soldiers were on French soil, and by May 20, they had broken through to the sea, to the coast of the English Channel. In effect German forces cut the Anglo-French troops in two.

The Germans prepared to surround and annihilate the Allied forces converging on the French seaport of Dunkirk. Between the end of May and early June 1940, however, the Allies managed to evacuate some three hundred and thirty-eight thousand of their own soldiers. Using merchant ships, motorboats, fishing boats, private yachts, destroyers, and any other craft they could muster, the British rescued their men from the beaches of Dunkirk while under continued attack from the Germans. They had no choice but to leave most of their equipment behind.

The British and their allies were not the only ones fleeing the German advance. In scenes reminiscent of Poland less than a year earlier, panicked Parisians streamed out of the city, heading for what they hoped would be safety in the countryside, searching for friends and family members, or just running from German fire. The writer Irène Némirovsky produced an unforgettable account of this flood of refugees in her novel, *Suite française*. As Némirovsky told it, chaos and fear did not bring out the best in people. She described a wealthy Frenchman to whom all that mattered was saving his collection of porcelain, a self-righteous Catholic priest who was killed by the delinquent boys in his care, and a bourgeois woman whose sense of charity vanished the moment her own children faced the possibility of shortage. As cars ran out of gas and trains were diverted or halted, people ended up jumbled together on the roads, where they pushed, shoved, and stole from one another. Only a few behaved nobly or even decently.

Némirovsky had seen such responses for herself: she was living in Paris with her husband and two daughters when the Germans invaded. She had previous experience as a refugee of war, too. Her father, a wealthy banker, had escaped the Russian Revolution and Civil War with his family, and in the 1920s, joined the large number of emigres and refugees in France.

The Némirovskys were Jewish, although Irène converted to Christianity in 1939 and had her children baptized as Catholics. In the tumultuous days of May and June 1940, whether one was Jewish or not made little difference for most people in France; everyone was under attack. Only in the provinces of Alsace and Lorraine, which Germany annexed, were Jews singled out immediately and expelled. So when Némirovsky wrote her description of events and reactions in the summer of 1940, she had no way of knowing that her fate and the fate of other Jews and people of Jewish ancestry in France would diverge sharply from that of their countrymen.

In July 1942, French police arrested Némirovsky. She was sent to Auschwitz, where she died of typhus. Her husband had tried everything to get her released but without success. He too was sent to Auschwitz, where he was gassed immediately. With the help of a former nanny, the couple's two daughters survived the war in France. Somehow they managed to hold onto the suitcase containing their mother's unfinished book, and in 2004, more than sixty years after Némirovsky's death, it appeared in print.

Massacres of Black Soldiers

German actions in the French campaign revealed the priorities of racial warfare. Some one hundred thousand men from French West Africa served in the French military in 1939–1940. During May and June 1940, the Germans captured thousands of these soldiers, whom they separated from their white counterparts and targeted for special abuse. Sometimes on orders from their officers or on their own initiative, German soldiers shot them or blew them up with grenades. Supported by a massive propaganda campaign from Berlin, these slaughters of an estimated three thousand black French soldiers within two months echoed German behavior in Poland and anticipated the massacres of millions of Soviet POWs that began a year later.

The photograph here, from the German military press service, documents the Wehrmacht's victory in France. Like many images, however, it invites questions that go beyond the photographer's intention. Look at the three white German soldiers on the right. Each has struck a different triumphant pose. One, who is looking straight at the camera, has his hand in the

French colonial troops and their German captors in a prisoner of war camp. In May and June 1940, members of the Wehrmacht captured and killed an estimated three thousand black French men, many of them from the units known as Tirailleurs Sénégalais. In all, the Germans, egged on by a vicious propaganda campaign, massacred about ten thousand black French soldiers.

top of his jacket, perhaps alluding to portraits of Napoleon. The man to his right seems to be scrutinizing one of the captives, and beside him a German has a mocking expression on his face. But it is the black men who hold the center of the photograph. Whether or not the photographer aimed for this effect, the four men on the left appear dignified and self-possessed, although their captors surround them. Here the subjects of the photograph assert their presence and communicate directly with the viewers, challenging the photographer's perspective.

The Fall of France

By June 14, German troops marched triumphantly into Paris. Visiting the city for the first time Hitler danced the jig that became famous from the newsreels. The French government, unlike its Norwegian and Dutch counterparts, did not go into exile. Instead it remained and signed an Armistice Agreement on June 22, 1940. Under the terms of the armistice the Germans divided France into two parts: an occupied zone and an unoccupied zone known as Vichy France because its capital was located in the small, southern city of Vichy. Much of the French army entered prisoner of war camps, whereas the navy remained intact.

The head of the Vichy state was Marshal Henri Philippe Pétain (1856–1951), a hero of World War I and by 1940, an old man. For part of the war Pétain's prime minister was Pierre Laval (1883–1945). Together those two names would become symbols of French collaboration with Nazi Germany. Some of the French, however, refused to accept defeat. Among those, General Charles de Gaulle (1890–1970) would emerge as leader of the Free French forces. In June 1940 he too escaped to London.

For a young boy named Saul Friedländer, the collapse of France in 1940 was not a national humiliation but a personal catastrophe that eventually put his parents in the clutches of the Nazis and left him an orphan. Friedländer was born in Prague in 1932. He and his parents, middle-class, secular Jews, had left Czechoslovakia in 1939, even as German troops were moving in. France seemed a safe destination, and it was hard enough to move that far, leaving behind property, career, and relatives. It would prove difficult, and for Friedländer's parents eventually impossible, to remain safe in a society where they were strangers, without money, friends, or connections.

In the years before 1940, France had been a haven for refugees from all over Europe. Many Communists and other supporters of the Spanish Republic had fled to France in 1939 when their side lost the civil war in Spain. Like the Friedländers, Jews from other parts of Europe had taken refuge in France as their homelands fell prey to German aggression. Now all of these people came into the hands of the Germans and their French partners. Vichy authorities incarcerated many of them in Gurs, Rivesaltes, and other camps in France. They also sent foreigners, including Jews, who had volunteered for and fought in the French army against Germany to work camps in Algeria and Morocco. Thousands of Jewish refugees, women and men, were interned in North Africa, many consigned to forced labor on the pan-Saharan railroad line.

Hans Landesberg, a Viennese doctor who had fought with the International Brigade in the Spanish Civil War, was arrested in France in 1939, interned at Gurs, and later sent to a camp in Algeria. He managed to get to Morocco, but police there only allowed refugees to remain at large for two weeks, so he was incarcerated again, until 1943, when he received a visa for the United States and moved to New York. Next time you watch the 1942 classic *Casablanca*, you might think of Landesberg. Much of the movie is based on fantasy—it was not filmed in Morocco but in a Hollywood studio—but it is realistic in depicting Casablanca in late 1941 as a city of refugees. Actual refugees and exiles played key roles in the movie: as Laszlo, the Czech resistance hero; Major Strasser, Carl the waiter, and the petty crook Ugarte. A host of smaller

Prisoners gather outside their barracks in the Gurs concentration camp in southwestern France, in 1939 or 1940. French authorities, not Germans, were in charge of Gurs. Originally set up for refugees from Franco's Spain, Gurs was used after 1940 to intern "foreign" Jews (non-French nationals) and other people deemed enemies of Vichy France. This photograph highlights the wide range of places that get grouped together under the label "Nazi camps."

parts—the pickpocket, the Viennese refugee couple, the croupier, most of the Nazis, the extras in the café and casino—were filled by actors and actresses, many of them Jewish, who had fled Nazi Germany and German-dominated Europe in the years since 1933.

The Battle of Britain

With the fall of France, most accounts will tell you that Britain stood alone against Germany. Indeed, Britain was the only European power both to declare war on Germany in 1939 and to stand firm until 1945. Neither the Soviet Union nor the United States entered the war against Germany until 1941.

The British, however, were not entirely alone. The Dominions—Australia, New Zealand, Canada, and, after considerable internal debate, South Africa—joined in declarations of war against Germany. The British-controlled

government of India also did so, although without consulting the Indian political parties or, for that matter, the Indian public. For its part, the Irish Free State
proclaimed its neutrality.

Support of the Allied cause by countries all over the world was significant,
both to the outcome of the war and after the fact, to the national pride of
citizens of the nations concerned. People in the Dominions would bear a
substantial burden in the war, and if the British Isles were to have fallen to the
Germans, there would still have been the possibility of continuing the war effort. In fact, the British leadership planned to do so from Canada and moved
large parts of Britain's gold reserves to Canada in case they would be needed
to finance the war.

Within Europe, Britain became the last refuge for many people fleeing
Nazi Germany. The Polish, Norwegian, and Dutch governments-in-exile were
surrounded by communities of people forced to flee their homelands. Czech
and French opponents of Germany also gathered in Britain, as did those Jews
from the continent who could make it in. Among the people who had arrived
before war began in 1939 were the ten thousand children of the Kindertransport and thousands of German Jewish adults, including many women who had
entered on visas that restricted them to work in domestic service, as maids,
nannies, housekeepers, or cooks.

In Britain, too, the situation of refugees was precarious. Families were
separated and unable to communicate. After the evacuation at Dunkirk,
British authorities began interning German-born adult males as enemy
aliens. Jews from Germany and Austria were included in this measure, which
put twenty-seven thousand men behind barbed wire, many of them on the
Isle of Man, and some in overflow camps in Canada and Australia. Hundreds
of Jewish teenage boys who had entered Britain with the Kindertransport
now found themselves categorized as "enemy alien" adults and confined to
internment camps. One young man from Hanover got to England on the
Kindertransport, was interned, shipped to Australia, and ended up serving in
the Australian army. At the time he and others dispatched to isolated sites
halfway across the world must have felt completely cut off from everything
they had known. Only in hindsight is it clear that what seemed a catastrophe
in 1940 ended up putting at least some Jews out of reach of Nazi German
destruction.

With the fall of France, Hitler saw the British as Germany's main enemy
in Europe. He proceeded with plans for an invasion, while British prime minister Winston Churchill rallied the British population against the Germans. One
of Churchill's most famous speeches included the following challenge: "The
Battle of Britain is about to begin. Upon this battle depends the survival of
Christian civilization. . . . If we fail then . . . all we have known and cared for

will sink into the abyss of a new Dark Age." After the evacuation of Dunkirk, Churchill's rousing words helped strengthen and inspire British determination:

> Even though large tracts of Europe and many old and famous states have fallen or may fall into the grip of the Gestapo and all the odious apparatus of Nazi rule, we shall not flag or fail. We shall go on to the end. We shall fight in France, we shall fight on the seas and oceans, we shall fight with growing confidence and growing strength in the air, we shall defend our island, whatever the cost may be. We shall fight on the beaches, we shall fight on the landing grounds, we shall fight in the fields and in the streets, we shall fight in the hills; we shall never surrender; and even if, which I do not for a moment believe, this island or a large part of it were submerged and starving, then our Empire beyond the seas, armed and guarded by the British Fleet, would carry on the struggle, until, in God's good time, the new world, with all its power and might, steps forth to the rescue and the liberation of the old. (quoted in Sachse, 314–15)

The German plan for landings in Britain had the code name Operation Sea-Lion. German planners were convinced that successful crossing of the English Channel and establishment of beachheads on the English coast depended on control of the skies, and Göring assured Hitler that the Luftwaffe could destroy the Royal Air Force (RAF).

In July 1940 the Luftwaffe began massive attacks on British air and naval installations. Every day for the next two months hundreds of planes fought in the skies over Britain. The Germans, however, could not gain the mastery they expected. On September 15, 1940, the RAF shot down sixty aircraft, and two days later, Hitler postponed the invasion "until further notice." He hoped among other things that invasion and defeat of the Soviet Union—both of which were already planned—would isolate and weaken Britain so that the Germans could come back later for an easy victory. Those late summer, early autumn months of 1940 became known as the Battle of Britain.

Throughout 1941, the Germans bombed British cities, industrial centers, and ports. Air raids became a nightly event, with the inhabitants of London, Coventry, Plymouth, and other cities seeking safety in subways, cellars, and homemade bomb shelters. German bombing took a heavy toll on civilian lives and property, but British morale remained firm. Meanwhile German air raids spurred the Allies to further develop radar technology that would play a crucial role in winning the war in the air.

As a Jewish refugee child in a boarding school in the south of England, Gerhard Weinberg saw bombs falling and heard and read of battles raging. All the while he knew most of his relatives—aunts, uncles, cousins—were trapped in Germany. Later he learned that they had been murdered. Now a renowned historian of World War II, Weinberg attributes his insistence on studying the Holocaust and the war together to his childhood experience. How could he not see that the war and the destruction of Jews were connected?

The Neutrals

Some countries in Europe remained neutral throughout World War II, most notably Switzerland, Sweden, Spain, Portugal, and Turkey. The neutrals would play different roles over the course of the war. At times they provided escape routes for victims of German persecution. For instance, in October 1943 the small Jewish community of Denmark was smuggled out to safety in neutral Sweden. Other neutrals, notably Switzerland, took some refugees but turned many away. Among those sent back at the border were Saul Friedländer's parents. In despair they ended up back in France, and eventually they were sent to Auschwitz and killed there.

Some of the neutrals profited considerably from the war. Swiss banks grew rich on stolen gold sent there by German authorities and on deposits from European Jews who hoped to protect some assets from the German predators. The Swedes delivered massive amounts of iron ore to Germany. Turkey offered refuge to some European Jews but charged special taxes intended to transfer wealth from the refugees to Turkish-born Turks. After the war Turkey also provided an escape route to the Middle East for many Nazi criminals. Neutral or not, no nation in Europe would be untouched by the war.

In 1940 Germany entered into the Three-Power Pact with Italy and Japan. Later that arrangement would be consolidated into a formal military alliance, although coordination among the three powers was minimal. For the time being the three states committed themselves to aid one another against their enemies.

Later in 1941, Hungary, Romania, Slovakia, Finland, Bulgaria, and Croatia would join the pact. Why were the leaders of these nations interested in allying themselves with Germany and Italy? A look at a map suggests an answer. All of these countries hoped to expand with German or Italian help at the expense of their neighbors. They operated on a common assumption: "the enemies of my enemies are my friends." By the end of World War II, that notion would prove disastrously false.

Soviet Assault on the Baltic States and Finland

As evident in the division of Poland in September 1939, Germany was not the only belligerent power in Europe. Under the leadership of Joseph

Stalin, the Soviet Union had its own expansionist program, linked to the goal of crushing all threats to internal security.

After seizing eastern Poland, Stalin turned his attention to the three Baltic states, Estonia, Latvia, and Lithuania. By October 1939 massive Soviet threats had compelled all three to accept Soviet military bases with tens of thousands of Red Army troops. In June 1940, as the victorious Wehrmacht marched into defeated Paris, Stalin grabbed the opportunity to transform those "bases" into a full-scale invasion and occupation of the Baltic states.

Along with Red Army tanks came the Stalinist system of terror, presided over by the NKVD (People's Commissariat for Internal Affairs) and its political police, known after 1941 as the NKGB (People's Commissariat for State Security) or simply KGB. Soviet authorities organized a wave of purges and deportations of local people of all ages. Hundreds of thousands of people simply vanished—into Soviet torture chambers, prisons, and labor camps in Siberia. In Latvia alone, 2 percent of the population "disappeared" as NKVD operatives sought to destroy the possibility of any national resistance. For the next year, Soviet interrogators and guards and local collaborators followed Stalin's injunction to "beat, beat, and again beat."

Likewise in June 1940, Stalin took advantage of the distraction provided by Nazi German invasions in western Europe to seize northern Bukovina and the province of Bessarabia in northern Romania. There too NKVD rule and ruthless state terror followed, with the same deadly consequences as in the Baltic states.

By the time the Germans launched their own invasions of these regions in mid-1941, the people of the Baltic states and northern Romania had been brutalized by deprivation and abuse. Small wonder that many of them in turn would seek revenge and scapegoats for their suffering by throwing their lot in with the Nazis. It can be tempting to set up competitions in evil between Hitler and Stalin. Who was worse? Who caused more murder and misery? This brief survey of the events of 1940, however, reminds us of an even more terrible reality; Nazism and Stalinism coexisted in time and place, and for many Europeans the horrors of one vicious system served to increase the destructive force of the other.

Already in November 1939 the Soviets had invaded Finland, another neighbor to the west. The gigantic attack was intended to overwhelm the 3.5 million Finns in rapid, blitzkrieg style. Instead the Finns mounted a resourceful, heroic resistance and held out until March 1940, when they were forced to sign a peace treaty and cede territories to the Soviet Union. In that conflict, known as the Winter War, Stalin again took advantage of British and French inability to aid the targets of his aggression and used the protective cover of German assaults elsewhere in Europe to pick up spoils of his own. At the same time, at least in the short run, Hitler and the Germans benefited from anything that further disrupted the stability of Europe and distracted attention from their own activities.

WAR AND ITS IMPACT INSIDE NAZI GERMANY

War had many repercussions inside Germany, too. For one thing, German military successes brought floods of luxury goods into the hands of Germans back home. Men sent furs and jewels to their wives and girlfriends; German museums and galleries acquired costly art treasures; the finest wines, chocolate, cheeses, pâtés, and other delicacies ended up on German tables. The wealthier the nation conquered, the richer the spoils of war.

In some ways, as the historian Robert Gellately has pointed out, war "revolutionized the revolution" in Nazi Germany. War allowed German authorities to increase the pace of change at home and take steps to silence critics. Restrictions on public meetings and control over the press tightened after 1939, and numbers of arrests continued to climb: for spreading so-called malicious rumors critical of the government or the Nazi Party, for violating state monopolies on information, for maintaining illegal organizations, and for engaging in other activities considered subversive. The population of the ever-expanding network of concentration camps and their satellites grew accordingly. At the same time, the Nazi regime's sensitivity to public opinion and its belief in the importance of keeping the home front happy put limits on how harshly it treated dissenters, at least those who were respected members of German society.

War exported Nazi policies including persecution of Jews and applied Nazi practices of divide and conquer in new territories. Already between 1933 and 1939 Hitler's regime had built on the principle that nothing succeeds like success. That notion proved extremely powerful in wartime. The prewar triumphs of Hitler's rule—for instance, the annexation of Austria and the seizure of the Sudetenland in 1938—had helped to bring some reluctant Germans in line. Germany's spectacular military successes in 1939 and 1940 turned out to be even more effective. German patriots of all kinds, including many who consistently had voted against Hitler, rejoiced with him at the destruction of Poland and the victory over France. To German nationalists these successes seemed to vindicate old desires for revenge and to legitimate German aggression.

The family of Alfons Heck, an eager member of the Hitler Youth, illustrates this particular effect of Germany's war. Before 1939 Heck's father, a committed Socialist, and his grandmother, a devout Catholic, had both opposed

Adolf Hitler. They also disapproved of Heck's enthusiastic involvement in the Hitler Youth. Nevertheless, both were thrilled with the German conquest of France in 1940. Living as they did near the border with France they were particularly aware of Germany's long enmity with its neighbor to the west. By mid-May 1940, Heck's father and grandmother had stopped complaining about Hitler's government and joined Alfons as supporters of the German war effort.

War brutalized life in ways that did not alter the goals of the German leaders but did transform what it was possible for them to achieve. War provided a cover for mass murder: remember Hitler's false dating of his order to murder the disabled to September 1, 1939, and the repeated claim that he had given his speech "predicting" annihilation of the European Jews not in January 1939 but in September of that year. War also made possible the training of large numbers of experienced killers, beginning in Poland in 1939.

War trapped the victims of Nazism inside Europe, making them ever more vulnerable. After September 1939 it became extremely difficult for Jews to leave Europe. By 1941 it was practically impossible. The German police regulation of September 1941 that required all people inside Germany who were defined as Jews to wear the identifying Star of David reinforced the obvious: Jews were now open targets.

War enabled Nazi propagandists to present attacks on innocent civilians of all ages as if they were defensive measures necessary to protect the German nation from its foes. For all these reasons, war was a necessary ingredient in what would develop into genocide—the deliberate effort to annihilate identifiable groups of people.

ASSAULT ON THE BALKANS—YUGOSLAVIA AND GREECE

In 1941, the Germans again turned east, first to the Balkans in southeastern Europe. Mussolini had gotten in over his head when he sent his Italian forces in to conquer Greece in 1940. Now he needed the Germans to bail him out.

The German attack on the Balkans was also linked to preparation for an assault on the Soviet Union. Hitler and his generals considered it necessary to control the Balkan states in order to secure their southeastern flank and safeguard access to Romanian oil. With Romania, Bulgaria, and Hungary already bound to Germany through diplomatic arrangements, only Yugoslavia and Greece remained to be brought into the Nazi sphere.

On April 6, 1941, the Luftwaffe launched an air raid on Belgrade. German forces surrounded the Yugoslav army, which capitulated on April 17. Italian,

Hungarian, and Bulgarian troops invaded Yugoslavia in aid of the Germans and to assert their own territorial claims. The Yugoslav king fled to Britain, where he too formed a government-in-exile.

Although the German offensive advanced rapidly, it faced tough resistance. Yugoslav partisans used the rugged terrain to their advantage and benefited from the effective, harsh leadership of Tito (Josip Broz, 1892–1980). Aid from the British in the form of supplies and intelligence helped too.

In Yugoslavia the German forces stooped to depths of organized brutality that rivaled their behavior in Poland. Here too they relied on familiar techniques of divide and conquer. Part of the country (Croatia, Bosnia, and Herzegovina) became an independent Croatian state under Ante Pavelic (1889–1959) and his fascist Ustasha movement. The Germans used their ally Pavelic to carry out their will. At the same time they gave him and his henchmen license to do what they wanted against enemies of their own, which meant above all the Serbs. Meanwhile the Germans annexed some northern

A Serbian gendarme guards a group of Roma on the way to their execution, sometime between 1941 and 1943. Note the bare feet of many of the prisoners. Did they not have shoes, or had their captors taken the shoes for themselves? Certainly being barefoot would make it harder to escape. Yugoslavia was the epicenter of the genocide of Roma during World War II, with tens of thousands murdered in Serbia and in Croatia.

parts of Yugoslavia (Slovenia) to the German Reich and set up a military government in occupied Serbia. Everywhere, they encouraged attacks on Jews, Roma, Communists, liberals, and anti-German nationalists of any kind.

The Nazi Germans' occupation policies ensured a steady flow of people into the partisan groups. In particular, the practice of reprisals aroused hatred. For every one German whom Yugoslav partisans attacked or killed, German authorities ordered a certain number of Yugoslavs shot. Sometimes the ratio was fifty to one; sometimes it was one hundred or even two hundred to one. The victims seized included people of all ages, female as well as male. Often the Germans took their first victims from among the local Jewish and Roma populations, but they also took hostage and shot many Serbs. There were Croats, Bosnian Muslims, and people with mixed backgrounds among those shot in reprisals too. Germans used reprisals—often based only on fear or suspicion of partisan actions—as an excuse to massacre hundreds of thousands of Yugoslavs. By allowing local partners and collaborators to select the targets of reprisal killings, German forces also deepened existing divisions and created new hatreds.

In Yugoslavia it was the regular military, not special SS units, who carried out mass shootings of civilians. In fact some of the most damning evidence of atrocities committed by the Wehrmacht during World War II comes out of Yugoslavia. Although soldiers were not forced to participate in the killings, there were always enough volunteers for such duties. Some of them took photographs of their exploits that they carried in their pockets or sent home to their girlfriends and wives. Like other images of atrocity, such photos served to disseminate knowledge of what was going on, even if those who saw them said nothing.

These two pictures, taken by German soldiers in Yugoslavia in 1941, also raise some questions specific to that setting. Were the photos meant to capture the familiarity or the strangeness of the scenes? For many in the Wehrmacht, Yugoslavia was not the "wild east" or some exotic, fantasy colonial space, but well-known terrain. Soldiers and especially officers from annexed Austria were prominent in the Yugoslavian campaign: it made sense to deploy units who knew the region, parts of which had been in the Habsburg Empire prior to World War I. During that war Serbia itself had been occupied by Austria, and according to historians, not particularly brutally. Did the men of the Wehrmacht in 1941 see their victims as somehow linked to the past or as the products of a completely new and unprecedented conflict?

Already in 1940, Hitler's Italian ally, Mussolini, had launched his own military campaign against Greece, but the Italian offensive bogged down until the spring of 1941, when the Germans took over. In April and May 1941 German forces overran Greece. Here too the Germans assaulted civilians as well

Germans pose near the bodies of recently murdered Serbian civilians in 1941 in Yugoslavia. In Yugoslavia, members of the regular military, not special SS units, were responsible for the massive death toll. In massive reprisal actions, entire villages were burned to the ground, their inhabitants of all ages murdered.

as members of the military. In so-called special actions, often in retaliation for resistance or partisan activity, they wiped out entire villages and towns.

On Hitler's orders, German soldiers tried to spare Greece's artistic treasures. Hitler had always been fascinated by Greek and Roman art. He held the notion that the best artistic achievements had been the work of "Aryans" who later migrated north and brought their superior creativity to Germany. According to Hitler, the Greeks of his own time were a lesser people unworthy of their country's glorious past. In Greece, as elsewhere, Hitler adjusted reality to fit his view of the world.

GERMAN ASSAULT ON THE SOVIET UNION

On June 22, 1941, German and other Axis troops invaded the Soviet Union. The invasion was given the code name Operation Barbarossa. With this step Nazi forces entered a new stage of what Hitler called the "war of annihilation."

War in the Soviet Union was extremely bloody. An estimated 27 million Soviet citizens were killed, two-thirds of them civilians. Carnage on this scale was no mere replay of Napoleon's failed invasion of Russia 129 years earlier.

German troops stand at the edge of a trench used as a mass grave for the bodies of Jews and Roma killed by the 750th Infantry Regiment in October 1941 in the Macva region of Yugoslavia. A German soldier sent this photograph to a woman friend in spring 1945. One wonders why he did so then: was he boasting about past exploits or trying to share knowledge of atrocities with someone back home?

The aim of the German assault was total destruction of the Soviet Union: seizure of its land, and colonization, enslavement, and murder of its people, in short, establishment of the Nazi new order.

By mid-1941 German forces were ready to wage a war of annihilation. Trained in conquest in Poland, proven capable of wholesale massacre of captured soldiers in France, flushed with successes in the west, and hardened by war on partisans and civilians in the Balkans, they were no longer likely to protest atrocities as some had in 1939. From day one German operations in the Soviet Union would be characterized by a level of violence that has led the historian Omer Bartov to speak of the "barbarization of warfare."

You may have heard people say that Germany would have won the war if Hitler had not made the mistake of attacking the Soviet Union. Given Hitler's worldview this claim makes little sense. For Hitler the whole point of the war was to conquer land and resources to support his purportedly superior "Aryan race." The *Lebensraum*—living space—he sought could only be found in the east. Hitler had always planned on war with the Soviet Union; it was only a question of when.

Some writers have contended that Hitler's assault on the Soviet Union was purely defensive. According to them, Stalin was poised to attack Germany, so Hitler ordered a preemptive strike. Neither German nor Russian archival records support such a notion. Hitler made his intentions against the Soviet Union very clear, not only in *Mein Kampf* and in his second, untitled book, but in numerous conversations and speeches. Most significant, German military planners had worked out the details of an offensive against the Soviet Union long before June 1941. Of course Stalin had his own violent plans for eastern and central Europe, but such schemes do not alter the fact of Hitler's aggression. Unfortunately there is no reason why two opponents cannot both be scoundrels.

What about the Molotov-Ribbentrop nonaggression pact of 1939? Like all of Hitler's diplomatic agreements it was made to be broken. The deal had served Nazi goals well; it enabled rapid defeat of Poland in 1939, freed up German forces to concentrate in the west in 1940, and bought almost two years of time to prepare for war with the Soviet Union. It seems unlikely that Hitler or his generals even gave it a thought in June 1941.

The maps that follow illustrate several points. Note the many "major killing sites" and how they coincide with German military advances. Also significant is the concentration of killing sites in the west, the region of "dual occupation." Many Jews lived there and most of them were killed there. Those who survived mostly did so in the Soviet interior, far to the east.

Evacuation and Escape

In the panic-stricken days that followed the German invasion, Soviet authorities organized mass evacuations of people and resources to regions far from the western borders. The goal was to make it possible to continue agricultural, industrial, and military production even if the Germans should succeed in overrunning the Soviet Union's European territories. Entire factories were hastily dismantled, packed up, and together with their workers transported to the Urals, Siberia, and Soviet Central Asia. These gigantic relocations were not designed to save Jews from the German onslaught, and indeed, it was high-ranking Communists, NKVD operatives, and their family and friends who got the highest priority.

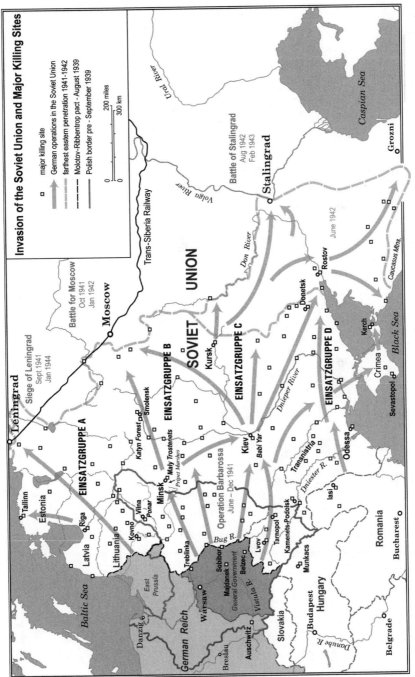

Invasion of the Soviet Union and Major Killing Sites

□ major killing site
German operations in the Soviet Union
farthest eastern penetration 1941-1942
Molotov-Ribbentrop pact - August 1939
Polish border pre - September 1939

0   200 miles
0   300 km

Trans-Siberia Railway

Leningrad
Siege of Leningrad
Sept 1941
Jan 1944

Battle for Moscow
Oct 1941
Jan 1942

Moscow

SOVIET UNION

Ural River

Volga River

Battle of Stalingrad
Aug 1942
Feb 1943

Stalingrad

Caspian Sea

EINSATZGRUPPE A
EINSATZGRUPPE B
EINSATZGRUPPE C
EINSATZGRUPPE D

Don River

June 1942

Rostov

Caucasus Mtns.

Grozni

Kursk

Smolensk
Katyn Forest
Maly Trostenets
Minsk
Pripet Marshes

Dnieper River

Donetsk

Kerch

Black Sea

Crimea

Sevastopol

Kiev
Babi Yar

Estonia
Tallinn
Riga
Latvia
Lithuania
Kovno
Vilna
Ponar

Treblinka
Bug R.
Sobibor
Majdanek
Belzec
General Government
Vistula R.

Operation Barbarossa
June – Dec 1941

Lvov
Tarnopol
Kamenets-Podolsk

Transnistria

Dniester R.

Odessa

Iasi

Munkacs

Romania

Bucharest

Baltic Sea

East Prussia

German Reich

Danzig

Warsaw

Breslau

Auschwitz

Slovakia

Budapest
Hungary

Danube R.

Belgrade

Map by Michael J. Fisher, cartographer

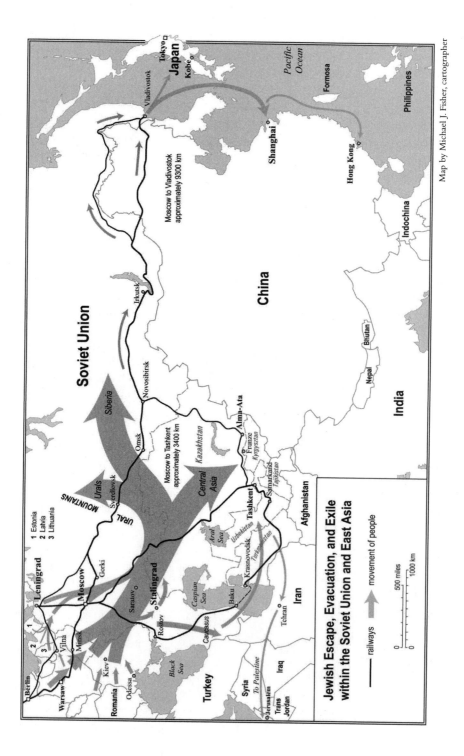

Jewish Escape, Evacuation, and Exile within the Soviet Union and East Asia

railways — movement of people

Map by Michael J. Fisher, cartographer

Nevertheless, many Soviet Jews and Jews from elsewhere who had fled to the Soviet Union earlier—from Germany, Austria, France, Poland, the Baltic States, and elsewhere—found ways to join the mass movement to the east. People packed themselves and their families into evacuation trains, begged and bribed their way onto trucks, cars, and any other moving vehicles, and when all else failed, took to the roads on foot. Scholarship on the wartime evacuations and specifically on the Jews who managed to be swept along by them is just starting to take off, but it is clear that by far the largest site of Jewish survival during World War II was behind Soviet lines. An estimated one million European Jews found refuge in the Soviet interior, though under conditions that were precarious at best and often deadly.

In Tashkent, Frunze, Samarkand, and other cities and towns in Central Asia substantial populations of Jews were able to establish and maintain a level of communal life that was impossible anywhere under German occupation. They set up schools and cultural institutions, produced literature and songs in Yiddish, and most of all did everything they could to maintain contact with the remnants of Jewish life in Europe and inform the wider world of their fate.

The many Jews who survived the war in the Soviet interior also included hundreds of thousands of people sent there by force. Stalin's terror had its Jewish victims, too, many of whom had been sent to Gulags in Siberia prior to June 1941. During the Soviet occupation of Eastern Poland and the Baltic States, large numbers of Jews there had been swept up in waves of arrests and deportations, and they too had been dispatched to labor and prison camps behind the Urals, to Kazakhstan, and other distant sites. Now even those places offered better chances for survival than Hitler's killing fields.

Caught between Stalin and Hitler

It is important to note that the Germans invaded the Soviet Union, not just Russia. The Soviet Union was a multinational empire that included many territories in addition to Russia. In fact some of the worst devastation of World War II occurred not in Russia but in eastern Poland, Ukraine, Belorussia, and the Baltic states of Latvia, Estonia, and Lithuania.

In June 1941, before the Germans reached Russia, they first entered territories that the Soviets had seized after the attack on Poland in 1939. As a consequence, people in eastern Poland, Lithuania, Latvia, and elsewhere experienced two rounds of invasion in less than two years. Starting in September 1939 Stalin's armies had moved in; Hitler's troops arrived in 1941.

Some people in those areas had greeted the Soviets in 1939 as bearers of Communism and protectors from Nazism. Almost all had become disillusioned by 1941. That year some people in eastern Europe welcomed the German invasion, expecting Hitler's forces to crush Communism and grant them in-dependence. For instance, there were Ukrainian nationalists who hoped the Nazis would let them set up their own state. They too would be disappointed. Most eastern Europeans quickly learned that they could expect only terror and destruction from a war fought not for them but on top of them.

The region of dual, and in some cases triple, occupations, proved par-ticularly deadly for Jews. The incoming Germans targeted Jews from the start and actively encouraged local people to join in the violence. In some com-munities, like the eastern Polish town of Jedwabne, non-Jews needed minimal prompting from the Germans to massacre their Jewish neighbors. In Lithuania there were some vicious attacks on Jews even before German troops arrived: people did not need detailed knowledge of Nazi plans to grasp that invasion signaled open season on Jews. Certainly many Jews understood and tried to outrun the rapidly advancing Wehrmacht. For non-Jews this tumultuous situ-ation created opportunities to grab property and possessions, settle old scores, and demonstrate loyalty to the new German masters. Not everyone gave in to those temptations, and why some individuals and communities attacked Jews in mid-1941 while others did not remains a persistent question in Holocaust studies.

An Account from Lvov

One person who experienced Soviet takeover in the fall of 1939 and then the German invasion in 1941 was Nelly Toll. Born in 1935, she was a little girl in 1939. Her family was among the one hundred and ten thousand Jews in the eastern Polish city of Lvov (now L'viv in Ukraine), home to Poland's third-largest Jewish community, after Warsaw and Lodz. About one million Jews lived in the surrounding region, called eastern Galicia.

Under Soviet rule more Jews streamed into the city to escape the Ger-mans, but Soviet control brought its own hardships. Nelly Toll's father went into hiding to avoid being sent to a labor camp in Siberia. As the wealthy owner of a dry goods store he was considered an enemy of Communism. Soviet officials seized much of the Tolls' property and took over their spacious apartment. Nelly remembers her family's relationship with the Red Army officers as a mixture of fear, friendliness, and contempt for people she and her relatives considered somewhat less civilized than themselves.

When the Germans came to Lvov in 1941 even some Jews there thought they might be an improvement over the Soviets. Nelly's grandfather, for example, at first regarded the German takeover as a good thing. In his view Germans were more cultured and intelligent than Russians. He was wrong: Hitler's Germans proved no less barbaric and more deadly than Stalin's Soviets.

In Lvov some of the local people saw arrival of the Germans as a chance to take revenge for all they had suffered under the Soviets. In particular Ukrainians in the region wanted to seize the chance to get back at the Russians as well as their Polish neighbors. Most of the Soviets had fled before the advancing Germans. So angry residents of Lvov attacked their Jewish neighbors as convenient scapegoats instead. They accused Jews of collaborating with the Soviets to oppress them. No doubt there had been Jews who supported the Soviet regime, but there had also been non-Jewish Poles and Ukrainians who had done the same.

As usual German authorities encouraged ethnic strife and rewarded pogroms. They urged local Ukrainians to take out their grievances against the Polish majority, in particular against those elements the Germans targeted too: intellectuals, Catholic priests, and other community leaders. They gave Ukrainians and Poles license to terrorize Jews and steal their possessions.

In June 1941 Ukrainians in Lvov arrested some Jews on the charge that they had committed crimes against Ukrainians during the Soviet occupation. Many of those Jews were executed in prisons and nearby forests. Others were taken to prison cells already stained with Jewish blood, forced to clean them, and then shot. Throughout July 1941 pogroms raged in the city, and thousands of Jews were killed. On one occasion Nelly Toll watched from the balcony with her cousins as German soldiers beat an old Jewish man. A crowd gathered to laugh and clap.

The chief rabbi of Lvov, Ezekiel Lewin, appealed for help to Metropolitan Andrey Sheptytsky, head of the Ukrainian Greek Catholic church. Sheptytsky called on Ukrainians to stop murdering Jews, but without effect. He invited the rabbi and his family to take refuge in his personal residence. Rabbi Lewin accepted on behalf of his children but thought his own place was with his people. Later that day rioters seized him, and a member of the Ukrainian militia shot him dead, in front of his son.

Nelly Toll was luckier than Rabbi Lewin. She lived through 1941, although children threw stones at her in the street, her mother was beaten black and blue by a Ukrainian policeman, and the family was forced into a ghetto. Eventually Nelly's mother sent her to hide with a Christian family. When that place proved too risky she returned to the ghetto to learn that her brother, aunt, and cousins had all been taken away by the Gestapo and put on a train. None of them returned.

In 1943, after more close calls and a failed attempt to escape to Hungary, Nelly and her mother went into hiding. They ended up with a Polish Catholic couple who sheltered them in exchange for money. The woman was kind and thoughtful but her husband was violent, paranoid, and antisemitic, abusive to his wife and over-attentive to Nelly's mother. It was a very difficult situation.

Somehow both Nelly and her mother survived the war, but they never saw Nelly's father again. Nelly Toll immigrated to the United States in 1951, where she became an artist and a counselor.

Crossing the Line to Annihilation

Hitler expected the campaign against the Soviet Union to be easy for the Germans. In this regard he and his military planners were caught in their own ethnic and racial stereotypes. They thought of Slavs as stupid and incompetent and believed that the Communist Soviet Union was in the grip of Jews, whom they viewed as cowardly and perfidious. Such attitudes caused the German leaders to make some severe miscalculations.

The German invasion did not turn out as planned. The Soviets were better equipped than German planners had thought; the Germans themselves were overextended and unprepared for winter. Contrary to what many German accounts claim, the winter of 1941 was neither unusually early nor extraordinarily harsh; it was more or less a typical Russian winter. Nor, as Gerhard Weinberg has pointed out, did it snow only on the Germans; the Soviets faced the same weather conditions. Hitler and his generals, however, had anticipated quick victory, another "lightning war" that they would win. They had not thought it necessary to prepare for winter.

From the beginning of war with the Soviet Union, the German leadership advocated ruthless measures. In instructions to the military and the SS, Hitler, Himmler, and Heydrich made it clear that no mercy was to be shown Germany's enemies, whether they were Jews, Communists, or resistors. High-ranking officers passed the message down to their men.

With the invasion of the Soviet Union the Nazi leadership would move to full implementation of their ideas of race and space on a massive scale. Their warfare reached new depths of brutality, especially against civilians but also against Soviet prisoners of war. Most noticeably they crossed the line from persecution and killing of Jews to a systematic attempt at total destruction.

Yet in many ways 1941 was not a radical break with earlier Nazi practices. All of the pieces were already in place. Hitler had spelled out the quest for Lebensraum in *Mein Kampf*. The Germans had begun to grab territory in Europe even before the war. They had assaulted civilians on a wide scale in occupied Poland since 1939; they had used their enemies as slave labor, forcibly relocated enormous numbers of people, and started to slaughter disabled people, Jews, and Roma. In 1940 in France they had massacred thousands of captured black soldiers. All of these terrible developments culminated in the Soviet Union in 1941 and the years to follow.

The Einsatzgruppen

Perhaps the most blatant sign of Germany's style of warfare in 1941 was the use of special murder squads. German authorities dispatched mobile killing units to follow the regular military into Soviet territory. The main units, known as the Einsatzgruppen, "special action groups," included between five hundred and one thousand men each, many of them well educated,—lawyers, theologians, and other professionals. The Einsatzgruppen worked together with more numerous German units known as the Order Police and with local collaborators. The Einsatzgruppen cooperated with the German military, something they had learned to do in 1938 in annexed Austria and especially in Poland a year later.

The task of the mobile killing units in 1941 was straightforward. They had instructions from Heydrich to kill Jews, prominent Communists, and anyone suspected of sabotage or anti-German activity. Officially their goal was to secure conquered territory by combating bolshevism and preventing guerrilla warfare. In fact, during the summer of 1941, they began to interpret their primary job as slaughter of all Jews, including women, children, and old people. The Einsatzgruppen and Order Police also murdered Roma and inmates of mental hospitals, although they seem to have been less systematic against those target populations.

Members of the mobile killing units often tried to involve local people in their work. Many non-German auxiliaries—Ukrainians, Latvians, ethnic Germans from eastern Europe, Belorussians, and others—helped in their grisly task. Threats, bribes, massive amounts of alcohol, and promises of privileges for recruits and their families all helped the Germans find accomplices. Even local conditions could be used to facilitate murder. The Pripet marshes, a massive swampy region in southern Belorussia and northern Ukraine became a site of horrendous slaughter. Himmler urged his commanders in the region to shoot all Jewish men and drive the women and children into the swamps.

The Einsatzgruppen and Order Police attempted to stir up pogroms wherever they went. In some cases locals did take unprompted action against Jews, but the mobile killing groups were less successful in this regard than the German leadership had hoped. Local individuals sometimes terrorized Jews and took the initiative to steal their property, but generally the impetus and organization for systematic killing came from the Germans.

Many of the actions of the mobile killing units more or less followed the same pattern. First they rounded up the Jews in a given area using various ruses to deceive them and relying on local collaborators for denunciations. The Germans ordered large pits dug in some convenient area—a local cemetery, nearby forest, or easily accessible field. Sometimes they forced the prisoners themselves to dig what would be their own graves, though in many cases they conscripted the labor of local non-Jews. At gunpoint they made the victims undress. Then they shot them by groups directly into the graves. In this manner the mobile killing units and their helpers massacred around a million people even before the establishment of major killing centers that killed with gas.

Such mass shootings in the open air could hardly be kept secret. Eyewitnesses of all kinds saw these massacres—German soldiers and workers, ethnic Germans who lived nearby, and Lithuanian, Polish, or Ukrainian families from the region. Some of those observers gave detailed, chilling accounts of what they saw. For example, a German builder named Hermann Graebe watched while mobile killing squads shot scores of people of all ages near Dubno in Ukraine. He was surprised to be allowed to stay, but he noticed three uniformed postal workers looking on as well. Elsewhere in Ukraine a fifteen-year-old Mennonite boy and his friends watched the slaughter of a group of Roma at a local cemetery. Later someone came around the village to distribute clothes taken from the murdered people. According to the eyewitness's account, written down decades later, no one in the community wanted that clothing.

The Kamenets-Podolsk Massacre

Members of the Einsatzgruppen quickly learned that they did not need to worry about widespread opposition from local populations. Enough people could always be recruited or coerced to take part in the killing operations—digging pits, sorting clothing and other items, burying the bodies, stamping down the dirt, even preparing lunch for the killers. Others came to watch, drawn by the spectacle or perhaps hoping to get something for themselves. But many—probably most—tried desperately to stay away, hunkered down in their houses with the doors and windows shut, terrified and traumatized.

Killing proved to be contagious, as officials of countries allied with Nazi Germany learned they too could solve their "problems" in this way. In late June 1941, Hungary declared war on the Soviet Union. Soon after, Hungarian authorities decided to expel foreign Jews from their territory. Most of these were Polish and Russian Jews, but there were also many refugees from western Europe. In Subcarpathian Rus', a region that had been part of Czechoslovakia until it was annexed by Hungary in 1939, very few Jews could document Hungarian citizenship, and entire communities were rounded up and loaded onto freight trains.

Under Hungarian guard, around eighteen thousand Jews were brought to what prior to 1939 had been the border with Poland and by mid-1941 separated Hungary from territory under German control. There the Hungarians handed them over to the Germans, who marched them to the city of Kamenets-Podolsk in occupied Ukraine (now Kamianets-Podilskyi).

Uncertain what to do next, German authorities in the region held a meeting. Friedrich Jeckeln, the Higher SS and Police Leader for the Southern Front, promised to resolve the issue. His "solution" was both simple and final: over several days at the end of August 1941, a detachment of Einsatzgruppe C, assisted by other German, Ukrainian, and Hungarian units, shot all of those people: children, women, and men alike. They rounded up thousands of Jews from the area and killed them, too. In all the Germans murdered 23,600 Jews in this action—Jeckeln provided the total in his report—an unprecedented number at that point in the Holocaust.

Some unusual photographs from Kamenets-Podolsk shed light on how genocide is documented. The Hungarian military units involved in the killing had with them at least one Hungarian Jew, who had been assigned to the army as a driver. Since early 1939, Jewish men in Hungary were drafted into labor service units. The driver, Gyula Spitz, was stationed in Kamenets-Podolsk and witnessed the round-ups and massacres there. Somehow he got his hands on a camera and took a series of photographs. In one, the top of the steering wheel and edge of the windshield are visible, showing that Spitz took the picture quickly, from inside his truck. He got closer to the Jews in the column for

Jews under German guard march through the streets of Kamenets-Podolsk in occupied Ukraine to a killing site outside the city in August 1941. The photographer, Gyula Spitz, was a Jew from Budapest. Assigned as a forced laborer to the Hungarian army, he was stationed in Kamenets-Podolsk when a mass killing of Jews by German SS and military personnel and Hungarian soldiers took place in August 1941.

Jewish men and women force-marched through Kamenets-Podolsk to a killing site outside of the city. This is another of the photographs taken by Gyula Spitz. Note that several of the men have noticed that they were being photographed and turned their heads in the direction of the photographer. As a Jew, Spitz made himself extremely vulnerable when he approached so close to the victims in order to document their fate.

another picture, and some of them appear to be looking at him, maybe even speaking to him. These photographs survived the war, but Spitz did not. He was arrested by the Germans and sent to Mauthausen, where he died.

Most information about the mass shootings comes from witnesses like Spitz or from the perpetrators themselves. Few victims lived to tell about their experiences. One of the exceptions is a man named Zvi Michalowsky, whose account appears in a book by Yaffa Eliach called *Hasidic Tales of the Holocaust*.

In 1941 on Rosh Hashanah, the Jewish new year, Germans and their local helpers murdered the Jews in a Lithuanian town called Eisysky. Michalowsky, a teenaged boy at the time, was among those forced to strip and wait at the edge of a grave for a bullet. A split second before the Germans fired, Zvi threw himself back into the pit. Miraculously he avoided serious injury.

For the rest of that day Zvi lay in the mass grave, feeling the bodies pile up on top of him. Only long after the shooting had stopped did he dare to climb out. He ran, naked and covered with blood, to the nearest house, but when he knocked, the terrified Polish Christians who lived there refused to let him in. Finally he approached an old woman. He told her he was Jesus Christ come down from the cross, and she opened the door to him. Zvi Michalowsky went on to found a resistance group in the woods, and he survived the war.

Babi Yar

The biggest slaughter carried out by the Einsatzgruppen and their helpers was the massacre at Babi Yar in Ukraine. In just two days in September 1941, German mobile killing units, working closely with the regular military and aided by Ukrainian-speaking collaborators, shot more than thirty thousand Jews and an unknown number of other people at Babi Yar, a ravine on the outskirts of Kiev. That act, just months after the invasion of the Soviet Union, was a deliberate attempt to eradicate all of the Jews in Kiev and its surrounding area.

Many of Kiev's Jews had already fled, terrified by rumors and reports of atrocities as the Germans advanced. But not everyone could run away. Pregnant women and mothers with small children, the elderly, people who were sick or disabled, those with no means of transportation or no idea where to go or who to turn to for help, people unwilling to be separated from family and friends—such people were left in the city. Threatened with death if they failed to comply, many of them answered the German summons to appear at designated assembly points, from which they were told they would be transported to labor and resettlement sites. Accounts from non-Jews describe the endless columns that moved through the city, people carrying bundles and babies, the lucky ones with carts or wheelbarrows to hold their possessions or bear family members unable to walk.

Guards, police, and soldiers of the German 6th Army force-marched the Jews of Kiev, some accompanied by non-Jewish family members and friends, to the ravines, made them remove their clothes, and machine-gunned them in batches. When it became too dark to shoot, they locked the people still left alive in sheds until the next morning, when they resumed killing.

The Babi Yar massacre has become emblematic of the carnage wrought by Nazi Germans in the Soviet Union generally and particularly in Ukraine. Germans continued to use Babi Yar as a killing field throughout the occupation. The majority of the dead were Jews, although others targeted by the German occupiers died at Babi Yar as well: Roma, prisoners of war, and victims of reprisal actions. In Soviet times state authorities put up a monument at the ravines. A plaque dedicated the memorial to the "more than one hundred thousand Soviet citizens" killed there. Nowhere did it mention that most of the dead were murdered solely because they were Jews. Here the official act of remembering also became a way of forgetting.

That peculiar combination continues to haunt the place of Babi Yar in Holocaust memory. Soon after Soviet troops liberated Kiev, the esteemed director Mark Donskoy made a feature film in which the massacre featured prominently. *The Unvanquished*, released in 1945, was unusual in its unflinching depiction of the slaughter at Babi Yar. Even more remarkable, it was filmed on location at the ravines, and among the actors were well-known Soviet Jews. Although the movie did not openly state that Babi Yar was an attack on Jews, it communicated this fact to its audience. Some images, notably scenes of people of all ages trudging along in a column, became a kind of symbol, repeated in many movies, of Nazi victimization of Jews.

The Role of the Military

The exact number of people killed by the mobile units cannot be known, although experts estimate a total of almost two million victims. Most were Jews—some 1.3 million—and there may have been as many as two hundred and twenty-five thousand Roma. The Einsatzgruppen and Order Police could not have carried out such an enormous number of killings without the knowledge and cooperation of the Wehrmacht. They followed the regular military and in many cases relied on them for provisions, security, and intelligence. How did the military respond?

At first it seems there might have been misgivings. One incident illustrates the forms such doubts might have taken. In mid-August 1941, German authorities in the Ukrainian town of Belaya Tserkov, more than two hundred miles east of Lvov, ordered local Jews to report for registration. Over the next few days, SS and German soldiers scoured the area for Jews, slaughtering hundreds of men and women. In the summer of 1941 some of the killers still seemed unclear as to whether their task included murder of all Jews, women and children as well as men. Perhaps for this reason, the shooters at Belaya Tserkov did not initially kill all the children. Instead they dumped about ninety of them and a handful of women in a school.

German soldiers in a field hospital nearby heard babies crying in the night. Uncertain what to do, they appealed to their military chaplains. The two German clergy, a Protestant pastor and a Catholic priest, went to see for themselves. They were appalled. It was hot, and the children were crammed into a small space without water, food, or adult care. Some of the mothers were locked in an adjoining room, from which they could see the misery of their children without being able to get to them.

The chaplains appealed to the local military commander, an elderly Austrian, to take pity on the children. Their effort failed, one of them later reported, because the man was a convinced antisemite. Together the chaplains convinced another German officer to intervene. He got Army High Command to agree to postpone shooting of the children, but SS representatives and military officers on the spot prevailed, citing instructions from Field Marshal Gerd von Rundstedt, commander of Army Group South, that they were to show no mercy. On August 21, 1941, the children were taken from the school and killed by members of German Sonderkommando 4a, part of Einsatzgruppe C.

Killings of civilians did not end in the summer or fall of 1941 but continued throughout the war. Presumably German soldiers and the military chaplains who ministered to them got used to the routine. The comfort of knowing they were backed by orders from above must have helped too.

The most widely circulated of such orders came from German Field Marshal Walter von Reichenau, Commander of the Sixth Army. Reichenau issued his statement just two weeks after the Babi Yar massacre, in which he and some of his men had been actively involved. Infantry divisions of the Sixth Army had helped arrest and confine Jews, and Reichenau had participated in a series of meetings where it seems the action was planned. (One outcome of those meetings was a requisition to print two thousand posters ordering the Jews of Kiev to report at certain places.) In his order issued on October 10, 1941, Reichenau admitted that there was "uncertainty" among the German troops as to the "current situation" in the east. However, he told his men, given the nature of the war and the need to eradicate what he called the "Jewish-bolshevist system," it was necessary to break the conventional rules of war, to show no mercy to those defined as Germany's enemies, above all to the people Reichenau labeled "Jewish subhumans."

It is certainly not common practice for military superiors to justify themselves and their decisions to the people under their command. Reichenau, however, did just that. His order implies that there was some uneasiness in the ranks about military involvement in slaughter of civilians. We can assume that those reservations were overcome sufficiently for the killings to continue with the necessary military support. Perhaps German soldiers accepted the justifications offered to them, that such excesses were a necessary part of the German struggle against partisans, or later on, that they were some kind of revenge for Allied bombings of German cities.

Of course neither of those rationalizations makes much sense. How could a baby be responsible for a partisan attack on German rail lines? What could an old Jewish woman more than a thousand miles away who spoke nothing but Yiddish have to do with British planes dropping bombs on Hamburg or Cologne? Nevertheless, these explanations may have helped men live with themselves once they were involved in killing. Many of their motivations for killing in the first place were undramatic: their comrades were doing it, and they did not want to stand out; they considered it part of their job; they had gotten used to it.

What we do know is that Germans were not forced to be killers. Those who refused to participate were given other assignments or transferred. To this day no one has found an example of a German who was executed for refusing to take part in the killing of Jews or other civilians. Defense attorneys of people accused of war crimes during World War II have looked hard for such a case because it would support the claim that their clients had no choice. The Nazi system, however, did not work that way. There were enough willing perpetrators so that coercive force could be reserved for those deemed enemies.

Romania and the Killing Fields in Transnistria

Extreme violence breeds more of the same. This point is evident if we look at Romania, one of Germany's World War II allies, in 1941. The Romanian army took an active part in the German offensive against the southern Soviet Union. In the areas conquered, German and Romanian armies cooperated with the Einsatzgruppen in massacring Jews and Roma.

The case of Jews in the Ukrainian city of Odessa is a case in point. In the fall of 1941, several days after German and Romanian forces occupied Odessa, an explosion rocked Romanian army headquarters there. In retaliation, Romanian leader Ion Antonescu ordered the execution of two hundred "Communists" for every Romanian officer killed and one hundred for each soldier. Most of the victims selected were Jews. Einsatzgruppen killers worked together with German and Romanian military, Ukrainian auxiliary police, and recruits from the local ethnic German population to slaughter some thirty-five thousand Jews. In February 1942, Odessa was proclaimed "Judenrein," or "cleansed of Jews."

Beginning in 1941, persecution of Jews also exploded within Romania. The Romanian government introduced laws restricting Jews in all kinds of ways, and pogroms resulted in the death of well over a thousand Romanian Jews. Antisemitism was not new to Romania, but the war and German leadership gave antisemites license to act on their hatreds in large-scale ways.

In the fall of 1941, Romanian authorities began moving Jews out of Romania proper and forcing them east across the Dniester River and then the Bug River into an area of intense Einsatzgruppen operations. First fifty thousand and then another one hundred and twenty thousand Romanian Jews were driven into the hands of the Germans and their accomplices in Transnistria in occupied Ukraine.

Among those expelled in this way was a young boy named Aharon Appelfeld. Separated from his father, he ended up in a makeshift Transnistrian camp. Somehow he escaped, dodged the killing fields of the Einsatzgruppen, and evaded the reach of local collaborators. Just nine years old in 1941, he survived for four years working as a shepherd, hiding in the woods, stealing, begging, and taking refuge with people who helped him. After the war Appelfeld moved to Israel. He is the author of many acclaimed works of fiction dealing with themes from the Holocaust.

Many Romanian Roma shared the fate of their Jewish compatriots. As a girl of about ten, Drina Radu survived expulsion to Transnistria. She remembers crossing the Dniester River into the part of Ukraine occupied by Romania. Everyone rushed to get on the first boatloads, she told the journalist Isabel Fonseca, not because they were eager to reach the other side but because, in her words, "the boats were made of paper." Hastily constructed from cheap, porous material, they became waterlogged and sank after three or four trips. That detail reveals the deadly cynicism of the Romanians in charge. Why go to any effort or expense to protect the lives of people they knew were slated for death anyway? Between 1941 and 1944, approximately thirty-six thousand Roma were killed in Transnistria.

For the Jews and Roma murdered in the killing fields of Transnistria, there was nothing ambiguous about their government's plan for them: it was deadly. But there were ways in which the Romanian situation was complex too. For one thing, German authorities did not always welcome Romanian initiatives, such as the expulsion of almost two hundred thousand Jews into territories the Germans held. They preferred to retain control themselves. Accordingly, Antonescu was told to stop striking out on his own and wait for Germans to take the lead.

Non-Jewish Romanians continued to have their own ideas about how to solve what they considered their "Jewish problem." The Romanian government set up an office to look after Jewish affairs. It tolerated the existence of Jewish mutual-aid activities and allowed them to try to help the expellees. Leaders of the Jewish community maintained relations with some heads of state and in some incidents even managed to mitigate anti-Jewish measures. There were prominent Romanians—including the queen—who approached the Germans on behalf of Romanian Jews, although those overtures were rejected.

In wartime Romania, traditional antisemitism and widespread persecution of Jews were the norm. Nevertheless, the Romanian leadership, for all its viciousness, did not show the same single-minded and systematic dedication to eradication of Jews that the Nazi Germans introduced in the countries they controlled. Traditional Jewish means of self-preservation—mutual aid, intercession with rulers, evasion, and bribery—continued to have some effect in Romania. In the killing zone of Transnistria, Jews like Aharon Appelfeld, who managed to escape from Romanian camps and evade German killing squads, sometimes found members of the local population willing to provide shelter or work. The historian Diana Dumitru maintains that in this region, which had been part of the Soviet Union, official measures to combat antisemitism had had some effect. Overall, for all the horrors of 1941 and the years to follow, a higher percentage of Jews in Romania would survive the war than would be the case in Poland or the Netherlands.

German Treatment of Soviet POWs

Hitler's war of annihilation against the Soviet Union included killing of prisoners of war on a massive scale. Of the millions of non-Jews killed in German camps, by far the largest group of dead was Soviet POWs. Their treatment violated every standard of warfare.

Statistics only begin to tell the story. Initial German successes in the summer and fall of 1941 brought an enormous number of POWs into German hands. In total, between June 22, 1941, and the end of the war, Germans took approximately 5.7 million Red Army soldiers prisoner. As of January 1945, about nine hundred and thirty thousand Soviet POWs remained in Wehrmacht prison camps. About one million had been released as helpers of the German military. Another estimated half million had escaped or been liberated by the Red Army. That still leaves 3.3 million—57 percent—unaccounted for. They were dead.

Such a staggering death rate was neither an accident nor an automatic result of war. It was deliberate policy. German treatment of Soviet POWs differed wildly from handling of POWs from Britain and the United States. Of the two hundred and thirty-one thousand British and American prisoners held by the Germans, only about eight thousand three hundred—3.6 percent—died before the end of the war.

Death came in various ways to the more than three million Soviet POWs who died in German hands. In the early stages of the conflict the Germans shot many of the prisoners they took. They had made few provisions to accommodate their captives; they simply disposed of them. Eventually they erected some makeshift camps, but the lack of proper food, clothing, and shelter took a terrible toll. By the end of 1941, epidemics—especially typhoid and dysentery—emerged as the big killers. In October 1941 alone, as many as four thousand six hundred Soviet POWs died per day. Death rates fell off somewhat in 1942 as German authorities decided POWs could be a useful source of wartime labor. In 1943 and 1944, however, they soared again, due above all to hunger.

Starvation of Soviet POWs was directly tied to the Nazi policy of making sure there was plenty of food for the German home front. No doubt Hitler and others remembered the food riots of World War I, a war they believed Germany had lost because of its weak home front. This time they intended to keep food supplies—and morale—up, even if it meant starvation of what one bureaucrat called "umpteen million people."

German authorities viewed Soviet POWs as a particular threat, regarding them not only as Slavic and "Asiatic" inferiors but as part of the "bolshevik menace," linked in their minds to some imaginary Jewish conspiracy. No mercy was to be shown to Soviet prisoners. In the camp of Gross-Rosen, in Germany, the commandant had sixty-five thousand Soviet inmates killed within six months by feeding them a soup made only of grass, water, and salt. In Flossenbürg, SS men burned Soviet POWs alive. In Majdanek, they shot them into trenches. In Mauthausen, in Austria, so many POWs were killed that people living near the camp complained about pollution of their water supply; for days the rivers and streams of the area ran red with blood.

The photograph on the next page, from official German sources, provides a glimpse of the enormous number of Soviet men taken prisoner of war. The picture also captures some tensions within Nazi propaganda. On the one hand, it aimed to illustrate German success and superiority. Note the small number of Germans—on horseback or motorized—shown as masters of the Soviet hordes. On the other hand, by highlighting how outnumbered the Germans were, the image also reveals German vulnerability. Another tension is between strangeness and similarity. The photograph seems designed to showcase the "otherness" of the Red Army captives: they have rags around their heads, their skin is dark, their clothing anything but uniform. And yet they are unmistakably men and soldiers, not so different from the friends, sons, brothers, husbands, and fathers of the Germans back home who were the audience of these photos. Perhaps such images came back to haunt them later in the war, when it was German men who were being captured en masse.

In a 1941 letter to his wife, Konrad Jarausch, a German staff sergeant who helped administer a POW camp, wrote that "not all Russians are really 'pigs' or 'beasts'." An intellectual and devout Protestant, Jarausch became attached to certain prisoners, who tutored him in Russian and with whom he discussed world literature. The starvation and disease in the camp distressed him, but he assured his wife that he himself was well fed. Nevertheless, like so many of his charges, he contracted typhus, and in January 1942 he died. The editor of Jarausch's letters gave the volume the title *Reluctant Accomplice*, an apt description of the role he and many other Germans played in atrocities.

Camps set up for Soviet POWs became part of the machinery for destruction of Jews. The notorious sites of Auschwitz, near Krakow, and Majdanek, by Lublin, were originally designated to hold Soviet POWs and exploit their labor for the industrial complexes Himmler planned there. In 1941 some fifteen thousand Soviet POWs were taken to those places; by the end of that year, only a few hundred remained alive. During the first months of 1942, Himmler filled those camps with one hundred and fifty thousand Jews and transformed them into parts of the killing complex.

In September 1941, a column of Soviet POWs heads toward the rear and internment. Most Soviet POWs were held—and killed—in facilities administered by the German military, not the SS. Such sites of detention hardly merited the label "camp" because in many cases they provided neither shelter nor food. The overwhelming speed and incredible success of the early months of Operation Barbarossa can be glimpsed in this photo, taken by Heinrich Hoffmann, Hitler's favorite photographer. Note the lone German on horseback guarding hundreds of captured Soviet soldiers.

It was when dealing with Soviet POWs at Auschwitz that camp commandant Rudolf Hoess and his assistants experimented with the means of killing that have become the symbol of Nazi genocide: Zyklon B. In early September 1941, six hundred Soviet prisoners selected for execution by the SS arrived at Auschwitz. In order to avoid the cumbersome task of shooting so many people, Hoess and his men decided to gas them with the pesticide Zyklon B, also known as hydrogen cyanide. While they were at it they included another two hundred and fifty inmates who had been designated unfit for work.

The T-4 killers had already experimented with gassing as a way to murder people considered disabled. Those lessons were subsequently applied to Soviet POWs and then to Jews. In December 1941 the SS opened its first killing center for Jews, at Chelmno, called Kulmhof by the Germans. Located just forty miles from Lodz, the Chelmno facility used specially equipped gas vans to kill Jews and also Roma. Guards loaded their victims into the cargo compartment and sealed the doors. As the van was driven, carbon monoxide was pumped into the back so that the people there were asphyxiated.

7

WAR AND GENOCIDE

DECISIONS AND DYNAMICS IN THE PEAK YEARS OF KILLING, 1942–1943

When it comes to human suffering, each year of a war tends to be worse than the year before. The passage of time adds further material deprivation, more wounded, and more dead to the accumulated misery of the people involved.

This observation certainly holds true for World War II. By the end of 1942 the Germans were heading into their fourth year of war. At least in the short term their victories insulated them from much of the hardship that war brings. The same was not true for the people they conquered. The devastation of Poland—economically, politically, socially—worsened as the Poles endured year after year of occupation. The Nazi German hand may have been less heavy on western Europe, but there too—in occupied Denmark, Norway, the Netherlands, Belgium, and France—adversity and demoralization continued to build. Meanwhile, in the Balkans and the Soviet territories overrun in 1941, German occupation practices produced escalating waves of brutality.

It was not just the normal dynamic of war that served to multiply human suffering as World War II continued. The Nazi principles of spatial expansion and "racial purification" meant that more and more killing was a direct goal of the German war effort. As Hitler's empire extended its reach, it confronted more people it deemed enemies—Jews above all, and others defined as dangerous or unwanted. Conquest, violent occupation, and genocide turned imagined enemies into real ones, and in this setting military triumph and failure alike fed the drive to destroy. For these reasons, 1942 and 1943—the years when German power reached its height and then began to wane—were also the peak years of killing.

In this period eradication of Jews emerged as the top priority of Nazi German decision-makers. They created procedures and facilities to annihilate Jewish communities and individual Jewish lives. These developments in turn generated changes in how perpetrators but also neighbors and witnesses perceived Jews. With such powerful forces bent on their elimination, Jews seemed to be doomed, people without a future, already dead, even if through some coincidence or exception they were still moving and breathing. In this climate, non-Jews got the message that anything they did to Jews was permitted, by the German occupiers, and even morally. Perhaps it did not seem so wrong to take the boots from a person who was dead anyway. Under a ruthless occupation non-Jews faced their own perils: hunger, forced labor, separation from family and community. Making humane choices and showing empathy to anyone outside the immediate circle of family and friends must often have seemed to be unaffordable luxuries.

This chapter examines the decisions and dynamics of 1942 and 1943. Policies and practices in the preceding years had established a framework in which killing became the go-to solution for the Germans and their collaborators. Decisions made in that context then ratcheted up the violence, which in turn was transformed by the scale of operations into something qualitatively different even from the carnage of 1941. As the conquerors moved into circumstances where everything seemed possible, their victims scrambled to comprehend what was happening and to make their own decisions, based on scraps of information and the impossibility of seeing into the future. Complicating everything was the war itself and the unforeseen consequences of massive military actions and reactions. In this phase of the war, even German setbacks and Allied successes could end up worsening the situation of Jews.

THE WANNSEE CONFERENCE—TAKING STOCK
OF DESTRUCTION

On January 20, 1942, fifteen men met in a beautiful villa in Wannsee, a suburb of Berlin. Among them were Hans Frank's deputy from the General Government, representatives of several branches of the SS including the Security Police/Einsatzgruppen, Nazi Party headquarters, the Foreign Office, Justice Ministry, and others. Reinhard Heydrich, who had called the meeting, presided. With the help of a stenographer, Adolf Eichmann, chief of the SS Reich

Security Main Office's Department of Jewish Affairs, produced the official report, now known as the Wannsee Protocol.

Why was the meeting at Wannsee significant? Many popular accounts, including the 2001 movie *Conspiracy*, claim it was here that the Nazis decided on the "Final Solution," the plan to murder all Jews. But by January 1942, mass murder was long underway. Hundreds of thousands of Jews had been starved, beaten, or worked to death in camps and ghettos, and hundreds of thousands more shot into mass graves. A killing facility dedicated to the murder of Jews was already operating at Chelmno. Methods and habits of killing had been honed in campaigns against other targets: the tens of thousands of disabled people killed inside Germany, the thousands of black French soldiers and eventually millions of Soviet prisoners of war. By the time those fifteen men convened at Wannsee, a decision was no longer necessary.

Most historians consider the Wannsee Conference important not for deciding on annihilation but for coordinating procedures. The participants, though powerful and important, were implementers and managers, not top-tier Nazi leaders. Neither Hitler, Himmler, Göring, nor Goebbels attended, nor were any field marshals, generals, or in fact any representatives of the Wehrmacht present. Heydrich opened the meeting by brandishing a letter from Reich Marshall Göring, charging him to "carry out all preparations with regard to organization, the material side and financial viewpoints for a final solution of the Jewish question in these territories in Europe which are under German influence." The SS, Heydrich made clear, was in charge of destroying Jews, but other agencies and offices also had key roles to play. Moreover, by their very presence those bureaucrats, party functionaries, and occupation authorities demonstrated that they understood what was going on and endorsed it.

No one at the conference objected to the policy and practice of annihilation, although it was presented openly, starting with the announcement that Estonia was now "free of Jews." Instead participants spent their time on practical matters, above all on who would be included in the category of Jews to be "evacuated to the East" for killing. Especially thorny and left partly unresolved was the question of so-called Mischlinge, Germans of mixed Jewish and non-Jewish parentage. Differences of opinion over how to handle these people were not expressed in terms of right and wrong or even primarily in racial terms. Rather the officials sought to minimize negative impact on public morale within Germany and avoid disruption for the "Aryan" relatives. This was the bureaucratic face of genocide, people's lives and deaths reduced to categories and lists.

The Wannsee Conference has an additional, wider significance: it reflected the worldwide dimensions of the genocidal project yet revealed how military developments had temporarily limited Nazi ambitions to Europe. As Gerhard Weinberg shows, the conference must be understood in the context of the war. Originally scheduled for December 1941, the meeting was postponed after the Japanese attack on Pearl Harbor and the German declaration of war on the United States. During those two months, December 1941 and January 1942, "all eyes were focused on the actual course of the fighting" (Weinberg 2008, 395). The Soviets spectacularly halted the German advance before Moscow, and additional German defeats at both ends of the Eastern Front made it clear this would not be another blitzkrieg. In North Africa, a British offensive pushed back Rommel's Afrika Korps. So the destruction of Jews, which its planners had assumed would be much further advanced by the end of the year, was confined to Europe, at least for the time being.

The Wannsee Conference gave Heydrich and the others an opportunity to report on the progress of destruction so far, to take stock of phase one of operations, the European phase. Eichmann presented a statistical tabulation of the eleven million Jews whose killing was under discussion. Included were Jews in Sweden, Switzerland, England, and Ireland, places not in German hands, although there were plans to invade the first two and an expectation that the latter two would eventually fall to Germany. Also on the hit list were Jews in the "European part" of Turkey but not in Anatolia; Jews in Italy, including Sardinia, but not on the island of Rhodes. Nor were the Jews of Palestine on the list, although Hitler was on record as having promised that they too would be killed. To Eichmann and his staff, Anatolia, Rhodes, and Palestine lay outside Europe and hence were not part of the current discussion. The implication was clear: Jews outside Europe were slated for destruction too, but in a subsequent phase to be made possible by renewed German victories.

In Nazi logic, all Jews everywhere were the enemy. This way of thinking gave the program of annihilation a worldwide dimension. Hitler knew that in the past Jews had been persecuted and expelled in many places but they had always come back. The Nazis' *final solution* was to be just that: final and total. There were to be no Jews left to return.

The Wannsee Protocol, like any official report, is selective, more an expression of what the meeting was supposed to achieve than evidence of what participants actually said. At his trial twenty years later, Eichmann testified that the men had spoken bluntly, "about methods for killing, about liquidation, about extermination." Given their jobs, those men could connect the dots. They would have grasped that listing only Turkey's "European part" did not mean Jews across the Bosphorus would be left alive. And they would have understood what it meant when Heydrich closed the meeting by asking them all for "appropriate assistance in the carrying out of the tasks involved in the solution" (Noakes and Pridham 3:541).

ABBA KOVNER AND THE MANIFESTO
OF JEWISH RESISTANCE

By the time Heydrich and the others met at Wannsee, most of the Jews in Lithuania had already been killed. Eichmann's table listed thirty-four thousand Jews there, targets of the "final solution of the European Jewish question." Half a year earlier, the invading Germans had encountered a quarter of a million Jews in Lithuania, many of them refugees from German-occupied Poland. Attacked by Germans and surrounded by hostile or cowed Lithuanians, Jews in Lithuania faced agonizing conditions and tormented choices that mostly ended in death.

Sometimes there was no time for any decisions at all. Sara Ginaite was a teenager in Kovno in June 1941, when a group of armed Lithuanians, the so-called White Armbanders, burst into the building where her relatives lived. Leading them was a janitor who knew her family. "Here is where all of the Jewish Communists are hiding," he announced. As Sara watched, horrified, the White Armbanders led her three uncles and two other Jewish men out into the yard and shot them dead.

In Vilna, Germans and Lithuanians working together had killed tens of thousands of Jews by mid-December 1941. Abba Kovner was a leading member of the Zionist-Socialist youth movement, Hashomer Hatzair (Young Guard) there. Together with some friends he found shelter in a Catholic convent, whose Polish Mother Superior, Anna Borkowska, tried to help as many Jews as she could. From that refuge Kovner heard rumors of mass shootings at Ponar, a forest outside the city. Most of the Jews in the ghetto believed that those who had been kidnapped or arrested had been sent to labor camps. They knew some people had been murdered but held out hope that the others were still alive somewhere.

Kovner first suspected then grew convinced that those who had vanished were dead. When a few people, including an eleven-year-old girl, managed to crawl out of a mass grave and return to the ghetto, Kovner was among those who listened and believed what they said. Meanwhile, some Jewish women found ways to pass outside the ghetto. From peasants who lived near Ponar they heard reports of barbed wire barricading the area and gunfire that lasted all day long, day after day.

Kovner's instinct told him the killing was not a local peculiarity but part of a massive scheme to destroy all the Jews of Europe. Tormented by this thought, he, his friends, and representatives of some other political and youth movements tried to work out a course of action. Some people urged escape, to Warsaw perhaps, or Bialystok. But Kovner and others came to believe that nowhere was safe. Certain that none of them would remain alive, they called for an uprising as the only way to die with honor.

They decided to issue a manifesto. Written in Yiddish by Kovner, a poet, it has become one of the most famous documents of the Holocaust. At a meeting in the ghetto on December 31, 1941, held under cover of a new year's party, he read it aloud. Its first message was excruciatingly clear. The Jews of Vilna were being annihilated:

Jewish youth, do not believe the perpetrators. Of the 80,000 Jews of the "Jerusalem of Lithuania" only 20,000 have remained. . . .
All those forced out of the ghetto never returned.
All the roads of the Gestapo lead to Ponar, and Ponar is death!
Throw away illusions. Your children, husbands and wives are all dead.
Ponar is not a camp—everyone was shot there.

The Manifesto's second claim was even more shocking: "Hitler has plotted to murder all of the Jews of Europe. The Jews of Lithuania are doomed to be first in line."

The only response, Kovner insisted, was to fight back:

Let us not go like lambs to the slaughter!
True, we are weak and helpless, but the only answer to the hater is resistance!
Brothers! Better fall as free fighters than live at our murderers' mercy!
Resist! Resist to the last breath. (quoted in Porat, 71)

In hindsight, it seems obvious that all Jews were under assault, targeted for destruction in the Nazis' so-called final solution. But it was remarkable that by January 1942, a group of young people, cut off from the world, isolated even from developments elsewhere in Lithuania, and desperate with grief over the disappearance of countless family members and friends, had arrived at this conclusion. It may have helped that Kovner, who was born in Sevastopol and spent the first years of his life in the Soviet Union, had a wide, international perspective. His intense charisma certainly played a role, along with the conviction that he had a mission, like the Jewish prophets and judges of old. The courageous efforts of Vitka Kempner and other women, who found ways to pass in and out of the ghetto, establishing and maintaining connections among Jews and between Jews and non-Jews, were also essential to gather information and piece it together.

But it was still an enormous leap from grasping the local fact of mass murder to seeing it as part of a program of total annihilation. Even in Vilna, in January 1942 most Jews rejected this idea. Still the Manifesto put that possibility into words and offered a way to respond. It did not, however, lay out a clear course of action: in the summer of 1943, the Vilna ghetto would be torn apart by differences over how, when, and where to fight back against the Germans. Kovner never led an uprising but along with Kempner and many of their close associates ended up leaving the ghetto to join Communist partisan units in the forest. After the war, he was a hero in Israel, although he was criticized, too, for decisions and actions at the time and for arrogance and grandiosity. He died in 1987 of cancer of the vocal cords.

THE NAZI "NEW ORDER"

One point is so obvious it is often not stated: Hitler and the Nazis planned to win the war. War, Hitler believed, would not merely defeat the enemy militarily; it would create a "new order."

German planners developed in detail the implications of their notion of *Lebensraum*—living space—in an initiative called the "General Plan for the East." An ambitious project directed by the Reich Security Main Office, it involved teams of bureaucrats and experts in geography, city planning, agriculture, and economics. Konrad Meyer, a professor of agronomy in Berlin and member of the SS, headed up the research unit. Among the historians who contributed was Theodor Schieder. After the war Schieder pursued an academic career in West Germany. Only after his death in the 1980s would his many students and admirers realize the use to which he and others like him had put their training and skills during the war.

General Plan for the East was a warrant for what is now called ethnic cleansing. Germans and ethnic Germans were to settle eastern Europe, where they would produce food and babies for the "Aryan race." To make such settlements possible, the plan demanded elimination of the people currently living there. Tens of millions of Poles, Ukrainians, Russians, and others were to be forced into less desirable areas, allowed to die of starvation or disease, or killed. A small percentage would be kept as slaves for the German empire. Jews were to disappear altogether.

Like so much Nazi writing, General Plan East was full of euphemisms. Instead of spelling out the goal as to kill people or make sure they died, the document talked about "reducing" or "removing" certain populations. Nevertheless, its intentions were obvious. It also made clear that German policies toward different population groups were connected. Settlement of Germans and ethnic Germans; expulsion, enslavement, and murder of Poles, Russians, Belorussians, Ukrainians, and others; and destruction of Jews were all parts of the same plan.

Germanization

The General Plan for the East envisioned "Germanization" of a vast territory that stretched eastward from the old German Reich to the Ural Mountains. Someday, according to the plan, hundreds of millions of people would live there: "Aryan" Germans and their slaves.

German population planners realized that even a massively increased birthrate could not produce enough children to achieve the rate of population growth they wanted. As a result, they proposed taking "racially valuable" children away from supposedly inferior parents in order to "Germanize" them. In other words, they intended to transform some of the children of non-Germans into members of the "Aryan race." So-called racial experts estimated that about 50 percent of Czech children were suitable for Germanization. They thought as many as 75 percent of the children in some parts of western Belorussia might be acceptable, but under no conditions were Jewish children to be Germanized.

Under a program code named Operation *Heuaktion,* the "hay action," German agencies kidnapped thousands of children and adolescents from eastern Europe and sent them to the Reich, in some cases to be raised by German families, in other cases to work in factories or handicrafts. Meanwhile, German doctors, many of them with access to concentration camps and inmates as subjects, experimented with methods of mass sterilization. Medical scientists working in Auschwitz must have known that Jews would not be the people intended for the new techniques of sterilization, because Jews were in the process of being annihilated. Sterilization and eventual extinction were to be the fate of the non-Jewish population of eastern Europe.

Germanization schemes remind us how contrived Nazi notions of blood and race were. The case of two Polish women provides an illustration. Although the parents of Johanna and Danuta W. were "pure Polish," the sisters applied for Germanization. No doubt they hoped to get the benefits that being classified as German rather than Polish would bring.

In 1944, SS racial authorities in one city approved Johanna's application, and she became officially recognized as an ethnic German. A similar office elsewhere rejected Danuta. Meanwhile both women went to work as housemaids in Germany. There Danuta became pregnant by an SS man. When her baby was born he received ethnic German status, but his mother was still classified as a Pole. The only reason German authorities gave for rejecting Danuta was that "she did not look so good."

Danuta's status caused practical problems because the sisters lived together. Under the terms of Nazi racial law, ethnic Germans such as Johanna were to have no social contact with Poles like Danuta. Nor was Danuta's child permitted to interact with his mother. The postwar fates of Johanna, Danuta, and her son are unknown.

Forced Labor

During 1942 and 1943 Germans enslaved millions of people, women as well as men, from the Soviet Union and elsewhere in eastern Europe. Some were forced to labor in the occupied areas; millions of others were sent to Germany to work in factories, on farms, and in private homes.

Hitler and other planners considered forced labor a way to keep the German home front happy. They did not want to introduce measures that might have been unpopular with many Germans: for example, recruiting large numbers of German women into factory work or curtailing supplies of food and consumer goods. After all, Hitler and others believed that discontent at home had led to German defeat in the last war. So they brought in millions of people they considered disposable and used them to make waging a war of annihilation as comfortable as possible for the German people.

The German occupiers also seized agricultural produce in the areas they controlled, causing famine and starvation among the people left behind. They took over whatever industrial production had not been evacuated by the Soviet Army as it had fled in 1941. In the name of fighting partisans, German forces burned entire villages, often along with many of the people who lived in them. Public hangings, torture, rape, and sexual slavery were all common occurrences in the occupied territories.

Anti-Partisan Warfare

Some German authorities worried that extreme brutality in the occupied areas was counterproductive because it sparked opposition that could have been avoided. As one high-ranking German official observed, many of the Soviet people had suffered terribly under Stalin. It would not have taken much to persuade them that their lives under German rule would be better. The viciousness of German occupation, however, convinced the vast majority of Soviets that even Stalin was preferable to Hitler.

Hitler and propaganda minister Goebbels paid lip service to the need to soften up in order to prevent an explosion of opposition, but German policies did not change. To the contrary, reprisals against guerrilla activity kept increasing in their ferocity. Meanwhile the Germans defined partisan activity, or "banditry," as they preferred to call it, more and more broadly.

Anti-partisan warfare developed a deadly dynamic. Brutal occupation practices drove people into partisan groups, and German fear of partisans served as justification for attacks on civilians. Public hangings were common as the Germans sought to intimidate potential opponents. Photography was also a weapon in the anti-partisan offensive. Germans took pictures to demonstrate their power and prove their effectiveness to their enemies, their superiors, and themselves. This picture, taken by a German soldier near Novgorod, captures the staged nature of a public execution. Camera in hand, a German officer arranges the scene.

A German soldier holding a camera directs the hanging of a Russian woman by unidentified collaborators in the Novgorod region, in 1943 or early 1944. The German "war of annihilation" against the Soviet Union meant that anyone suspected of partisan activity or supporting the partisans could be executed, their families killed, and their villages burned to the ground. Public hangings were often spectacles witnessed by soldiers and civilians alike. Such spectacles were choreographed not only to terrorize the population but also to demonstrate for authorities back in Germany the merciless treatment being meted out to opponents of the occupation.

SS leader Himmler summed up prevailing German views in a speech to top SS men in October 1943:

> We must be honest, decent, loyal, and comradely to members of our own blood and to nobody else. What happens to a Russian or to a Czech does not interest me in the slightest. What the nations can offer in the way of good blood of our type we will take, if necessary by kidnapping their children and raising them here with us. . . . Whether 10,000 Russian females fall down from exhaustion while digging an anti-tank ditch interests me

only in so far as the anti-tank ditch for Germany is finished. We shall never be rough and heartless when it is not necessary, that is clear. We Germans, who are the only people in the world who have a decent attitude towards animals, will also assume a decent attitude towards these human animals. But it is a crime against our own blood to worry about them and give them ideals, thus causing our sons and grandsons to have a more difficult time with them. (Noakes and Pridham 3:919–20)

In Himmler's mind Russians and Czechs merited nothing more than the self-interested care one would show a beast of burden.

CONCENTRATION CAMPS

The vast network of camps had been expanding since Hitler came to power, and during 1942 and 1943, the Germans incarcerated huge numbers of people from all over Europe. The total number of Nazi German camps of various kinds is not known, but it must be in the thousands. Millions of people passed through these sites.

Territorial conquests brought new kinds of prisoners. German political prisoners, Communists, Jehovah's Witnesses, homosexual men, common criminals, so-called asocials, and recalcitrant Catholic priests were joined by Polish and French Communists and Socialists as well as members of resistance groups from all over Europe. These inmates were not gassed, but they were beaten, starved, used for experiments, and forced to do backbreaking labor. Some survived only a few weeks, others lived for months, and still others made it longer, often because they wrangled a privileged position in the camp.

Camps that housed political prisoners included Gross-Rosen, Stutthof, Bergen-Belsen, Flossenbürg, Buchenwald, Ravensbrück for women, and many others. Each name could encompass a vast network of facilities; Buchenwald, for example, had 134 satellite camps.

Another type of mass-detention facility was the labor camps. Many of their inmates were non-Jewish women and men from conquered nations. German authorities used them for work connected to military requirements, in factories, mines, quarries, and production of armaments. One example was Dora-Mittelbau, a camp in north-central Germany not far from the city of Göttingen. In its extensive underground facility slave laborers built V-2 rockets.

The German state viewed slave workers as a renewable resource; their lives had no value. Death tolls in such camps were astronomical. Toward the end of the war, as more Jews were kept alive for labor, they died at even higher rates than other prisoners. Camp organizers quartered the Jews separately, gave them less food, and treated them more harshly than they did the non-Jews.

Concentration camps specialized in brutality, with an eye to comfort and ease for the staff. Buchenwald had a zoo; many had gardens and, beginning in 1943, brothels staffed by sex slaves from the occupied territories. Sometimes camp authorities also assigned German "asocial" women—lesbians, Communists, and criminals—to brothels. Clients included staff and especially privileged male prisoners.

All of the big camps, even places such as Dora-Mittelbau, had orchestras. Often they included Roma, popular as entertainers in Europe, or trained classical musicians. There was no shortage of candidates; Europe in the 1940s was a very musical place. Orchestras performed to entertain the guards, to send the prisoners off to work, and sometimes during executions. They played well-known marches, arias, folk songs, and even Christmas carols. The cynicism of those behind the camp system is evident in other ways too. A sign over the gate of Auschwitz read *Arbeit macht frei*, "work liberates." Buchenwald, built in 1937, had its own slogan: *Jedem das Seine*, "to each his own."

Camp Personnel

Authorities recruited for high-ranking positions at the camps from within the German police. They hired unskilled or semiskilled workers to be guards at the lower levels. At Ravensbrück, for example, women guards were recruited through ads that promised job security, a responsible position, and wages higher than many nonskilled positions. Successful candidates underwent a short training course.

Outside of Germany, SS men took the top positions in the camps. Often they had been trained at Dachau. Lowlier guards commonly came from subject populations, for example, ethnic Germans from eastern Europe, Ukrainians, Latvians, and Croats. Many auxiliary police and guards were recruited from captured Soviet POWs processed and trained at the SS camp of Trawniki. Jobs in the camps gave some individuals a chance to improve their circumstances at the expense of the inmates. They also provided opportunities to lord it over one's own enemies. For example, the Germans hired Croats to guard Serbs, Roma, and Jews; they often used Ukrainians against Poles. Working conditions that tolerated and even encouraged drunkenness and rape appealed to sadists and thugs and served to brutalize others.

At the lower levels women occupied many of the same positions that men did. Generally women prisoners had women guards. There were also female SS units, usually assigned to communication duties and housekeeping for SS men at the front. It was no secret that these women, chosen on the basis of their supposedly valuable "blood," were expected to help German SS men resist the temptation of sexual liaisons with "non-Aryans."

About two thousand female guards assisted the SS at the Ravensbrück camp for women. Some women, like some men, were notorious for cruelty. Most infamous were Irma Grese, a guard at Auschwitz, and the "Bitch of Buchenwald," Ilse Koch, wife of Commander Karl Koch. Koch, though not herself a guard, was active in the camp. After the war, wild rumors circulated about her sexual deviancy and fondness for lampshades and other household decorations made of tattooed human flesh. Some of the most horrific stories about Ilse Koch were never proven, but what seems clear is that to prisoners and outside observers alike, the involvement of women emblemized the grotesqueness of the Nazi system.

Prisoner Hierarchies

German authorities in the camps also appointed some prisoners to supervise and control other inmates. Such prisoner functionaries became known as kapos. Often the leaders of labor gangs, kapos had access to some power and privilege. At the same time they remained answerable to camp authorities.

The use of kapos encouraged development of hierarchies of power within the camps. Such divisions, of course, benefited the Nazis, who needed to invest less time and energy to control prisoners who were at odds with one another. By rewarding kapos for brutality against fellow prisoners, German officials continued to undermine solidarity. Every kapo realized that he or she could be replaced at a moment's notice. There were plenty of prisoners eager to improve their chances by accepting positions of privilege within the camp.

To reinforce divisions among prisoners, camp officials introduced a system of colored badges to identify various groups. Criminals wore a green triangle; Communists received red. Roma and "asocials" were marked with a black badge, and Jehovah's Witnesses with purple. A pink triangle designated homosexual men. A yellow triangle—or two triangles together to form a six-pointed star—identified Jews.

Camp authorities recruited most kapos from the green and red triangles, the groups at the top of the hierarchy. Kapos from the other groups were not unknown, but it was hard for people to assert authority over those considered above them. Jews, marked as they were for death, were at the bottom. Often the other prisoners ostracized and tormented homosexual men in particularly vicious ways. Nevertheless, there were cases of Jews and homosexuals serving as kapos or in similar positions.

The perpetrators devised humiliations for members of each of their victim groups, and even the same treatment was experienced in different ways by people whose values and taboos set them apart from one another. German aggressors often launched attacks on Jews on the Jewish holidays. Camp officials frequently put kapos known as homophobes in charge of gay prisoners. Nakedness of adults in front of their own children was taboo among Roma, so orders to strip carried extra shame for members of that group.

Efforts to Maintain Solidarity

Camp officials tried to divide and conquer their prey. They set people against one another by forcing competition for absurdly small prizes—a crust of bread, a button, a piece of string. Some of the most powerful stories of the camps explain how inmates countered such efforts to isolate them. Primo Levi tells how he reminded himself and a fellow prisoner in Auschwitz of their humanity by reciting from Dante's *Divine Comedy*: "Think of your breed; for brutish ignorance / Your mettle was not made; you were made men, / To follow after knowledge and excellence." Sara Nomberg-Przytyk, a Polish Jewish Communist, attributes her survival to a stranger in the next train car who sacrificed her blanket so Sara would not freeze to death.

Bogumila Babinska (Jasiuk), a prisoner in Ravensbrück, shows wounds inflicted by German doctors who used her for medical experimentation. A member of the Polish underground, Babinska and her friends documented the abuses through photographs they took clandestinely. In early 1945 Babinska evaded execution, survived a death march, and managed to return to Warsaw.

Photography proved valuable in resistance efforts. It offered a way to document crimes and in some cases identify perpetrators for future retribution. In Ravensbrück, a group of women connected to the Polish underground got a camera from another prisoner in exchange for bread. They used it in secret to take pictures of the wounds inflicted by German doctors who used prisoners as "rabbits" (guinea pigs) for medical experimentation. Here Bogumila Babinska displays her injured leg. The women also documented the experiments with invisible messages written in urine.

In Mauthausen, a group of Spanish prisoners found another way to use photography as resistance. One of them, a trained photographer, was assigned to the lab, where his duties included developing pictures taken by the SS photographer and making copies to be attached to various reports and files. He made contact with another prisoner, a Pole who had been making an addi-

The corpse of a German Jew who committed suicide by running into the electrified barbed-wire fence at Mauthausen. This photograph was one of several hundred taken by SS personnel but copied by inmates who worked in the camp photo lab—first by the Polish prisoner Grabowski, and later by two Spaniards, Antonio Garcia and Francisco Boix. Through a series of intermediaries, the photographs were hidden and preserved outside of the camp until liberation. Recognizing the importance of photographic evidence of German crimes, Allied authorities invited Boix to testify at the Nuremberg Trials, the only Spaniard to do so.

tional print of key photographs and stashing them in a secret archive. With the help of an Austrian Socialist who lived nearby, members of the underground managed to smuggle all of the photographs out of the camp. Some were even presented as evidence to the Nuremberg Tribunal.

HOMOSEXUALS—THE "MEN WITH THE PINK TRIANGLE"

Since its early years in power Hitler's regime had harassed and persecuted gay men and men suspected of homosexuality. Between 1933 and 1945 German courts convicted fifty thousand men on charges related to Paragraph 175, which criminalized sexual relations between men. The year 1942 brought a record number of arrests, mostly of Germans. Nazi ideology regarded homosexuals, particularly men, as a threat to "Aryan racial health" because they did not take part in producing children for the fatherland. Many people also believed gay men undermined military effectiveness. In wartime, especially in 1942 and 1943, as German casualties began to climb, the leadership took these issues very seriously, and police arrested thousands of men accused of homosexual activity. Between five and seven thousand of these men perished in World War II, perhaps half of them in concentration camps.

Like every group targeted by Nazi Germany, gay men had experiences particular to them. For one thing, Nazi theorists and practitioners were confused as to whether homosexuality was biological or acquired. So German officials vacillated between treating accused homosexuals as racial enemies and handling them as candidates for reeducation. In 1933 Himmler had estimated there were between one and four million homosexually inclined men in Germany, but even the homophobic Himmler never mounted a systematic effort to wipe out homosexuality as such. Instead police made arrests on the basis of denunciations and raids.

By 1942 many concentration camps had homosexual inmates. Sachsenhausen and Buchenwald housed the largest numbers, at times in separate "queer blocks." Gay men, like Jews and Roma, fell near the bottom of the camp hierarchy. Viewed even by many fellow prisoners as the scum of humanity, they suffered torture, beating, and medical experimentation. Perhaps their isolation explains the high death rate among homosexual inmates in Nazi camps: it was about 60 percent as compared to 41 percent for political prisoners and 35 percent for Jehovah's Witnesses.

As the war went on and German demands for labor increased, officials allowed some of the accused homosexuals in Sachsenhausen to be released as civilian laborers, but there were strings attached. In order to be pronounced "cured," a candidate for rehabilitation had to perform "properly" with a prostitute from the camp brothel. If he failed but agreed to castration, he might still be released for heavy labor. Some gay men also won release by volunteering for special penal units sent to the worst areas of the front. Few of those individuals survived.

Harry Pauli, an actor from Berlin, was one of the exceptions. Sentenced on grounds of homosexual activity to twenty months' imprisonment, he served eight months before being drafted into the Wehrmacht. Ridiculed and abused by the other men, he tried to desert but was caught. His punishment was a year with the penal battalion Dirlewanger. Thanks to a nonfatal wound, he witnessed the end of the war from a military hospital in Prague.

In significant ways persecution of homosexual men in Nazi camps continued what went on outside. After liberation in 1945, occupation authorities rearrested some gay men and sent them back to prison. Homosexual activity remained a criminal act in both East and West Germany, as in many other jurisdictions, until the 1960s. Illegality and social stigma account for the silence that shrouded the treatment of gay men in Nazi Germany until the 1970s and 1980s.

MILITARY DEVELOPMENTS AND NONMILITARY REPERCUSSIONS

The vast majority of Jews murdered by Nazi Germans—about 95 percent—came from outside Germany. Without military conquests the perpetrators would never have got those victims in their hands.

Yet even during the war, many people on the Allied side did not see the links between the German war effort and mass murder. Soviet, British, and American military planners tended to take a fairly narrow view of events. Their goal was to win the war, whatever that meant; their objectives were military ones. It is probably fair to say that they devoted little thought to what seemed bizarre, nonmilitary "sideshows" on the part of the Germans, such as attacks on disabled people, Roma, and Jews. In many cases they disbelieved or discounted the reports that came in about those atrocities. Nevertheless, military decisions and developments in 1942 and 1943 had repercussions far beyond the military sphere. We will consider three examples: developments surrounding Stalingrad, North Africa, and Italy.

The Battle of Stalingrad

From 1941 to 1943 most of the combat in Europe occurred between German and Soviet forces on Germany's eastern front. In 1941, the Red

Army had checked the Germans and their Axis partners, but by mid-1942 the Germans took the offensive again.

The new German offensive had two prongs. One entered the Caucasus region with an eye to the oil fields there. The other moved toward the city of Stalingrad—later Volgograd—on the lower Volga River. What is now known as the Battle of Stalingrad began in the late summer and fall of 1942 as the defending Red Army blocked the advancing Germans.

Hitler instructed the German 6th Army under General (later Field Marshal) Friedrich Paulus to take Stalingrad. In September the 6th Army and the 4th Panzer Army advanced into the outskirts; by mid-November they had captured much of the city.

Fighting was extraordinarily fierce. The Soviets, ordered by Stalin to defend the city with everything they had, contested every inch. Losses on both sides were staggering. From August to mid-October 1942, the German 6th Army suffered some forty thousand casualties. In late November, a Soviet offensive cut off the 6th Army, parts of another German army, and two Romanian armies in the Stalingrad area, and the Red Army surrounded them. German attempts to relieve their forces in December failed, and the Soviets demanded capitulation.

The Red Army had some remarkable photographers, many of them Jewish. Georgy Zelma, who took this picture, was an assimilated Jew from Uzbekistan. He worked for the newspaper *Izvestiia* throughout the war and did his most famous work at the Battle of Stalingrad. Note that the photographer here is in the middle of the action.

Assault units of the 62nd Soviet Army battle the Germans in Stalingrad. Fierce, close-combat fighting took place from late 1942 until February 1943, when remnants of the German 6th Army surrendered. The defeat at Stalingrad marked a military and symbolic turning point for the Third Reich, but in the short run it also contributed to an intensified focus on the destruction of Jews. Decades after the fact, the Battle of Stalingrad remains enormously significant as a sign of Russian invincibility and a triumph of the Soviet liberator soldier.

Already earlier, some of Hitler's generals had advised a withdrawal, but he and others were determined to hold on. The territory had been won at such a high cost, and Stalingrad was an important hub of Soviet transport. Hitler did agree to retrenchment in the Caucasus, so it is not the case that he never authorized retreats. With Stalingrad, however, he did not give in.

On January 31, 1943, the German southern contingent under Paulus capitulated. A few days later the northern contingent followed. The Soviets took ninety thousand German prisoners of war; there were hundreds of thousands dead on both sides.

Even after the Battle of Stalingrad, the outcome of the war was far from a foregone conclusion. Just a month later, in late February 1943, the Germans mounted a successful counteroffensive at the southern part of their eastern front. Still, in hindsight, Stalingrad appears to have been an important military and symbolic turning point.

Impact on the German Home Front

Back home Goebbels's propaganda machine presented Stalingrad as a strategic retreat, but few were fooled. The Red Army victory at Stalingrad marked a visible departure from the way the war had gone so far for Germany, and at least some Germans were scared. SS reports indicate that the Nazi Party began to lose support. Many Germans had lost family members at Stalingrad; now they wanted the war to end as soon as possible.

Discontent for the most part did not translate into open opposition. Instead the German public became more cynical and withdrawn. Distracted by increasing Allied air raids on their cities, Germans at home busied themselves with the practical matters of staying alive and keeping their families together. The regime did make some concessions to try to boost public spirits; it eased restrictions on the churches and slackened its campaign against cigarette smoking.

Reports prepared by the Nazi Security Service, the SD, indicate that many Germans knew quite a lot about the atrocities their country was committing. In 1943, when mass graves of Polish officers and soldiers shot by the Soviets were found at the Katyn Forest, there was little reaction within Germany. The Soviets would soon find plenty of mass graves of murdered Jews, some muttered, so it was better not to draw too much attention to crimes on the other side.

In the meantime, the German leadership worried about its critics at home. Beginning in early 1943, offenses such as "defeatism" could be punished by death. The sister of Erich Maria Remarque, author of the World War I classic *All Quiet on the Western Front,* was condemned to death for remarking that Hitler should resign. German authorities also introduced draconian measures against accused deserters and traitors in the military, at least twenty-five thousand of whom they had shot over the course of the war, mostly in its later stages.

The Rosenstrasse Protest

Still, being defined as "Aryan" continued to offer considerable protection for Germans. An important case involves a group of German women in Berlin who were married to German Jewish men. In early 1943, Goebbels planned to remove the last Jews from the city and send them east to be killed. Most of Germany's Jews had already been sent away and murdered, beginning in late 1941. Many of those who remained were married to non-Jews.

German officials had long been uncertain as to how to proceed against German Jews married to "Aryans." On the one hand, according to Nazi logic, any Jew alive represented the possible pollution of generations of "Aryan blood." On the other hand, practical considerations made it dangerous to strike against Jews married to "Aryan" Germans or to attack the "half-Jewish" offspring of such unions. Any "mixed" families had a "pure Aryan" side, which meant relatives who would be antagonized by the expulsion and murder of their husband, uncle, son-in-law, niece, granddaughter, or so forth. During wartime the regime was reluctant to risk stirring up discontent among its public and its fighting men. Outside Germany of course the matter was easy. German officials hardly cared if they alienated Polish or Ukrainian gentiles or mistakenly included some of them among the people they defined as Jews. Inside Germany the situation demanded much more delicacy.

By early 1943 Nazi planners decided the remaining Berlin Jews had to go. Police arrested most of the men at the factories where they worked and locked them in a building on the Rosenstrasse—German for "Street of Roses." From there they were to be deported and killed.

In a spontaneous show of disobedience, the non-Jewish wives of those men gathered in the Rosenstrasse to protest the arrest of their husbands and demand their release. Sympathizers joined them until there were several thousand people milling about. Hitler and Goebbels were furious, but they did not dare order police or military to open fire on a crowd of Germans. Instead they allowed the men to be released. Many of the internees of the Rosenstrasse survived the war. The historian Nathan Stoltzfus recounts these events in his book *Resistance of the Heart*.

Maintaining Morale

The Nazi leadership tried in various ways to prevent discontent within the military and their families and communities back home. Some top Nazis, including Himmler, were suspicious of Christianity, which they considered an offshoot of Judaism that encouraged weakness. In wartime, however, they were reluctant to deprive Germans of the comfort of traditional religion. Accordingly they allowed Christian military chaplains—Catholic and Protestant—to minister to the men of the Wehrmacht. Accounts from these German clergy give another perspective on conditions during the war.

One Catholic chaplain buried 120 German soldiers during the first few months of 1942. In a report to superiors he admitted that the "long duration of the war and the many dead have brought a certain indifference to death." If the Germans had become numb toward their own casualties, how much less must they have cared about anyone else?

Christian clergy also heard confessions of terrible crimes. For example, a German Catholic priest stationed in Ukraine met a wounded soldier who confided to him about his past. The man had taken part in a mass shooting of Jews near Sevastopol in the Crimea. According to the priest, the soldier was ruined by his experience. He described the Jews, lined up, naked—women, children, and men. Although he had manned one of the machine guns he insisted he had only shot in the air. What should he have done, he asked the priest?

We do not know what the priest answered, but it seems evident that at least some Germans could not tolerate conditions in the east. Desertions and self-mutilations were not uncommon, although military authorities punished them severely, even with death. Nervous breakdowns generally led to transfers to less trying duties.

When it came to his top military men, Hitler used bribery to make sure that their consciences did not protest too loudly. Every month, on orders from the Führer, German generals received special tax-free supplements of between two thousand and four thousand Reich Marks. They had their pick of the finest estates in Poland and elsewhere, stolen, of course, from the original owners. On special birthdays—when a general turned fifty, for example—he received a bonus of as much as two hundred and fifty thousand Reich Marks. Such sums made the German generals fabulously wealthy. In contrast, German infantry who cleared mines during the war—an extremely dangerous job—received supplements to their regular incomes of only one mark per day.

The Impact of Stalingrad on the Situation of Jews

In the case of Stalingrad, a military setback for the Germans did not improve the immediate situation of European Jews or, for that matter, of other civilians under the German yoke. However, it may have helped to break down the myth of the invincible Germans and to encourage resistance.

The defeat at Stalingrad changed the dynamic between the Nazi regime and its Axis partners. In 1942, at German insistence, Romanian and Hungarian troops had also been included in the advance on Stalingrad. Improperly armed and trained, those satellite forces were crushed in the Red Army offensives. Small wonder that by 1943 the leadership of those countries began looking for ways to get out of the war. Suddenly the alliance with Germany seemed more a liability than an advantage.

After Stalingrad, Romanian and Hungarian leaders also became less willing to turn over the Jews among their populations to the Germans to be killed. It was not that those authorities suddenly became humanitarian. Rather they recognized that should they need to negotiate with the Allies, Jews might be useful bargaining chips. Perhaps, they reasoned, they could barter Jewish lives for things they needed. Thus, the German setback at Stalingrad might have had the unanticipated effect of prolonging and maybe even saving the lives of some Romanian and Hungarian Jews. On the whole, however, Stalingrad left the situation of Jews in Europe even more catastrophic than it had been before.

The Battle of Stalingrad is often described as the beginning of the end for Nazi Germany, but it signaled no change in the assault on the Jews. To the contrary, Stalingrad occurred right in the peak of the killing process. Military setbacks gave the guards, SS men, and bureaucrats who were attached to the program for killing Jews a new reason to step up their efforts. For them it was clearly preferable to be in the camps and offices overseeing mass murder of unarmed people than to face the Red Army. The chances of living through the war seemed quite good for Germans engaged in the slaughter of defenseless civilians. The odds were much lower for those assigned to fight armed opponents.

Even after Stalingrad the Germans had substantial military resources and a solid eastern front. Germany still held Poland and the killing centers built there—Chelmno, Belzec, Sobibor, Treblinka, and Auschwitz. Forced to begin to pull back from the east, the Germans concentrated their destructive energies on the territories they still controlled. From that base of power the Nazi leadership would launch the effort in late 1943 to destroy the last remnants of the Jewish communities in Poland.

People often wonder why Nazi Germans wasted manpower and other resources slaughtering Jewish civilians when there was a war to be won. According to Nazi logic, however, murder of the Jews was as much part of the war effort as were offensives against the Soviet Union. As Hitler had proclaimed in January 1939, and as Nazi propaganda insisted, Jews purportedly pulled the strings behind the Allied war effort. Military setbacks in 1943 did not slow down the killing operations; if anything, they speeded them up.

A German poster (from after December 7, 1941) with the slogan: "Behind the enemy powers: the Jew." Nazi propaganda insisted that the Allied war effort was only a cover for an international Jewish plot to destroy Germany. This accusation offered a way for killers to justify mass murder of Jews, as if the Holocaust were a defense of the German nation. The imagery here is typical, with "the Jew" hiding behind the British, American, and Soviet flags. As Minister for Popular Enlightenment and Propaganda, Goebbels presented himself as uniquely able to pull back the veils behind which Jews concealed themselves in order to educate the German public about the dangers Jews allegedly posed.

In the fall of 1943, the Germans launched a new offensive against the remaining Jews of Poland. Its code name was Harvest Festival. Within just a few days in November 1943, Germans and their accomplices massacred forty-two thousand Jews in the Lublin area, near Majdanek. The Harvest Festival relied heavily on mass shootings. In special "Jew hunts," the German Order Police and Einsatzgruppen worked with local collaborators to locate and kill as many Jews as they could. By the end of 1943, of the several million Jews who had

An antisemitic poster produced in Italy in 1942. The aggressive figure, clearly meant to be Jewish, wears a red star, a symbol of Soviet communism; in the background is New York City, the center of American capitalism. Antisemites saw a Jewish plot behind every movement they detested. This Italian poster and the preceding German image both associate Jews with an international conspiracy but they differ in emphasis. This design, perhaps reflecting the war-weariness of Italians by 1942, shows "the Jew" as pugilist, punching his way off the page to attack the viewer. Implied is that he is to blame for the war and its hardships. On the German poster "the Jew" appears cowardly yet cunning, using others to fight and take risks for him.

lived in the region, only some tens of thousands remained. Many of those were in hiding or fighting in partisan units. For economic reasons German officials allowed some to remain in the Lodz ghetto, and others survived in work camps.

North Africa

The years 1942 and 1943 also brought German setbacks in North Africa. In this case too, military developments had enormous nonmilitary results.

Africa had long been the focus of Fascist Italian ambitions, and particularly since 1935 when Mussolini's forces invaded Ethiopia. By 1940, the Italians requested German help against the British and their Allies in North Africa. The following year saw formation of the German Africa Korps under the popular General Erwin Rommel (1891–1944), the "Desert Fox."

In late October and early November 1942, the British 8th Army under Bernard L. Montgomery (1887–1976) defeated Rommel's German-Italian forces at El Alamein. At the same time, the American and British "Operation Torch" landed one hundred and six thousand Allied forces in Morocco and Algeria under the command of General Dwight D. Eisenhower. Soon Allied troops had pushed the Axis back into Tunisia and a small part of Libya.

The Germans managed to halt the initial Anglo-American advance and reinforce their position. By March 1943, however, Rommel was unable to supply his troops. He flew to Hitler's headquarters to request an evacuation, but Hitler refused. In May 1943 Tunis, the last Axis outpost in Africa, fell to the Allies, who took more than two hundred and thirty thousand soldiers prisoner. About half of them were German.

The reverberations of military action in North Africa were felt all over the world. Already in 1942 Hitler had blamed his Vichy French collaborators in North Africa for capitulating to the Allies, and in November of that year, he ordered German occupation of Vichy France. From then on Germans would administer the territory directly, as they did the rest of France. There would be no more concessions to French independence.

Developments in North Africa also generated a chain reaction that affected the Soviet Union. Thanks to massive reinforcements in November 1942, the Germans held their bridgehead in Tunisia until May 1943. As a result, the Allies had to mount a campaign to crush those remaining Axis forces in North Africa. In turn it became impossible for the Allies to undertake the long-awaited invasion of northwestern Europe in 1943.

Stalin nonetheless continued to call for the western Allies to invade northwestern Europe as soon as possible. Since 1941 the Soviet Union had borne the brunt of German power, and Stalin and the Red Army were desperate for relief. But the western Allies could not liberate Tunisia and make the switch to operations in northwestern Europe during the same year. Instead British and American planners decided for landings in Sicily, then on the Italian mainland for 1943, and postponed invasion of France until 1944.

In the meantime, during 1943 and 1944, Germans in Soviet territories and elsewhere slaughtered millions of people: Red Army soldiers, Soviet civilians, and Jews from all over Europe. Military developments in North Africa, worked out by both sides with little regard to the impact on Soviet civilians,

Jews, or Italians, had enormous—and unforeseen—consequences for all those groups of people.

In 1942 and 1943, the territory that in 1948 became the State of Israel was still part of the British mandate of Palestine. Arabs as well as some Jews lived in the area. During meetings with Arab leaders, most notably the Grand Mufti of Jerusalem, Hajj Amin al-Husseini, Hitler had promised that German forces would drive the British out of Palestine, occupy the territory, and slaughter the Jews there. An Einsatzkommando had already been created for the purpose, with the plan to attach it to Rommel's headquarters. Its members had been recruited and trained, but because of the military situation they never deployed.

Thanks to Allied victories in North Africa, the Germans never occupied the British mandate of Palestine, so the Jews there remained alive. Allied military planners and the soldiers fighting in Allied armies, including hundreds of thousands of men from India, probably gave no thought to the fate of the world's Jews as they battled the Axis in North Africa. Nevertheless, their triumphs there in 1942 and 1943 made possible the eventual establishment of a Jewish state in Israel by saving the lives of those Jews already in the area.

War 1939–1945. Limburg. Stalag XIIA, prisoners of war camp. Indian prisoners. Representatives of the International Red Cross took this picture of Indian POWs during an inspection of the camp in Limburg, Germany. It serves as a reminder of the long reach of the Holocaust as global history.

Italy

Military developments in North Africa also affected Italy, Germany's longest-standing alliance partner. After the Stalingrad debacle, the loss of North Africa completed Italy's disillusionment with the Axis. German demands, German arrogance, and German contempt for Italian officials and the Italian armed forces had also led to growing discontent.

In July 1943, Allied forces landed on Sicily, and soon they were advancing northward through the Italian peninsula. Committed Italian Fascists and their German backers retreated to the north of Naples, around the top of the ankle on the Italian boot.

After more than twenty-one years, Benito Mussolini's regime collapsed. In July 1943 the Italian king assumed supreme command, dismissed Mussolini from office, and had him arrested. A new Italian government under Marshal Pietro Badoglio dissolved the Fascist Party and surrendered to the Allies. Badoglio's government then fled to southern Italy and abandoned most of the country, as well as the Italian-occupied portions of France, Yugoslavia, Albania, and Greece, to the Germans.

The Germans took severe countermeasures. German troops occupied Rome and disarmed Italian soldiers, discharged them from service, or placed them in POW camps. By December 1943, the Germans had interned seven hundred and twenty-five thousand Italian soldiers and had sent six hundred and fifteen thousand Italian men to Germany as forced laborers.

Badoglio's government declared war on Germany. Meanwhile the Germans managed to free Mussolini by using a special paratroop unit and install him in a puppet state in northern Italy. Not until the end of April 1945 did the German forces in Italy capitulate. That month Italian partisans shot Mussolini and his mistress as they tried to flee to Switzerland.

Events in Italy had devastating effects for Jews in Yugoslavia, Albania, Greece, and France. In those countries the Germans had divided occupation duties with their Italian allies. The Italians tended to be less brutal than the Germans as occupiers, at least when it came to the genocide of Jews. Many Italian military and diplomatic officials would not cooperate with the Germans in what some described as a barbaric procedure unworthy of a civilized society. On the whole they did not show the same reticence about atrocities against Ethiopians and Slovenes.

During 1941 and 1942, many Jews from German-occupied areas fled into the Italian zones. When the Germans took over in 1943, those refuges disappeared. Already in the spring, Nazi Germans had begun to destroy the ancient Sephardic Jewish communities in Greece and Yugoslavia, transporting their members to Auschwitz to be killed. Now, with the Italians out of the way, the job could be completed. The Germans murdered forty thousand Jews from Salonika and even sent boats to take the last elderly Jews from remote Greek islands, including Rhodes.

Until 1943, Jews in Italy had been relatively safe. In the late 1930s, under German pressure and for reasons of his own, Mussolini had introduced legislation to limit Jews' activities and expel or incarcerate foreign Jews. In contrast to the leadership in Slovakia and Vichy France—partners who cooperated eagerly with German plans—Italians had been reluctant to turn over "their Jews" for killing, although the population proved quite willing to take Jewish property. Beginning in 1943, Germans came into Italy and took the Jews out themselves. Most of the Italian Jews murdered in the Holocaust died in 1944 or early 1945.

Primo Levi

Primo Levi, an Italian survivor of the Holocaust, produced some of the most insightful reflections written on that event. Born in Turin in 1919, Levi was arrested with his Italian partisan group in December 1943. When his German captors discovered he was Jewish, they sent him to Auschwitz.

Levi survived, but almost all of the inmates he knew in the camp did not. His closest friend in Auschwitz was another Italian named Alberto. Levi and Alberto shared what little food they received or "organized" for themselves. They encouraged each other to muster the will to try to stay alive, both physically and in some deeper, moral way that meant retaining an awareness of themselves as human beings.

Thanks to Levi's prewar training as a chemist, he got a job in the camp that protected him from some of the harshest conditions there. Somehow he survived. Alberto, however, did not. He too was a resourceful, intelligent young man full of the desire to live. In early 1945, as the Red Army advanced from the east, the Germans evacuated the camp at Auschwitz. Guards marched Alberto, along with most other inmates, out of the camp to the west. Levi, sick in the infirmary at the time, was left behind with others too weak to walk. Who could have known that what seemed the chance for life—leaving the camp at last—would be Alberto's death, whereas Levi, abandoned by the guards as almost dead, would survive?

In his writings about the Holocaust, Levi described the camp as above all a place of inhumanity. The English translation of Levi's memoir is called *Survival in Auschwitz*, but he originally titled the book *Se questo è un uomo*, "If this is a man." For Levi, to be human meant more than to eat and breathe. It meant having an identity, relationships with others, ties to a past and a future, and a sense of decency and dignity.

The camp took all that away. Physical abuses heaped on the prisoners—starvation, beatings, exposure—together with the many humiliations they suffered attacked their sense of themselves. In the camp, prisoners lost their names and became numbers. Emaciated, sick, shorn, and forced to wear rags, they looked nothing like their former selves. Brutality and deprivation turned them against one another; pain and despair made them forget the values and ideals they had cherished. It was this destruction of people's humanity that Levi considered the most terrible crime of the Holocaust.

After the war Levi did everything he could to share his insights and to warn against brutality and genocide in the postwar world. Already in Auschwitz he had nightmares that people "outside" would not listen to his story. Toward the end of his life he expressed frustration that the world refused to learn from the past. Primo Levi died in 1987 when he fell down the stairs in his home. Many people believe he committed suicide.

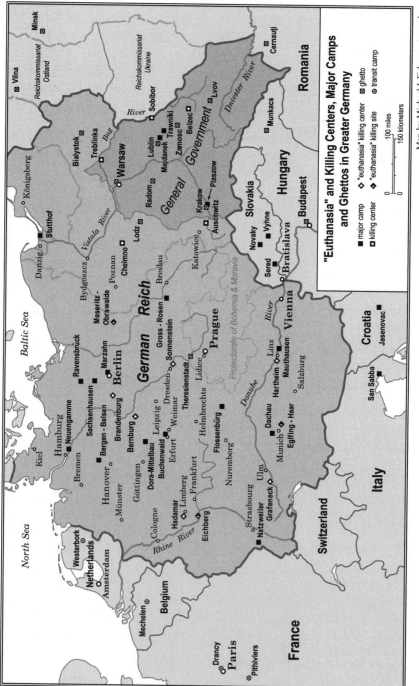

"Euthanasia" and Killing Centers, Major Camps and Ghettos in Greater Germany

■ major camp	⬙ "euthanasia" killing center
☐ killing center	◆ "euthanasia" killing site
⊠ ghetto	⊙ transit camp

0   100 miles
0 150 kilometers

Map by Michael J. Fisher, cartographer

8

FLASHOVER

THE KILLING CENTERS, 1942–1944

Although it may have seemed impossible, for Jews in Europe, 1942 and 1943 went even beyond the horrors of the years before. In early 1942, even after three years of war, ghettoization, hunger, forced labor, and massacres, 75 percent of the Jews who would be murdered in the Holocaust were still alive. By the spring of 1943, about 75 percent of the approximately 6 million who would be killed were already dead.

This chapter examines the developments that made this accelerated rate of destruction possible, above all the establishment of killing centers. What were those facilities? Who planned them and who ran them? How did the people targeted to be sent there act and react?

In the beginning of this book I compared the Holocaust to a burning house. Preexisting prejudices formed the dry timber, Hitler and the Nazi leadership lit the spark, and the winds of war fanned the flames. That metaphor can be extended to capture the theme of this chapter: the killing centers as a flashover. In the fire service, "flashover" refers to the near-simultaneous ignition of all combustible material in a space. Put simply, flashover is the transition from a fire in a room to a room on fire. The build-up of heat is rapid and intense—temperatures can reach 2000 degrees F—and witnesses often describe the fire as exploding. Survival of anyone inside the space is highly unlikely, people elsewhere in the building are suddenly in severe danger, and those outside can do little except try to extinguish the fire.

By comparing the Holocaust in the peak years of killing to a flashover I do not mean to suggest it was inevitable or to downplay the role of human actions and decisions. To the contrary. Perpetrators of all kinds—instigators, organizers, and hands-on killers—created that genocidal explosion. They adapted approaches that had worked for them on a smaller scale—methods of killing and disposing of bodies, ways of recruiting and training killers, means of financing operations and profiting from destruction—and continued to seek ways to increase outputs and improve their efficiency. They were like arsonists, pleased to see the fire they lit become an inferno. For Jews inside the kill zone, the volatile environment was practically nonsurvivable, and merely the effort to live could be a form of resistance.

THADDEUS STABHOLZ: SEVEN HELLS

Thaddeus Stabholz lived through many of the events addressed in this chapter. "Teddy" grew up in a middle-class, assimilated Jewish family in Poland and was a medical student in Warsaw when World War II began. Months after the Germans invaded, Teddy, his father, his grandmother, and the rest of his relatives were forced to move into the Warsaw ghetto. Teddy's mother had died in 1938 of cancer; his father was killed by Germans in 1941.

Teddy was left alone "like a homeless dog," he wrote later. With his fiancée, Fredzia, he survived as best he could on food they scrounged. He cared for his grandmother too, until January 1943, when Germans beat her to death in the street. By that time, many of the Jews—especially the old, very young, and sick—had already been taken out of the ghetto and sent to the gas chambers of Treblinka.

In early 1943 some young Jews left in the Warsaw ghetto organized an uprising against the Germans. Teddy and Fredzia were among them. They fought desperately with whatever weapons they had, but they were no match for the SS firepower. The Germans burned the ghetto, killed many of the people in it, and sent most of those remaining to Treblinka. There Fredzia was murdered, but Teddy was sent on to Majdanek. He remained a prisoner of the Germans in various camps for two more years.

Through extraordinary luck—if one can speak of good fortune in the context of genocide—Teddy Stabholz survived. At Majdanek guards selected him to be killed but at the last minute pulled him out of the group and made him a medic. He was sent on to Auschwitz-Birkenau, where he was starved, beaten, and forced to carry enormous loads of water and cement. He almost died of pneumonia. For a time he had a "job" delousing the body hair of fellow prisoners with Zyklon B, the same pesticide used in the gas chambers. Stabholz managed to win the favor of some senior prisoners and guards by "operating" on the corns and calluses on their feet. In the late summer of 1944, he witnessed the murder of all of the Roma in Auschwitz.

Stabholz endured excruciating work, plagues of typhus and lice, and transfers to camps farther from the front lines. At one point he resigned himself to death, but a vision of his father and mother encouraged him and revived his will to live.

In April 1945 American troops fighting their way through southern Germany found Stabholz and some fellow prisoners who had escaped from the SS and hidden in the woods. After spending time in a displaced persons camp in occupied Germany, Teddy came to the United States. He graduated from medical school in Vermont and later opened a practice in Ohio. Dr. Stabholz's memoir of the Holocaust is called *Seven Hells*.

ANNIHILATION, DEPORTATION, LIQUIDATION

Historians differ about when, where, and how the Nazi leadership made the decision for total annihilation of Jews. Some argue that it was the euphoria of victory in the early months of the war against the Soviet Union that made implementation of what had been vague ideas to "cleanse" the German living space suddenly realizable. Others point to military developments later in the year as crucial: with the Wehrmacht's advance halted before Moscow, they contend, the option of postponing a "solution" to the "Jewish question" until defeat of the Soviet Union disappeared, and genocide moved to the top of the Nazis' priorities.

Who made the decision is also contested. Was it the leadership in Berlin, above all Hitler, who called the shots? Or was it primarily German forces on the ground in the occupied areas whose actions radicalized the situation? And what was the nature of the decision? Did it occur in stages: first a "solution" to the "Jewish problem" in the Soviet Union, then a wider European program of annihilation? Or was it not really a decision at all but a policy or practices that evolved in response to changing conditions?

Since Hitler never signed an order regarding the genocide of Jews comparable to his authorization of the so-called euthanasia killings, these questions remain open. In any case, the prevailing interpretations are not mutually exclusive. The general idea that Jews would somehow disappear, whether by forcible removal, attrition, or destruction, was present from the outset of Nazi rule. Possibilities of implementing that notion expanded in tandem with German conquests, which also increased the scope and scale of the "problem," that is, the number of people to be eliminated. By 1942, the Nazi practitioners of genocide were groping their way forward into uncharted terrain but they did so guided by previous experience. In conditions saturated with violence, pressure built to such intensity that the rate of killing exploded in a number of different places at the same time. In a word, this was flashover.

The Perpetrators' Problems and Their Solutions

By the autumn of 1941 it was evident that some problems of the Germans' own making had become urgent. One was a problem of numbers. There were so many Jews in the territories under German control, Jews languishing in ghettos and labor camps, starving, sick, and unable to work. To the conquerors they posed a threefold threat. First, they constituted a drain on the food supply. Even the pitiful amounts allocated to Jews were regarded as an unacceptable loss to the Germans. Second, they spread disease. Forced to live in filthy, crowded conditions, Jews were vulnerable to contagious diseases including dysentery, cholera, and typhus. The Germans were particularly nervous about typhus, which had been widespread in central and eastern Europe during World War I, and is carried by lice. Their obsession with typhus is a reminder that the perpetrators understood very well that their victims were human beings, just like them. Third, to the Germans, Jews constituted a security threat. The closer they were to enemy lines, the more dangerous the Jews appeared.

For the Nazis, efforts to solve the "Jewish problem" in one place created new problems somewhere else. In the fall of 1941, German police rounded up tens of thousands of German, Austrian, and Czech Jews and transported them to ghettos and ad hoc camps in the east. But this measure only exacerbated the threats around food, disease, and security. Many of the Jews from the west were dumped in ghettos and camps in and around Riga. The SS had prepared for their arrival by slaughtering Jews from the area, and then continued the killing of both groups. At the Rumbula massacre of November and December 1941 they murdered twenty-five thousand people, among them almost all of the Jews from Riga and about one thousand German Jews. In charge of the operation was Friedrich Jeckeln, the same SS commander who headed up the slaughter of Jews at Kamenets-Podolsk three months earlier.

Another self-made problem for the Germans involved efficiency. By the end of 1941, they had killed a lot of people in open-air shootings: Jews and Soviet POWs in the largest numbers, also Roma and partisans. But this method had drawbacks. For one thing, it was too porous; so many people were involved and even more witnessed or saw evidence of the massacres. In the short run, such public violence could serve to intimidate subject peoples, but in the longer term, it risked alienating them. Why would they not assume that they could be next? Also as terrible as the carnage was, it was never complete. People managed to run away, to hide, and some even emerged alive from mass graves. They became enemies of Nazi Germany in a visceral way, sworn to revenge and with nothing to lose.

Mass shootings at close range raised other complications. The procedure was labor intensive. It required a lot of weapons and ammunition, and each shooter could only kill one victim at a time, although there are accounts of efforts to save bullets by grouping victims together. Many of the killers found it physically and psychologically challenging to do this grisly work. They finished their shifts covered with blood, and massive consumption of alcohol and attempts to generate a carnival atmosphere could not silence all their unease. In unguarded moments, even some of the worst killers admitted that parts of the job bothered them. One man confessed to a member of his unit that after killing children, he found it hard to touch his own child. Commanders also worried about the effects on the morale and discipline of their men. By all accounts, however, the killers and their superiors expressed these concerns not as moral issues but as practical, technical problems.

Obvious solutions were at hand, with proven leaders and managers in charge. Himmler had Hitler's full confidence and as head of the SS presided over all aspects of the genocide. In July 1941, Göring explicitly tasked Heydrich with the "final solution of the Jewish problem." These men were the top architects of genocide, and competition between and among them furthered the cause of destruction. At their disposal were vast resources and personnel, including SS and special killing units, police forces, auxiliaries recruited from conquered peoples, and of course unlimited slave labor. By 1942, Himmler, Heydrich, and their associates were well positioned to recognize "best practices" in mass murder.

One source of lessons was the destruction of Soviet prisoners of war. The combination of death by neglect, starvation, and disease with direct killing proved potent: it wiped out more than two million lives within six months with no major outbreaks of resistance. The practice of sorting victims into those able to work and hence to be destroyed through labor and those to be killed immediately proved transferable, too. Soviet POWs also served as guinea pigs to test methods of killing. One experiment, mass murder using explosives, was deemed a failure; another, the use of Zyklon B, was judged a success.

Another site of innovation was the territory of Galicia. Under the Molotov-Ribbentrop arrangement, this region was under Soviet control until the Germans arrived in the summer of 1941. Galicia had a large Jewish population, with some two hundred thousand Jews in Lvov alone, many of whom had fled to the city in 1939 from German-occupied Poland. The German invasion unleashed a wave of violence that evolved into a system of negative triage.

Jews were divided into three groups: skilled workers and craftsmen, laborers, and "superfluous" people: the weak, sick, and old, children, and mothers. Those deemed useless were killed immediately, the others put to work. Many of those judged fit were assigned to a massive project to build a road to the east for future German settlement. The planners intended workers to die along the way and be replaced with new victims.

The "euthanasia" program proved to be an especially fruitful training ground for the new phase of killing. Several years of murdering people with disabilities produced experts with experience in methods of killing and disposing of bodies. In August 1941, on Hitler's order, the gassing phase was halted and the killing decentralized to more than one hundred, smaller sites across Greater Germany. Under a new code name, 14f13, the program now targeted different groups, including prisoners in concentration camps who could no longer work, Jewish and so-called Mischling orphans, and habitual offenders. This new set-up did not require all the experienced managers that the "euthanasia" program had produced, so many of them were available for new positions. Himmler arranged for about one hundred of these people to be transferred to the east where they played key roles in setting up the killing centers for destroying Jews.

Rather than a moment of decision, the development of killing centers was a process. For the German leadership it functioned like an equation: take a problem, add experience and initiatives, and the result is a solution. As the pieces came together, the idea of bringing the victims to the killers rather than vice versa gained favor. Two sites were identified for the new facilities: Chelmno, near Lodz, and Belzec in the General Government, which from 1941 included Galicia. Odilo Globocnik, the Higher Police and SS Leader in Lublin District and a favorite of Himmler, who affectionately referred to him as "Globus," was chosen to head up the gigantic project of eradicating Jews in the General Government. Slated for destruction under Operation Reinhard, as it was known, were two million people.

Convergence of East and West

Over the course of 1942 and 1943, the situations of Jews across Europe, so different in the earlier years of the war, converged as all were swept into the program of destruction. German and Austrian Jews, as well as many Czech Jews, had not been confined to ghettos, but now they were transported by the tens of thousands to transit camp-ghettos in the General Government. The largest of these were in and around the town of Izbica. Starvation and disease, particularly typhus, took a heavy toll even before facilities for killing with gas were ready in nearby Belzec.

Authorities in Slovakia were the first of Germany's partner states to hand over Jews from their jurisdiction. By the end of March 1942, transports of Slovakian Jews to Auschwitz for killing were underway. The Germans required the Slovak government to pay 500 marks per head to cover the costs, and the Slovaks agreed, even paying extra to make sure children would be included. Their concern was that orphaned Jewish children might attract sympathy from non-Jews, causing complications. It was easier if they "disappeared" with the adults. For the staunchly Catholic Slovak leaders, this approach also had a moral advantage: they could claim to be respecting family bonds.

Meanwhile, in the Netherlands Jews were not even required to wear the identifying star until April 1942. In France, that regulation was imposed even later, in June. Months after Germans began gassing Polish, Slovak, and German Jews, many French and Dutch Jews were still living in their own homes. Some, like Hélène Berr, a brilliant student of English literature, were attending university in Paris. Others, like Salomon Schrijver in Amsterdam, were getting married and making plans for the future.

Hlinka guardsmen load Slovak Jews onto a train, probably headed to Auschwitz. As can be seen here, collaborators in Slovakia played an important role in organizing and overseeing the round-ups and transports of their Jewish neighbors. Such was the case across Europe, in the Netherlands, France, Hungary, and elsewhere. Note how close the guardsmen are to their victims. Proximity served greed and sometimes benevolence. In the last moments before the trains departed, guards robbed Jews on the platform or climbed right into the cars to demand watches and other valuables. Yet a sympathetic guard might agree to carry a message to loved ones or even help an individual escape.

This photo, from Schrijver's wedding day, is a reminder of how different conditions were for Jews west and east—and how quickly those differences dissolved. By early 1942, Jews in many parts of occupied Poland had been confined to ghettos for more than two years. They had lost their livelihoods and possessions, and in most cases, their health, family members, and friends. Only a very few, the most privileged and well connected, would have been able to muster the clothing, flowers, make-up, and jewelry evident here—not to mention hire a photographer. But by that summer, round-ups of Jews were in full swing, in Germany and in the occupied west and east.

In July 1942, French police confined thirteen thousand Jews, most of them foreign born, in the Vélodrome d'Hiver, a sports arena in Paris. From there they were sent to the transit camp of Drancy and then to Auschwitz, where most were murdered. Transports of Jews from the Netherlands to killing centers began that summer, too. Schrijver and his new wife were sent to Westerbork, a Dutch transit camp, and from there to Sobibor, where they were killed in 1943.

Wedding portrait of Salomon Schrijver and his bride, Flora Mendels, in the Jewish quarter of Amsterdam, sometime in 1942. Note the yellow star marked "Jood" sewn onto the groom's jacket; the requirement that Jews in the Netherlands wear the star was imposed in late April of that year. Another photograph of the couple shows the bride is also wearing a star, attached to her wedding dress. Here it is covered by her bouquet. Both Schrijver and his wife were murdered in Sobibor.

Ghetto "Liquidations"

As the Germans ramped up the killing operations, they shut down most of the ghettos in occupied Poland, a process they called "liquidation." The term suggests a financial decision in the context of a business venture—one thinks of liquid assets or liquidation sales. But the Nazi process was far from an exercise in accounting. Liquidation of a ghetto involved massive violence: SS and police stormed in, tearing families apart, selecting some strong individuals for labor, killing others on the spot, and consigning the rest to killing centers. Sometimes they forced the Jewish leadership and Jewish police to assist in the process, with promises that they and their loved ones would be spared. Eventually they killed the ghetto elites, too, though often in a later round of destruction. Liquidation terminated the authority of the Jewish councils, Jewish police, and any other elements of self-administration.

Liquidation of ghettos had a material side, too, as the Germans in charge seized any remaining property and possessions. Sometimes they burned down buildings but in other cases they took them over for their own purposes. Non-Jews in the surrounding area who caught wind of impending liquidations used that knowledge in various ways. Some tipped off people they knew inside the ghetto, who might be able to escape or arrange hiding places for their children or themselves. Many ethnic Poles assisted Jews in these ways. Often it was friends, coworkers, or employees who helped—nannies and housekeepers frequently played this role—but there were also generous strangers who risked not only their own lives but those of their family members.

Other non-Jews grabbed the chance to steal things before the Germans claimed it all. Many Jewish survivors tell of Volksdeutsche, Poles, Ukrainians, Czechs, and Hungarians who suddenly appeared demanding boots, coats, jewelry, even books. "You won't be needing that where you're going," they explained. Yet even such shows of greed and contempt could serve as a warning.

How much did the inmates of ghettos know about the fate that awaited them? This question, which seems straightforward, is in fact difficult to answer. Rumors spread like wildfire, carried by those few individuals who crawled out of mass graves, jumped from transport trains and trucks, or otherwise evaded their captors. Incredibly, the postal service inside and even in and out of the ghettos functioned, if sporadically, and people tried to share what they knew with friends and family. Non-Jews involved, as police, local officials, laborers, or witnesses were also sources of information.

But it was impossible for people to make sense of it all. There were deep emotional reasons to block out or compartmentalize news of mass killing: how does one live without hope? And there were enough variations and exceptions to make patterns of genocide hard to discern. For every horrific tale of gassing or shooting, there were also reports of Jewish men who were in a labor camp somewhere or young people who had joined partisan groups in the forest.

Photographs from the time reflect this in-hindsight incomprehensible blend of knowing and not knowing. In Lodz, two talented photographers, Henryk Ross and Mendel Grossman, worked for the Jewish council, to document various aspects of life and death in the ghetto. Both used their access to cameras, film, and a darkroom to take pictures for purposes of their own, including to record round-ups and transports out of the ghetto. This photo, taken by Grossman, shows a young woman writing what the description provided by the U.S. Holocaust Memorial Museum calls her "last letter." But did she really know that? Did Grossman regard her as practically already dead? Through the lens of his camera, she appears very much alive. Meanwhile, the photograph itself attests to the photographer's vitality. The woman presumably was murdered at Chelmno. Grossman escaped that fate but died on a death march in April 1945.

A woman in the Lodz ghetto writes a letter before being transported to the killing center at Chelmno. Such letters and notes, written on scraps of paper, cloth, wood, or anything else available, were thrown out windows, stuffed through cracks in freight cars, or scattered along roadsides in an attempt to make contact with the world of the still-living.

THE KILLING CENTERS

Within months of the Wannsee Conference in January 1942, four new killing centers were in operation, all of them, like Chelmno, in areas that had
significant Jewish populations. Contrary to widespread notions, German
mass killing of Jews was not some perfectly coordinated, "clean" enterprise.
Like the entire Nazi regime it was characterized by confusion and rivalry,
which only served to exacerbate the horror. Nor were the killing centers
sites of painless, automated, assembly-line extermination; the camps were
sites of torture, rape, and corruption. Killing was hands-on, close-up, and
messy—many accounts describe the stench that surrounded the camps. For
this reason I avoid the labels "extermination camp," which suggests the killing
of some kind of vermin, not human beings, and "death camp," which creates
the impression of primarily a camp with deadly conditions rather than a site
dedicated to killing.

Chelmno

The killing center at Chelmno was located in the incorporated territory,
that is, the part of Poland annexed to the Reich and earmarked for Germanization. Chelmno was a small village on a railway branch line. An unoccupied
castle proved useful as headquarters for the killing process.

Trains brought Jews, mostly from the surrounding area, to Chelmno,
and then trucks drove them to the courtyard of the castle. There an SS man
addressed them. They were to be sent to Germany, he told them, but first they
had to take a shower. Ordered to strip, they were handed towels and soap and
pushed through a corridor labeled "washroom" into the gas vans.

About ninety people were forced into a van at once. The vans drove
slowly for a few miles into the forest. There personnel opened the doors and
dumped the bodies. Guards shot anyone who was still alive.

The Germans kept a few Jews around to unload the corpses and bury the
bodies. Known as the *Sonderkommando*, "special unit," this small group of men
handled twelve to thirteen vans—about one thousand bodies—each day. Jews
were also assigned to sort the clothing left behind and clean out the vans. The
more lucrative task of extracting any gold teeth went to the Nazis' Ukrainian
helpers.

Most members of the Jewish Sonderkommando did not hold that position for long. As additional shipments of Jews arrived the German guards
selected new workers and killed the old ones. Some of the Jewish workers tried
to escape, and a few succeeded. The Germans responded to those attempts by
chaining the legs of Sonderkommando members.

By the spring and summer of 1942, the area around Chelmno was filled with the stink of rotting bodies. German officials ordered ovens brought in so that the mass graves could be opened and the bodies exhumed and burned. Of course they delegated this gruesome job to members of the Jewish Sonderkommando.

Mordechai Podchlebnik, a Jewish man assigned to the task, found the bodies of his wife and two children in a mass grave. He begged the SS guards to shoot him, and when they refused, he tried to commit suicide. This time his comrades stopped him. Eventually he escaped. One of very few survivors of the killing center at Chelmno, Podchlebnik later served as a central witness at the postwar Chelmno trial.

Rumors about the killing center at Chelmno soon spread. Jews in the region struggled to know how to react, but their options were extremely limited. In December 1941, German authorities demanded that Rumkowski, head of the Jewish Council at Lodz, hand over twenty thousand members of his community for "special treatment." Aware that selection most likely meant death, Rumkowski and his committee tried to fill their list with outsiders and people considered asocial. Among those early victims were the remainder of some five thousand Roma who had been sent to Lodz from the Reich. Located in a separate part of the ghetto, many had already died from hunger and disease. Now those left would be murdered in Chelmno.

By mid-1942, the German district commander reported to Himmler that in the next two to three months, the "special treatment" of some one hundred thousand Jews from the area would be complete. Given the "success" of the project, he suggested a similar program for Poles with tuberculosis.

From December 1941 to the end of 1942, Germans and their henchmen killed about one hundred and forty-five thousand people, most of them Jews, in the gas vans at Chelmno. In late 1942 the SS closed the killing center until 1944, when it was reactivated briefly in order to finish destroying the Lodz ghetto. Its job in the area had been completed.

Belzec

The number of inmates of the killing center at Belzec who survived the war can be counted on one hand. Located on the rail line between Lvov and Lublin, two cities with large Jewish populations, Belzec began operations in March 1942. German governor Hans Frank of the General Government in Poland had boasted that Jews in his territory would be the first victims of the so-called Final Solution. To that end, after the Wannsee Conference, the labor camp at Belzec was outfitted as a killing center.

Belzec was one of three Operation Reinhard camps. It is often assumed that the operation was named after Reinhard Heydrich, Himmler's deputy and the driving force at the Wannsee Conference, but we do not know for sure. Although Heydrich was assassinated by Czech partisans in May 1942, the escalation of killings continued as planned.

Belzec had a fixed installation for gassing that used diesel engines to generate carbon monoxide. On April 1, 1942, the first night of the Jewish holiday of Passover, the SS brought more than fifteen thousand Jews from Lvov to Belzec to be killed. By the time the camp was dismantled in the spring of 1943, over four hundred thousand Jews had been murdered there, along with an unknown number of Roma and Poles.

We have an early account of a gassing at Belzec from an unusual source: an SS man named Kurt Gerstein. Gerstein was a Nazi Party member and devout Protestant. He had served a brief term in a concentration camp himself for criticizing the anti-Christian attitudes of the Hitler Youth. Nevertheless, thanks to family connections, he was able to have his name cleared and join the SS.

Drawing by an unidentified artist of camp guards watching prisoners die in a gas chamber. In 1942, Kurt Gerstein, an SS man, watched through a peephole at Belzec as hundreds of Jews were murdered using diesel fumes. The image of guards and other perpetrators looking through a peephole as people suffocated occurs in many films and other representations of the Holocaust. Film critics have pointed out that this motif replicates for viewers the powerful, voyeuristic gaze of the perpetrators.

Gerstein was an engineer with training in sanitation and medical matters. Accordingly he received a post as SS chief disinfection officer. Early in 1942, a deputy of Eichmann's assigned Gerstein to transport Zyklon B to a secret place. The destination was Belzec.

At Belzec the commandant, Dr. Christian Wirth, an old T-4 expert, invited Gerstein to witness the killing of Jews. That day the diesel motor broke down. About eight hundred Jews were forced to wait naked for nearly three hours until the gassing began. The killing itself took thirty-two minutes; Gerstein timed it with his stopwatch. The image of killers watching through a peephole as their victims suffocate is captured in this drawing by an unidentified artist.

Horrified by what he had seen, Gerstein decided to try to use his position to stop the killings. He destroyed some of the Zyklon B he was supposed to deliver to Auschwitz, and he tried to get the word out about German mass murder of Jews in Poland. When he met a Swedish diplomat on a train, Gerstein blurted out the whole story. He went to the papal nuncio—the Vatican's representative—in Berlin to pass the news to the pope, but Gerstein's efforts met with little response.

At the end of the war, Gerstein was captured by the French. Arrested and charged with war crimes, he died in prison, either by his own hand or as a victim of foul play. Only half a century later, due to efforts by his family, did he gain a reputation as a hero.

Gerstein's story is instructive. A lone individual who tried to sabotage a murderous process from within, he ended up caught in the system himself and destroyed. He did not have the public backing within Germany that allowed Bishop von Galen to protest the killing of the disabled with some effect. Nor would or could the foreigners he told about what he knew grasp what must have seemed to them the ravings of a madman.

Sobibor

The camp at Sobibor was constructed solely for the purpose of killing Jews. Its first commandant was an Austrian named Franz Stangl, a policeman trained in the T-4 program. Slaughter of Jews at Sobibor began in April 1942 and continued until October 1943. Sobibor was the second of the Operation Reinhard camps to begin operations.

At Sobibor, Germans and their accomplices murdered two hundred and fifty thousand Jews from eastern Poland, the occupied Soviet Union, and other European countries. For instance, many Dutch Jews were killed there. Trains brought the victims right into the camp. Guards selected some Jews as workers in the killing process, and the rest they gassed immediately.

In October 1943 Sobibor was the site of an uprising by its Jewish workers, who staged a mass escape. Most were recaptured and killed, but some survived the war. The Germans closed the camp shortly after the revolt. It is not clear whether the revolt hastened the camp's closure, but by the time Sobibor stopped operations, most of the Jews in the territories from which it had drawn its victims were already dead.

Treblinka

The third Operation Reinhard camp, Treblinka began operations as a killing center in July 1942. A forced labor camp nearby had existed since 1941. Just eighty miles from Warsaw, Treblinka became the grave of a staggering number of Polish Jews. Its first victims were some three hundred thousand Jews from Warsaw, but Roma who had been in the Warsaw ghetto and Jews from all over central Poland, Germany, Austria, Czechoslovakia, and Greece were killed there, too. An estimated nine hundred thousand Jews and two thousand Roma were murdered at Treblinka.

Treblinka also had its Sonderkommando, more than eight hundred Jews who worked in the camp. They included craftspeople employed by the SS as well as men assigned to work in the gas chambers, cutting hair and burying and burning bodies. In August 1943 Jewish workers at Treblinka revolted, after which German authorities gradually shut the camp down.

A number of high-ranking Nazi officials visited Treblinka, including Eichmann. He described the fake railway station that greeted arrivals to Treblinka as looking "just like Germany." Camp organizers intended the facade to create a semblance of normalcy so that people would not suspect they were about to be killed. Eichmann also saw guards chase Jews into the gas chambers through a path between barbed-wire fences that the Germans in charge of the camp called the "hose," the "funnel," or the "road to heaven."

Treblinka was far from perfectly organized. Often corpses littered the train tracks both inside and outside the compound. Eventually, the commandant of Sobibor, Franz Stangl, was transferred to Treblinka to clean the place up. Even Stangl's "improvements"—increased efficiency and a beautification scheme that included planting flower beds—could not conceal the unbearable smell that surrounded the place. Fields came right up to the security fence, so that Polish farmers who lived nearby could see much of what happened inside. No one in the area could be unaware of the massive killing operations at Treblinka.

Auschwitz-Birkenau

Auschwitz-Birkenau was the last site established as a killing center, but it functioned the longest in that capacity. Like Belzec and Treblinka, Auschwitz started as a labor camp. Its first inmates in 1940 were Polish political prisoners from Tarnów. Facilities for mass killing were added later as were a number of factories using slave labor drawn from the camp; the chemical company IG Farben had a plant at Auschwitz III (Buna-Monowitz) to produce artificial rubber.

In the summer of 1941—before the Wannsee meeting—Himmler decided to transform the camp at Auschwitz into a killing center. He assigned a man named Rudolf Hoess, trained at Dachau, to the task. Auschwitz seemed an ideal location to Himmler. It was near the small town of Oswiecim and convenient to rail lines yet securely distant from the front. The prisoners already on hand provided a ready source of manpower.

Germans conducted some early trial gassings at Auschwitz. In September 1941 they killed nine hundred Soviet POWs using Zyklon B. By March 1942 Jews were being sent there from the surrounding area to be gassed. The killing center was known as Auschwitz II or Birkenau. Eventually, Birkenau would be the destination of Jews rounded up for killing from Slovakia, France, and then all over Europe. Thousands of Roma would be gassed at Birkenau too.

The killing procedure at Auschwitz-Birkenau was similar to that elsewhere. Often German officials met the transports of Jews right at the ramp as they came off the trains. There they made their "selections"—the decision as to who would go immediately to the gas and who would be kept alive for a time as laborers in the camp or outside.

Many survivors remember selections conducted by Josef Mengele. Mengele was a scientist and SS doctor who had his own special projects that involved experiments with dwarfs, twins, and others. Mengele's abusive experiments killed the vast majority of his subjects. With a wave of the hand, Mengele and his counterparts sorted those deemed useful from those considered fit only for killing. Children, women with children, pregnant women, older men and women, the sick, and the weak were sent to one side and then on to the gas. Others were admitted into the camp.

The officials who presided over the killing process developed a series of tricks and deceits to keep their victims calm. Often SS men addressed those selected for gassing in polite, helpful tones as they entered the gas chambers. "You have been on a journey, and you are dirty," the SS informed their victims. "You will take a shower." Sometimes they even handed out soap and towels before cramming the people in the "Shower Room." Hoess was proud of arrangements at his camp; he had a sense that he had perfected procedures.

At Auschwitz as elsewhere in the Holocaust, killing went hand in hand with plunder. In the large storage area that for some reason became known in camp slang as "Canada," prisoner workers sorted through heaps of eyeglasses, suitcases, photographs, shoes, and everything else people brought with them on transports. The most valuable items—cash, jewelry, luxury goods—were claimed by the higher-ups in the camp; privileged prisoners who worked at the unloading ramps helped themselves to the leftovers. In an era before cheap mass production, clothing and shoes were expensive and hard to come by, and even well-off people were used to hand-me-downs and second-hand clothes. Anything deemed usable was to be sent to Germany or collected for distribution to German settlers or cooperative people in the occupied territories. Rags, mismatched shoes, and the like were used as prison "uniforms."

Many Holocaust museums and memorials display piles of shoes or photographs of them as a way to convey the magnitude of destruction and the humanity and individuality of the victims. Already in 1943, the great Yiddish poet Abraham Sutzkever wrote about a load of shoes transported, without their wearers, from the Vilna ghetto to Berlin:

"The cartwheels rush,
quivering.
What is their burden?
Shoes, shivering. . . .
"Slippers and pumps,
look, there are my mother's:
her Sabbath pair,
in with the others." (quoted in Roskies, 493)

The photograph on page 255 was found by a prisoner working in "Canada." She recognized the young man as the son of another inmate, Rosa Lieberman. In 1938 the Liebermans had been expelled from Berlin and moved to Bedzin, where Rosa had been born. The family survived liquidation of the ghetto in 1943 by hiding in a bunker but they were caught the following year and sent to Auschwitz-Birkenau. Alex, the son, was killed on arrival, and his father was also soon sent to the gas chamber. Mrs. Lieberman and her daughter were chosen for work. For more than half a year, Rosa Lieberman managed to keep the photo, hiding it in her mouth during every roll-call and search. She, her daughter, and the picture of her son survived Auschwitz, a series of death marches, and a stint in Ravensbrück, to be liberated by the Allies in May 1945.

As the last and largest of the killing centers, Auschwitz-Birkenau represented refinement of the Nazi system. From early in the process officials had worried about conflicts between German economic interests and the goal of annihilating Jews. In Auschwitz, those two aims were combined. The SS found they could make money by essentially renting out slave laborers to manufacturers and industrialists. Employers need not worry about keeping their workers alive; there were always more where they came from. In addition to the

At a warehouse in Auschwitz-Birkenau, female prisoners in the *Aufräumungskommando* (clean-up commando) sort through shoes taken from a May 1944 transport of Jews from Subcarpathian Rus'. Top administrators in the camps had first dibs on the victims' property, and mid- and lower-level camp functionaries and privileged prisoners also helped themselves. Everything else was sorted and funneled through a vast distribution network until it ended up in the hands of individuals and various economic branches of the Nazi empire. This photograph comes from the Auschwitz album, a collection put together by camp personnel to document the "processing" of one transport of Jews from their arrival to just outside the gas chamber.

concentration camp and the killing center known as Birkenau, the Auschwitz system included a massive industrial complex and labor camp called Monowitz. There was also a model town where thousands of employees and their families, Germans and ethnic Germans, enjoyed the fruits of state-of-the-art urban planning.

Bizarre as it may seem, some Germans made a pleasant life for themselves at the killing centers. Ambitious medical scientists had an endless supply of disposable human subjects on whom to conduct experiments. Commandants and other high-ranking administrators often brought their wives and children to be near them. They had access to every luxury and of course to free labor. Hoess's wife supposedly said about Auschwitz, "Here I want to live until the end of my days." Himmler authorized fish farms, gardens, brothels, and even zoos on the sites for the employees' enjoyment. As for the guards, assignment to a killing center was certainly safer than being sent to the front.

A portrait of Alex Lieberman, a German Jew who fled with his family to Poland in 1938 and was later murdered at Auschwitz-Birkenau. This basic, passport-style picture, damaged and scarred by folds, reflects the enormous value of photographs as objects that connected people to those they loved. Rosa Lieberman preserved this photo of her son by hiding it in her mouth during every search and selection while she was a prisoner at Auschwitz and on death marches to Ravensbrück and Neustadt-Gleve. She and her daughter Ella were liberated in May 1945.

Secrecy, Denial, Disbelief

German authorities tried to contain knowledge of the killing centers, just as they had attempted earlier to conceal the murder of disabled people and the mass shootings of Jews, but in no case was secrecy really possible. The killing operations were too big and involved too many people to keep them quiet.

Local populations watched full trains pull in and saw them depart empty. The air for miles around was thick with the ashes of burning bodies and putrid with the stink of death. Civilians came from Germany and elsewhere for jobs in the camps. There were guards, of course, but also architects and engineers, suppliers, telephone operators, and secretaries. What did the German and Polish women think whose job it was to type up lists of the dead and prepare statistics of the numbers of people killed?

Perpetrators, bystanders, and onlookers found ways to live with their knowledge of the killing. One account illustrates some of the forms denial and rationalization could take. Teresa Stangl was married to Franz Stangl, commandant first of Sobibor and then of Treblinka. A devout Catholic, she had initially opposed her husband's involvement with the Nazi Party. According to Mrs. Stangl, she had never really understood his position in the T-4 program; she claimed she did not know the nature of the programs he administered.

Later Teresa Stangl moved to Sobibor to be near her husband. From their house near the camp she could not see the activities inside. One day a drunken coworker of her husband's called on her and told her the details of Franz's job. Horrified Mrs. Stangl confronted her husband. He denied any direct connection with killing and assured his wife that he was just responsible for routine administration. Nevertheless, she found herself unable to have sexual relations with him for some time. Eventually, she moved away, and they continued their marriage from a distance.

Despite her misgivings Mrs. Stangl stood by her husband. He loved her and would have done anything for her, she said. Once, she admitted in an interview that he would have chosen her over his work if she had given him an ultimatum, but later she insisted that she could have done nothing.

What of the Jews? What could Jews in Europe know in 1942 and 1943 of the killing centers? The answer is complicated by geography. Clearly Jews farther away—in Greece, for example—had access to little reliable information, but even Polish Jews, at least in the early stages of the killing centers' operation, could have problems grasping the reality of genocide. The word "genocide" did not even exist until after World War II.

Perhaps one account can illustrate. Piotrków Trybunalski, in the incorporated territories, was home to about 11,400 Jews, some 22 percent of the overall population. Since October 1939 the Jews of Piotrków had been confined to a ghetto.

In the spring of 1942, two young men escaped from Chelmno. They arrived in Piotrków and revealed the truth about German gassings of Jews. Most people refused to believe their ears. Why, during wartime, when it was well known that Germany had a serious shortage of labor, would the Germans try to slaughter every Polish Jew?

The leaders of the community met. Desperate to reassure themselves, they decided that the excesses the men had witnessed must be regional aberrations. Everyone knew that the SS commander Odilo Globocnik in Lublin was exceptionally vicious. Surely nothing so terrible could happen in their district.

Were the Jewish leaders of Piotrków naive? Maybe, but perhaps that innocence is to their credit. Who could imagine mass gassings as part of a systematic annihilation of Jews? Such a thing had never happened. Nazi planners in turn exploited that inability to believe the worst.

Hope, even when based on an illusion, had some advantages over despair. One of the chroniclers of the Warsaw ghetto wrote, "It is good that we console ourselves, for even if these are false hopes, they keep us from collapsing." For the most part those Jews who grasped German intentions toward them could do nothing anyway. In the summer of 1942, Adam Czerniaków was head of the Jewish Council in Warsaw. When the Germans ordered him to hand over the children of the ghetto, he knew that they would be killed. Powerless to stop the slaughter, Czerniaków took the only way out still left to him: he committed suicide.

ROMA

The killing centers marked the culmination of the process of destruction. In all, an estimated 3 million Jews were murdered at the five sites outlined above. The number of Roma killed with them is even harder to pin down, but it was certainly in the tens of thousands. Approximately twenty thousand Roma died in Auschwitz-Birkenau alone—two-thirds of them from starvation, disease, experimentation, beatings, and shootings; the rest in the gas chambers.

Almost every Jewish memoir about Auschwitz mentions Roma. For Roma, like Jews, 1942 and 1943 were the peak years of killing. As German forces consolidated their hold on subject territories, they located more and more groups of Roma. In all, German perpetrators and their accomplices killed an estimated one-quarter to half a million Roma, including many children and old people. Thousands of others were sterilized.

Nazi ideology considered Roma impure and dangerous. One of the absurdities of the situation was that according to Nazi terminology, Roma were in fact more "Aryan" than the Nordic Germans. The Rom people originated in India, home of the original Aryan tribe, whose name was appropriated by European racists for their own purposes. The Romani language even bears some similarity to Indian languages.

SS leader Himmler was fascinated by Sinti and Roma. He set up an office within the German Ministry of Health called the Racial Hygiene and Population Research Center. Its main task was to study the approximately thirty thousand Sinti (German Rom), draw up genealogies of them, and identify those considered "pure." The information gathered made it possible to locate Sinti and Roma and sterilize or kill them.

Initially Himmler wanted to preserve some supposedly "pure Gypsies" in a kind of reservation or zoo, where they could be examined by future German scientists. "Experts" estimated that between 3 and 4 percent of the Roma would fall into that category. Later Himmler abandoned that idea. The German government provided generous funding for research on the Roma, and many scientists got involved in the project, especially anthropologists and other social scientists.

Roma shared many of the experiences of Jews in the Holocaust. Classified, dispossessed, deported, forced into ghettos, shot into mass graves, and gassed, they too were marked for annihilation, but Nazi authorities never devoted the same fanatical energy to killing Roma as they did to eradication of Jews. They seemed to regard Sinti and Roma as a nuisance rather than part of a diabolical conspiracy. Still, they were targeted for murder.

The experience of Nazi persecution highlighted how isolated Roma were within Europe. Church leaders in Germany protested the killing of people deemed disabled in 1941. In the 1943 Rosenstrasse protest in Berlin, the non-Jewish wives of German Jewish men forced cancellation of plans to transport their husbands to the east to be killed. In occupied Poland, the Netherlands, Ukraine, Yugoslavia, and elsewhere, non-Jews risked their lives to hide Jewish children and adults, sometimes for years. Who protested on behalf of the Roma? Who beyond their own circles sheltered Rom children from death? There were some people who did so, for instance a priest in Croatia intervened on behalf of Christian Roma, but such stories are almost unknown.

OTHER SITES OF DESTRUCTION

As the perpetrators honed their skills, they developed sites of destruction in response to particular circumstances and needs. Two such places, Majdanek and Theresienstadt, do not fit easily into the familiar categories of ghetto, concentration camp, or killing center. But they were nonetheless important parts of the machinery of annihilation, and their distinctive features say something about how the system functioned.

Majdanek

Majdanek combined a labor camp with a massive depot or site for sorting property and people. Just a mile from the city of Lublin, the camp, modeled after Dachau in Germany, was built in the winter of 1940–1941 for prisoners of war. In fact, the Jewish POWs from the Polish army who were its first inmates did much of the construction.

In July 1941 the Germans brought Soviet POWs to Majdanek. Over time they added many Poles, especially political prisoners. They built gas chambers in 1942, but gas vans and shooting were also used at Majdanek. All of Majdanek's inmates were subjected to terrible abuses, and many were worked to death. Most of the Soviet POWs died from torture and starvation. The SS men in Majdanek were known as sadists who enjoyed killing children in front of their mothers and forcing prisoners to engage in deadly "sports."

Many prisoners, Jews and non-Jews, passed through Majdanek before being dispatched to other destinations. The SS used the site to hold Jews marked for destruction until space was available at one of the killing centers; they also kept prisoners of various kinds there while awaiting assignments to labor camps and projects. It was all the better for those in charge if their captives died in the meantime.

In late 1942 Eichmann visited Majdanek. Guards forced the inmates to spend the entire day on parade. Eichmann looked at them and said, "Get rid of the whole lot." In Nazi eyes, the lives of prisoners at Majdanek were worth less than nothing. On just one day in November 1943, guards at Majdanek mowed down some seventeen thousand people with machine gun fire and forced the few left alive to conceal the evidence. In all, around two hundred thousand people were killed in the camp, two-thirds of them Jews. Because of the large number of non-Jews among the dead and because Majdanek was among the first large sites of destruction liberated by the Red Army, it became a potent symbol of Nazi assault on all the peoples of eastern Europe.

Theresienstadt

Theresienstadt (also known by the Czech name, Terezín) was a transit ghetto in the Protectorate of Bohemia and Moravia, not far from Prague. Nazi Germans sent more than one hundred and forty thousand Czech, German, Austrian, Dutch, Danish, Slovak, and Hungarian Jews to Theresienstadt, where around one-quarter of them died. Elderly people had a particularly high death rate there. Many more people—some eighty-seven thousand—were sent on from Theresienstadt to the east to sites of killing: Riga, Lodz, and ghettos in the Lublin district, Treblinka, and Auschwitz-Birkenau.

Like Majdanek, Theresienstadt served multiple purposes, but in contrast to Majdanek, Theresienstadt was exclusively a site of Jewish suffering. It was a prison and a ghetto for Czech Jews, a transit point for Jews from all over central and western Europe, and a so-called advantage ghetto. As Heydrich explained at the Wannsee Conference, Theresienstadt was to be the destination for groups

deemed exceptions, among them elderly German Jews and prominent individuals who might attract international attention. In this respect, Theresienstadt
served a propaganda function for the Germans, because it existed as "proof"
that transports to the east were indeed to labor camps. Otherwise why would
the elderly and prominent artists and scientists be exempted? Of course most
of them were murdered too, but Theresienstadt provided a convenient delay
and cover. To this end the SS twice permitted the International Red Cross to
visit the site, which temporarily became a showcase of the supposedly humane
treatment of Germany's Jewish prisoners.

EFFORTS TO LIVE

People targeted for destruction tried to stay alive, but their options were
perilously few. Gender, age, nationality, class, and even physical appearance all
affected the possibilities of making it through any given situation. But no qualities guaranteed survival, and Jews in particular faced horrific odds.

Gender and Genocide

Women's and men's experiences in the Holocaust converged and
diverged in significant ways, summed up in the scholar Myrna Goldenberg's
phrase "different horrors, same hell." Jewish men were more likely to be killed
in labor camps in occupied Poland in 1939 and 1940, but more women were
among the groups "selected" from the ghettos in 1942 for transport to killing
centers. In Auschwitz, men generally had a better chance of being chosen for
work; SS authorities regularly consigned women, particularly if pregnant or
with small children, directly to the gas. Toward the end of the war, however,
the balance shifted, because the Germans considered young men too dangerous
and preferred women laborers.

Accounts by Jewish women in Nazi camps often emphasize the physical
transformation that their bodies underwent. Isabella Leitner, a survivor from
Hungary, described her feelings in Auschwitz in May 1944:

> Our heads are shaved. We look like neither boys nor girls. We haven't
> menstruated for a long time. We have diarrhea. No, not diarrhea—typhus.
> Summer and winter we have but one type of clothing. Its name is "rag."
> Not an inch of it without a hole. Our shoulders are exposed. The rain is
> pouring on our skeletal bodies. The lice are having an orgy in our armpits,
> their favorite spots. Their bloodsucking, the irritation, their busy scurrying
> give the illusion of warmth. We're hot at least under our armpits, while our
> bodies are shivering. (Rittner and Roth, 67)

The process of crushing people's sense of dignity and worth often began with destroying their identity and honor as women or men.

Jews in Hiding

Not all Jews targeted in the Holocaust ended up in killing centers. Many fled, taking refuge where they could. Others hid, and still others "passed" as gentiles. An estimated eighty thousand to one hundred and twenty thousand Jews were hidden in Poland; maybe half of those people survived the war.

Many of the Jews hiding and passing were children. It was easier to persuade non-Jews to have pity on children than on adults, who took up more space, ate more, and whose presence was harder to explain. It tended to be more difficult to find places for Jewish boys than for girls. In Europe few Christians had their sons circumcised, so Jewish boys had their religion marked on their bodies. It was not uncommon for police or local collaborators hunting for Jews to demand that men or boys pull down their pants to reveal if they had been circumcised.

The decision to put a child into hiding was agonizing for parents. Who could one trust? When was hiding the best option? Was it not better to stay together? How could one leave a child one might never see again? Only as adults have many of the people hidden as Jewish children during the war recounted their experiences publicly. Here are two of their stories.

Henia Wisgardisky (now Henia Lewin) was the daughter of Lithuanian Jews from Kovno. When she was just a year and a half old, she and her parents were forced to move into the ghetto. For more than two years Henny's parents hid her in a small room that had been a walk-in pantry, but when she developed whooping cough it became too risky to keep her there. So they arranged for a Lithuanian Christian family outside the ghetto to take her in.

Henny's mother also arranged a hiding place for her two-year-old niece, Shoshana Bluma Berk (now Sarid), after Germans shot the little girl's father. She made contact with a Lithuanian priest who got false papers for Shoshana and placed her in a convent. Later the nuns passed her on to a family of pig farmers. Against all odds, Shoshana, Henny, and Henny's parents survived the war. Henia Lewin went on to become a renowned Jewish educator in the United States, and a translator and instructor of Hebrew and Yiddish.

Rudy, a little boy in the Netherlands, survived the war in about twenty different hiding places, most of them in rural Holland. He remembers spending three days with a Jewish family in the woods while Germans searched the area. He heard German vehicles and dogs at night but stayed hidden under branches and leaves, and they did not find him. Later two young women hid him with a group of ten other children. Several times a local Dutch policeman

Two girls in the Kovno ghetto wearing Stars of David that were fashioned out of wood by their uncle. Pictured are cousins Henia Wisgardisky (right) and Bluma Berk. This photo was taken in July 1943, a few months before Henia's mother smuggled the girls out of the ghetto. Both children were hidden by Lithuanian families and survived the war. Henia's parents also fled the ghetto and hid in a root cellar on a potato farm. Reunited after the war, the family immigrated to Palestine and later moved to Canada. The father of Bluma (now Shoshana Sarid) was shot by the Germans at the Fourth Fort in Kovno in 1941. Her mother was sent to Stutthof but survived.

warned them of an impending raid. Once, they stayed in a cave for two days until it was safe to return. Eventually, the group had to be split up. Only after the war, as adults, did some of them find one another again. Rudy, who returned to his original name, Yehudi Lindeman, had little contact with other former hidden children or with study of the Holocaust until the 1980s, when he cofounded "Living Testimonies," a video archive of survivor accounts in Montreal.

Accounts of hiding involve rescue, heroism, and survival, but they are also entangled with betrayal, collaboration, and loss. Henry Friedman survived the Holocaust as a teenager, hidden in a hayloft in eastern Poland with his mother, brother, and school teacher. His memoir, *I'm No Hero*, makes it clear that he owes his life to the Ukrainian woman who sheltered them. Her husband did not know she was hiding Jews, nor would he have approved.

Also unaware of the Jews in the barn, just a wall away from the woman's bedroom, was her lover, the head of the local Ukrainian police and a notorious antisemite and killer. His active collaboration provided unintentional cover for her act of rescue. Their affair, for anyone watching, may also have helped explain the gold earrings she loved to wear outside, although Friedman's mother, who had given them to her, begged her to leave them home. Gentiles who suddenly acquired jewelry or money attracted suspicion for harboring Jews.

Unbeknownst to Friedman and his brother, their mother was pregnant when they went into hiding, and eventually it was time for the baby to be born. By his account, the denizens of the loft took a vote regarding what to do. The results were three to one (Friedman's mother dissenting) to have her deliver the baby, the teacher would then kill it, and the Ukrainian woman would bury the body. This is what occurred. By Friedman's account, "the decision we made has haunted me ever since. I wake in the middle of the night, crying. My brother still denies that he voted" (Friedman, 27). As Friedman's account reveals, in circumstances saturated in violence, collaboration was ubiquitous, intermingled with greed, brutality, and sometimes heroism.

Resistance

All over Europe people resisted Nazism in many ways. There were individual acts of defiance and heroism; there was sabotage and rescue of people targeted for killing. The Communist Party organized resistance groups, often with backing from the Soviet Union. The British Special Operations Executive supported nationalist guerrilla movements from France to Yugoslavia and Greece.

Any discussion of resistance has to define the term. Does opposition need to be effective to count as resistance? Does it need to be organized? Armed? Unmixed with collaboration or opportunism? I define "resistance" as any actions taken with the intent of thwarting Nazi German goals in the war, actions that carried with them risk of punishment. Under this definition, resistance could be individual or group, armed or unarmed. Whether we talk about intelligence as resistance, Jewish resistance, or resistance within Germany, all discussion of resistance serves to counter some popular misconceptions about World War II.

The Spread of Information as Resistance

Resistance can take many forms. Many anti-Nazi organizations took enormous risks to collect and transmit information that would undermine the German war effort. One of the most remarkable examples of intelligence as resistance involved a member of the Polish underground named Jan Karski.

Born in 1914 Karski made a career before the war in the Polish Foreign Service. He joined the Polish army in 1939 and was taken prisoner of war by the Soviets. Karski escaped and became part of the Polish underground. In the fall of 1942, Karski was charged with a mission to London. He was to carry a report to the Polish government-in-exile that described the situation in German-occupied Poland.

Leaders of two Jewish organizations learned of Karski's impending trip to London and asked if he would also carry a report for them. Karski agreed. The Jews of Poland were being annihilated, the Jewish leaders told Karski. Eventually, Hitler would lose the war, they said, but he would win his war against Polish Jewry. The Jewish leaders asked Karski to tell the highest circles of the Allied governments that Hitler planned to kill every Jew regardless of the outcome of the war. Polish Jews and even Polish gentiles were helpless to stop the destruction. Only the Allied governments could save the Jews.

Before they sent him off with their message, the Jewish leaders wanted Karski to see for himself what they meant. They smuggled him, disguised as a Ukrainian guard, into the transit ghetto of Izbica. Karski was devastated by what he saw. After an hour he broke down and had to be taken out, vomiting blood. Karski became one of the first eyewitnesses to present the whole truth about the fate of the Jews in occupied Poland.

Karski delivered his reports as promised. He met with British, American, and Polish representatives; he spoke directly with Prime Minister Churchill in Britain and President Roosevelt in the United States and sought out journalists and other opinion leaders.

All of Karski's perseverance and heroism did not get the results he so desperately wanted. People simply did not comprehend. After U.S. Supreme Court Justice Felix Frankfurter listened to Karski's report, he responded that he could not believe it. Frankfurter did not mean he thought Karski was lying; he simply could not grasp the enormity of what he had heard. Karski found no effective help for the Jews of Poland from any nation, government, or church. Only a few courageous individuals were willing to act. Karski survived the war and moved to Washington, DC, where he taught political science for many years. He died in 2000.

Jan Karski's experience highlights the issue of Allied knowledge of Nazi crimes. What did the British or the Americans know and when? By late 1942, when Karski prepared his report, at least some people within the Allied leadership had access to a great deal of information about German atrocities. Already in 1941 British code breakers, building on Polish intelligence, were reading German dispatches, including those from the Soviet Union describing murders of Jews and other civilians by the Order Police. Reports from eyewitnesses and individuals who had managed to escape from Nazi prisons and camps reached world leaders through various channels, and every government had its own sources of intelligence. The press offered considerable detail for the reading public—in the United States, Canada, Switzerland, and elsewhere.

Nevertheless, a number of factors prevented the Allies from broadcasting their knowledge of slaughter of Jews and other people. Most important, there was a war to be won, a war whose outcome was by no means clear in 1942 or even 1943. No doubt some individuals were indifferent to the fate of Europe's Jews or even had antisemitic notions of their own. But it is probably fair to assume that many people simply could not grasp the unprecedented nature of this war of annihilation, and even those who could tended to be preoccupied with their own issues and struggles.

Jewish Resistance

Jewish resistance of various kinds was more widespread than many people used to assume. It is worth contemplating why Jewish resistance has often been downplayed. Certainly Germans at the time wanted to show Jews as weak, to highlight their own strength and portray Jewish death as almost inevitable. For observers afterward the notion that Jews were passive, even fatalistic about their destruction, could serve to soften the horror. The image of fighting Jews also complicates a narrative of genocide as slaughter of the innocents. Some Jews at the time accused others of failing to resist as a way to try to recruit fighters. Abba Kovner, writing in Vilna in January 1942, spoke of the "shameful" behavior of "Jewish youth" who gave in to the temptation of hope instead of realizing there was no hope. It was Kovner who used the phrase "like sheep to the slaughter" in his call on Jews in the ghetto to die fighting.

Heroic gestures aside, the most effective form of resistance was involvement in military action. Jews participated in all of the armies that fought and in the end defeated Nazi Germany: the Polish, French, British, Canadian, Soviet, and U.S. militaries all included Jewish soldiers. In the cases where those militaries were defeated, Jews were among those most likely to seek ways to fight on, with the Free French forces, Soviet partisan units, or underground armies. In fact Jews were statistically overrepresented in resistance groups, notably so in the early stages of the war when the Germans seemed invincible. In North Africa, for example, Jews played a crucial role in gathering and transmitting intelligence that facilitated the 1942 Allied landings codenamed Operation Torch. Anyone at risk of being considered a Jew had a high incentive to understand what was at stake if Germany won the war.

The largest numbers of Jews served in the Red Army, as regular soldiers and as officers. Like their non-Jewish fellows they experienced terrible casualty rates and deadly treatment if captured. Soviet Jews also faced additional dangers, because the Germans singled them out for immediate killing. In some units from Central Asia, with the support of their comrades, Soviet Jews succeeded in "passing" as Muslims and thereby increasing their chances of survival. Trapped in their own stereotypes, Germans were unprepared for Sephardic Jews who did not speak Yiddish or look like the Nazi image of a Jew. Like Jews, Muslims traditionally practice circumcision and do not eat pork. But in the Soviet context, many members of both religions did not observe those traditions. So neither circumcision nor its absence was a reliable marker of ancestry.

Jews also participated in special units organized by the Soviets to fight Nazi Germany. Many Polish Jewish refugees fought in the Polish Armed Forces in the East, known as Anders' Army, after its commander, Wladyslaw Anders. After World War II, in the climate of the Cold War, the memory of Jewish soldiers who helped the Soviets defeat Nazism was suppressed. Photos like this one, of three Polish Jewish refugees who served in Anders' Army, taken in November 1944 in liberated Warsaw, judging from the background in a photographer's studio, turned from being a sign of honor to something to be forgotten.

All across German-occupied Europe, Jews and other opponents of Nazism took to the woods, often forming partisan units to combat the Germans. But Jewish and non-Jewish resistance differed considerably with regard to timing. For Jews, armed resistance tended to emerge from hopelessness: as the Germans' genocidal intentions became clear over the course of 1942, many Jews, especially young people, concluded like Kovner that they had nothing to lose, so they might as well die fighting. For non-Jews, armed resistance came from the opposite impulse. After the German defeats at Stalingrad and in North Africa, it became clear that there was something to gain by fighting: a role in the liberation and future of one's homeland. As a result, Jewish resistance gained momentum earlier, when German power was at its peak. Resistance by non-Jews gathered steam later, as the Germans were retreating.

The existence of Jewish partisans was precarious. They lived from hand to mouth, stealing when necessary, arranging secret deliveries of food, and spending hours and even days in holes in the ground when danger threatened. Afraid that the presence of Jews nearby would jeopardize their own security, non-Jews often denounced or even killed their Jewish counterparts. Nevertheless, as German police records for 1943 indicate, Jews in the woods of eastern Europe managed to acquire explosives and weapons and to perform acts of

Ignac Greenbaum (right), from Sosnowiec, with two other Jewish refugees who joined the Polish Army that was formed in the Soviet Union during the war. According to the U.S. Holocaust Memorial Museum Photo Archives, this picture was taken in Warsaw in November 1944, a month after German forces crushed the Polish uprising and before the Soviets entered the city in January 1945. The backdrop suggests the photo was taken in a studio, if an improvised one. At the end of the war, enterprising photographers set up shop in some unlikely places, including in newly liberated towns and concentration camps. People paid to have photographs taken that they could send to worried family members or use to document their wartime roles.

sabotage. Young Jewish men and women even married in the woods and gave birth to children there.

In Lithuania in early 1942, about ten thousand Jewish men and women were fighting as partisans. Among there were Sara Ginaite and her husband Misha Rubinson. At least thirty different Jewish partisan groups existed in the General Government alone. Thousands of Jews revolted in the ghettos and labor camps around Bialystok. In general, the groups that banded together

On the front line. Partisans Sara Ginaite and Ida Vilenchiuk walk down a street of Vilna during its liberation in July 1944. Ginaite's partisan unit, "Death to the Occupiers," operated in the forests near Vilna, eventually assisting in the city's liberation from Nazi German rule. For obvious reasons, photos of partisans in action are rare, and many iconic images were in fact taken after liberation, by Soviet photographers. This picture is unusual because it was not staged or posed; Ginaite herself was unaware it existed until 2015, when she came across it on the internet.

were desperate, pitifully small, and barely armed. Their chances of success were minimal, but still they defied Nazi power.

Even in camps and killing centers, under the most adverse conditions, people fought back. Members of the Sonderkommando in Auschwitz-Birkenau took a series of graphic photographs to try to convey the reality of mass murder to the world. Numerous survivors tell of the beautiful dancer in Auschwitz who seized a gun from an SS man and shot him. Both Sobibor and Treblinka had revolts in 1943. In May 1944, Roma defied efforts to liquidate the so-called Gypsy family camp in Birkenau, and in October, Jewish prisoners blew up one of the camp's crematoria. Starved, isolated, and destitute, Jews were in a weak position to offer resistance to the Germans. Nevertheless, like others they did resist—violently, passively, spiritually, physically, and emotionally—throughout the entire process of the "Final Solution."

The Warsaw Ghetto Uprising

The Jewish ghetto in Warsaw must have been one of the last places the Germans expected an uprising in the spring of 1943. By then 80 percent of the population of the Warsaw ghetto was already gone, most of them murdered at Treblinka in the summer of 1942.

Initially the Warsaw Jewish rebels had little support even within their own community. The Jewish Fighting Organization had fewer than five hundred fighters. Another, better connected but now less well-known resistance movement, the Jewish Military Union, may have had more people in its ranks. Armed only with gasoline bombs, hand grenades, pistols, a very few submachine guns, and some rifles, these men and women must have seemed unlikely to accomplish anything other than mass suicide. Yet, they managed to mount the largest armed resistance organized by any targets of Nazi mass murder during World War II. What happened?

In January 1943 German SS planned to liquidate the Warsaw ghetto. To their surprise they met with armed resistance from ghetto Jews. Unwilling to risk casualties in the wake of the defeat at Stalingrad, they gave up the attempt after a few days.

Four months later, on April 19, 1943, the Germans returned much better prepared. More than two thousand men came with armored vehicles, artillery, flame throwers, heavy-caliber machine guns, and aircraft. For their part Warsaw Jews had prepared an elaborate system of bunkers and underground passages. Determined to make a stand they held off the Germans for four weeks.

The SS burned down buildings, dynamited, and smoked out the Jews' bunkers until they won the upper hand. The Jewish fighters' tenacity was astounding, especially because the ghetto was sealed off and it was almost impossible to get weapons or supplies. The Nazis crushed the uprising at a huge cost in human lives, almost all of them Jewish. The SS commander reported sixteen German dead; the actual number may have been slightly higher.

Small pockets of Jewish resistance continued for weeks, but in the end, more than fifty-six thousand Jews surrendered. The Germans shot many on the spot and transported the others to killing centers and labor camps. Thousands of Jewish dead remained buried in the rubble. The commander in charge, SS Major General Jürgen Stroop, prepared a report that he titled "The Warsaw Ghetto Is No More." Bound in leather and intended as a souvenir album for

SS troops walk past a block of burning buildings in April 1943 during the suppression of the Warsaw ghetto uprising. This photograph was one of fifty-two included in the Stroop Report, compiled to document the destruction of the ghetto and intended as a souvenir album for Himmler. Its original caption read, "An assault squad."

Himmler, it included numerous photographs, among them this one of casually triumphant SS men.

Another picture, taken clandestinely by the Polish photographer Tad Brezkis, offers a different perspective on events. Brezkis shot this photo from a window looking down on Sienna Street, on the edge of the recently destroyed ghetto. Here the Germans march in tight formation, intimidating yet vulnerable on all sides. Is this an image of strength or weakness?

The Warsaw ghetto uprising marked the first large-scale urban revolt against German occupation. It did not save many, if any, Jewish lives. In fact it convinced the Germans to use more force more quickly in the future when they set out to liquidate ghettos. Given their intention to kill the Jews anyway, however, it could hardly have worsened the Jews' situation. Certainly its moral and symbolic importance as an assertion of life cannot be underestimated.

Resistance within Germany

Examples of widespread resistance within Germany are few although so-called Aryan Germans were in the strongest position to oppose the Nazi regime. The early years of Hitler's rule had paralyzed organizations that might have been

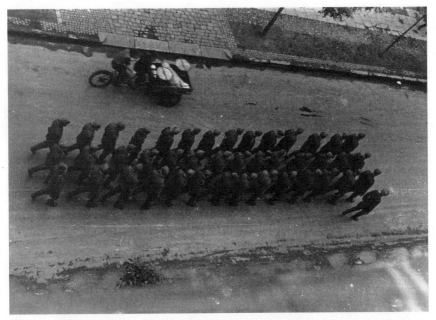

German troops on Sienna Street shortly after the destruction of the Warsaw ghetto, in mid-1943. This photograph was part of a series of nearly forty pictures taken secretly by Tad Brezkis, a Polish gentile. After witnessing the destruction of the ghetto, Brezkis returned a few months later with his camera. This is a remarkable composition, especially given that he was working in haste. Note how the soldiers are looking in different directions, uneasy about their surroundings, perhaps, or curious.

the focal point of opposition. Members of the Communist Party, for example, had been dispersed, although they managed to retain some links to one another and preserve some pockets of resistance. The time to oppose Nazism had been in the first phases of its rule in Germany. By 1942 and 1943 the stakes were much higher. Only in 1944, once Germany was clearly losing the war, would more opponents of the regime be emboldened to acts of resistance.

Still there were important incidents earlier on. In the winter of 1942 a professor and a handful of students at the University of Munich formed an oppositional group. The key figures were Kurt Huber, a professor of philosophy; Willi Graf, a devout Catholic; Alexander Schmorell, son of a Russian woman; Christoph Probst and Hans Leipelt, both of whom had Jewish family members; and a brother and sister, Hans and Sophie Scholl. Both Scholls had been enthusiastic Nazis as children, but as students they broke with those ideas. Hans's tour of duty as a medical orderly on the eastern front gave him firsthand exposure to the horrors of Nazi German warfare.

Under the name "the White Rose," the group printed a series of leaflets decrying the crimes of Nazism. The last issue, dated February 1943, was called "The Spirit Lives!" In it the students protested the moral destruction of Germany. Nazism, they wrote, had turned German youth into godless, shameless, unscrupulous murderers.

Police caught Hans and Sophie Scholl along with three of their friends, including Professor Huber. They were interrogated and tried for spreading malicious and defeatist rumors against the state. Sophie, a 22-year-old philosophy student at the time, addressed the court as guards led her away: "What we have written is in all your minds, but you lack the courage to say it aloud."

Hans and Sophie Scholl and Christoph Probst were executed in February 1943. Schmorell, Huber, Graf, and Leipelt were tried and put to death later. Their university remained silent; there was neither protest nor a show of solidarity from administrators, faculty, or students on behalf of these members of their community. After the war the University of Munich named its main quadrangle after the Scholl siblings.

Obstacles to Resistance

There were enormous barriers to resistance, especially for members of groups targeted for persecution and death. One of the most significant was the Nazi policy of exacting reprisals. The Germans made entire communities suffer for acts of resistance on a scale massively out of proportion to the supposed offense.

In June 1942 members of the Czech underground, with support from the British Special Operations Executive, assassinated Reinhard Heydrich. The Germans responded with total destruction of the town of Lidice, near Prague. They murdered all 199 men there as well as many of the women and children. Those remaining were removed for Germanization.

In 1943, a group of Jewish fighters from Vilna escaped from the ghetto to join partisans in the forest. Somehow they got their hands on a few weapons and attacked some Germans outside the city. In retaliation, the Gestapo seized the entire family of each Jewish fugitive or everyone who lived with him or her. They also arrested the leaders of all of the Jewish work parties in the vicinity, together with their families. All of those people were shot.

The policy of reprisals was a major deterrent. It probably explains why revolts in the Jewish ghettos often occurred only after the rebels were certain that death was planned for them and those close to them anyway.

Divisions within communities could present another obstacle to resistance. What would be the prospects? What were the best tactics? Were some would-be heroes risking increased horror for other people?

After years of war and occupation few people had the prerequisites for resistance. Overwhelmed by events, isolated, exhausted, and hungry, they could not hope for much success when it came to stopping Nazi Germany. Given those conditions we should perhaps be surprised at how much rather than how little resistance there was under German occupation.

The topic of resistance easily lends itself to manipulation and stereotypes. For decades the insistence of the postwar French governments that they were the heirs of the heroic French resistance made it impossible to face the realities of French collaboration. The fact that Jews were vastly overrepresented among French resisters was rarely acknowledged.

It is tempting to offer resistance as a sort of antidote to the depressing subject of World War II and the Holocaust, but some caution is in order. For one thing, a focus on heroism—those "lights in the darkness" who dared to defy the Nazi juggernaut—can serve both as an inspiration and a reminder of how many people participated in the crimes of the Third Reich. It is also important to keep in mind that resistance did not change the course of the war. It was military might that defeated Nazi Germany; with very few exceptions it was the Red Army and the western Allies that liberated occupied territories from German control.

Nevertheless, resistance had a crucial impact. To other conquered peoples it sent a message that they were not alone and that the Germans were not invincible. Resistance also left a positive legacy for a postwar world in which so many people had been compromised by collaboration and opportunism or paralyzed by fear.

9

DEATH THROES AND KILLING
FRENZIES, 1944–1945

If the Germans were to lose the war, Hitler once said, they would bring down with them "a world in flames." Hitler kept that promise. The last stage of the war in Europe, from 1944 until May 1945, brought German retreat, defeat, and collapse, but the Nazi Empire remained bloody and destructive until its end.

At the beginning of 1944, many Germans still expected to win the war. By the end of the year, few persisted in that hope. Germany was under assault—from the air, from the Red Army in the east, and, after D-Day in June, from the Allies in the west. Even internally there were some signs of weakening, but it still took until May 1945 for total collapse.

The death throes of the Third Reich were deadly themselves, though far less for the privileged elite of the regime than for its victims. Even as defeat became ever more certain, killing went on in many settings. The Allies, both eastern and western, had to fight hard and suffer many casualties to advance. When a plot to assassinate Hitler and stage a coup failed in July 1944, the Nazi regime responded with a vicious crackdown on its own population.

Well into 1945, Nazi programs of mass murder continued in the ever-shrinking territories that Germany controlled. The Roma who remained in Auschwitz were gassed in 1944. The murder of almost four hundred thousand Hungarian Jews took place that summer too. Throughout the last year of the war, the Germans kept opening new labor camps. As they abandoned killing

A group of Jewish women and children see their fathers, husbands, sons, and brothers as they are driven away from the deportation assembly point in Ioannina, Greece. Of the ten people who have been identified in this March 1944 photograph only one, Elda Levi, survived. It is not known who took the picture, but the photographer was clearly standing closer to the police and soldiers than to the Jewish family members. And yet the focus is on their agonized reactions, not on the men in charge, two of whom frame the image on the left.

centers and camps in areas lost to Allied advances, guards sent the inmates still left alive on murderous treks known as death marches.

None of that killing halted the disintegration of German power, but it ensured that the defeat of Nazism was accompanied by the maximum amount of carnage. This chapter surveys developments in the last stage of the war. How did the Nazi German Reich, the Holocaust, and the war in Europe end?

ATTACKS ON THE NAZI REGIME

The Soviet Advance

From late 1943, the Soviets remained on the offensive against Germany. The Red Army made rapid advances in 1944. On the third anniversary of Operation Barbarossa—in June 1944—the Soviets launched a massive offensive against the German Army Group Center.

By the end of 1944, odds on Germany's eastern front were heavily in favor of the Soviets. Against the total German strength of between 2 and 3.5

million men loomed 6 million Red Army soldiers. A German disadvantage of one German to every five Soviets was common; in some places the odds were closer to one to thirty or forty.

Still the Soviets fought at a tremendous cost. Even at the end of 1944, the Germans were still killing or wounding four Soviets for every casualty of their own. The huge Soviet advantage in replacements—and the need to send in wave after wave of those troops—itself implied the staggering death toll that the fighting took on the Red Army. It is estimated that the battle for Berlin alone cost half a million people their lives or their health. Small wonder that as soon as it could, the Soviet leadership would demand massive territorial gains and enormous reparations from the Germans.

Allied Bombing and Conditions in Germany

Air raids on Germany by the Royal Air Force and the U.S. air force peaked between January 1944 and January 1945. In the words of U.S. president Franklin Roosevelt, "Fortress Europe" had no roof. American planes alone made some seven hundred and fifty-five thousand sorties that year and dropped 1.4 million tons of bombs on Germany and German-controlled territories. Much of that aerial bombing was inaccurate, so that planes often dropped their loads indiscriminately in and around major German cities. Allied bombing may have killed as many as five hundred thousand German civilians.

Attacks from the air hit the petroleum and chemical industries hard. By September the Germans could supply only 10 percent of their needs in aviation fuel. By early 1945, the flow of fuel and ammunition to the German fronts had almost stopped.

Nevertheless, the German war machine demonstrated remarkable resilience to the assault from the air. Electric power stations continued to function, and German war production persisted during the last stage of the war. Of course a regime obsessed with public opinion ensured that these achievements were accompanied by massive "armaments propaganda." Did manufacturing of fighter planes peak in late 1944? Was total German military output in 1944 really more than the country's 1939 level? Eager to depict Germany as invincible in the face of economically superior enemies, Goebbels and his minions exaggerated and celebrated the triumphs of mass production and trumpeted the imminent appearance of new miracle weapons.

Such claims were encouraged and supported by Albert Speer (1905– 1981), Hitler's minister of armaments and war production from 1942. A trained architect and a friend and confidante of Hitler, Speer also indulged the Führer's passion for designing giant buildings for the Nazi world of the future. The

Allies captured Speer at the end of the war and brought him to trial for his role in German crimes against foreign labor. As Minister of Armaments and Munitions he exploited millions of forced laborers, many of whom were killed or died in the process. Convicted at Nuremberg for war crimes and crimes against humanity, he served twenty years in prison. Speer published memoirs and a diary. Unlike almost all of his Nazi counterparts, it appears that by the end of his life Speer was repentant toward the victims of the Third Reich and regretted his role in German crimes.

The real key to German wartime production, as Speer's career suggests, was the massive use of slave labor. In 1939 there were about three hundred thousand forced laborers in Germany. By 1944 that number had skyrocketed to 7.5 million. It was above all these non-Germans—from Russia, Ukraine, Belorussia, Poland, France, the Netherlands, Italy, Hungary, and elsewhere—who bore the tremendously high human cost involved in outfitting the German war machine.

The impact of the attack from the air on the morale of German civilians is hard to gauge. Certainly air raids alone did not destroy German support of Hitler's regime, although it is possible that the destruction of German cities made it easier for Germans to recognize defeat and surrender at the end of the war. Much easier to measure was the physical impact of the bombing. Allied raids destroyed between 4.5 and 5 million habitations, so that Germans experienced an incredible shortage of housing in the last stages of the war. Production of consumer goods fell dramatically at the same time.

By 1944 the German economy was in serious trouble. Hitler's insistence on protecting the home front from the costs of war meant deficit financing on a huge scale. The idea, of course, was that the vanquished would pay for the war. As long as the Germans were victorious they supported themselves through theft and plunder. Once the tide of the war turned, however, they were left with the hollowness of their own economy. Printing large amounts of money sparked inflation. Rapidly rising prices, in conjunction with stringent wage and price controls, led—as that particular combination always does—to the emergence of an active black market. In the German case, even before the war was over cigarettes began to overtake the official currency as the preferred medium of exchange.

D-Day—Allied Invasion from the West

On June 6, 1944, in a massive action with the code name Operation Overlord, the western Allies landed in Normandy in northwestern France. D-Day, as it became known, was the greatest amphibious assault ever. The numbers alone are staggering. More than four thousand Allied ships landed one hundred and seventy-six thousand troops after ten thousand aircraft dropped ten thousand tons of explosives on the German defenders of the French coast.

The Germans fought fiercely, but they could not stop the Allies. The historian Yaron Pasher links this failure directly to the Holocaust. In the month before D-Day, the Germans transported about three hundred thousand Jews from Hungary to Auschwitz. Those same trains, Pasher shows, could have been used instead to bring almost an entire army—more than one hundred thousand soldiers—to fight the Allies in Normandy. Pasher concludes that the Nazi German program of annihilation of Jews had a significant and demonstrable impact on the German military effort. Top decision-makers nevertheless chose to devote energy and resources to murdering Jews, not because they were stupid or tactically incompetent, but because that act of destruction was their first priority.

By the end of July, after heavy casualties, Allied forces broke out of the beachheads and began to drive the Germans eastward. In August 1944 the Allies liberated Paris. The next month the western Allies under General Dwight Eisenhower crossed the German border. Germany's new "wonder weapons"—the V-1 and V-2 rockets—were deadly enough for those targeted, and for the slaves who had built them, but they were no match for the onslaught of Soviet, British, and American artillery and tanks during 1944.

In the wake of D-Day and the Soviet offensive of June 1944, Hitler named Goebbels the Reich Plenipotentiary for Total War. Together the Führer and his loyal associate painted a gruesome picture for the Germans of what lay in store if they were defeated. Germans could expect only the harshest of treatment from the vengeful Allies, they warned. Their scare tactics assumed widespread knowledge of the atrocities that Germans had committed throughout the preceding years, especially in the east. It was as if Hitler and Goebbels were taunting the German public with its complicity—we Germans are all in this together, they insisted, and all of us will have to pay the price if we surrender.

Meanwhile Hitler and Goebbels instructed the German press to keep blaming the Jews for the war. U.S. President Roosevelt held out to Europeans the promise of the four freedoms: freedom of speech, freedom of worship, freedom from want, and freedom from fear. Hitler, for his part, threatened the German public with his own version of what Allied victory would mean: "Jewish poison, Bolshevik slaughter, capitalist exploitation, and Anglo-American Imperialism."

It was not love for his people that motivated Hitler's raving but an obsessive fixation on his own goals of race and space. "I will shed no tears for the German people," he had once said in contemplating what defeat would mean.

According to Hitler's logic, any people that allowed itself to be conquered proved its own unworthiness to wear the mantle of the master race.

The Plot of July 20, 1944

Not internal dissension but military defeat eventually brought down the Nazi regime. Nevertheless there was one important attack from within Germany during the last year of the war: the assassination attempt of July 20, 1944.

The plot was the work of a fairly disparate network of opponents of Hitler's regime. The conspirators included high-ranking military men who resented the way Hitler was conducting the war effort. Some of them hoped to overthrow his government and then join up with the western Allies against the Communist Soviet Union. Others more loosely involved in the plan had moral and humanitarian motivations. Appalled by German crimes against civilians in the east, such people saw no option but overthrow of the dictator if Germany's soul was to be saved.

Typical of the humanistic side of the opposition to Hitler was Count Helmuth James von Moltke (1907–1945), a lawyer and devoted Christian who, from 1939 to 1944, was a war administration counselor in the international law section of the German Armed Forces Supreme Command. Moltke organized a group of anti-Nazi friends and like-minded individuals who met during the war to make plans for a new, democratic Germany. Moltke, who struggled with the ethical implications of violence, did not support assassination, but he did urge military leaders to overthrow Hitler. Arrested already in January 1944, Moltke was hanged in Berlin-Plötzensee a year later.

Anti-Communists, conservatives, liberals, monarchists, and dedicated Christians all numbered among those who hoped to see Hitler assassinated or at least removed in July 1944. Although their visions for a reorganized Germany differed, they all saw the need to replace Hitler's rule with a government that would seek peace with the Allies and introduce reforms at home.

The plan for July 20, 1944, itself was straightforward. A high-ranking General Staff officer, Colonel Claus Schenck von Stauffenberg (1907–1944), would plant a bomb at a meeting in the "Wolf's Lair," Hitler's East Prussian headquarters. The death of Hitler would then give the signal for a coup d'état in Berlin.

The plan failed. Stauffenberg set the bomb in his briefcase, placed it under the table around which the meeting was taking place, and then left the building. As he drove toward Berlin he heard the explosion and assumed Hitler had been killed. In fact only part of the explosives went off, and Hitler was barely injured. Instead of a successful coup the conspirators experienced the Führer's terrible revenge.

Stauffenberg was captured and shot by firing squad on the evening of July 20, 1944. He went to his death shouting, "Long live Germany!" Others accused of participation in the plot were hauled before the so-called People's Court, publicly humiliated, and sent to prison. Hitler had many of them killed, some immediately, others only after some months. The assassination attempt provided an excuse for a general crackdown within Germany on anyone suspected of opposition.

A WORLD IN FLAMES

The Volkssturm

In September 1944, Hitler ordered full deployment of Germany's resources against the enemy through creation of a Volkssturm, a "people's storm." The Volkssturm was to mobilize all men between the ages of fifteen and sixty, adding a total of 1.5 million men under arms. Not just intended for local defense, Volkssturm units were to close gaps in the regular Wehrmacht and engage the enemy in combat.

Some of the Volkssturm boys and men fought valiantly and desperately against the Red Army and the western Allies. Some units were well organized and fairly well equipped. Others were thrown together; thirteen-year-old boys stood on bridges expecting to take on men in tanks, and men in their sixties took up arms to try to hold their villages. Some units took appalling losses of life; others collapsed in the face of the Allied advance.

By early 1945 even Nazi true believers had to see that the war was lost. The German army was falling apart. Increasing numbers of men deserted, although military authorities continued to shoot those they caught and in many cases to arrest members of their families. Special courts-martial were set up with the intent of frightening the German troops into reckless resistance. Propaganda announced the existence of the Werewolf organization to continue Nazi efforts behind enemy lines. Roving SS units sought out and punished German civilians who expressed defeatism, advised surrender, or made contact with the enemy. None of these measures stopped the Allied advance, but they did reveal for anyone who had not yet noticed the heartless ruthlessness of National Socialism.

On March 19, 1945, Hitler gave what became known as the Nero Order. He instructed Germans fleeing before the advancing Allies to destroy everything they left behind and leave nothing for the enemy. The Nero Order called for the destruction of all installations serving military purposes, transportation, communication, industry, and supply. At the same time Hitler ordered the defense of German cities under threat of the death penalty for anyone disobeying his orders. When Speer suggested that the Germans too would starve if such measures were implemented, Hitler showed no concern.

The Warsaw Uprising

The unraveling of German power emboldened the regime's opponents in occupied Europe. Once again, as in 1943, the city of Warsaw was the site of a major revolt. By August 1944 the Red Army was approaching Warsaw from the east. Leaders of the Polish Home Army decided to try to liberate the city from the Germans themselves. The Home Army was the independent Polish resistance linked to the Polish military and the government-in-exile. Drawing on an armed force of about sixty thousand fighters, Home Army leaders launched a large-scale uprising.

Instead of continuing their advance into Warsaw, Red Army units stopped on the east bank of the Vistula River and waited. Perhaps they did not want to risk confrontation with the Germans massing on Warsaw, or Stalin preferred to let German forces wipe out the Polish resistance inside the city to clear the way for a Communist takeover. Whatever the reason, the Soviets abandoned the Polish insurgents and turned their attention toward the Balkans.

German forces outnumbered and vastly outgunned the struggling Poles. Throwing everything they had into the effort, the Germans crushed the revolt by October 2, 1944. In the process they killed some one hundred and seventy thousand people in Warsaw. Among the victims were many Jews who were hiding or passing in the city.

By the fall of 1944 the Germans' overall position was weak. Nevertheless, they still had the might to wreak terrible destruction, especially on civilians. Soon after the Warsaw Uprising began, Hitler ordered the city leveled, and German forces carried out the command. Unlike Moscow and Leningrad, which the Germans never conquered, or Paris, which they spared, Warsaw was flattened. It was an act of revenge unique even in the gory history of World War II, but typical of the killing frenzies of the last stage of Hitler's war.

Germany's Allies and the Jews of Hungary

The year 1944 also brought dramatic changes within those countries that had been partners in the German war effort. In September Finland signed an armistice with the Soviet Union and withdrew from the war. Finnish authorities had never handed over the small community of Jews in their country to the Germans to be killed. There had even been a few Finnish Jewish soldiers fighting alongside the Wehrmacht against the Soviet Union. The history of World War II and the Holocaust is full of such strange twists.

For some time already the authoritarian regimes in Romania and Hungary had been eager to get out of the war. By mid-1944 the Germans had to abandon hope of getting their hands on Romanian oil. By the fall of 1944 the Soviets occupied Romania and Bulgaria and were moving toward Hungary and Yugoslavia. Both Romania and Bulgaria signed armistices with the Soviet Union and declared war on Germany.

In March 1944 the Germans took steps to prevent Hungary from capitulating. That month German forces occupied Hungary, their ally, to keep control of the territory and safeguard access to its resources. In October 1944, when the Hungarian leader Admiral Miklos Horthy was caught trying to cut a deal with the Soviets, Hitler had him overthrown. The Germans installed a Hungarian Fascist regime dependent on their support.

Until the spring of 1944 the Jews of Hungary had managed to stay out of German hands. In March 1944, however, when German forces moved into Hungary, they brought with them Adolf Eichmann and a team of experts who were intent on making sure that Hungarian Jews, too, would be annihilated.

In the summer of 1944, Germans and Hungarian collaborators worked together to transport a large proportion of Hungary's Jewish population to Auschwitz-Birkenau to be killed. In hindsight it is clear that the war was lost for the Germans. Nevertheless, they continued to pursue their goal of destruction in those areas still in their control. Between May 15 and July 9, German and Hungarian police crammed some four hundred and thirty-seven thousand Hungarian Jews into 147 transports and sent them north to Auschwitz. As usual, Roma from Hungary shared that fate.

One of those Roma was fifteen-year-old Karoly Lendvai, who came from a town near Budapest. Rounded up by Hungarian police, he and his family walked 40 miles to an internment camp, where they stayed for two weeks. Decades later Lendvai remembers his hunger and the pits overflowing with corpses as typhus raged among the prisoners. Among his most vivid memories is the double-barreled curse a Hungarian guard shouted at him: "Rot, you Jew-Gypsy!"

Aranka Siegal was among the Jews sent from Hungary to Auschwitz-Birkenau, together with her mother and sisters. They came from the town of Berehovo (Beregszász), in Subcarpathian Rus', a region annexed to Hungary in March 1939. In the spring and early summer of 1944, German experts began the deportation process there, moving next to another recently acquired territory, Northern Transylvania. The Hungarian leadership, as well as the Germans, preferred to deal first with Jews they considered "foreign," assuming non-Jews were less likely to protest anything done to these people. The same tendency was evident in France and Bulgaria, where most "foreign Jews" were sent to be killed, whereas the majority of French- and Bulgarian-born Jews survived.

In April 1944, Jews from Berehovo and the surrounding area were confined in ghettos and a month later forced to assemble in two brickyards on the city's outskirts. Neighbors seized the opportunity to plunder their homes, and the Hungarian police and gendarmes who guarded the brickyards took whatever they had with them. Aranka Siegal, who was thirteen at the time, describes having a man at the gate subject her to a crude cavity search.

The two photographs here come from *The Auschwitz Album*, a book of photographs documenting the arrival, selection, and processing of one or more of the transports of Jews from Subcarpathian Rus' that arrived at Auschwitz-Birkenau in May 1944. The album includes 193 photographs. SS men in charge of the Auschwitz photographic laboratory produced the album as a presentation volume for the camp commandant. In the process they no doubt used the labor of the prisoners who worked for them.

Women and children from a May 1944 transport of Jews from Subcarpathian Rus' on the platform at Auschwitz-Birkenau. This photograph was part of a series taken for the Auschwitz album, one of the rare occasions in which photography was allowed in a killing center. Clearly the people shown here were aware of the camera and likely had been arranged and told to look at the photographer. The only man visible, on the right in the striped uniform, is a privileged prisoner, a member of the commando that unloaded the trains. Notice the warm coats many of the people were wearing, not because it was cold but because they wanted to be prepared for what might lie ahead.

Years after the war, Siegal spoke at a workshop for Holocaust educators. When one of the participants brought out a copy of *The Auschwitz Album*, she quickly left the room. She could not bear to open that book, she told me, because she was afraid she would see her mother. Siegal's mother and younger sister had been sent directly to the gas chambers. She did not want an image of how they must have looked moments before their deaths to replace her memories of their faces as she had known them.

Because of the acute shortage of labor, German officials decided to postpone the killing of some of the Hungarian Jews until they had been exploited as slave workers. In 1944 Hitler allowed Himmler and Speer to bring some Jews into Germany to add to the labor force needed for military production. Under those terms, about one hundred thousand Hungarian Jews slated for killing were brought to German labor camps. There these men and women were used to excavate underground bunkers and make armaments. Conditions were terrible, but they had at least a chance to live, something denied to their

Women and children who have been selected for death walk toward the gas chambers at Auschwitz-Birkenau, May 1944. This photograph, like the preceding one, comes from the Auschwitz album. Presented to the camp commandant, the album was found after liberation in an SS barracks by Lili Jacob (later Zelmanovic, now Meier), who appears in one of the pictures. She also recognized her rabbi in a photograph, as well as other members of her community, including her two little brothers.

more than three hundred thousand relatives and friends sent immediately to the gas at Auschwitz-Birkenau.

Why did the Germans persist in the slaughter of the Hungarian Jews? Some scholars have suggested that such determination even in the face of impending defeat showed just how deeply committed many Germans were to the annihilation of Jews. Many German functionaries, however, showed similar dedication in the last stages of the war in their efforts against other victim groups: Poles, slave laborers, and Soviet POWs.

At least some of these last-minute brutalities were motivated by the common drive of self-preservation. By 1944 and 1945 the prospect of the front looked worse all the time. Many German guards, police, and officials of various kinds who were involved in attacks on civilians worked feverishly to prove how crucial their jobs were—jobs they could do in relative safety. Even in Nazi Germany, cowards were probably more common than fanatics.

Some Hungarian Jews survived within Hungary, thanks to rescue efforts on the part of many people, including foreign diplomats and international Jewish groups. The most famous rescuer in Hungary was Raoul Wallenberg, a Swedish businessman and diplomat who helped thousands of Hungarian Jews avoid deportation. Using money raised largely from the Jewish community in the United States, Wallenberg set up safe houses under the jurisdiction of the Swedish embassy, issued Swedish passports, bribed German and Hungarian officials, and even rescued some Jews from transports slated for Auschwitz.

At the end of the war Wallenberg wound up in Soviet hands. His fate is unknown, but it seems likely that he was sent to Siberia as a suspected spy and perished there.

Elie Wiesel is no doubt the best-known Jewish survivor from Hungary, or more precisely Northern Transylvania. His book *Night* is probably the single most widely read personal account of the Holocaust. It recounts the experiences of Wiesel, an adolescent at the time, in the hell of Auschwitz in the deadly last months of the war.

Another Hungarian survivor is Judith Magyar Isaacson, who recorded her experiences in *Seed of Sarah*. Like Wiesel, just a teenager in 1944, Judith Magyar landed in Auschwitz with her mother and a young aunt. Somehow the three women managed to stay together. Once, Judith faced down an SS man who tried to send her to one side of a selection, her mother to another. He let her go with her mother. Camp functionaries offered Judith a position as kapo, but she refused. Judith, her mother, and her aunt were among the Hungarian Jews taken out of Auschwitz and sent as slave laborers to Germany. Beaten, half-starved, and terrified of rape, Judith lived through the final stages of the war. Later she married an American soldier and moved to Maine, where she taught mathematics and served as dean of students at Bates College until she retired.

The Hungarians suspended transports of Jews to Auschwitz in July 1944, and it was only in November that the new Arrow Cross government installed by the German coup ordered the Jews remaining in Budapest into a closed ghetto. The Arrow Cross was brutal: over the next two months its men shot twenty thousand Jews and dumped their bodies into the Danube River. But it could not approach the efficiency of Auschwitz-Birkenau. When the Red Army liberated Budapest in February 1945, there were one hundred thousand Jews still alive in the city.

Auschwitz at the End of the War

The killing center of Auschwitz reached new records of destruction in the final phase of the war. In the summer of 1944, as the transports from Hungary poured in, camp functionaries murdered as many as twelve thousand Jews per day. To mark their achievement, the SS men in charge of the photo lab had another album created, this one with pictures of camp staff enjoying special occasions and leisure activities together. In 2007, an anonymous donor mailed the album to the U.S. Holocaust Memorial Museum.

SS officers and women auxiliaries in 1944 in Solahütte, the SS retreat center outside of Auschwitz. Karl Hoecker, adjutant to the camp commandant, appears in the middle. This photograph was included in an album prepared by or for Hoecker in 1944. Although the pictures were taken during the peak of killings at Auschwitz-Birkenau, none of the photos showed prisoners. Likewise, the pictures of victims in the Auschwitz album excluded guards and administrators, as if the camp's victims and those who victimized them somehow occupied separate worlds.

There was a large operation against Roma that summer too, in which the entire "Gypsy family camp" was wiped out in one night. Of the twenty-three thousand Roma sent to Auschwitz, almost twenty thousand died there. By August 2, 1944, more than thirteen thousand were already dead. That night the remaining six thousand Roma in the camp were gassed. Now that transports of Jews from Hungary had been suspended, camp functionaries had time to kill Roma. German military setbacks, however severe, did not save the lives of those thousands of Roma any more than they spared the Jews of Hungary.

The last year of the war also saw several important incidents of armed resistance within German camps and killing centers. In mid-May 1944, when SS and camp workers first tried to annihilate the Roma camp at Auschwitz-Birkenau, they encountered violent resistance. Roma inside the camp improvised weapons as best they could or fought with their bare hands. Otto Rosenberg, the Sinto teenager from Berlin, was there and remembers the unbelievable tension as the people in his barracks grabbed tools and prepared to die, but the guards and kapos backed down. That defiance may have helped postpone killing of all the Roma in Auschwitz until early August 1944. Meanwhile, Rosenberg and some others, like Judith Magyar, were selected for labor camps.

The most dramatic example of resistance within Auschwitz came in October 1944, when Jewish Sonderkommando prisoners blew up and destroyed Crematorium IV. Some of the necessary explosives were provided by a young Polish Jewish woman named Roza Robota. Assigned to work in an ammunition factory, Robota, along with some other women, began to smuggle small amounts of explosives to the Sonderkommando. The SS arrested and tortured her, but she refused to divulge any information. Robota was hanged in January 1945, shortly before the arrival of the Red Army.

The Race against Destruction

In this stage of the war, the situation changed extremely quickly, and a week, even a day could mean the difference between life and death. In mid-1944, in a camp in Estonia, a Jewish prisoner named Herman Kruk urgently parsed the fragments of news he could gather. Kruk had been a librarian in Warsaw before the war and subsequently in the Vilna ghetto, and perhaps those skills helped him now. Somehow he learned of the attempt to kill Hitler, which added to the urgency he expressed to his diary on July 23, 1944:

> Yesterday was a day of some tension. Today new rumors are spreading: the men will be castrated, the women sent to Königsberg. [. . .] Since the latest events on the eastern Front, since the assassination attempt on H., since Estonia and the entire Baltic has been surrounded, our situation seems to

be coming to a head. We are so upset, our nerves choke us, and every day is superfluous. Everything is more and more irritating. We count not just the days, but the hours and minutes: any minute we may get out of hell. When I write about it, I can hardly believe it. (Kruk, 697–98)

Kruk was shot by the Germans and his body burned, in September 1944, one day before Red Army units reached the area.

In July 1944, Sara Ginaite and other members of her partisan unit participated in the liberation of Vilna. Not far away, the Germans had prepared to retreat by destroying the Kovno ghetto. They used dynamite to explode buildings and force anyone out of hiding. An estimated two thousand people were shot or burned alive. When Sara returned to what had been her home some weeks later, a cloud of smoke still hung over the area. Digging in the ruins she found a few of her family's belongings—a pair of glasses, a kettle, and many photographs. Later she learned that her mother had died in Stutthof. Other relatives had been burned in the ghetto, died on a death march, or at Dachau. Sara's husband's sister survived until liberation but died a day later. Only five

Ruins of the Kovno ghetto, photographed in August 1944 by George Kadish (born Zvi Kadushin). In July 1944, the Germans transported over six thousand Jews from Kovno to Stutthof and other concentration and labor camps. They then razed the ghetto area, doused the ruins with gasoline, and incinerated thousands of people who had evaded the round-ups. Only about one hundred Jews survived the destruction of Kovno ghetto. One of them was Kadish, an amateur photographer who had taken many pictures in the ghetto, some through the buttonhole of his coat. He was also able to retrieve a cache of negatives he had hidden. Kaddish died in 1997.

A new family, including three survivors of the destroyed Kovno ghetto: Tanja, who survived hidden by a non-Jewish Lithuanian woman; Sara Ginaite, a partisan fighter; Misha Rubinson, partisan fighter and leader; and Anja, born after the war. This photograph was taken in 1955.

members of her family remained alive: Sara's sister and brother-in-law; Sara and her husband Misha, and three-year-old Tanya, hidden by a Lithuanian woman.

THE DEATH MARCHES

Beginning in the fall of 1944, as the Germans lost control of much of the territory they had occupied, they began to evacuate many of the camps and killing centers. At the same time, they opened new labor camps in areas still safe from Allied advance. On orders from Himmler, camp officials began to empty the camps of prisoners. They sent the inmates, under guard, marching in columns toward places farther from the ever-advancing front. Throughout late 1944 and early 1945, these trails of half-dead prisoners made their way through the German, Austrian, and Czech countrysides. Their presence brought the Holocaust home to regions that had until then been spared the ravages of war.

Because of the awful numbers killed and dying along the way, the treks have come to be known as death marches. A masterful study by Daniel Blatman traces the contorted journeys of thousands of prisoners and their motley guards. In some respects all of the episodes are similar: hungry, sick men and women forced to walk or ride in open trains and trucks, the weakest and least cooperative of them shot or abandoned to die; brutal, confused guards, many of them hastily recruited from among local police, reserve officers, and soldiers, driving their charges at a murderous pace away from the rapidly advancing fronts, although the swirling chaos of those final four months of the war perilously impaired the information they received and their judgment; the stunned, scared inhabitants of the areas through which the prisoners and their

Prisoners pass through a village on a death march from Dachau to Wolfratshausen, April 1945. As the Allies advanced from east and west and the Third Reich collapsed, hundreds of thousands of prisoners were marched from camp to camp and away from the front lines. Those who moved too slowly or were too sick to continue were shot by guards at the side of the road. As can be seen in this photograph, taken clandestinely by Benno Gantner through the upstairs window of the house he lived in, the death marches brought the horror of Nazi rule into full view of Germans. One of the prisoners in this photo has been identified: in the middle is Katharina Goldstein (Prevost) from Budapest.

guards zigzagged, hunkered down to await the worst and lashing out in panic at the prisoners who embodied their worst fears.

The death marches occurred in agonizing stages. To give just one example: in the late fall of 1944, Germans sent about a thousand Jewish women, many of them Hungarian, from Auschwitz to Gross-Rosen. There the women were forced to dig antitank ditches, in the snow, with little or nothing to eat, and often without shoes.

In early January 1945, as the front advanced, that camp too was evacuated. Guards forced the remaining women to begin a new march. In eight or nine days they had covered only about 60 miles. One hundred and fifty of the women died along the way. Perhaps 20 succumbed to starvation; guards shot another 130.

They were soon evacuated again from their next destination, along with about a thousand additional prisoners. The group was divided, with half of the women being marched toward Helmbrechts in Bavaria, a satellite camp of Flossenbürg. In the middle of winter those women walked about 300 miles. After five weeks, 621 of them arrived at the camp. A few had escaped, and around two hundred had remained at various camps along the way. Another two hundred prisoners did not survive that march. Many were shot by guards.

The camp at Helmbrechts was quite new. Established in the summer of 1944, it housed women prisoners set to work for an armaments firm. As always, they suffered brutal beatings and deadly privation.

In April 1945 Helmbrechts too was emptied. German guards forced some eleven hundred women on yet another trek to nowhere. The group was about half Jewish and half gentile. Guards refused them food and water and forbade inhabitants of the surrounding area to help the prisoners. By many accounts Jewish women received even worse treatment than the others. Around two hundred of the Jewish women died during this stage of the march, just weeks before the war ended. Every one of them would have died had they not been liberated by American forces.

On April 15, 1945, the same day that British troops reached the concentration camp of Bergen-Belsen, SS and camp guards forced tens of thousands of women and men to march westward from the concentration camps of Ravensbrück and Sachsenhausen into territories still in German hands. Hundreds of women died of exhaustion on the march from Ravensbrück. Retreating guards and SS men shot hundreds of others. Some were killed by Allied bombs. Having made it so long, thousands died by the roadside just days away from the end of the war. Death marches continued right up until the German surrender on May 8, 1945. In all, an estimated two hundred and fifty thousand to three hundred and seventy-five thousand people died in such forced marches.

FINAL COLLAPSE

On the military front too, Hitler's Germans exacted a high price from their enemies. At the end of December, Hungary finally completed the reversal of its allegiances. Declaration of war on Germany was followed a month later by an armistice with Moscow.

The Germans came back with a final onslaught in the west. The Ardennes Offensive, called the Battle of the Bulge by the Allies, began in December 1944. That grandiose effort failed, but only after it had cost many lives on both sides.

By early March 1945 the German front in the west had collapsed. U.S. and British forces were advancing in the north, center, and south. German authorities responded by lowering the age for the draft to include boys born in 1929.

In the last months things unraveled quickly. March brought a partisan offensive by Tito's forces against German troops in Yugoslavia. By April the Red Army was in Vienna, and German forces in Italy capitulated at the end of that month. In early May, Czechs revolted against German occupation in Prague. In this climate, even the death of U.S. President Roosevelt on April 12, 1945, did not weaken the Allies' demand for Germany's unconditional surrender.

Finally, in the last stage of the war, many Germans came to feel something of the reality of the conflict their leadership had inflicted on Europe. More Germans died in bombings, expulsions, and the collapse of the military fronts in the last six months of war than in the previous four years together. Approximately one hundred and sixty thousand German soldiers died in 1940–1941. In 1944 that number increased almost fourfold to some six hundred thousand. The all-or-nothing mentality of Hitler's Social Darwinism made all lives cheap, including those of the German people.

If you look at textbooks on Nazi Germany you will notice that many of them label the last days of the Third Reich the *Götterdämmerung*, or "twilight of the gods." The reference is to the end of the ring cycle, a group of operas by Richard Wagner. Hitler loved those operas, and the massive, tragic cataclysm at the end fit his own obsession with heroic death. That morbid fascination came to the fore in the last months of Hitler's regime.

T. S. Eliot's poem "The Hollow Men" (1925) includes the following lines: "This is the way the world ends, not with a bang but a whimper." That description could be applied to the Third Reich, which ended with both an explosion of death and destruction and a whimper of cowardice and defeat.

In a small way, Hitler reaped what he had sown with the principle of divide and conquer when it came to the behavior of his inner circle in the last days. Whimpering treachery turned out to be more characteristic of Hitler's henchmen than that iron loyalty they had loved to espouse. Everyone, it turns out, seemed to have a plan as to how to salvage the Reich—and of course, save his own neck. In February 1945, Goebbels suggested that Hitler should remain head of state but appoint a new chancellor and foreign minister. Goebbels's preferred candidate for the job: himself, obviously. In deference to Himmler's control of the SS empire, Goebbels proposed Himmler for minister of war.

Himmler himself had toyed for a long time already with the idea of a separate peace with Britain. He used his contacts to test the waters, but they were icy cold. Efforts on the part of Luftwaffe commander Göring and German foreign minister Ribbentrop to negotiate a separate peace with the western powers also failed.

Hitler was determined to continue the fight, but on April 22, 1945, two days after his birthday, he fell into depression. Hitler realized that the war was lost, and he knew he could not negotiate a peace himself. Göring, he decided, was the man for the job.

When Göring heard about Hitler's remarks he decided it meant he was to take over. Outraged by that presumption, Hitler denounced Göring as a traitor, dismissed him from his many posts, and had him arrested by the SS. Göring would eventually be captured and brought to trial at Nuremberg, where he committed suicide before his scheduled execution.

Just days after he dismissed Göring, Hitler got word of Himmler's treachery. Furious, he ordered the arrest of the SS leader as well, but Himmler slipped through his hands. Himmler too would manage to kill himself before the Allies could exact justice. In the last days of April, Hitler swung briefly from depression into a kind of manic activity. He ordered a massive counterattack to drive the Soviets back from Berlin. He announced that the western Allies would soon be at war with the Soviet Union and that Germany would be saved. Nothing came of any of these notions.

On April 29, 1945, holed up in his bunker in Berlin, Hitler dictated one final document: his last will and political testament. In it he admonished Germans "punctiliously to observe the racial laws" and to fight on against "the poisoner of all the nations of the world, international Jewry." True to form he blamed the entire course of the lost war on "international Jewry and its helpers." Consistent to the end, Hitler described annihilation of the Jews of Europe as his greatest achievement.

That same day Hitler married Eva Braun. On April 30 the "first soldier of the German Reich" deserted by committing suicide in his bunker. Dead beside him by their own hands were his new wife, the loyal Goebbels, and Goebbels's wife and six children. Hitler's war would end as it had started—with a lie. His chosen successor, Admiral Karl Dönitz, reported by radio to the nation that its Führer had sustained "heroic death in battle." Two days later, the city of Berlin surrendered to the Soviets. Hitler's successors signed documents of unconditional surrender on May 8, 1945.

The reality of how Nazi rule ended sweeps away the myth of order that has grown up around Hitler's regime. There was neither order nor glory to his demise. No heroic struggle marked his death, only cowardice, the ruin of his own people, and lies.

The Nazi revolution had promised a new awakening. Instead it brought destruction and death far beyond the borders of Germany. An estimated 55 million people died worldwide in World War II. Among them were more than 5 million German soldiers. At least 27 million Soviet citizens were dead, as well as millions of Poles, perhaps a million Yugoslavs, and scores of other people from all over Europe. Close to 6 million Jews were murdered, and Jewish civilization was almost eradicated from Europe.

Still, even in the spring of 1945, Jews celebrated Passover. The U.S. Army Chaplain Max Eichhorn held services in a synagogue in France, in territory still behind German lines. Thousands of miles to the east, a group of Polish Jewish refugees celebrated Passover in Soviet Central Asia. The photograph shows something quite remarkable, and in April 1945 possible only in the Soviet interior: Polish Jewish children, smiling and healthy, together with their parents, baking matzah.

Jewish refugees from Poland who survived World War II in the Soviet interior bake matzah for the Passover holiday. Pictured are members of the Bankir and Szczukowski families. The Szczukowkis fled Lodz in 1939, first to Siberia and in 1941 to the Zamin district of Uzbekistan.

Conclusion

LEGACIES OF ATROCITY

Deciding how to end a history of the Holocaust may be even more difficult than choosing where to begin. The Holocaust and its repercussions extend beyond May 1945 in so many ways. And what about the fundamental question: is the ending happy or sad? Do we conclude with uplifting and inspiring themes—liberation, survival, resilience, success, justice—or with grief, loss, and the suffering and failure evident in displacement, persistent antisemitism, and subsequent genocides?

Reflection on the Holocaust, its reverberations, and legacies suggests that resilience and devastation, survival and loss, life and death cannot really be separated, not in this case. With destruction of such magnitude, every outcome, no matter how triumphant, is steeped in sadness. At the same time, even the most horrific accounts seem to include some spark of light—a gesture of kindness, expressions of defiance and dignity, the miracle of survival. Efforts to conclude a history of the Holocaust neatly or to achieve closure oversimplify the past and its influence on the present and future. Even worse, such attempts often end up appropriating the power of the past for current agendas.

Returning to the personal account with which this book began illustrates some long-term echoes of the Holocaust. Henry Friedlander lived through Nazi Berlin, the Lodz ghetto, Auschwitz-Birkenau, and a series of death marches that passed through the camps of Ravensbrück and Neuengamme. His is a story of survival against all odds. But Friedlander never called himself a survivor. He disliked that label because of the way it was used to imply something heroic or remarkable. Survival, he insisted, was only a matter of chance.

Friedlander emerged from Hitler's Europe alone. His mother was killed in Birkenau; his father chose to stay in Germany rather than go to Canada with his teenaged son. Yet Friedlander built a full and successful life. He made many friends, got married twice, and had children and grandchildren. He became an American citizen and a renowned historian of the Holocaust whose most important contribution was to demonstrate the connections between Nazi murders of the disabled and of Jews. He advocated including the Roma into understandings of the Holocaust as well. An expert on postwar trials, Friedlander carried his commitment to pursuing justice into the contemporary world. He taught for a time at a historically black college in Louisiana and was an outspoken opponent of racism. For years he was the key instructor in a course for state trial court judges across the United States, called "When Justice Fails," designed to examine the case of Nazi Germany in order to educate judges about what can be at stake in applying certain laws. The German state of Lower Saxony awarded him a medal of honor for his leadership in redesigning the Bergen-Belsen memorial.

But Friedlander was always conscious of the limits to understanding the Holocaust. "When all is said and done," he wrote, "I am still unable to fathom why seemingly normal men and women were able to commit such extraordinary crimes." In his view, attempts to replicate what they did in a laboratory—he mentioned the famous Milgram experiment—could not succeed, because the "antiseptic experimental setting" was too distant from the "grisly reality of the killing centers." The T-4 killers, he continued, "confronted real human beings as victims and saw their agony." The subjects in Milgram's experiment might not grasp the pain that they could inflict, "but the Nazi killers, even if they lacked all imagination, could not avoid knowing what they were doing. They understood the consequences of their deeds" (Friedlander, 249).

Only toward the end of his life did Henry Friedlander speak in public about his personal experience of the Holocaust. Even many colleagues and friends had no idea he had been in Auschwitz. In 2008, at a conference of Holocaust scholars, Friedlander asked to say a few words at the closing banquet. "Everyone who survived was rescued by someone," he began. "To save oneself didn't happen at all." Friedlander's rescuer in Birkenau was a Communist prisoner, a kapo. They bonded because they came from the same district of Berlin and spoke the same dialect. One day Friedlander got caught in a round-up of boys to be sent to the gas. He thought he was finished until he saw "his kapo" with a group of other privileged prisoners and guards. He approached the man and blurted out the first words that came to his mind: "I don't belong here." How absurd, he recounted, as if anyone belonged in that place.

The kapo told Friedlander to hide in his barracks and not make a sound. Lying on the floor, afraid even to breathe, the fourteen-year-old heard the trucks and then the screams of the other boys. "I can tell you, sometimes I still hear those screams today," he said. "I'm a historian," he told the scholars in the room. "I know how to write about the Holocaust. But how do I write about that?"

Friedlander had a few more chances to talk about his experience of the Holocaust, including to the Parliament of Lower Saxony. In early 2009, he suffered a massive stroke that left him unable to speak. He died in October 2012.

Liberation and Loss

The arrival of Allied forces and the collapse of Nazi Germany could not undo or even immediately stop the spiral of destruction unleashed by years of brutality. Although in hindsight it is easy to speak of liberation, for many individuals and groups of people, the end of the war meant continued and

Jewish youth liberated at Buchenwald lean out of a train as it pulls away from the station, June 1945. The train, marked with the phrase, "Hitler kaput" (Hitler is finished), was en route to a home in France run by the Oeuvre de Secours aux Enfants, a Jewish humanitarian organization. This photo comes from the collection of Romek Wajsman (later Robert Waisman), from Poland, one of one thousand Jewish child survivors found by American troops when they arrived at Buchenwald in April 1945. It is a joyous image, but there is also something restrained about the boys, moving into an unknown future, many of them quite alone.

even new forms of misery. The defeat and total collapse of Hitler's Germany unleashed a movement of people within Europe, some of it voluntary, much of it coerced. Wartime atrocities created urgent demands for justice, even as the enormity of the crimes committed and the overwhelming death and destruction made any kind of restitution painfully inadequate and often impossible. Whether they had been victims, perpetrators, or bystanders in Nazi barbarity—and many Europeans had reason to count themselves in more than one of those categories—people faced the challenge of building lives for themselves and what was left of their families and communities with scarce resources and restricted freedom, and in a climate of distrust and grief.

As Allied troops moved into German-held territory in the last stages of the war, they encountered shocking scenes. The Soviets were the first to reach the major killing centers. Even they, many of whom had experienced and witnessed Nazi German brutality firsthand, were stunned by the horror of

Jewish refugees who had fled to Bukhara during the war gather for a meeting on Victory Day, May 9, 1945 (observed a day later in the Soviet Union than in the West). Saloman (Salek) Liwer, who is credited with this photograph, fled with his family from Bedzin in western Poland to Lvov in September 1939, only to be deported in 1940 by the Soviets to Archangel in northern Siberia. A year later they were allowed to move to Tashkent, but food shortages forced them to relocate to Bukhara in Uzbekistan, where they survived the war. Liwer returned to Poland, then spent several years in DP camps in Austria before immigrating to Israel in 1949. Looking up at the photographer, the faces of the people assembled here suggest not euphoria but uncertainty, relief, and cautious optimism. Where next?

Soviet troops lead German POWs past the Majdanek crematoria and the remains of prisoners killed there. Horrified by the scenes they encountered in camps in Poland, Austria, and Germany, the Allies often forced captured German soldiers and local civilians to view the remains of murdered prisoners and bury their bodies. In a role reversal, a Soviet soldier can be seen here filming the Germans as they file by the grisly display.

Majdanek and Auschwitz. Soldiers from the United States and Great Britain who fought their way into Germany from the west were even less prepared for what they found: mass graves, abandoned camps, boxcars full of corpses, and emaciated, dying people.

On April 15, 1945, the first British tanks entered the concentration camp of Bergen-Belsen. Terrorized and enfeebled, inmates of the camp could not believe they were free. And in fact, freedom did not come easily. After initial contact, the British moved on. For the next forty-eight hours, the camp was only nominally under British control. Hungarian soldiers whom the Germans had stationed there as guards remained in command. In two days they shot more than eighty prisoners, Jews and non-Jews, for such offenses as taking potato peels from the kitchen. Even after British and Canadian troops entered Belsen in force, for more than two weeks three hundred inmates continued to die daily of typhus and starvation. Suffering on the scale of the Holocaust did not simply disappear with the arrival of the Allied liberators.

The images captured on film by photographers and journalists who accompanied and followed Allied forces horrified people back home, just

A young Hungarian Jew identifies the body of his father, who was among the prisoners from Flossenbürg shot in the woods on a death march. As Allied forces approached, inmates of Flossenbürg were sent by train toward Dachau, only to be forced on foot when Allied bombers destroyed the trains and rail lines. Those eventually liberated had survived not only beatings and mass executions perpetrated by their guards but also attacks from Allied planes pursuing the fleeing Germans. Notice the American with a camera on the left and the German civilians moving corpses on the right. Here the headgear differentiates Americans from the Hungarian and the Germans.

as the sights themselves stunned and sickened the soldiers who saw them firsthand. Decades later those images continue to haunt us and to shape the way we perceive and present atrocities in our own time. The questions they raise remain pressing even though they have almost become clichés: How could human beings do such things to other people? How can we go on living in a world where crimes and agony of such magnitude are possible?

The fate of N. highlights several issues in the aftermath of the Holocaust and World War II. Like many stories that end in death, the details can only be pieced together in a fragmentary way, but they are nonetheless significant. This account begins in the mid-1930s in the Soviet Union. Frightened by manifestations of antisemitism under Stalin, a young Russian Jew whom we will call N. decided to leave his home and head west. He settled in France, where he built a life for himself until the Germans invaded in 1940, and his existence again became precarious.

For a while N. succeeded in evading the Nazi dragnet, but sometime in 1942 or 1943 German or French police rounded him up, along with many other foreign Jews living in France, and sent him east to a Nazi camp. Against terrible odds, N. survived more than a year as a prisoner and slave of Nazi Germany. In mid-April 1945, when British troops arrived at the concentration camp Bergen-Belsen, N. was one of the inmates liberated.

Under the terms of an Allied agreement, N., a citizen of the Soviet Union, was turned over to Soviet authorities. Instead of relief from years of torment at Nazi German hands, he soon found himself again on a deportation transport, this time to Siberia. Suspicious of the loyalty of Soviet citizens who had spent years outside the country, Stalin had tens of thousands of people like N.—Jews, POWs, forced laborers—sent directly from their "liberation" to labor camps and prisons in remote regions, where they toiled in massive industrialization projects.

N. did not survive this second round of abuse. N.'s son, who lived through the war in France and later moved to New York, spent years trying to trace his father through the Red Cross and other international organizations. Decades after the war ended, he received the news he had long feared: his father had died in Siberia.

For those who survived, the end of World War II brought the realization of all that had been destroyed. Alone, without family or friends, often far from what had been their homes, many survivors, particularly Jews, had nowhere to go. Separated from their parents for years, some Jewish children no longer knew their birth names or even that they came from Jewish families. Many Jews had seen their gentile neighbors turn against them, denouncing them to Nazi officials and stealing their possessions. Could they now simply go back as if nothing had happened? In Poland, Ukraine, Hungary, and elsewhere, Jewish survivors who returned home to search for family members or reclaim their property often met with hostility from the new "owners." Some Jews were attacked and beaten; some were killed.

Non-Jewish victims of Nazism faced their own problems as they discovered that true liberation was impossible in hostile surroundings. Roma and Sinti who had managed to live through the Nazi assault were no more welcome in many places after May 1945 than they had been before or during the war. Few non-Romany people realized or cared that Nazi Germany had singled out the Roma for particular abuse. Only decades after the war would Roma gradually begin to be acknowledged legally and unofficially as victims of Nazism. In some places—for example, in the western zones of occupied Germany—homosexual men were released from Nazi prisons and concentration camps only to be arrested again and incarcerated under old or new laws that criminalized homosexuality. Jehovah's Witnesses, thousands of whom endured imprisonment in Hitler's Germany, faced renewed persecution, especially under Communism, such as in the eastern zone of Germany, subsequently East Germany. Looking back at Nazism and the Holocaust, we often vow "never again," but for the Jews hounded out of Czech, Polish, and Hungarian cities and towns in 1945 and 1946, the Jehovah's Witnesses sitting in Communist jails in the 1950s, and the Roma crippled and left homeless by arson attacks in Romania in the 1990s, a more apt slogan might have been "Still?"

Displacement and Rebuilding

World War II sparked the movement of the largest number of people in the shortest period of time that the world had ever known. Refugees, fugitives, displaced persons, deportees, and expellees jammed the roadways and waterways of Europe and spilled over into Central Asia and the Americas. Hundreds of thousands of people, like the Russian Jew N., were transported eastward, against their will, as prisoners and laborers of the Soviet Union. More of the wave of motion, however, was westward. An estimated 10 million refugees poured into the western zones of occupied Germany alone, those parts controlled by the United States, Britain, and France.

The motivations of those fleeing west varied. Some had experienced Communism in Stalin's Soviet Union and would risk anything to avoid a return to that misery. Some were ethnic Germans whose families had lived in eastern Europe for generations. Nazi authorities had begun evacuating them already before the war ended, aware that they would be targets for revenge. Many ethnic Germans had eagerly served the cause of race and space and benefited from the deprivation and expropriation of their neighbors. In some cases, Soviet and local authorities expelled ethnic Germans, both to remove potential troublemakers and to free up space for resettlement programs of their own. Ethnic Germans were forced out of western Poland, for example, at least partly because the Soviets needed homes for Poles they had pushed out of the eastern parts of the country, territories annexed to the Soviet Union after 1945.

Other east Europeans—those Latvians, Lithuanians, Ukrainians, and others, who like many ethnic Germans had collaborated with Nazism, also had reasons to flee west, now that their German protectors had retreated. Fearing the wrath of their neighbors, they sought security or at least anonymity. The Red Army's horrific record of rape and plunder as its troops penetrated deeper into central Europe added another urgent reason for many people to try to escape westward.

Throughout 1945 masses of weary travelers crisscrossed Europe—Hungarian Jews trying to go home; ethnic Germans from the Sudetenland making their way north and west; demobilized soldiers, prisoners of war, former slave laborers from Ukraine and Poland. Amid the chaos it is no surprise that war criminals and other fugitives often found it easy to blend in and evade detection. Under such conditions, whose documentation was in order anyway? Who would know if a former SS man or high-ranking Nazi Party boss, or even Heinrich Himmler himself, had simply buried or burned his papers, put on old clothing, and assumed a new identity? Paradoxically, the Nazis, with their obsession with race, blood, and homeland, had created a situation where all of those identities were in flux.

Building on creation during the war of the U.N. Relief and Rehabilitation Administration, the United Nations tried to address some of the most pressing humanitarian concerns stemming from the refugee crisis. U.S. occupation authorities set up camps for displaced persons (DPs) in their zone, which became the first destination of many Jewish survivors. Initially DPs were organized by country of origin, so that Jews, ethnic Germans, and non-German collaborators might find themselves grouped together as Ukrainians, Poles, or Yugoslavs. Subsequently the Americans set up separate facilities for Jews, who had different needs and options from most gentiles.

By late 1946 more than one hundred and fifty thousand Jews lived in DP camps in the U.S. zone, bringing a Jewish presence to parts of Germany that previously had been home to relatively few Jews. Jewish DP camps were sites of Zionist activity, as survivors, especially young people, were urged to leave Europe for Palestine and, after 1948, Israel. Many Jews preferred to wait for visas to the United States, Canada, or Australia, and some accepted options that were often quicker, such as relocation to South Africa, South America, or the Caribbean. An estimated twenty thousand Jews remained in Germany even after the last Jewish DP camp finally closed in 1957. Some of them were too old or sick to travel or be granted visas; some had ties to Germany.

Jewish DP camps were more than just holding places for people waiting to exit. They developed an internal leadership and communal spirit, with cultural and religious activities, educational opportunities, and social and family life. The immediate postwar years saw a baby boom as the birthrate among Jewish DPs rose to remarkable heights, especially in contrast to the unusually low rates for other people in Germany. Those Jewish children must have represented faith in new beginnings and hope for life after so much death.

Justice and Injustice

Despite the urgent demands of daily existence, many people in postwar Europe concerned themselves with questions of justice. Perpetrators and organizers of Nazi crimes went to immense lengths to avoid being brought to account for their deeds. They set up self-help networks and used connections in Turkey, the Middle East, South America, Canada, and the Vatican to get themselves to safety. For example, Franz Stangl, former T-4 operative and subsequently commandant of Sobibor and Treblinka, fled via Turkey and the Middle East to Argentina, where Hitler's expert on Jews and transportation/deportation, Adolf Eichmann, also found refuge. Josef Mengele, the doctor and medical scholar whose vicious experiments at Auschwitz killed thousands of people, made his way to Brazil, where he died in the 1980s.

Of course those victimized by Nazism had very different interests in justice. No acts of revenge or restitution could make up for the deaths of millions, the annihilation of Jewish life in much of Europe, the destruction of property, and the shattering of trust and coexistence. Nevertheless survivors had to begin new lives, and for that they required at least minimal material resources, some acknowledgment of their suffering, and a measure of confidence in the world around them. Seeing some key criminals brought to justice could begin to address those needs as well as combat the sense of meaninglessness that must have threatened to overwhelm many survivors.

People who had been victimized during the war also tried to see some kind of justice done toward members of their own communities who had collaborated with the enemy, or were seen to have done so. The Soviets were actively and often brutally committed to the identification and punishment of traitors. The many investigations, hearings, and commissions they undertook, even before the war was over, were designed to strengthen Stalin's rule at any price, but they also brought to light many atrocities by the Germans and their fellow travelers. In Poland, France, Yugoslavia, and elsewhere there were waves of trials as well as personal and collective acts of retribution against individuals and groups accused of disloyalty to the nation. Women were especially vulnerable to accusations of so-called horizontal collaboration or sleeping with the enemy.

Jews in DP camps set up honor courts that tried individuals deemed to have betrayed the Jewish people. Those who had served as kapos in the camps or as police or members of the Jewish councils in the ghettos were most likely to come under investigation, but suspected denouncers and informants also attracted attention. After establishment of the State of Israel in 1948, there were a number of sensational cases tried in courts, or in the court of public opinion, there.

Already during the war Allied leaders had agreed that the defeated Germany must be denazified and top perpetrators brought to justice. Doing so was necessary for postwar stability, at least some of them believed, because it would make it possible to effect some kind of separation between "Nazis," who needed to be punished, and "Germans," who could and should be integrated into a peaceable world. The International Military Tribunal with the Nuremberg Trials of 1945–1946, a joint effort of all the Allies, served this purpose.

Contrary to what detractors claimed, the trial of twenty-one major war criminals and a handful of central Nazi German organizations at Nuremberg was not sham "victors' justice" or a reflection of some Allied notion of German "collective guilt." Although the trials were not perfect, and Allied cooperation

In June 1945, German civilians from Burgsteinfurt watch a film in the local cinema about the atrocities of the Bergen-Belsen and Buchenwald concentration camps. Some British soldiers called Burgsteinfurt the "village of Hate" because of its silent but noticeable resentment of the Allied occupation. In late May the military government began screening a documentary on the concentration camps. When few residents turned up, British military authorities ordered all four thousand townspeople to attend showings. They were assembled and marched to the cinema.

was severely strained at times, they were real legal proceedings, with witnesses, massive amounts of documentation, and counsels for the defense—and without torture. Some individuals and organizations were acquitted, and those convicted received varying sentences, including death sentences in about half of the cases. The most famous defendant, Hitler's favorite, Hermann Göring, committed suicide in his cell before the order for his execution could be carried out.

The Nuremberg Trials were just one step. The occupying powers, and subsequently local authorities, including Germans and foreign governments—like Israel with the Eichmann trial in 1961—conducted their own hearings,

German civilians from Burgsteinfurt exit the cinema in their town where they were forced to see a film showing atrocities perpetrated in Buchenwald and Bergen-Belsen, May 1945. After the war the Western Allies and Soviets alike made extensive use of photographs and films in public education programs and in trials to draw attention to Nazi crimes.

trials, and deportation proceedings of camp guards, doctors, bureaucrats, members of the Einsatzgruppen, and former SS men accused of lying on their immigration applications to the United States, Canada, and elsewhere. Property of all kinds—art, gold, land, buildings, factories—has been grounds for other kinds of legal cases, commissions, and occasionally settlements. These processes are all important, although they can never bring closure to a past that remains an open wound despite remarkable—perhaps unprecedented—efforts by Germans to come to grips with their nation's cruel past.

In a 1948 photo taken in Linz, Austria, David Greenfield sits in the center of a large Star of David. An estimated million and a half Jewish children were murdered in the Holocaust. In the years immediately following the war, Jewish survivors living in DP camps produced an extraordinary baby boom. Little David's parents and the photographer must have been keenly aware of the significance of this picture, taken in what was once Hitler's hometown, in the year the State of Israel was established.

An Open-Ended History

This history has no uplifting message of redemption. It leaves us only with human beings, with their startling capacities for good and evil, and with an awareness of the complex ties that connect the fates of people and nations all over the world.

One final account may best express these points. This time the story begins in the Netherlands with the birth of a baby girl in 1943. When she was two weeks old, her Jewish parents and older brother were rounded up by German and Dutch police, sent to the transit camp of Westerbork, and from there to Sobibor, where they were murdered.

Somehow the baby escaped that fate. Perhaps her parents hid her or a sympathetic policeman took pity on her. Either way, someone brought her to a beauty parlor run by two young women with connections to the Dutch underground, including people who helped find hiding places for Jewish children.

Here the details become even blurrier. According to one version of events, the women found a family to take the baby, but the arrangement fell through, possibly because the couple would not promise to surrender the girl when the war was over. Meanwhile, the young women had fallen in love with the baby, and—after a coin toss to decide between them—one of them took the child herself and cared for her until 1947, when an uncle from New York managed to locate his niece. Although the Dutch woman could not bear to lose her daughter, she gave the girl up and never saw her again. Growing up in the United States, the girl remembered little from her early years, and her uncle and his wife discouraged all contact with her Dutch foster mother, who subsequently suffered severe emotional problems and died quite young. Only decades later would the twice-orphaned girl, now a mother and grandmother herself, find a way to restore contact with members of her Dutch family. In the process she met people who had known her parents and brother, saw photographs of them, and even was given a few of their belongings.

One could present this account as an inspirational example of heroism and resilience, and those are indeed messages to take away from a study of the Holocaust. At least as significant, however, are the crushing themes of violence and loss, and the unavoidable, heartbreaking decisions that no one should have to make, decisions the scholar Lawrence Langer has dubbed "choiceless choices." These are the realities of the Holocaust and its bitter legacy, a history specific and unique but at the same time firmly embedded in the all-too-familiar global experiences of war and genocide.

SOURCES AND SUGGESTIONS FOR FURTHER READING

Note: Books are listed in the first chapter to which they directly relate. Many of the titles given in one place are helpful elsewhere too. Some relevant movies appear at the end of each chapter list. To the extent possible, I have limited myself to works available in English. I included materials that influenced me or that I consider useful; this does not mean I necessarily agree with everything in them.

WEBSITES

Through the website of the U.S. Holocaust Memorial Museum in Washington, DC, one can access some of the Museum's collections of photographs, maps, documents, and oral testimonies as well as the Holocaust Encyclopedia:

http://www.ushmm.org/

The website of Yad Vashem, the Holocaust Martyrs' and Heroes' Remembrance Authority in Jerusalem, is another valuable resource:

http://www.yadvashem.org/

More than fifty-two thousand survivor accounts are available through the University of Southern California Shoah Foundation Visual History Archive. The full collection can be accessed only at a subscribing institution, but some materials can be viewed on the website:

https://sfi.usc.edu/

INTRODUCTION: HOLOCAUST, WAR, AND GENOCIDE: THEMES AND PROBLEMS

Aly, Götz. *Into the Tunnel: The Brief Life of Marion Samuel, 1931–1943*. Translated by Ann Millin. New York: Metropolitan Books/Henry Holt, 2008.

Bauer, Yehuda. *Rethinking the Holocaust*. New Haven, CT: Yale University Press, 2001.

Berenbaum, Michael, and Abraham J. Peck, eds. *The Holocaust and History: The Known, the Unknown, the Disputed, and the Reexamined*. Bloomington: Indiana University Press in association with the U.S. Holocaust Memorial Museum, 1998.

Bloxham, Donald. *The Final Solution: A Genocide*. New York: Oxford University Press, 2009.

Botwinick, Rita S. *A History of the Holocaust: From Ideology to Annihilation*. 5th ed. Boston: Pearson Education, 2014.

Crane, Susan. "Choosing Not to Look: Representation, Repatriation, and Holocaust Atrocity Photography." *History and Theory* 47, no. 3 (October 2008): 309–30.

Crowe, David. *The Holocaust: Roots, History, and Aftermath*. Boulder, CO: Westview Press, 2008.

Didi-Huberman, Georges. *Images in Spite of All: Four Photographs from Auschwitz*. Translated by Shane B. Lillis. Chicago: University of Chicago Press, 2008.

Friedlander, Henry. *The Origins of Nazi Genocide: From Euthanasia to the Final Solution*. Chapel Hill: University of North Carolina Press, 1995.

Friedländer, Saul. *Nazi Germany and the Jews*. Vol. 1, *The Years of Persecution*. New York: HarperCollins, 1997.

———. *The Years of Extermination: Nazi Germany and the Jews, 1939–1945*. New York: HarperCollins, 2007.

Gerlach, Christian. *Extremely Violent Societies: Mass Violence in the Twentieth-Century World*. Cambridge: Cambridge University Press, 2010.

Goda, Norman J. W. *The Holocaust: Europe, the World, and the Jews 1918–1945*. Boston: Pearson, 2013.

———, ed. *Jewish Histories of the Holocaust: New Transnational Approaches*. New York: Berghahn, 2014.

Hayes, Peter, ed. *How Was It Possible? A Holocaust Reader*. Lincoln: University of Nebraska Press and the Jewish Foundation for the Righteous, 2015.

Hayes, Peter, and John K. Roth, eds. *The Oxford Handbook of Holocaust Studies*. New York: Oxford University Press, 2010.

Heineman, Elizabeth D., ed. *Sexual Violence in Conflict Zones: From the Ancient World to the Era of Human Rights*. Philadelphia: University of Pennsylvania Press, 2011.

Herzog, Dagmar, ed. *Brutality and Desire: War and Sexuality in Europe's Twentieth Century*. London: Palgrave Macmillan, 2009.

Hilberg, Raul. *The Destruction of the European Jews*. 3 vols. 3rd ed. New Haven, CT: Yale University Press, 2003.

————, ed. *Documents of Destruction: Germany and Jewry, 1933–1945.* Chicago: Quadrangle, 1971.

Hirsch, Marianne. *Family Frames: Photography, Postmemory, and the Holocaust.* Cambridge, MA: Harvard University Press, 1997.

Jaskot, Paul B. "'Realism'? The Place of Images in Holocaust Studies." In *Lessons and Legacies X: Back to the Sources: Reexamining Perpetrators, Victims, and Bystanders,* edited by Sara R. Horowitz, 68–88. Evanston, IL: Northwestern University Press, 2012.

Kiernan, Ben. *Blood and Soil: A World History of Genocide and Extermination from Sparta to Darfur.* New Haven: Yale University Press, 2007.

Knowles, Anne Kelly, Tim Cole, and Alberto Giordano, eds. *Geographies of the Holocaust.* Bloomington: Indiana University Press, 2014.

Marrus, Michael R. *The Holocaust in History.* New York: Meridian, 1989.

Milton, Sybil. "The Context of the Holocaust." *German Studies Review* 13, no. 2 (1990): 269–83.

Morgan, Michael L., ed. *A Holocaust Reader: Responses to Nazi Extermination.* New York: Oxford University Press, 2001.

Naimark, Norman. *Fires of Hatred: Ethnic Cleansing in Twentieth-Century Europe.* Cambridge, MA: Harvard University Press, 2001.

Pergher, Roberta, Mark Roseman, Jürgen Zimmerer, Shelley Baranowski, Doris L. Bergen, and Zygmunt Bauman. "The Holocaust: A Colonial Genocide? A Scholars' Forum." *Dapim: Studies on the Holocaust* 27, no. 1 (2013): 40–73.

Petropoulos, Jonathan, and John K. Roth, eds. *Gray Zones: Ambiguity and Compromise in the Holocaust and Its Aftermath.* New York: Berghahn, 2005.

Shneer, David. *Through Soviet Jewish Eyes: Photography, War, and the Holocaust.* New Brunswick, NJ: Rutgers University Press, 2011.

Spicer, Kevin, ed. *Antisemitism, Christian Ambivalence, and the Holocaust.* Bloomington: Indiana University Press, 2007.

Stoltzfus, Nathan, and Doris L. Bergen. "In Memoriam: Henry (Heinz Egon) Friedlander, 1930–2012." *German Studies Association Newsletter* 37, no. 2 (Winter 2012–2013): 61–79.

Stone, Dan. *Histories of the Holocaust.* New York: Oxford University Press, 2010.

Struk, Janina. *Photographing the Holocaust: Interpreting the Evidence.* London: Tauris, 2004.

Waxman, Zoë Vania. *Writing the Holocaust: Identity, Testimony, Representation.* New York: Oxford University Press, 2006.

Weinberg, Gerhard L. *Germany's War for World Conquest and the Extermination of Jews.* Joseph and Rebecca Meyerhoff lecture. Washington, DC: U. S. Holocaust Memorial Museum, 1995.

Weiss-Wendt, Anton, ed. *The Nazi Genocide of the Roma: Reassessment and Commemoration.* New York: Berghahn, 2013.

Weitz, Eric D. *A Century of Genocide: Utopias of Race and Nation.* Princeton, NJ: Princeton University Press, 2003.

Wiese, Christian, and Paul Betts, eds. *Years of Persecution, Years of Extermination: Saul Friedländer and the Future of Holocaust Studies.* London: Continuum, 2010.

Wieviorka, Annette. *The Era of the Witness.* Translated by Jared Stark. Ithaca, NY: Cornell University Press, 2006.

Yahil, Leni. *The Holocaust: The Fate of European Jewry.* Translated by Ina Friedman and Haya Galai. New York: Oxford University Press, 1990.

Zemel, Carol. *Looking Jewish: Visual Culture and Modern Diaspora.* Bloomington: Indiana University Press, 2015.

1. DRY TIMBER: PRECONDITIONS

Arendt, Hannah. *The Origins of Totalitarianism.* New York: Harcourt Brace, 1951.

Baranowski, Shelley. *Nazi Empire: German Colonialism and Imperialism from Bismarck to Hitler.* Cambridge: Cambridge University Press, 2011.

Bartov, Omer. *Mirrors of Destruction: War, Genocide, and Modern Identity.* New York: Oxford University Press, 2000.

Beachy, Robert. *Gay Berlin: Birthplace of a Modern Identity.* New York: Knopf, 2014.

Berkowitz, Michael. *The Crime of My Very Existence: Nazism and the Myth of Jewish Criminality.* Berkeley: University of California Press, 2007.

Breitman, Richard. *The Architect of Genocide: Himmler and the Final Solution.* New York: Knopf, 1991.

Burleigh, Michael. *Death and Deliverance: "Euthanasia" in Germany c. 1900–1945.* New York: Cambridge University Press, 1997.

Burleigh, Michael, and Wolfgang Wippermann. *The Racial State: Germany 1933–1945.* New York: Cambridge University Press, 1991.

Confino, Alon. *A World without Jews: The Nazi Imagination from Persecution to Genocide.* New Haven: Yale University Press, 2014.

Crowe, David M. *A History of the Gypsies of Eastern Europe and Russia.* New York: Palgrave Macmillan, 1995.

Eley, Geoff. *Nazism as Fascism: Violence, Ideology, and the Ground of Consent in Germany, 1930–1945.* New York: Routledge, 2013.

Engel, David. *Historians of the Jews and the Holocaust.* Stanford, CA: Stanford University Press, 2010.

Fout, John C. *Forbidden History: The State, Society, and the Regulation of Sexuality in Modern Europe.* Chicago: University of Chicago Press, 1992.

Gay, Peter. *My German Question: Growing Up in Nazi Berlin.* New Haven, CT: Yale University Press, 1998.

Gellately, Robert, and Nathan Stoltzfus, eds. *Social Outsiders in Nazi Germany.* Princeton, NJ: Princeton University Press, 2001.

Ginaite-Rubinson, Sara. *Pro Memoria: Moments in Time, 1911–2012.* A photographic album of the Virovichius, Ginas, Rubinsonas and Benjaminovichius (Benn) families. Toronto: Self-published, 2012.

Gitelman, Zvi. *A Century of Ambivalence: The Jews of Russia and the Soviet Union, 1881 to the Present.* 2nd ed. Bloomington: Indiana University Press, 2001.

Hamburg, Gary, Thomas Sanders, and Ernest Tucker, eds. *Russian-Muslim Confrontation in the Caucasus: Alternative Visions of the Conflict between Imam Shamil and the Russians, 1830–1859.* London: Routledge Curzon, 2004.

Hancock, Ian. "The Roots of Antigypsyism: To the Holocaust and After." In *Confronting the Holocaust: A Mandate for the 21st Century,* edited by C. Jan Colijn and Marcia Sachs Littell, 19–49: *Studies in the Shoah* 19. Lanham, MD: University Press of America, 1997.

Hanebrink, Paul. *In Defense of Christian Hungary: Religion, Nationalism, and Antisemitism, 1890–1944.* Ithaca, NY: Cornell University Press, 2006.

Hochschild, Adam. *King Leopold's Ghost: A Story of Greed, Terror, and Heroism in Colonial Africa.* New York: Mariner, 1999.

Hochstadt, Steve, ed. *Sources of the Holocaust.* New York: Palgrave Macmillan, 2004.

Hull, Isabel. *Absolute Destruction: Military Culture and the Practices of War in Imperial Germany.* Ithaca, NY: Cornell University Press, 2005.

Jelinek, Yeshayahu A. *The Carpathian Diaspora: The Jews of Subcarpathian Rus' and Mukachevo, 1848–1948.* Translated by Joel A. Linsider. Boulder, CO: Eastern European Monographs. 2007.

King, Christine Elizabeth. *The Nazi State and the New Religions: Five Cases in Non-Conformity.* New York: Edwin Mellen, 1982.

Kopp, Kristin Leigh. *Germany's Wild East: Constructing Poland as Colonial Space.* Ann Arbor: University of Michigan Press, 2012.

Kramer, Alan. *Dynamic of Destruction: Culture and Mass Killing in the First World War.* Oxford: Oxford University Press, 2007.

Langbehn, Volker, and Mohammad Salama, eds. *German Colonialism: Race, the Holocaust, and Postwar Germany.* New York: Columbia University Press, 2011.

Langmuir, Gavin I. *History, Religion, and Antisemitism.* Berkeley: University of California Press, 1990.

Lemkin, Raphael. *Axis Rule in Occupied Europe: Laws of Occupation, Analysis of Government, Proposals for Redress.* Edited by Samantha Power. Clark, NJ: Lawbook Exchange, 2005.

Levy, Richard S., ed. *Antisemitism in the Modern World: An Anthology of Texts.* Lexington, MA: Heath, 1991.

Lipton, Sara. *Dark Mirror: The Medieval Origins of Anti-Jewish Iconography.* New York: Metropolitan, 2014.

Liulevicius, Vejas. *War Land on the Eastern Front: Culture, National Identity and German Occupation in World War I.* Cambridge and New York: Cambridge University Press, 2000.

Marhoefer, Laurie. *Sex and the Weimar Republic: German Homosexual Emancipation and the Rise of the Nazis.* Toronto: University of Toronto Press, 2015.

Marks, Sally. "Black Watch on the Rhine: A Study in Propaganda, Prejudice, and Prurience." *European Studies Review* 13, no. 3 (1983): 297–334.

Mazower, Mark. *Dark Continent: Europe's Twentieth Century.* New York: Knopf, 1998.

Meyerson, Mark D. *A Jewish Renaissance in Fifteenth-Century Spain.* Princeton, NJ: Princeton University Press, 2004.

Mosse, George. *The Nationalization of the Masses.* New York: Howard Fertig, 1975.

Müller-Hill, Benno. *Murderous Science: Elimination by Scientific Selection of Jews, Gypsies and Others in Germany, 1933–1945.* Translated by George R. Fraser. Plainview, NY: Cold Spring Harbor Laboratory Press, 1998.

Nirenberg, David. *Anti-Judaism: The Western Tradition.* New York: Norton, 2013.

———. *Communities of Violence: Persecution of Minorities in the Middle Ages.* Princeton, NJ: Princeton University Press, 1996.

Penslar, Derek. *Jews and the Military: A History.* Princeton, NJ: Princeton University Press, 2013.

Petrovsky-Shtern, Yohanan. *The Golden Age Shtetl: A New History of Jewish Life in East Europe.* Princeton, NJ: Princeton University Press, 2014.

Poliakov, Léon. *Harvest of Hate: The Nazi Program for the Destruction of the Jews of Europe.* New York: Holocaust Library, 1979.

Polonsky, Antony. *The Jews of Russia and Poland: A Short History.* Abridged ed. Oxford: Littman, 2013.

Pomerantz, Jack, and Lyric Wallwork Winik. *Run East: Flight from the Holocaust.* Urbana: University of Illinois Press, 1997.

Poore, Carol. *Disability in Twentieth-Century German Culture.* Ann Arbor: University of Michigan Press, 2007.

Probst, Christopher J. *Demonizing the Jews: Luther and the Protestant Church in Nazi Germany.* Bloomington: Indiana University Press, 2012.

Rodrigue, Aron. "Sephardim and the Holocaust." Occasional paper. Washington, DC: U.S. Holocaust Memorial Museum, 2005.

Roseman, Mark, Devin Pendas, and Richard Wetzell, eds. *Beyond the Racial State.* New York: Cambridge University Press, 2016.

Shternshis, Anna. *Soviet and Kosher: Jewish Popular Culture in the Soviet Union, 1923–1939.* Bloomington: Indiana University Press, 2006.

Siegal, Aranka. *Upon the Head of the Goat: A Childhood in Hungary, 1939–1944.* New York: Puffin, 1981.

Stern, Fritz. *The Politics of Cultural Despair.* Berkeley: University of California Press, 1961.

Stopes, Marie Carmichael, and Ruth E. Hall, eds. *Dear Dr. Stopes: Sex in the 1920s.* London: Deutsch, 1978.

Wasserstein, Bernard. *On the Eve: The Jews of Europe before the Second World War.* New York: Simon & Schuster, 2012.

Weiss, Sheila Faith. *The Nazi Symbiosis: Human Genetics and Politics in the Third Reich.* Chicago: University of Chicago Press, 2010.

Wette, Wolfram. *The Wehrmacht: History, Myth, Reality.* Translated by Deborah Lucas Schneider. Cambridge, MA: Harvard University Press, 2007.

Wistrich, Robert M. *Antisemitism: The Longest Hatred.* New York: Pantheon, 1992.

Zimmerer, Jürgen. "The First Genocide of the Twentieth Century: The German War of Destruction in South-West Africa (1904–1908) and the Global History of Genocide." Translated by Martina Cucchiara. In *Lessons and Legacies VIII*, edited by Doris L. Bergen, 34–64. Evanston, IL: Northwestern University Press, 2008.

Films

Aferim! Directed by Radu Jude. Romania, 2015.

The Longest Hatred: The History of Anti-Semitism. Directed by Rex Bloomstein. United Kingdom, 1993.

Namibia: Genocide and the Second Reich. Directed by David Adetayo Olusoga. United Kingdom, 2005.

Paragraph 175. Directed by Jeffrey Friedman and Rob Epstein. United Kingdom/Germany/United States, 2000.

A People Uncounted: The Untold Story of the Roma. Directed by Aaron Yeger. Canada, 2011.

Theologians under Hitler. Directed by Steven D. Martin. United States, 2005.

2. LEADERSHIP AND WILL: HITLER, THE NATIONAL SOCIALIST GERMAN WORKERS' PARTY, AND NAZI IDEOLOGY

Abel, Theodore. *Why Hitler Came into Power.* 1938. Reprint, Cambridge, MA: Harvard University Press, 1986.

Allen, William Sheridan. *The Nazi Seizure of Power.* Rev. ed. New York: Watts, 1984.

Brown, Timothy S. *Weimar Radicals: Nazis and Communists between Authenticity and Performance.* New York: Berghahn, 2009.

Burrin, Philippe. *Hitler and the Jews: The Genesis of the Holocaust.* Translated by Patsy Southgate. London: Arnold; New York: Routledge, Chapman and Hall, 1994.

Fischer, Conan. *Stormtroopers: A Social, Economic, and Ideological Analysis, 1929–35.* London: George Allen & Unwin, 1983.

Haffner, Sebastian. *The Meaning of Hitler.* Translated by Ewald Osers. Cambridge, MA: Harvard University Press, 1983.

Hamann, Brigitte. *Hitler's Vienna.* Translated by Thomas Thornton. New York: Oxford University Press, 1999.

Hastings, Derek. *Catholicism and the Roots of Nazism: Religious Identity and the Early Nazi Movement in Munich.* Oxford: Oxford University Press, 2009.

Hitler, Adolf. *Hitler's Second Book: The Unpublished Sequel to Mein Kampf.* Edited by Gerhard L. Weinberg, 1st English language ed. Lancaster: Gazelle, 2003.

———. *Hitler's Table Talk, 1941–1944: His Private Conversations.* Edited by Norman Cameron, R. H. Stevens, H. R. Trevor-Roper, and Gerhard L. Weinberg. Translated by Norman Cameron. New updated ed. New York: Enigma Books, 2008.

Jäckel, Eberhard. *Hitler's World View: A Blueprint for Power.* Cambridge, MA: Harvard University Press, 1981.

Kershaw, Ian. *Hitler: 1889–1936, Hubris.* New York: Norton, 1998.

———. *Hitler: 1936–1945, Nemesis.* New York: Norton, 2000.

———. "'Working towards the Führer': Reflections on the Nature of the Hitler Dictatorship." In *Hitler, the Germans, and the Final Solution,* 29–48. New Haven: Yale University Press, 2008.

Lochner, Louis P., ed. *The Goebbels Diaries 1942–43.* Translated by Louis P. Lochner. Garden City, NY: Doubleday, 1948. A complete edition of the diaries is available in German. See *Die Tagebücher von Joseph Goebbels,* edited by Elke Fröhlich. Part I: *Aufzeichnungen 1923–1941.* 14 vols. Part II: *Diktate 1941–1945.* 15 vols. Munich: K.G. Saur, 1993–2006.

Longerich, Peter. *Goebbels: A Biography.* Translated by Alan Bance, Jeremy Noakes, and Lesley Sharpe. New York: Random House, 2015.

Marks, Sally. "The Myths of Reparations." *Central European History* 11, no. 3 (1978): 231–35.

Noakes, Jeremy, and Geoffrey Pridham, eds. *Nazism, 1919–1945. Vol. 1: The Rise to Power, 1919–1934: A Documentary Reader.* Exeter: University of Exeter, 1998.

Reck-Malleczewen, Friedrich Percyval (Fritz Percy). *Diary of a Man in Despair.* Translated by Paul Ruebens. New York: Macmillan, 1970.

Rosenbaum, Ron. *Explaining Hitler: The Search for the Origins of His Evil.* New York: Random House, 1998.

Rosenfeld, Gavriel D. *Hi Hitler! How the Nazi Past is Being Normalized in Contemporary Culture.* Cambridge: Cambridge University Press, 2015.

Sax, Benjamin, and Dieter Kuntz, eds. *Inside Hitler's Germany.* Lexington, MA: Heath, 1992.

Schleunes, Karl A. *The Twisted Road to Auschwitz: Nazi Policy toward German Jews, 1933–39.* Champaign, IL: University of Illinois Press, 1990.

Stoltzfus, Nathan. *Hitler's Compromises: Coercion and Consensus in Nazi Germany.* New Haven, CT: Yale University Press, 2016.

Weber, Thomas. *Hitler's First War: Adolf Hitler, the Men of the List Regiment, and the First World War.* Oxford: Oxford University Press, 2011.

Weinberg, Gerhard L. *Germany, Hitler, and World War II: Essays in Modern German and World History.* New York: Cambridge University Press, 1995.

Films

The Architecture of Doom. Directed by Peter Cohen. Sweden, 1991.

The Dark Charisma of Adolf Hitler. Written and Produced by Laurence Rees. United Kingdom, 2012.

The Great Dictator. Directed by Charles Chaplin. United States, 1940.

Triumph of the Will. Directed by Leni Riefenstahl. Germany, 1934.

3. FROM REVOLUTION TO ROUTINE: NAZI GERMANY, 1933–1938

Bajohr, Frank. *"Aryanization" in Hamburg: The Economic Exclusion of Jews and the Confiscation of Their Property in Nazi Germany.* Translated by George Wilkes. New York: Berghahn, 2001.

Bankier, David. *The Germans and the Final Solution: Public Opinion under Nazism.* Cambridge, MA: Basil Blackwell, 1992.

Baranowski, Shelley. *Strength through Joy: Consumerism and Mass Tourism in the Third Reich.* Cambridge: Cambridge University Press, 2004.

Barkai, Avraham. *From Boycott to Annihilation: The Economic Struggle of German Jews, 1933–1943.* Hanover: University Press of New England, 1989.

Bergen, Doris L. *Twisted Cross: The German Christian Movement in the Third Reich.* Chapel Hill: University of North Carolina Press, 1996.

Bergerson, Andrew Stuart. *Ordinary Germans in Extraordinary Times: The Nazi Revolution in Hildesheim.* Bloomington: Indiana University Press, 2004.

Breitman, Richard, Barbara McDonald Stewart, and Severin Hochberg, eds. *Advocate for the Doomed: The Diaries and Papers of James G. McDonald, 1932–1935.* Bloomington: Indiana University Press, 2007.

Bridenthal, Renate, Atina Grossmann, and Marion Kaplan, eds. *When Biology Became Destiny: Women in Weimar and Nazi Germany.* New York: Monthly Review Press, 1984.

Caplan, Jane, ed. *Nazi Germany.* New York: Oxford University Press, 2008.

Dawidowicz, Lucy S., ed. *A Holocaust Reader.* West Orange, NJ: Behrman House, 1976.

Dean, Martin. *Robbing the Jews: The Confiscation of Jewish Property in the Holocaust, 1933–1945.* Cambridge: Cambridge University Press, 2008.

Dillon, Christopher. *Dachau and the SS: A Schooling in Violence.* Oxford: Oxford University Press, 2015.

Dwork, Debórah, and Robert Jan van Pelt. *Flight from the Reich: Refugee Jews, 1933–1946.* New York: W.W. Norton, 2009.

Engelmann, Bernd. *Inside Hitler's Germany.* Translated by Krishna Wilson. New York: Pantheon, 1985.

Ericksen, Robert P. *Complicity in the Holocaust: Churches and Universities in Nazi Germany.* New York: Cambridge University Press, 2012.

Ericksen, Robert P., and Susannah Heschel, eds. *Betrayal: German Churches and the Holocaust.* Minneapolis, MN: Fortress, 1999.

Evans, Richard. *The Third Reich in Power, 1933–1939.* New York: Penguin, 2005.

Fritzsche, Peter. *Life and Death in the Third Reich.* Cambridge, MA: Belknap Press of Harvard University Press, 2008.

Fromm, Bella. *Blood and Banquets: A Social Diary.* New York: Harper and Brothers, 1942.

Gellately, Robert. *The Gestapo and German Society: Enforcing Racial Policy, 1933–1945.* New York: Oxford University Press, 1990.

Gerwarth, Robert. *Hitler's Hangman: The Life of Heydrich.* New Haven, CT: Yale University Press, 2011.

Giles, Geoffrey. "'The Most Unkindest Cut of All': Castration, Homosexuality, and Nazi Justice." *Journal of Contemporary History* 27, no. 1 (1992): 41–61.

———. *Why Bother about Homosexuals? Homophobia and Sexual Politics in Nazi Germany.* J. B. and Maurice C. Shapiro Annual Lecture, May 31, 2001. USHMM.

Heck, Alfons. *A Child of Hitler.* Frederick, CO: Renaissance House, 1985.

Jaskot, Paul B. *The Architecture of Oppression: The SS, Forced Labor, and the Nazi Monumental Building Economy.* New York: Routledge, 2000.

Johnson, Eric A. *Nazi Terror: The Gestapo, Jews, and Ordinary Germans.* New York: Basic, 2000.

Iggers, Georg, and Wilma Iggers. *Two Lives in Uncertain Times: Facing the Challenges of the Twentieth Century as Scholars and Citizens.* New York: Berghahn, 2006.

Kaplan, Marion. *Between Dignity and Despair: Jewish Life in Nazi Germany.* New York: Oxford University Press, 1998.

Kaplan, Thomas Pegelow. *The Language of Nazi Genocide: Linguistic Violence and the Struggle of Germans of Jewish Ancestry.* New York: Cambridge University Press, 2009.

Kirkpatrick, Clifford. *Nazi Germany: Its Women and Family Life.* New York: Bobbs-Merrill, 1938.

Klemperer, Victor. *I Will Bear Witness: A Diary of the Nazi Years, 1933–1941.* Translated by Martin Chalmers. New York: Random House, 1998.

———. *Language of the Third Reich: LTI, Lingua Tertii Imperii.* Translated by Martin Brady. New York: Athlone, 2000.

Koehn, Ilse. *Mischling, Second Degree: My Childhood in Nazi Germany.* New York: Bantam, 1977.

Koonz, Claudia. *Mothers in the Fatherland: Women, the Family, and Nazi Politics.* New York: St. Martin's, 1987.

———. *The Nazi Conscience.* Cambridge, MA: Harvard University Press, 2003.

Longerich, Peter. *Heinrich Himmler.* Translated by Jeremy Noakes and Lesley Sharpe. Oxford: Oxford University Press, 2012.

Marcuse, Harold. *Legacies of Dachau: The Uses and Abuses of a Concentration Camp, 1933–2001.* Cambridge: Cambridge University Press, 2001.

Maschmann, Melitta. *Account Rendered.* Translated by Geoffrey Strachan. London: Abelard-Schuman, 1964.

Massaquoi, Hans J. *Destined to Witness: Growing Up Black in Nazi Germany.* New York: Perennial, 2001.

Matthäus, Jürgen, and Mark Roseman. *Jewish Responses to Persecution, 1933–1946.* 4 vols. Lanham, MD: AltaMira Press in association with the U.S. Holocaust Memorial Museum, 2010.

Mosse, George. *Confronting History: A Memoir.* Madison: University of Wisconsin Press, 2000.

Neumann, Franz. *Behemoth: The Structure and Practice of National Socialism, 1933–1944.* Introduction by Peter Hayes. Chicago: Ivan R. Dee in association with the U.S. Holocaust Memorial Museum, 2009; originally published 1942.

Opitz, May, Katharina Oguntoye, and Dagmar Schultz, eds. *Showing Our Colors: Afro-German Women Speak Out.* Translated by Anne V. Adams. Amherst: University of Massachusetts Press, 1992.

Owings, Alison. *Frauen: German Women Recall the Third Reich.* New Brunswick, NJ: Rutgers University Press, 1993.

Peukert, Detlev. *Inside Nazi Germany: Conformity, Opposition, and Racism in Everyday Life.* New Haven, CT: Yale University Press, 1987.

Patterson, Orlando. *Slavery and Social Death: A Comparative Study.* Cambridge, MA: Harvard University Press, 1985.

Rosenberg, Otto. *A Gypsy in Auschwitz.* Edited by Ulrich Enzenberger. Translated by Helmut Bögler. London: London House, 1999.

Ryan, Donna F., and John S. Schuchman, eds. *Deaf People in Hitler's Europe.* Washington, DC: Gallaudet University Press, 2002.

Saidel, Rochelle G. *The Jewish Women of Ravensbrück Concentration Camp.* Madison: University of Wisconsin Press, 2006.

Spicer, Kevin P. *Resisting the Third Reich: The Catholic Church in Hitler's Germany.* DeKalb: Northern Illinois University Press, 2004.

Steinweis, Alan. *Studying the Jew: Scholarly Antisemitism in Nazi Germany.* Cambridge, MA: Harvard University Press, 2006.

Szobar, Patricia A. "Telling Sexual Secrets in the Nazi Courts of Law: Race Defilement in Germany, 1933 to 1945." *Journal of the History of Sexuality* 11, nos. 1/2 (January/April 2002): 131–63.

Thimme, Annelise. "Geprägt von der Geschichte. Eine Aussenseiterin." In *Erinnerungsstücke: Wege in die Vergangenheit,* edited by Hartmut Lehmann and Gerhard Oexle, 153–223. Vienna: Boehlau, 1997.

Wachsmann, Nikolaus. *KL: A History of the Nazi Concentration Camps.* New York: Farrar, Strauss, and Giroux, 2015.

Films

Elisabeth of Berlin. Directed by Steven D. Martin. United States, 2008.

Jehovah's Witnesses Stand Firm against Nazi Assault. Directed by Watchtower Bible & Tract Society of New York. United States, 1996.

The Nazis: A Warning from History. Directed by Laurence Rees. United Kingdom, 1997.

Der Olympische Sommer. Directed by Gordian Maugg. Germany, 1993.

The People Next Door. Directed by Tim Hunter. USA, 1996.

Storm Troopers of Christ: The Jews and Baptism in Nazi Germany. Directed by Steven D. Martin. USA, 2007.

4. OPEN AGGRESSION: IN SEARCH OF WAR, 1938–1939

Abella, Irving, and Harold Troper. *None Is Too Many: Canada and the Jews of Europe, 1933–1948.* Toronto: Lester and Orpen Denys, 1982. Republished University of Toronto Press, 2012.

Ascher, Carol. *Afterimages: A Family Memoir.* Teaneck, NJ: Holmes & Meier, 2008.

Barnett, Victoria J. *Bystanders: Conscience and Complicity during the Holocaust.* Westport, CT: Greenwood, 1999.

Boehling, Rebecca L., and Uta Larkey. *Life and Loss in the Shadow of the Holocaust: A Jewish Family's Untold Story.* New York: Cambridge University Press, 2011.

Bryant, Chad. *Prague in Black: Nazi Rule and Czech Nationalism.* Cambridge, MA: Harvard University Press, 2007.

Bukey, Evan Burr. *Hitler's Austria.* Chapel Hill: University of North Carolina Press, 2000.

Cesarani, David. *Becoming Eichmann: Rethinking the Life, Crimes, and Trial of a "Desk Murderer."* Cambridge, MA: Da Capo Press, 2006.

Felstiner, Mary Lowenthal. *To Paint Her Life: Charlotte Salomon in the Nazi Era.* New York: HarperCollins, 1995.

Gellately, Robert. *Backing Hitler: Consent and Coercion in Nazi Germany.* New York: Oxford University Press, 2001.

Glatshteyn, Yankev. *Emil and Karl.* Translated by Jeffrey Shandler. New Milford, CT: Roaring Brook, 2006. Originally published in 1940. (Note: this is a work of fiction based on contemporary research.)

Goeschel, Christian. *Suicide in Nazi Germany.* Oxford: Oxford University Press, 2009.

Goldstein, Susy, Gina Hamilton, and Wendy Share. *Ten Marks and a Train Ticket: Benno's Escape to Freedom.* Toronto: League for Human Rights of B'nai Brith Canada, 2008.

Grau, Günter, ed. *Hidden Holocaust? Gay and Lesbian Persecution in Germany, 1933–1945.* Translated by Patrick Camiller. London: Cassell, 1995.

Gruner, Wolf. *Jewish Forced Labor under the Nazis: Economic Needs and Racial Aims, 1938–1944.* Translated by Kathleen Dell'Orto. New York: Cambridge University Press, 2008.

Gruner, Wolf, and Jörg Osterloh, eds. *The Greater German Reich and the Jews: Nazi Persecution Policies in the Annexed Territories, 1935–1945.* New York: Berghahn, 2015.

Hammel, Andrea, and Bea Lewkowicz, eds. *The Kindertransport to Britain 1938/39: New Perspectives.* Amsterdam: Yearbook of the Research Centre for German and Austrian Exile Studies, 13 (2012).

Heilbronner, Oded. *Catholicism, Political Culture, and the Countryside: A Social History of the Nazi Party in South Germany.* Ann Arbor: University of Michigan Press, 1998.

Heschel, Susannah. *The Aryan Jesus: Christian Theologians and the Bible in Nazi Germany.* Princeton, NJ: Princeton University Press, 2008.

Hesse, Hans, ed. *Persecution and Resistance of Jehovah's Witnesses during the Nazi-Regime, 1933–1945.* Bremen, Germany: Edition Temmen, 2001.

Hochstadt, Steve. *Exodus to Shanghai: Stories of Escape from the Third Reich.* New York: Palgrave Macmillan, 2012.

Horwitz, Gordon J. *In the Shadow of Death: Living Outside the Gates of Mauthausen.* New York: Free Press, 1990.

Jennings, Eric T. "Writing Madagascar back into the Madagascar Plan." *Holocaust and Genocide Studies* 21, no. 2 (Fall 2007): 187–217.

Klein, Ruth, ed. *Nazi Germany, Canadian Responses: Confronting Antisemitism in the Shadow of War.* Montreal: McGill-Queen's University Press, 2012.

Kluger, Ruth. *Still Alive: A Holocaust Girlhood Remembered.* New York: Feminist Press, 2001.

Kotkin, Stephen. *Stalin: Paradoxes of Power, 1878–1928.* Part I. New York: Penguin, 2014.

Kühne, Thomas. *Belonging and Genocide: Hitler's Community, 1918–1945.* New Haven: Yale University Press, 2010.

Leff, Laurel. *Buried by the Times: The Holocaust and America's Most Important Newspaper.* New York: Cambridge University Press, 2005.

Lipstadt, Deborah. *Beyond Belief: The American Press and the Coming of the Holocaust.* New York: Simon and Schuster, 1986.

Mann, Fred. *A Drastic Turn of Destiny.* Toronto: Azrieli Foundation, 2009.

McFarland-Icke, Bronwyn Rebekah. *Nurses in Nazi Germany: Moral Choice in History.* Princeton: Princeton University Press, 1999.

Meyer, Beate, Hermann Simon, and Chana Schütz, eds. *Jews in Nazi Berlin: From Kristallnacht to Liberation.* Chicago and London: University of Chicago Press, 2009.

Ogilvie, Sarah A., and Scott Miller. *Refuge Denied: The St. Louis Passengers and the Holocaust.* Madison: University of Wisconsin Press, 2006.

Opfermann, Charlotte, and Robert A. Warren. *Charlotte, a Holocaust Memoir: Remembering Theresienstadt. As Shared with Robert A. Warren.* Santa Fe: Robert A. Warren, 2006. (Note: this book is not a commercial publication.)

Phayer, Michael. *The Catholic Church and the Holocaust.* Bloomington: Indiana University Press, 2000.

Preston, Paul. *The Spanish Holocaust: Inquisition and Extermination in Twentieth-Century Spain.* New York: Norton, 2012.

Quack, Sibylle, ed. *Between Sorrow and Strength: Women Refugees of the Nazi Period.* New York: Cambridge University Press, 1995.

Rigg, Bryan Mark. *Hitler's Jewish Soldiers.* Lawrence: University Press of Kansas, 2002.

Roseman, Mark. *A Past in Hiding: Memory and Survival in Nazi Germany.* New York: Picador, 2000.

Safrian, Hans. *Eichmann's Men.* Translated by Ute Stargardt. Cambridge and New York: Cambridge University Press, 2010.

Salomon, Charlotte, and Judith C. E. Belinfante. *Life? Or Theatre?* Zwolle: Waanders, 1998.

Sofsky, Wolfgang. *The Order of Terror: The Concentration Camp.* Translated by William Templer. Princeton, NJ: Princeton University Press, 1997.

Steinhoff, Johannes, Peter Pechel, and Dennis Showalter, eds. *Voices from the Third Reich: An Oral History.* Washington, DC: Regnery Gateway, 1989.

Steinweis, Alan E. *Kristallnacht 1938.* Cambridge, MA: Belknap Press of Harvard University Press, 2009.

Tooze, Adam. *The Wages of Destruction: The Making and Breaking of the Nazi Economy.* London: Allen Lane, 2006.

Voticky, Anka. *Knocking on Every Door.* Toronto: Azrieli Foundation, 2010.

United States Holocaust Memorial Museum Encyclopedia of Camps and Ghettos, 1933–1945. Vol. I: *Early Camps, Youth Camps, and Concentration Camps and Subcamps under the SS-Business Administration Main Office (WVHA).* Bloomington: Indiana University Press, 2009.

Weilbach, S. *Singing from the Darktime: A Childhood Memoir in Poetry and Prose.* Montreal: McGill-Queen's University Press, 2011.

Wünschmann, Kim. *Before Auschwitz: Jewish Prisoners in the Prewar Concentration Camps.* Cambridge, MA: Harvard University Press, 2015.

Films

Garden of the Finzi-Continis. Directed by Vittorio De Sica. Italy/West Germany, 1970.

Into the Arms of Strangers: Stories of the Kindertransport. Directed by Mark Jonathan Harris. United Kingdom/United States, 2000.

A Jewish Girl in Shanghai. Directed by Wang Genfa. China, 2010.

My Knees Were Jumping: Remembering the Kindertransports. Directed by Melissa Hacker. United States, 1996.

Nowhere in Africa. Directed by Caroline Link. Germany, 2001.

Professor Mamlock. Directed by Adolf Minkin and Herbert Rappaport. USSR, 1938.

Shanghai Ghetto. Directed by Dana Janklowicz-Mann and Amir Mann. United States, 2002.

Voyage of the Damned. Directed by Stuart Rosenberg. United Kingdom, 1976.

5. BRUTAL INNOVATIONS: WAR AGAINST POLAND AND THE SO-CALLED EUTHANASIA PROGRAM, 1939–1940

Adelson, Alan, and Robert Lapides, eds. *Lodz Ghetto: Inside a Community under Siege.* New York: Viking, 1989.

Aly, Götz. *"Final Solution": Nazi Population Policy and the Murder of the European Jews.* Translated by Belinda Cooper and Allison Brown. London: Arnold, 1999.

Arendt, Hannah. *Eichmann in Jerusalem: A Report on the Banality of Evil.* New York: Viking, 1963.

Bauman, Zygmunt. *Modernity and the Holocaust.* Ithaca, NY: Cornell University Press, 1989.

Bergen, Doris L. "Instrumentalization of *Volksdeutschen* in German Propaganda in 1939: Replacing/Erasing Poles, Jews, and Other Victims." *German Studies Review* 31, no. 3 (2008): 447–70.

———. "Studying the Holocaust: Is History Commemoration?" In *The Holocaust and Historical Methodology*, edited by Dan Stone, 158–77. New York: Berghahn, 2012.

Bluman, Barbara Ruth. *I Have My Mother's Eyes: A Holocaust Memoir across Generations.* Vancouver: Ronsdale, 2009.

Browning, Christopher. *Remembering Survival: Inside a Nazi Slave-Labor Camp.* New York: W.W. Norton, 2010.

Chary, Frederick. *The Bulgarian Jews and the Final Solution, 1940–1944.* Pittsburgh: University of Pittsburgh Press, 1972.

Dobroszycki, Lucjan, ed. *The Chronicle of the Lodz Ghetto, 1941–1944.* Translated by Richard Lourie, et al. New Haven, CT: Yale University Press, 1984.

Engelking, Barbara, and Jacek Leociak. *The Warsaw Ghetto: A Guide to the Perished City.* Translated by Emma Harris. New Haven, CT: Yale University Press, 2009.

Epstein, Catherine. *Model Nazi: Arthur Greiser and the Occupation of Western Poland.* New York: Oxford University Press, 2010.

Friedlander, Henry. *The Origins of Nazi Genocide: From Euthanasia to the Final Solution.* Chapel Hill: University of North Carolina Press, 1995.

Friedländer, Saul. *Pius XII and the Third Reich: A Documentation.* Translated by Charles Fullman. New York: Knopf, 1966.

Gotfryd, Bernard. *Anton the Dove Fancier and Other Tales of the Holocaust.* New York: Washington Square, 1990.

Griech-Polelle, Beth A. *Bishop Von Galen: German Catholicism and National Socialism.* New Haven, CT: Yale University Press, 2002.

Gross, Jan T. *Neighbors: The Destruction of the Jewish Community in Jedwabne, Poland.* Princeton, NJ: Princeton University Press, 2001.

———. *Polish Society under German Occupation: The Generalgouvernement, 1939–1944.* Princeton, NJ: Princeton University Press, 1979.

Grossman, Mendel. *With a Camera in the Ghetto.* Edited by Zvi Szner and Alexander Sened. Translated by Mendel Kohansky. Tel Aviv: Ghetto Fighters' House, 1970.

Harvey, Elizabeth. *Women in the Nazi East: Agents and Witnesses of Germanization.* New Haven, CT: Yale University Press, 2003.

Heberer, Patricia. "'Exitus heute in Hadamar': The Hadamar Facility and 'Euthanasia' in Nazi Germany." PhD dissertation, University of Maryland, 2001.

Hilberg, Raul, Stanislaw Staron, and Josef Kermisz, eds. *The Warsaw Diary of Adam Czerniakow: Prelude to Doom.* Translated by Stanislaw Staron and the staff of Yad Vashem. New York: Stein and Day, 1979.

Horwitz, Gordon J. *Ghettostadt: Łódź and the Making of a Nazi City.* Cambridge, MA: Harvard University Press, 2010.

Kaplan, Chaim A. *Scroll of Agony: The Warsaw Diary of Chaim A. Kaplan.* Translated and edited by Abraham I. Katsh. Bloomington: Indiana University Press, 1999.

Kassow, Samuel D. *Who Will Write our History? Emanuel Ringelblum, the Warsaw Ghetto, and the Oyneg Shabes Archive.* Bloomington: Indiana University Press, 2007.

Kater, Michael H. *Doctors under Hitler.* Chapel Hill: University of North Carolina Press, 1989.

Kogon, Eugen, Hermann Langbein, and Adalbert Rückerl, eds. *Nazi Mass Murder: A Documentary History of the Use of Poison Gas.* Translated by Mary Scott and Caroline Lloyd-Morris. New Haven, CT: Yale University Press, 1993.

Kornberg, Jacques. *The Pope's Dilemma: Pius XII Faces Atrocities and Genocide in the Second World War.* Toronto: University of Toronto Press, 2015.

Krakowski, Shmuel, and Israel Gutman. *Unequal Victims: Poles and Jews during World War Two.* Translated by Ted Gorelick and Witold Jedlicki. New York: Holocaust Library, 1986.

Kulkielko, Renya. *Escape From the Pit.* New York: Sharon Books, 1947.

Kuntz, Dieter, and Susan Bachrach, eds. *Deadly Medicine: Creating the Master Race.* Chapel Hill: University of North Carolina Press, 2006.

Lifton, Robert Jay. *The Nazi Doctors: Medical Killing and the Psychology of Genocide.* New York: Basic Books, 2000.

London, Louise. *Whitehall and the Jews, 1933–1948: British Immigration Policy, Jewish Refugees and the Holocaust.* New York: Cambridge University Press, 2000.

Lukas, Richard C. *Did the Children Cry? Hitler's War against Jewish and Polish Children.* New York: Hippocrene, 1995.

————, ed. *Out of the Inferno: Poles Remember the Holocaust.* Lexington: University Press of Kentucky, 1989.

Matthäus, Jürgen, Jochen Böhler, and Klaus-Michael Mallman. *War, Pacification, and Mass Murder, 1939: The Einsatzgruppen in Poland.* Lanham, MD: Rowman and Little-field, 2014.

Melson, Robert. *False Papers: Deception and Survival in the Holocaust.* Urbana: University of Illinois Press, 2000.

Michlic, Joanna Beata. *Poland's Threatening Other: The Image of the Jew from 1880 to the Present.* Lincoln: University of Nebraska Press, 2006.

Michman, Dan. *The Emergence of Jewish Ghettos during the Holocaust.* New York: Cambridge University Press, 2011.

Nicosia, Francis R., and Jonathan Huener, eds. *Medicine and Medical Ethics in Nazi Germany: Origins, Practices, Legacies.* New York: Berghahn, 2002.

Noakes, Jeremy, and Geoffrey Pridham, eds. *Nazism, 1919–1945.* Volume 3: *Foreign Policy, War and Racial Extermination: A Documentary Reader.* Exeter, UK: University of Exeter Press, 2001.

Paulsson, Gunnar S. *Secret City: The Hidden Jews of Warsaw, 1940–1945.* New Haven, CT: Yale University Press, 2002.

Polonsky, Antony, and Joanna B. Michlic, eds. *The Neighbors Respond: The Controversy over the Jedwabne Massacre in Poland.* Princeton, NJ: Princeton University Press, 2004.

Rosenfarb, Chava. *The Tree of Life: A Trilogy of Life in the Lodz Ghetto.* Translated from Yiddish by the author with Goldie Magentaler. Madison: University of Wisconsin Press, 2004–2005. (Note: this is a work of fiction based on the author's personal experience.)

Rossino, Alexander B. *Hitler Strikes Poland: Blitzkrieg, Ideology, and Atrocity.* Lawrence: University Press of Kansas, 2003.

Rutherford, Phillip T. *Prelude to the Final Solution: The Nazi Program for Deporting Ethnic Poles, 1939–1941.* Lawrence: University Press of Kansas, 2007.

Schalkowsky, Samuel, ed. *The Clandestine History of the Kovno Jewish Ghetto Police.* Translated by Samuel Schalkowsky. Washington, DC: in association with the U. S. Holocaust Memorial Museum, 2014.

Sierakowiak, Dawid. *The Diary of Dawid Sierakowiak: Five Notebooks from the Łódź Ghetto.* Edited by Alan Adelson. Translated by Kamil Turowski. New York: Oxford University Press, 1996.

Snyder, Timothy. *Bloodlands: Europe between Hitler and Stalin.* New York: Basic, 2010.

Steinert, Marlis. *Hitler's War and the Germans: Public Mood and Attitude during the Second World War.* Edited and translated by Thomas E. J. de Witt. Athens: Ohio University Press, 1977.

Strauss, Elizabeth C. "'Cast me not off in my time of old age . . .' The Aged and Aging in the Łódź Ghetto, 1939–1944." PhD Dissertation, University of Notre Dame, 2013.

Szwajger, Adina Blady. *I Remember Nothing More.* Translated by Tasja Darowska. New York: Pantheon, 1990.

Tec, Nechama. *Defiance: The Bielski Partisans.* New York: Oxford University Press, 1993.

Wildt, Michael. *An Uncompromising Generation: The Nazi Leadership of the Reich Security Main Office.* Translated by Tom Lampert. Madison: University of Wisconsin Press, 2010.

Winstone, Martin. *The Dark Heart of Hitler's Europe: Nazi Rule in Poland under the General Government.* London: Tauris, 2014.

Zelkowicz, Josef. *In Those Terrible Days: Writings from the Lodz Ghetto.* Edited by Michal Unger. Translated by Naftali Greenwood. Jerusalem: Yad Vashem, 2002.

Zubrzycki, Geneviève. *The Crosses of Auschwitz: Nationalism and Religion in Post-Communist Poland.* Chicago: University of Chicago Press, 2006.

Zyskind, Sara. *Stolen Years.* Translated by Marganit Inbar. Minneapolis: Lerner, 1981.

Films

Deadly Medicine: Creating the Master Race (oral history interviews of the exhibition collection). United States Holocaust Memorial Museum Oral History Branch Institutional Archives (2002–2003). *USHMM.org.* http://collections.ushmm.org/search/?q=2003.485&search_field=Accession+Number

Europa Europa. Directed by Agnieszka Holland. Germany/France/Poland, 1990.

A Film Unfinished. Directed by Yael Hersonski. Germany/Israel, 2010.

Healing by Killing. Directed by Nitzan Aviram. Israel, 1996.

In the Shadow of the Reich: Nazi Medicine. Directed by John J. Michalczyk. United States, 1997.

To Be Or Not To Be. Directed by Ernst Lubitsch. USA, 1942.

Why We Fight. Directed by Frank Capra. USA, 1942–1945.

6. EXPANSION AND SYSTEMATIZATION: EXPORTING WAR AND TERROR, 1940–1941

Aly, Götz. *Hitler's Beneficiaries: Plunder, Racial War, and the Nazi Welfare State.* Translated by Jefferson Chase. New York: Henry Holt, 2008.

Ancel, Jean. *The History of the Holocaust in Romania.* Lincoln: University of Nebraska Press, 2011.

Aronson, Shlomo. *Hitler, the Allies, and the Jews.* New York: Cambridge University Press, 2004.

Bartov, Omer. *The Eastern Front, 1941–1945: German Troops and the Barbarisation of Warfare.* London: St. Martin's, 1985.

Beorn, Waitman Wade. *Marching into Darkness: The Wehrmacht and the Holocaust in Belarus.* Cambridge, MA: Harvard University Press, 2014.

Berkhoff, Karel. *Harvest of Despair: Life and Death in Ukraine under Nazi Rule.* Cambridge, MA: Belknap, 2004.

Bos, Pascale, "'Her flesh is branded: "For Officers Only"': Imagining and Imagined Sexual Violence against Jewish Women during the Holocaust." In *Lessons and Legacies XI: Expanding Perspectives on the Holocaust in a Changing World*, edited by Hilary Earl and Karl A. Schleunes, 59–85. Evanston, IL: Northwestern University Press, 2014.

Breitman, Richard. *Official Secrets: What the Nazis Planned and What the British and Americans Knew.* New York: Hill and Wang, 1998.

Breitman, Richard, and Allan J. Lichtman. *FDR and the Jews.* Cambridge, MA: The Belknap Press of Harvard University Press, 2013.

Browning, Christopher R. *The Origins of the Final Solution: The Evolution of Nazi Jewish Policy, September 1939-March 1942.* With contributions by Jürgen Matthäus. Lincoln: University of Nebraska Press, 2004.

Dallin, Alexander. *German Rule in Russia 1941–1945: A Study of Occupation Policies.* 2nd ed. London: Macmillan, 1981.

David-Fox, Michael, Peter Holquist, and Alexander Martin, eds. *The Holocaust in the East: Local Perpetrators and Soviet Responses.* Pittsburgh, PA: University of Pittsburgh Press, 2014.

Donat, Alexander. *The Holocaust Kingdom: A Memoir.* New York: Holocaust Library, 1978.

Dumitru, Diana. *The State, Anti-Semitism, and the Holocaust: Romania and the Soviet Union.* New York: Cambridge University Press, 2015.

Eliach, Yaffa. *Hasidic Tales of the Holocaust.* New York: Vintage, 1988.

Epstein, Barbara. *The Minsk Ghetto, 1941–1943: Jewish Resistance and Soviet Internationalism.* Berkeley: University of California Press, 2008.

Fonseca, Isabel. *Bury Me Standing: The Gypsies and Their Journey.* New York: Knopf, 1995.

Frank, Anne. *The Diary of a Young Girl.* Edited by Otto H. Frank and Mirjam Pressler. Translated by Susan Massotty. New York: Bantam Books, 1997.

Friedländer, Saul. *When Memory Comes.* Translated by Helen R. Lane. New York: Farrar, Straus, Giroux, 1979.

Gerlach, Christian. "Failure of Plans for an SS Extermination Camp in Mogilev, Belorussia." Translated by Deborah Cohen and Helmut Gerlach. *Holocaust and Genocide Studies* 11, no. 1 (1997): 60–78.

Gershenson, Olga. *The Phantom Holocaust: Soviet Cinema and Jewish Catastrophe.* New Brunswick, NJ: Rutgers University Press, 2013.

Ginaite-Rubinson, Sara. *Resistance and Survival: The Jewish Community in Kaunas, 1941–1944.* Oakville, Ontario: Mosaic, 2005.

Heer, Hannes, and Klaus Naumann, eds. *War of Extermination: The German Military in World War II, 1941–1944.* New York: Berghahn Books, 2000.

Himka, John-Paul. *Ukrainians, Jews, and the Holocaust: Divergent Memories.* Saskatoon, SK: Heritage Press, 2009.

Hirschfeld, Gerhard, ed. *The Policies of Genocide: Jews and Soviet Prisoners of War in Nazi Germany.* London: Allen and Unwin, 1986.

Hoenicke Moore, Michaela. *Know Your Enemy: The American Debate on Nazism, 1933–1945.* Cambridge: Cambridge University Press, 2009.

Ioanid, Radu. *The Holocaust in Romania: The Destruction of Jews and Gypsies under the Antonescu Regime, 1940–1944.* Chicago: Ivan R. Dee, 2000.

Jarausch, Konrad. *Reluctant Accomplice: A Wehrmacht Soldier's Letters from the Eastern Front.* Edited by Klaus Jochen Arnold, Eve M. Duffy, and Konrad Hugo Jarausch. Princeton, NJ: Princeton University Press, 2011.

Knappe, Siegfried. *Soldat: Reflections of a German Soldier, 1936–1949.* Edited by Ted Brusaw and Susan Davis McLaughlin. New York: Orion Books, 1992.

Kopstein, Jeffrey S., and Jason Wittenberg. "Deadly Communities: Local Political Milieus and the Persecution of Jews in Occupied Poland." *Comparative Political Studies* 44 (March 2011): 259–83.

Lower, Wendy. *Nazi Empire-Building and the Holocaust in Ukraine.* Chapel Hill: University of North Carolina Press, 2005.

Lower, Wendy, and Ray Brandon, eds. *The Shoah in Ukraine: History, Testimony, Memorialization.* Bloomington: Indiana University Press, 2008.

Mazower, Mark. *Inside Hitler's Greece: The Experience of Occupation, 1941–1944.* New Haven, CT: Yale University Press, 1993.

Megargee, Geoffrey. *Inside Hitler's High Command.* Lawrence: University Press of Kansas, 2000.

Merridale, Catherine. *Ivan's War: Life and Death in the Red Army, 1939–1945.* New York: Metropolitan, 2006.

Minear, Richard H. *Dr. Seuss Goes to War: The World War II Editorial Cartoons of Theodor Seuss Geisel.* New York: New Press, 2001.

Montague, Patrick. *Chełmno and the Holocaust: The History of Hitler's First Death Camp.* Chapel Hill: University of North Carolina Press, 2012.

Mühlhäuser, Regina. "The Historicity of Denial: Sexual Violence against Jewish Women during the War of Annihilation, 1941–1945." In *Lessons and Legacies XI,* edited by Hilary Earl and Karl Schleunes, 31–58. Evanston, IL: Northwestern University Press, 2014.

Némirovsky, Irène. *Suite Française.* Translated by Sandra Smith. New York: Knopf, 2006. (Note: this is a work of fiction based on contemporary research and personal experience.)

Pieper, Henning. *Fegelein's Horsemen and Genocidal Warfare: The SS Cavalry Brigade in the Soviet Union.* London: Palgrave Macmillan, 2014.

Poznanski, Renée. *Jews in France during World War II.* Translated by Nathan Bracher. Waltham, MA: Brandeis University Press in association with the U. S. Holocaust Memorial Museum, 2001.

Ramras-Rauch, Gila. *Aharon Appelfeld: The Holocaust and Beyond*. Bloomington: Indiana University Press, 1994.

Rubenstein, Joshua, and Ilya Altman, eds. *Unknown Black Book: The Holocaust in the German-Occupied Soviet Territories*. Translated by Christopher Morris and Joshua Rubenstein. Bloomington: Indiana University Press, 2008.

Sachse, William L., ed. *English History in the Making: Readings from the Sources*. Vol. 2. *Since 1689*. New York: Wiley, 1970.

Sarfatti, Michele. *The Jews in Mussolini's Italy: From Equality to Persecution*. Translated by John and Anne C. Tedeschi. Madison: University of Wisconsin Press, 2006.

Scheck, Raffael. *Hitler's African Victims: The German Army Massacres of Black French Soldiers in 1940*. New York: Cambridge University Press, 2006.

Sebastian, Mihail. *Journal, 1935–1944*. Edited by Radu Ioanid. Translated by Patrick Camiller. Chicago: Ivan R. Dee, 2000.

Shapiro, Paul A. *The Kishinev Ghetto, 1941–1942: A Documentary History of the Holocaust in Romania's Contested Borderlands*. Tuscaloosa, AL: University of Alabama Press, 2015.

Shepherd, Ben. *Terror in the Balkans: German Armies and Partisan Warfare*. Cambridge, MA: Harvard University Press, 2012.

———. *War in the Wild East: The German Army and Soviet Partisans*. Cambridge, MA: Harvard University Press, 2004.

Shternshis, Anna. "Between Life and Death: Why Some Soviet Jews Decided to Leave and Others to Stay in 1941." *Kritika: Explorations in Russian and Eurasian History* 15, no. 3 (Summer 2014): 477–504.

Sommer, Robert. "Situational Homosexual Slavery of Young Adolescent Boys in Nazi Concentration Camps." In *Lessons and Legacies XI*, edited by Hilary Earl and Karl Schleunes, 86–103. Evanston, IL: Northwestern University Press, 2014.

Steinberg, Jonathan. *All or Nothing: The Axis and the Holocaust: 1941–1943*. London: Routledge, 1990.

Steinhart, Eric C. *The Holocaust and the Germanization of Ukraine*. New York: Cambridge University Press, 2015.

Tec, Nechama. *Dry Tears*. New York: Oxford University Press, 1984.

Toll, Nelly S. *Behind the Secret Window: A Memoir of a Hidden Childhood during World War Two*. New York: Dial, 1993.

Tolstoy, Nikolai. *Stalin's Secret War*. New York: Holt, Rinehart and Winston, 1982.

Weinberg, Gerhard L. *A World at Arms: A Global History of World War II*. 2nd ed. New York: Cambridge University Press, 2005.

Weiss-Wendt, Anton. *Murder Without Hatred: Estonians and the Holocaust*. Syracuse, NY: Syracuse University Press, 2009.

Westermann, Edward B. *Hitler's Police Battalions: Enforcing Racial War in the East*. Lawrence: University Press of Kansas, 2005.

Films

Broken Silence. Children from the Abyss. Directed by Pavel Chukhraj, et al. United States/
  Argentina/Czech Republic/Hungary/Poland/Russia, 2002.

Casablanca. Directed by Michael Curtiz. United States, 1942.

Generation War (Unsere Mütter, unsere Väter). Directed by Philipp Kadelbach. Germany,
  2013.

Ladies' Tailor (Damskiy portnoy). Directed by Leonid Gorovets. USSR, 1990.

Mrs. Miniver. Directed by William Wyler. USA, 1942.

The Pianist. Directed by Roman Polanski. France/Poland/Germany/United Kingdom,
  2002.

Shoah. Directed by Claude Lanzmann. France/United Kingdom, 1985.

Spell Your Name. Directed by Sergey Bukovsky. Ukraine/United States, 2006.

The Sorrow and the Pity: Chronicle of a French Town during the Occupation. Directed by
  Marcel Ophuls. France/Switzerland/West Germany, 1969.

The Unvanquished (Napokorennye). Directed by Marc Donskoy. USSR, 1945.

Why We Fight. Chapter III: *Divide and Conquer;* Chapter IV: *The Battle of Britain.*
  Directed by Frank Capra. USA, 1943.

7. WAR AND GENOCIDE: DECISIONS AND DYNAMICS IN THE PEAK YEARS OF KILLING, 1942–1943

Achcar, Gilbert. *The Arabs and the Holocaust: The Arab-Israeli War of Narratives.* Translated
  by G. M. Goshgarian. New York: Metropolitan, 2009.

Arad, Yitzhak. *Ghetto in Flames.* New York: Holocaust Library, 1982.

Beck, Gad. *An Underground Life: Memoirs of a Gay Jew in Nazi Berlin.* Edited by Frank
  Heibert. Translated by Allison Brown. Madison: University of Wisconsin Press,
  1999.

Browning, Christopher R. *Ordinary Men: Reserve Police Battalion 101 and the Final Solution in Poland.* New York: HarperCollins, 1992.

Case, Holly. *Between States: The Transylvanian Question and the European Idea during World
  War II.* Stanford, CA: Stanford University Press, 2009.

Dean, Martin. *Collaboration in the Holocaust: Crimes of the Local Police in Belorussia and
  Ukraine, 1941–44.* New York: St. Martin's Press, 2000.

Faulkner Rossi, Lauren. *Wehrmacht Priests: Catholicism and the Nazi War of Annihilation.*
  Cambridge, MA: Harvard University Press, 2015.

Fenelon, Fania. *Playing for Time.* Edited by Marcelle Routier. Translated by Judith
  Landry. Syracuse, NY: Syracuse University Press, 1976.

Garbarini, Alexandra. *Numbered Days: Diaries and the Holocaust.* New Haven: Yale University Press, 2006.

Gerlach, Christian. "The Wannsee Conference, the Fate of German Jews, and Hitler's Decision in Principle to Exterminate All European Jews." *The Journal of Modern History* 70, no. 4 (1998): 759–812.

Gilbert, Shirli. *Music in the Holocaust: Confronting Life in the Nazi Ghettos and Camps.* Oxford: Clarendon Press, 2005.

Goda, Norman J.W. "Black Marks: Hitler's Bribery of His Senior Officers during World War II." *Journal of Modern History* 72, no. 2 (2000): 413–52.

———. *Tomorrow the World: Hitler, Northwest Africa, and the Path toward America.* College Station: Texas A&M University Press, 1998.

Grabowski, Jan. *Hunt for the Jews: Betrayal and Murder in German-Occupied Poland.* Bloomington: Indiana University Press, 2013.

Heger, Heinz. *The Men with the Pink Triangle.* Translated by David Fernbach. Boston: Alyson, 1980.

Herbermann, Nanda. *The Blessed Abyss: Inmate #6582 in Ravensbrück Concentration Camp for Women.* Edited by Hester Baer and Elizabeth R. Baer. Translated by Hester Baer. Detroit: Wayne State University Press, 2000.

Herf, Jeffrey. *The Jewish Enemy: Nazi Propaganda during World War II and the Holocaust.* Cambridge, MA: Harvard University Press, 2006.

———. *Nazi Propaganda for the Arab World.* New Haven, CT: Yale University Press, 2009.

Klee, Ernst, Willi Dressen, and Volker Reiss, eds. *The Good Old Days: The Holocaust as Seen by Its Perpetrators and Bystanders.* Translated by Deborah Burnstone. New York: Simon & Schuster, 1991.

Klemperer, Victor. *I Will Bear Witness: A Diary of the Nazi Years, 1942–1945.* Translated by Martin Chalmers. New York: Random House, 1999.

Koker, David. *At the Edge of the Abyss: A Concentration Camp Diary, 1943–1944.* Edited by R. J. van Pelt. Translated by Michiel Horn and John Irons. Evanston, IL: Northwestern University Press, 2012.

Laks, Szymon. *Music of Another World.* Translated by Chester A. Kisiel. Evanston, IL: Northwestern University Press, 1989.

Laska, Vera, ed. *Women in the Resistance and the Holocaust.* Westport, CT: Greenwood, 1983.

Levi, Primo. *Survival in Auschwitz: The Nazi Assault on Humanity.* Translated by Stuart Wolf. New York: Collier-Macmillan, 1958.

Lower, Wendy. *Hitler's Furies: German Women in the Nazi Killing Fields.* Boston: Houghton Mifflin Harcourt, 2013.

Mallmann, Klaus-Michael, and Martin Cüppers. *Nazi Palestine: The Plans for the Extermination of the Jews in Palestine.* New York: Enigma, 2010.

Noakes, Jeremy, and Geoffrey Pridham, eds. *Nazism, 1919–1945.* Volume 3: *Foreign Policy, War and Racial Extermination: A Documentary Reader.* Exeter, UK: University of Exeter Press, 2001.

Nomberg-Przytyk, Sara. *Auschwitz: True Tales from a Grotesque Land.* Translated by Roslyn Hirsch. Chapel Hill: University of North Carolina Press, 1985.

Porat, Dina. *The Fall of a Sparrow: The Life and Times of Abba Kovner.* Translated by Elizabeth Yuval. Stanford, CA: Stanford University Press, 2009.

Przyrembel, Alexandra. "Transfixed by an Image: Ilse Koch, the 'Kommandeuse of Buchenwald.'" Translated by Pamela Selwyn. *German History* 19, no. 3 (2001): 369–99.

Rodogno, Davide. *Fascism's European Empire: Italian Occupation during the Second World War.* New York: Cambridge University Press, 2006.

Seel, Pierre. *I, Pierre Seel, Deported Homosexual: A Memoir of Nazi Terror.* Translated by Joachim Neugroschel. New York: Basic, 1995.

Shneidman, N. N. *The Three Tragic Heroes of the Vilnius Ghetto: Witenberg, Sheinbaum, Gens.* Toronto, ON: Mosaic, 2002.

Stargardt, Nicholas. *Witnesses of War: Children's Lives under the Nazis.* London: Jonathan Cape, 2005.

Stoltzfus, Nathan. *Resistance of the Heart: Intermarriage and the Rosenstrasse Protest in Nazi Germany.* New York: Norton, 1996.

Todorov, Tzvetan. *The Fragility of Goodness: Why Bulgaria's Jews Survived the Holocaust.* Translated by Arthur Denner. Princeton: Princeton University Press, 2001.

Weinberg, Gerhard L. "Two Separate Issues? Historiography of World War II and the Holocaust." In *Holocaust Historiography in Context: Emergence, Challenges, Polemics, and Achievements,* edited by David Bankier and Dan Michman, 379–401. New York: Berghahn, 2008.

Zuccotti, Susan. *Under His Very Windows: The Vatican and the Holocaust in Italy.* New Haven, CT: Yale University Press, 2000.

Films

Amen. Directed by Costa-Gavras. France/Germany/Romania, 2002.

Come and See. Directed by Elem Klimov. USSR, 1985.

Conspiracy. Directed by Frank Pierson. United Kingdom/United States, 2001.

Divided We Fall (Musíme si pomáhat). Directed by Jan Hřebejk. Czech Republic, 2000.

Goodbye, Children (Au revoir les enfants). Directed by Louis Malle. France/West Germany/Italy, 1987.

A Love in Germany. Directed by Andrzej Wajda. France and West Germany, 1983.

Partisans of Vilna. Directed by Josh Waletzky. United States, 1986.

Playing for Time. Directed by Daniel Mann. United States, 1980.

Rosenstrasse. Directed by Margarethe von Trotta. Germany/Netherlands, 2003.

The Round Up (La Rafle). Directed by Rose Boch. France/Germany/Hungary, 2010.

Sarah's Key. Directed by Gilles Paquet-Brenner. France, 2010.

8. FLASHOVER: THE KILLING CENTERS, 1942–1944

Arad, Yitzak. *Belzec, Sobibor, Treblinka: The Operation Reinhard Death Camps.* Bloomington: Indiana University Press, 1987.

Berr, Hélène. *The Journal of Hélène Berr.* Translated by David Bellos. New York: Weinstein Books, 2008.

Birn, Ruth Bettina. "Austrian Higher SS and Police Leaders and Their Participation in the Holocaust in the Balkans." *Holocaust and Genocide Studies* 6, no. 4 (1992): 351–72.

Blatt, Thomas (Toivi). *Sobibor: The Forgotten Revolt.* Issaquah, Washington: H.E.P., 1998.

Borowski, Tadeusz. *This Way for the Gas, Ladies and Gentlemen.* Translated by Barbara Vedder. New York: Penguin, 1976. (Note: this is written in the form of short stories.)

Delbo, Charlotte. *None of Us Will Return.* Translated by John Githens. Boston: Beacon, 1967.

Dwork, Debórah, and Robert Jan van Pelt. *Auschwitz, 1270 to the Present.* New York: Norton, 1996.

Friedländer, Saul. *Kurt Gerstein: The Ambiguity of Good.* Translated by Charles Fullman. New York: Knopf, 1969.

Friedman, Henry. *I'm No Hero: Journeys of a Holocaust Survivor.* Seattle: University of Washington Press, 1999.

Fulbrook, Mary. *A Small Town Near Auschwitz: Ordinary Nazis and the Holocaust.* Oxford: Oxford University Press, 2012.

Greenberg, Gershon. "The Theological Letters of Rabbi Talmud of Lublin, 1942." In *Ghettos 1939–1945: New Research and Perspectives on Definitions, Daily Life, and Survival,* 113–28. Washington, DC: U.S. Holocaust Memorial Museum, 2005.

Greif, Gideon. *We Wept without Tears: Testimonies of the Jewish Sonderkommando from Auschwitz.* New Haven, CT: Yale University Press, 2005.

Grossman, Vasily Semenovich. *The Road: Stories, Journalism, and Essays.* Edited by Elizabeth Chandler, et al. Translated by Robert and Elizabeth Chandler with Olga Mukovnikova. New York: New York Review Books, 2010.

Heberer, Patricia. *Children during the Holocaust.* Lanham, MD: AltaMira Press in association with the U.S. Holocaust Memorial Museum, 2011.

Hedgepeth, Sonja M., and Rochelle G. Saidel, eds. *Sexual Violence against Jewish Women during the Holocaust.* Lebanon, NH: University Press of New England, 2010.

Herbert, Ulrich, ed. *National Socialist Extermination Policies: Contemporary German Perspectives and Controversies.* New York: Berghahn, 2000.

Hillesum, Etty. *An Interrupted Life: The Diary of Etty Hillesum.* New York: Pocket Books, 1981.

———. *Letters from Westerbork.* Translated by Arnold J. Pomerans. New York: Pantheon, 1986.

Hoess, Rudolf. *Commandant of Auschwitz: The Autobiography of Rudolf Hoess.* Translated by Andrew Pollinger. Buffalo, NY: Prometheus, 1992.

Hájková, Anna. "Sexual Barter in Times of Genocide: Negotiating the Sexual Economy of the Theresienstadt Ghetto." *Signs: Journal of Women in Culture and Society* 38, no. 3 (Spring 2013): 503–33.

Karski, Jan. *Story of a Secret State: My Report to the World.* New York: Houghton Mifflin, 1944. Republished by Georgetown University Press, 2013.

Kerenji, Emil, ed. *Jewish Responses to Persecution.* Vol. 4: *1942–1943.* Lanham, MD: Rowman & Littlefield, 2015.

Korczak, Janusz. *Ghetto Diary.* Edited and translated by H. Goldsmitz. New York: Holocaust Library, 1978.

Lanzmann, Claude. *Shoah: An Oral History of the Holocaust: The Complete Text of the Film.* New York: Pantheon, 1985.

Lindeman, Yehudi, ed. *Shards of Memory: Narratives of Holocaust Survival.* Westport, CT: Praeger, 2007.

Mailänder, Elissa. *Female SS Guards and Workaday Violence: The Majdanek Concentration Camp, 1942–1944.* Translated by Patricia Szobar. East Lansing: Michigan State University Press, 2015.

Millu, Liana. *Smoke over Birkenau.* Translated by Lynne Sharon Schwartz. Evanston, IL: Northwestern University Press, 1991. (Note: written in the form of short stories.)

Moore, Bob. *Survivors: Jewish Self-Help and Rescue in Nazi-Occupied Western Europe.* Oxford: Oxford University Press, 2010.

Muller, Filip. *Eyewitness Auschwitz.* Edited and translated by Susanne Flatauer. Chicago: Ivan R. Dee in association with the U.S. Holocaust Memorial Museum, 1999.

Paulovicova, Nina. "Rescue of Jews in the Slovak State, 1939–1945." PhD dissertation, History. University of Alberta, Edmonton, Canada, 2012.

Pawelczynska, Anna. *Values and Violence in Auschwitz: A Sociological Analysis.* Translated by Catherine S. Leach. Berkeley: University of California Press, 1979.

Perechodnik, Calel. *Am I a Murderer? Testament of a Jewish Ghetto Policeman.* Edited and translated by Frank Foxed. Boulder, CO: Westview, 1996.

Ringelheim, Joan. "Women and the Holocaust: A Reconsideration of Research." *Signs: Journal of Women in Culture and Society* 10 (1985): 741–61.

Rittner, Carol, and John Roth, eds. *Different Voices: Women and the Holocaust.* New York: Paragon House, 1993.

Roma and Sinti, Under-Studied Victims of Nazism: Symposium Proceedings. Washington, DC: United States Holocaust Memorial Museum, 2002.

Roskies, David G., ed. *The Literature of Destruction: Jewish Responses to Catastrophe.* Philadelphia: Jewish Publication Society, 1989.

Rotem, Simha. "Kazik." In *Memoirs of a Warsaw Ghetto Fighter,* translated by Barbara Harshav. New Haven, CT: Yale University Press, 1994.

Scholl, Inge. *The White Rose: Munich, 1942–1943.* 2nd ed. Translated by Arthur R. Schultz. Hanover, NH: Wesleyan University Press, 1983.

Seidman, Hillel. *The Warsaw Ghetto Diaries.* Translated by Yosef Israel. Southfield, MI: Targum, 1997.

Sereny, Gitta. *Into That Darkness: An Examination of Conscience.* New York: Vintage, 1983.

Shapiro, Amy H., and Myrna Goldenberg, eds. *Different Horrors, Same Hell: Gender and the Holocaust.* Seattle: University of Washington Press, 2013.

Shik, Na'ama. "Infinite Loneliness: Some Aspects of the Lives of Jewish Women in the Auschwitz Camps According to Testimonies and Autobiographies from 1945–1948." In *Lessons and Legacies VIII*, edited by Doris L. Bergen, 125–56. Evanston, IL: Northwestern University Press, 2008.

Spiegelman, Art. *Maus: A Survivor's Tale.* 2 vols. New York: Pantheon, 1986. (Note: family memoir in the form of a graphic novel.)

Stabholz, Thaddeus. *Seven Hells.* Translated by Jacques Grunblatt and Hilda R. Grunblatt. New York: Holocaust Library, 1990.

Steinbacher, Sybille. *Auschwitz: A History.* Translated by Shaun Whiteside. New York: HarperCollins, 2006.

Suhl, Yuri, ed. *They Fought Back: The Story of Jewish Resistance in Nazi Europe.* New York: Schocken, 1967.

Tec, Nechama. *Resilience and Courage: Women, Men, and the Holocaust.* New Haven: Yale University Press, 2003.

———. *When Light Pierced the Darkness: Christian Rescue of Jews in Nazi-Occupied Poland.* New York: Oxford University Press, 1986.

Troller, Norbert. *Theresienstadt: Hitler's Gift to the Jews.* Edited by Joel Shatzky. Translated by Susan E. Cernyak-Spatz. Chapel Hill: University of North Carolina Press, 1991.

Walke, Anika. *Pioneers and Partisans: An Oral History of Nazi Genocide in Belorussia.* New York: Oxford University Press, 2015.

Weiss-Wendt, Anton, ed. *The Nazi Genocide of the Roma: Reassessment and Commemoration.* New York: Berghahn, 2013.

Wood, E. Thomas, and Stanislaw M. Jankowski. *Karski: How One Man Tried to Stop the Holocaust.* New York: Wiley, 1994.

Films

As If It Were Yesterday (*Comme si c'était hier*). Directed by Myriam Abramowicz and Esther Hoffenberg. Belgium, 1980.

Auschwitz: Inside the Nazi State (also known as *Auschwitz: The Nazis and the "Final Solution"*). Directed by Lawrence Rees. United Kingdom, 2005.

Defiance. Directed by Edward Zwick. United States, 2008.

Diamonds in the Snow. Directed by Mira Reym Binford. United States, 1994.

Distant Journey (*Daleká cesta*). Directed by Alfréd Radok. Czechoslovakia, 1950.

Escape from Sobibor. Directed by Jack Gold. United Kingdom/Yugoslavia, 1987.

Hélène Berr, une jeune fille dans Paris occupé. Directed by Jérôme Prieur. France, 2013.

In Darkness: Sous Terre. Directed by Agnieszka Holland. Poland/Germany/Canada, 2011.

Jacob the Liar. Directed by Frank Beyer. East Germany/Czechoslovakia, 1975.

Korczak. Directed by Andrzej Wajda. Poland/Germany/United Kingdom, 1990.

The Last Stage (Ostatni etap). Directed by Wanda Jakubowska. Poland, 1948.

Latcho Drom: (Bonne Route). Directed by Tony Gatlif. France, 1993.

Schindler's List. Directed by Steven Spielberg. United States, 1993.

Secret Lives: Hidden Children and Their Rescuers during WWII. Directed by Aviva Slesin. United States, 2002.

The Shop on Main Street (Obchod na korze). Directed by Ján Kadár and Elmar Klos. Czechoslovakia, 1965.

Train of Life. Directed by Radu Mihaileanu. France/Belgium/Netherlands/Israel/Romania, 1998.

The White Rose (Die Weiße Rose). Directed by Michael Verhoeven. West Germany, 1982.

9. DEATH THROES AND KILLING FRENZIES, 1944–1945

Bessel, Richard. *Germany 1945: From War to Peace.* London: Simon & Schuster, 2009.

Blatman, Daniel. *The Death Marches: The Final Phase of Nazi Genocide.* Translated by Chaya Galai. Cambridge, MA: Belknap Press of Harvard University Press, 2011.

Braham, Randolph L. *The Politics of Genocide: The Holocaust in Hungary.* Condensed ed. Detroit: Wayne State University Press, 2000.

Braham, Randolph, and Scott Miller, eds. *The Nazis' Last Victims: The Holocaust in Hungary.* Detroit: Wayne State University Press, 1998.

Celinscak, Mark. *Distance from the Belsen Heap: Allied Forces and the Liberation of a Nazi Concentration Camp.* Toronto: University of Toronto Press, 2015.

Elias, Ruth. *Triumph of Hope: From Theresienstadt and Auschwitz to Israel.* Translated by Margot Bettauer Dembo. New York: Wiley, 1998.

Fein, Helen. *Accounting for Genocide: National Responses and Jewish Victimization During the Holocaust.* Chicago: University of Chicago Press, 1984.

Fritz, Stephen G. *Endkampf: Soldiers, Civilians, and the Death of the Third Reich.* Lexington: University Press of Kentucky, 2004.

Goldhagen, Daniel Jonah. *Hitler's Willing Executioners.* New York: Knopf, 1996.

Grier, Howard D. *Hitler, Dönitz, and the Baltic Sea: the Third Reich's Last Hope, 1944–1945.* Annapolis, MD: Naval Institute Press, 2007.

Gutman, Israel, and Michael Berenbaum, eds. *Anatomy of the Auschwitz Death Camp.* Bloomington: Indiana University Press in association with U.S. Holocaust Memorial Museum, 1994.

Hackett, David A., ed. *The Buchenwald Report.* Translated by David A. Hackett. Boulder, CO: Westview, 1995.

Herzberg, Abel J. *Between Two Streams: A Diary from Bergen-Belsen.* Edited by the European Jewish Publications Society. Translated by Jack Santcross. New York: St. Martin's, 1997.

Hoffmann, Peter. *Stauffenberg: A Family History, 1905–1944*. 3rd ed. Montreal: McGill-Queen's University Press, 2008.

Isaacson, Judith Magyar. *Seed of Sarah: Memoirs of a Survivor*. Urbana: University of Illinois Press, 1990.

Kertész, Imre. *Fatelessness: A Novel*. Translated by Tim Wilkinson. New York: Vintage International, 2004.

_____. *Dossier K*. Edited by Zoltán Hafner. Translated by Tim Wilkinson. Brooklyn: Melville House, 2013.

Klein, Gerda Weissmann. *All But My Life*. New York: Hill and Wang, 1995.

Kofman, Sarah. *Rue Ordener, Rue Labat*. Translated by Ann Smock. Lincoln, NE: University of Nebraska Press, 1996.

Kruk, Herman. *The Last Days of the Jerusalem of Lithuania: Chronicles from the Vilna Ghetto and the Camps, 1939–1944*. Edited by Benjamin Harshav. Translated by Barbara Harshav. New Haven, CT: YIVO Institute for Jewish Research, 2002.

Lévy-Hass, Hanna. *Diary of Bergen-Belsen, 1944–1945*. Chicago: Haymarket, 2009.

Meier, Lili, and Peter Hellman. *The Auschwitz Album: A Book Based upon an Album Discovered by a Concentration Camp Survivor, Lili Meier*. New York: Random House, 1981.

Moltke, Helmuth James von. *Letters to Freya 1939–1945*. Edited and translated by Beate Ruhm von Oppen. New York: Knopf, 1990.

Neufeld, Michael J., and Michael Berenbaum, eds. *The Bombing of Auschwitz: Should the Allies Have Attempted It?* New York: St. Martin's, 2000.

Pasher, Yaron. *Holocaust versus Wehrmacht: How Hitler's Final Solution Undermined the German War Effort*. Lawrence, KS: University Press of Kansas, 2014.

Prusin, Alexander Victor. "'Fascist Criminals to the Gallows!': The Holocaust and Soviet War Crimes Trials, December 1945–February 1946." *Holocaust and Genocide Studies* 17, no. 1 (2003): 1–30.

Robins, Marianne Ruel. "A Grey Site of Memory: Le Chambon-sur-Lignon and Protestant Exceptionalism on the Plateau Viverais-Lignon." *Church History* 82, no. 2 (June 2013): 317–52.

Sereny, Gitta. *Albert Speer: His Battle with Truth*. New York: Knopf, 1995.

Siegal, Aranka. *Grace in the Wilderness: After the Liberation, 1945–1948*. New York: Farrar, Straus, Giroux, 1985.

Speer, Albert. *Inside the Third Reich: Memoirs*. Translated by Richard Winston and Clara Winston. New York: Macmillan, 1970.

Stargardt, Nicholas. *The German War: A Nation under Arms, 1939–1945*. New York: Basic Books, 2015.

Venezia, Shlomo. *Inside the Gas Chambers: Eight Months in the Sonderkommando of Auschwitz*. Edited by Béatrice Prasquier and Jean Mouttapa. Translated by Andrew Brown. Cambridge, UK: Polity, 2009.

Volavková, Hana, ed. *I Never Saw Another Butterfly: Children's Drawings and Poems from Terezin Concentration Camp, 1942–1944*. 2nd ed. New York: Pantheon, 1994.

Wallenberg, Raoul. *Letters and Dispatches: 1924–1944.* Translated by Kjersti Board. New York: Arcade, 1995.

Weinberg, Gerhard L. *Visions of Victory: The Hopes of Eight World War II Leaders.* New York: Cambridge University Press, 2005.

Wells, Leon Welickzer. *The Janowska Road.* New York: Macmillan, 1999.

Wiesel, Elie. *Night.* Translated by Marion Wiesel. New York: Hill and Wang, 2006.

Yelton, David K. *Hitler's Volkssturm: The Nazi Militia and the Fall of Germany, 1944–1945.* Lawrence: University Press of Kansas, 2002.

Films

Aimee & Jaguar. Directed by Max Färberböck. Germany, 1999.

Blind Spot: Hitler's Secretary. Directed by André Heller and Othmar Schmiderer. Austria, 2002.

The Courage to Care: Rescuers of Jews during the Holocaust. Directed by Robert H. Gardner. United States, 1985.

Fateless (Sorstalanság). Directed by Lajos Koltai. Hungary/Germany/United Kingdom/Israel/France, 2005.

The Last of the Unjust. Directed by Claude Lanzmann. France/Austria, 2013.

Life is Beautiful. Directed by Roberto Benigni. Italy, 1997.

The Long Way Home. Directed by Mark Jonathan Harris. United States, 1997.

Majdanek – Cmentarzysko Europy (English version). Directed by Aleksander Ford. Poland, 1945.

Majdanek 1944: Victim and Perpetrator. Compiled by Irmgard and Bengt von zur Mühlen. West Germany, 1986.

One Survivor Remembers. Directed by Kary Antholis. United States, 1996.

Son of Saul (Saul Fia). Directed by László Nemes. Hungary, 2015.

Three Days in April (Drei Tage im April). Directed by Oliver Storz. Germany, 1995.

Three War Films: A Generation; Kanal; Ashes and Diamonds. Directed by Andrzej Wajda. United States, 2005.

Sunshine. Directed by István Szabó. Germany/Austria/Canada/Hungary/France, 1999.

Weapons of the Spirit. Directed by Pierre Sauvage. France, 1987.

CONCLUSION: LEGACIES OF ATROCITY

Abzug, Robert H. *Inside the Vicious Heart: Americans and the Liberation of Nazi Concentration Camps.* New York: Oxford University Press, 1985.

Améry, Jean. *At the Mind's Limits: Contemplations by a Survivor on Auschwitz and Its Realities.* Translated by Sidney Rosenfeld and Stella P. Rosenfeld. New York: Schocken, 1986.

Auerbach, Karen. *The House at Ujazdowskie 16: Jewish Families in Warsaw after the Holocaust.* Bloomington: Indiana University Press, 2013.

Bar-On, Dan. *Fear and Hope: Three Generations of the Holocaust.* Cambridge, MA: Harvard University Press, 1995.

Bartov, Omer. *Erased: Vanishing Traces of Jewish Galicia in Present-Day Ukraine.* Princeton, NJ: Princeton University Press, 2007.

Bartov, Omer, Atina Grossmann, and Mary Nolan, eds. *Crimes of War: Guilt and Denial in the Twentieth Century.* New York: The New Press, 2002.

Brenner, Michael. *After the Holocaust: Rebuilding Jewish Lives in Postwar Germany.* Translated by Barbara Harshav. Princeton, NJ: Princeton University Press, 1997.

Byford, Jovan. "Shortly afterwards, we heard the sound of the gas van! Survivor Testimony and the Writing of History in Socialist Yugoslavia." *History and Memory* 22, no. 1 (2010): 5–47.

Cohen, Beth B. *Case Closed: Holocaust Survivors in Postwar America.* New Brunswick, NJ: Rutgers University Press, 2007.

Connelly, John. *From Enemy to Brother: The Revolution in Catholic Teaching on the Jews, 1933–1965.* Cambridge, MA: Harvard University Press, 2012.

Dinnerstein, Leonard. *America and the Survivors of the Holocaust.* New York: Columbia University Press, 1982.

Diner, Hasia. *We Remember with Reverence and Love: American Jews and the Myth of Silence after the Holocaust.* New York: New York University Press, 2009.

Douglas, Lawrence. *The Memory of Judgment: Making Law and History in the Trials of the Holocaust.* New Haven: Yale University Press, 2001.

———. *The Right Wrong Man: John Demjanjuk and the Last Great Nazi War Crimes Trial.* Princeton, NJ: Princeton University Press, 2016.

Earl, Hilary. *The Nuremberg SS-Einsatzgruppen Trial, 1945–1958: Atrocity, Law, and History.* New York: Cambridge University Press, 2009.

Feinstein, Margarete Myers. *Holocaust Survivors in Post-War Germany, 1945–1957.* New York: Cambridge University Press, 2010.

Friedlander, Henry. "The T4 Killers: Berlin, Lublin, San Sabba." In *The Holocaust and History: The Known, the Unknown, the Disputed, and the Reexamined,* edited by Michael Berenbaum and Abraham J. Peck, 243–51. Bloomington: Indiana University Press in association with the U.S. Holocaust Memorial Museum, 1998.

Friling, Tuvia. *A Jewish Kapo in Auschwitz: History, Memory, and the Politics of Survival.* Waltham, MA: Brandeis University Press, 2014.

Frommer, Benjamin. *National Cleansing: Retribution against Nazi Collaborators in Postwar Czechoslovakia.* New York: Cambridge University Press, 2005.

Gigliotti, Simone, and Monica Tempian, eds. *The Young Victims of the Nazi Regime: Migration, the Holocaust and Postwar Displacement.* London: Bloomsbury, 2016.

Gross, Jan T. *Fear: Anti-Semitism in Poland after Auschwitz.* New York: Random House, 2006.

Gross, Jan T., and Irena Grudzińska Gross. *Golden Harvest: Events at the Periphery of the Holocaust*. New York: Oxford University Press, 2012.

Grossmann, Atina. *Jews, Germans, and Allies: Close Encounters in Occupied Germany*. Princeton, NJ: Princeton University Press, 2007.

Heberer, Patricia, and Jürgen Matthäus, eds. *Atrocities on Trial: Historical Perspectives on the Politics of Prosecuting War Crimes*. Lincoln: University of Nebraska Press, 2008.

Hébert, Valerie Geneviève. *Hitler's Generals on Trial: The Last War Crimes Tribunal at Nuremberg*. Lawrence: University Press of Kansas, 2010.

Herzog, Dagmar. *Sex After Fascism: Memory and Morality in Twentieth-Century Germany*. Princeton, NJ: Princeton University Press, 2005.

Himka, John-Paul, and Joanna Beata Michlic, eds. *Bringing the Dark Past to Light: the Reception of the Holocaust in Post-Communist Europe*. Lincoln: University of Nebraska Press, 2013.

Hirsch, Marianne. *The Generation of Postmemory: Writing and Visual Culture After the Holocaust*. New York: Columbia University Press, 2012.

Hoffman, Eva. *After Such Knowledge: Memory, History and the Legacy of the Holocaust*. New York: Public Affairs, 2004.

Horowitz, Sara. "The Gender of Good and Evil: Women and Holocaust Memory." In *Gray Zones: Ambiguity and Compromise in the Holocaust and its Aftermath*, edited by Jonathan Petropoulos and John K. Roth, 165–84. New York: Berghahn, 2005.

Jardim, Tomaz. *The Mauthausen Trial: American Military Justice in Germany*. Cambridge, MA: Harvard University Press, 2012.

Jockusch, Laura. *Collect and Record! Jewish Holocaust Documentation in Early Postwar Europe*. New York: Oxford University Press, 2012.

Jockusch, Laura, and Gabriel N. Finder, eds. *Jewish Honor Courts: Revenge, Retribution, and Reconciliation in Europe and Israel after the Holocaust*. Detroit: Wayne State University Press, 2015.

Judt, Tony. *Postwar: A History of Europe since 1945*. New York: Penguin, 2005.

Kellenbach, Katharina von. *The Mark of Cain: Guilt and Denial in the Post-War Lives of Nazi Perpetrators*. New York: Oxford University Press, 2013.

Langer, Lawrence. *Holocaust Testimonies: Ruins of Memory*. New Haven, CT: Yale University Press, 1991.

Levi, Primo. *The Drowned and the Saved*. Translated by Raymond Rosenthal. New York: Summit, 1988.

Mankowitz, Zeev W. *Life Between Memory and Hope: The Survivors of the Holocaust in Occupied Germany*. New York: Cambridge University Press, 2002.

Marrus, Michael R. *Lessons of the Holocaust*. Toronto: University of Toronto Press, 2016.

———. *The Nuremberg War Crimes Trial 1945–46: A Documentary History*. Boston: Bedford Books, 1997.

_____. *Some Measure of Justice: The Holocaust Era Restitution Campaign of the 1990s.* Madison: University of Wisconsin Press, 2009.

Meng, Michael. *Shattered Spaces: Encountering Jewish Ruins in Postwar Germany and Poland.* Cambridge, MA: Harvard University Press, 2011.

Miller, Judith. *One, by One, by One: Facing the Holocaust.* New York: Simon and Schuster, 1990.

Moyn, Samuel. *A Holocaust Controversy: The Treblinka Affair in Postwar France.* Hanover, NH: University Press of New England, 2005.

Naimark, Norman. *The Russians in Germany: A History of the Soviet Zone of Occupation, 1945–1949.* Cambridge, MA: Belknap, 1995.

Niewyk, Donald L., ed. *Fresh Wounds: Early Narratives of Holocaust Survival.* Chapel Hill: University of North Carolina Press, 1998.

Novick, Peter. *The Holocaust in American Life.* Boston: Houghton Mifflin, 1999.

Pendas, Devin O. *The Frankfurt Auschwitz Trial, 1963–1965: Genocide, History, and the Limits of the Law.* Cambridge: Cambridge University Press, 2006.

Pfefferkorn, Eli. *The Muselmann at the Water Cooler.* Boston: Academic Studies Press, 2011.

Rosen, Alan. *The Wonder of Their Voices: The 1946 Holocaust Interviews of David Boder.* New York: Oxford University Press, 2010.

Rothberg, Michael. *Multidirectional Memory: Remembering the Holocaust in the Age of Decolonization.* Stanford, CA: Stanford University Press, 2009.

Rubenstein, Richard L. *After Auschwitz: History, Theory, and Contemporary Judaism.* Baltimore: Johns Hopkins University Press, 1992.

Segev, Tom. *The Seventh Million: The Israelis and the Holocaust.* Translated by Haim Watzman. New York: Hill & Wang, 1993.

Seidman, Naomi. *Faithful Renderings: Jewish-Christian Difference and the Politics of Translation.* Chicago, IL: University of Chicago Press, 2006.

Shenker, Noah. *Reframing Holocaust Testimony.* Bloomington: Indiana University Press, 2015.

Stangneth, Bettina. *Eichmann before Jerusalem: The Unexamined Life of a Mass Murderer.* Translated by Ruth Martin. New York: Alfred A. Knopf, 2014.

Steinlauf, Michael. *Bondage to the Dead: Poland and the Memory of the Holocaust.* Syracuse, NY: Syracuse University Press, 1997.

Stone, Dan. *The Liberation of the Camps: The End of the Holocaust and Its Aftermath.* New Haven, CT: Yale University Press, 2015.

Trials of War Criminals before the Nuremberg Military Tribunals under Control Council Law No. 10, October 1946–April 1949. 42 vols. Nuremberg: U.S. Government Printing Office, 1947–1949.

Wiese, Christian, and Paul Betts, eds. *Years of Persecution, Years of Extermination: Saul Friedländer and the Future of Holocaust Studies.* New York: Continuum, 2010.

Wittmann, Rebecca. *Beyond Justice: The Auschwitz Trial*. Cambridge, MA: Harvard University Press, 2005.

Young, James E. *The Texture of Memory: Holocaust Memorials and Meaning*. New Haven, CT: Yale University Press, 1993.

Zahra, Tara. *The Lost Children: Reconstructing Europe's Families after World War II*. Cambridge, MA: Harvard University Press, 2011.

Films

2 or 3 Things I Know about Him (2 oder 3 Dinge, die ich von ihm weiß). Directed by Malte Ludin. Germany, 2005.

Dark Lullabies. Directed by Irene Angelico. Canada, 1985.

Everything's for You. Directed by Abraham Ravett. United States, 1989.

The Flat. Directed by Arnon Goldfinger. Israel / Germany, 2011.

Hotel Terminus: The Life and Times of Klaus Barbie. Directed by Marcel Ophuls. West Germany/France/United States, 1988.

Hannah Arendt. Directed by Margarethe von Trotta. Germany/Luxembourg/France/Israel, 2012.

Ida. Directed by Paweł Pawlikowski. Poland/Denmark/France/United Kingdom, 2013.

Judgment at Nuremberg. Directed by Stanley Kramer. United States, 1961.

Memories of the Eichmann Trial. Directed by David Perlov. Israel, 1979.

The Murderers Are Among Us (Die Mörder sind unter uns). Directed by Wolfgang Staudte. Germany, 1946.

Numbered. Directed by Dana Doron and Uriel Sinai. Israel, 2012.

Primo Levi's Journey (La strada di Levi). Directed by Davide Ferrario. Italy, 2006.

Punch Me in the Stomach. Directed by Francine Zuckerman. Written and performed by Deb Filler. New Zealand / Canada, 1997.

Sister Rose's Passion. Directed by Oren Jacoby. United States, 2004.

Unzere Kinder. Directed by Natan Gross and Shaul Goskind. Poland, 1948. Released in the United States as *It Will Never Happen Again*. Also available as *Our Children*.

INDEX

14f13, 164, 242

AB-Aktion, 137

Abel, Theodore, 82

Africa, 121, 146, 174. *See also* Ethiopia; North Africa; South Africa; Southwest Africa

African soldiers, 175; in occupation of Germany after World War I, 35–36; as victims of killings in 1940, 174–75

Afrika Korps, 210, 231

Afro-Germans, 35–36, 75–76, 94–95

Against the Jews and their Lies, 17

air raids: Allied: 277–78; German: 99, 170–71, 179–80, 183. *See also* Blitzkrieg; Luftwaffe

alcohol, 80, 81, 88, 108, 139, 144, 195, 218, 241, 256

Albania, 233

Algeria, 176, 231

Allied forces/Allies, 173–74, 177–79, 225, 230–33; and Jews, 223, 264–65; in the last year of war, 277, 293–94, 300–2; in post-war: 306–9. *See also* Britain, Soviet Union, United States, World War II

Alsace-Lorraine, 42, 174

Alten, Mark, 154

Americans. *See* United States

Amsterdam, 170–71, 243–44

Anders' Army, 266–67

Anders, Wladyslaw, 266

Ansbach, 162

Anschluss (annexation of Austria), 103–4. *See also* Austria; Germany

antisemitism, 14–18, 49; as center of Nazi ideology, 3, 53–56, 210; Hitler's, 53–56; linked to other Nazi prejudices, 18, 25–37, 28, 32, 35–37, 41, 53; outside Germany, 15–18, 134–35, 155, 202–3; redemptive antisemitism, 3, 54–55

anti-Slavic attitudes, 39–40

Antonescu, Ion, 202–3

Antwerp, 171

appeasement, 106–7

Appelfeld, Aharon, 202–3

Ardennes Offensive. *See* Battle of the
    Bulge
Arendt, Hannah, 150, 157
Argentina, 306
armistice agreement, German-French,
    175–76
Arrow Cross, 287
Article 48, Weimar Constitution, 66–67
Article 231, Treaty of Versailles, 42
"Aryans," 76–79, 186, 188, 213–14,
    226, 257; as a constructed category,
    52–53, 92; and western and northern
    Europeans, 157, 169
Ascher, Carol, 112
"asocials," 32–33, 80–82; in
    concentration camps, 114–15, 217–19
Augspurg, Anita, 119–20
Auschwitz (and Auschwitz-Birkenau),
    2–3, 9–10, 155, 214, 219, 220, 228,
    251–55, 260; and deportations
    from ghettos, 148, 152, 154; and
    deportations from western Europe,
    170, 174, 180, 233–35, 243–44; at
    the end of the war, 287–88, 292,
    301; Hungarian Jews and, 143, 279,
    282–87; other Jews in, 233, 243;
    resistance in, 288; Roma in, 30, 257,
    288; Soviet POWs in, 205–6. *See also*
    killing centers
Auschwitz album, 254, 284–85
Australia, 79, 121, 177–78, 305
Austria, 42, 47–50, 107; Anschluss and,
    103–4; Jews from, 113, 149, 171
Austria-Hungary, 40, 63
Axis, Rome-Berlin, 117

Babinska, Bogumila, 220–21
Babi Yar, 199–201
Bach-Zelewski, Erich von dem, 60
Baden Baden, 110, 112
Badoglio, Pietro, 233
Baeck, Leo, 79–80
Balkans, 183–86. *See also* Greece;
    Yugoslavia

Baltic States, 118. *See also* Estonia; Latvia;
    Lithuania
Bartov, Omer, 187
Battle of Britain, 177–80
Battle of the Bulge, 293
Battle of Stalingrad, 223–25, 228
Bavaria, 49–51, 56, 159, 165, 292
Beer Hall Putsch, 50, 65, 110
Belaya Tserkov, 200
Belgian Congo, 38
Belgium, 38, 62–63, 170–73
Belgrade, 183
Belorussia, 155, 191, 195, 214. *See also*
    Soviet Union
Belzec, 228, 242, 248–50. *See also* killing
    centers.
Benjamin, Kate, 122
Berehovo (Beregszász), 283–84
Bergen-Belsen, 2, 170, 217, 292, 298,
    301, 307–8. *See also* concentration
    camps
Berk, Shoshana Bluma (Sarid), 261–62
Berlin, 1–2, 96, 98, 294,
    298; concentration camps nearby, 101,
    114; gay community, 33–34, 73; Jews
    in, 111, 226, 253; T-4 program, 159–60
Berlin-Plötzensee, 280
Bernburg, 164
Berr, Hélène, 243
Bessarabia, 181
Bialystok, 149, 267
Bielski partisans, 145
Bielski, Tuvia, 145
Binding, Karl, 27, 42
Blaskowitz, Johannes, 144
Blatman, Daniel, 290
Blitzkrieg, 130–33, 168, 194, 210. *See also*
    Germany, Poland
Boix, Francisco, 221
Blomberg, Werner von, 99
Bolsheviks/Bolshevism, 40–41. *See also*
    communism, communists; Russia;
    Soviet Union
Borkowska, Anna, 211

Bosnia, 184. *See also* Yugoslavia

Bouhler, Philipp, 127, 159, 162

boycott, anti-Jewish, 76–79

Brandenburg, 160, 164

Brandt, Karl, 127, 159, 162

Brauchitsch, Walter von, 99

Braun, Eva, 294

Braunau am Inn, 47

Brazil, 306

Brecht, Bertolt, 84, 121

Breitman, Richard, 60

Brest Litovsk, Treaty of, 42

Brezkis, Tad, 270–71

Britain, 97; Battle of, 108–10; final stages of war, 277, 293; as imperial power, 37–39; Jews and, 78, 114, 125–26, 178–80, 264–65; navy, 168; as occupying power, 299–301, 305–9; partisans and, 263; pre-war relations with Germany, 106–7, 117; World War I, 42, 64; World War II, 131, 168–73, 177–80

brothels, 141, 218, 223, 254

Bruckberg, 162

Brüning, Heinrich, 66

Brussels, 171

Bryan, Julien, 85–86

Buchenwald, 114, 217–18, 299, 307–8. *See also* concentration camps

Budapest, 287

Budisavljevi□, Diana, 10

Bug River, 202

Bukhara, 300

Bukovina, 181

Bulgaria, 180, 183, 283–84

Buna rubber works, 252

Burgsteinfurt, 307–8

Bydgoszcz (Bromberg), 137–38, 160

Canada, 2, 23, 177–78, 265, 306; as a destination for refugees and fugitives, 79, 121, 124–25, 298, 305; as storage area in Auschwitz, 252–53

Capra, Frank, 171

Caribbean, 121, 305

Casablanca (movie), 176–77

Catholic Church, 75, 143; in Germany, 86–87, 115; protest against and legitimation of Nazi measures, 81, 86–87, 163–65. *See also* Christianity; Clemens August von Galen; Pius XI; Pius XII; protest; Vatican

Caucasus, 119, 224–25

Central Asia (Soviet), 22, 119, 135, 188, 191, 266, 295

Chamberlain, Neville, 106–7

chaplains, military, 200–1, 224–25, 227, 295

Chelmno (Kulmhof), 8, 149, 206, 209, 228, 242, 246–48, 256. *See also* killing centers

children: Germanization of, 214, 272; Jehovah's Witnesses' taken away, 116; Jewish children, 10, 19, 93–94, 171–73, 214, 243, 252, 262, 309; post-war, 303, 305; Jewish children rescued and hidden, 125–26, 245, 261–62; Roma children killed, 257–58; in Volkssturm, 281

China, 121–22

Christianity, 77–78; antisemitism and Jews and, 15–17; Nazi suspicion of, 57, 115, 227; role in protests against Nazi measures, 106–7, 163–65. *See also* Catholic Church; Protestant church in Germany

Churchill, Winston, 178–79, 264

circumcision, 20, 261, 266

code-breaking, 168, 264–65

collaboration, 169–170, 176, 184, 216, 231, 243, 263, 273; post-war fate of, 304, 306

communism, 40–41; Hitler and, 56, 99; Jews and, 41, 134–35; papacy and, 86, 143. *See also* Communist Party; communists; Soviet Union; Stalin

Communist Party, Germany, 41, 65–67, 73–74, 119; attacked under Nazism, 70–73, 114–15; resistance and obstacles, 70–71. See also communism; communists

Communist Party, Soviet Union, 119

communists, 217, 219; Soviet purges of, 119; as targets of Nazism, 70–73, 114–15

concentration camps: in pre-war Germany, 71, 83–84, 101, 114–17; in World War II, 138–39, 217–22, 290–92

Concordat, with Vatican, 86–87, 115. See also Catholic Church; Pius XII

Conti, Leonardo, 159–161

conversion/converts from Judaism to Christianity, 16–17, 19, 76–77, 102, 174

Coventry, 179

Crimea, 227

criminals, imprisoned in concentration camps, 83–84, 217–19. See also "asocials"

Croatia, 10, 180, 184, 258. See also Yugoslavia

Cuba, 124–25

Czechoslovakia, 63, 293; German minority in, 40, 106; Jews from, 142, 149, 176;

resistance in, 272; Sudetenland crisis, 106–7

Czerniaków, Adam, 153, 257

D-Day, 278–80

Dachau, 61, 71, 83–84, 114–15, 126, 164, 252, 258, 289, 291, 302. See also concentration camps

Dante Alighieri, 220

Danube River, 287

Danzig (Gdansk), 134

death marches, 290–92, 302

de Gaulle, Charles, 176

Delmez, Marie-Thérèse, 171–73

Denmark, 117, 157, 169–70; rescue of Jews from, 180

denunciations, 96–97

deportations, 181, 191, 239–46, 282–87. See also ghettos; killing centers; resettlement schemes

deserters, Wehrmacht, 225–26, 281

Dietrich, Marlene, 79, 121

Dirlewanger, penal battalion, 223

disabled: attitudes toward, 25–27, 95; children killed, 126–27; as first victims of killing program, 3–4, 25, 126–27; 1933 and 1935 laws, 80–82, 95; protests against killing, 163–65. See also "Euthanasia"; T-4 program

displaced persons, 304–5

displaced persons camps, 305–6

Divine Comedy, 220

Dniester River, 202–3

Dominican Republic, 124

Dönitz, Karl, 294

Donskoy, Mark, 199

Dora-Mittelbau, 217–18

Drancy, 244

Dresden, 102

dual occupation, 133–36, 188, 191–92

Dubno, 196

Dumitru, Diana, 203

Dunkirk, 173, 178

East Prussia, 121, 280

Eckstein, Lilli, 93

Eglfing-Haar, 159

Egypt, 38

Ehrhardt, Sophie, 31

Eichberg, 164

Eichhorn, Max, 295

Eichmann, Adolf, 142–43, 208–11, 283, 306, 308; visits to killing centers, 251, 259

Einsatzgruppen, 138, 195–200, 202, 229–30, 232. See also Order Police, SS

Einstein, Albert, 84, 121

Eisenhower, Dwight D., 231, 279

Eisenstaedt, Alfred, 59–60

Eisysky, (Eishyshok), 198

El Alamein, 231

Eliach, Yaffa, 198
Eliot, T. S., 293
Elser, Georg, 5
Enabling Law, 71–73
Engelmann, Bernd, 87–88
Estonia, 117–18, 141, 181, 191, 209, 288
ethnic Germans: as beneficiaries of Nazi measures, 145, 157–58; involved in persecution and killing, 195–96, 202; in Poland, 140–42, 149; post-war displacement, 304; resettlement plans for, 141–42, 213; in Sudetenland, 106
Ethiopia, 231, 233
eugenics, 25–27
Eulenburg-Hertefeld, Philip zu, 33
"Euthanasia", 3, 129–30, 159–65, 242; children's program, 126–27, 159. *See also* disabled; T-4 program
Evian Conference, 124
experiments, Nazi medical, 159, 214, 217, 220–21, 252, 254

Fascists, Italian, 47, 65, 233. *See also* Italy; Mussolini
Finland, 180–82, 282
Fiszman, Joseph, 123
Flossenbürg, 205, 217, 292, 302
Fonseca, Isabel, 203
forced labor, 214–15, 233, 277–78
Foreign Office, German, 146
Four-Year Plan, 58, 98
France, 97, 106–7, 108–9, 114; invaded, 173–77; Jews and Roma in, 29, 50, 174, 243, 283–84, 302–3; killing of black soldiers in, 174–75; resistance in, 273; Rhineland and, 97–98; post-war, 62–63, 273; World War I and, 41–42, 62; World War II and, 131, 168–169, 173–77, 278–79
Franco, Francisco, 98–99, 107
Frank, Anne, 9, 79, 170–71
Frank, Hans, 134, 136, 143, 208, 248. *See also* General Government
Frank, Otto, 171

Frankfurt, 79, 164, 170
Frankfurter, Felix, 264
Free French forces, 176, 265
Freemasons, 36–37
Freikorps (Free Corps), 40
Frick, Wilhelm, 70, 80
Friedlander, Henry, 1–3, 27, 297–99
Friedländer, Saul, 3, 54, 176, 180
Friedman, Henry, 263
Fritsch, Werner von, 99
Führer principle, 57
functionalists, 46

Galen, Clemens August von, 163–65
Galicia, 192–94, 241–42
Gantner, Benno, 291
Garcia, Antonio, 221
gas, use of poison: on disabled, 160; on Jews, 247–54; on Soviet POWs, 206; vans, 160, 206, 247, 259
Gay, Peter (Fröhlich), 21, 111
Gellately, Robert, 97, 182
General Government, 134, 141–43, 208, 242, 248, 267. *See also* Poland
General Plan for the East, 213–14
genocide, 38–39, 58, 183, 235, 256, 260–61
Gens, Jacob, 153–54
German-Soviet Non-Aggression Pact. *See* Hitler-Stalin Pact
Germanization, 135, 149, 213–14, 247
Germans, popular opinion among: during war's end and post-war, 290–92; Nazi sensitivity toward, 73, 76–79, 127, 182, 204, 209, 215, 226, 277; in 1938, 104, 111–12; programs against disabled, 127; regarding homosexuals, 73–74; regarding Nazi revolution, 73–79, 81–82, 87–88, 89–90, 100; and war, 102–3, 130–31, 182–83, 225–26, 277–78
Germany: anti-black and anti-Slavic attitudes in, 35–36, 39–40; before Hitler, 29, 33, 35–36, 41–42, 61–67;

declarations of war on, 131, 168; East
Germany, 223, 304; as imperial power
in Africa, 38–39; Nazi revolution and
routinization in, 69–97; occupied,
293–309; pre-war expansion,
114–15; rearmament, 87, 97; wartime
conditions in, 225–27, 277–78; West
Germany, 213, 223; World War I and,
41–42 *See also* Germans; World War II
Gerstein Kurt, 249–50
Gestapo, 58, 90, 96–97, 130; roles outside
Germany, 212, 272
ghettos/ghettoization, 16, 145–46,
259; Jewish Councils and Jewish
police in, 149–54, 245; in Poland,
145–54, 244, 245–46; resistance in,
267, 269–70; Roma and Sinti in,
149, 248
Ginaite, Sara, 22–24, 211, 267–68,
289–90
Gleichschaltung, 82–83
Globocnik, Odilo, 60, 242, 257
Goebbels, Joseph, 57–60, 84, 107–10,
215, 226; death of, 294; jokes about,
53, 96; propaganda efforts of, 225,
229, 277, 279. *See also* propaganda
Goebbels, Magda, 59, 294
Göring, Hermann, 58–60, 70–72, 99,
143, 209, 241; Four-Year Plan and, 58,
98, 136; Luftwaffe and, 58, 169, 179;
war's end and suicide, 294, 308
Göttingen, 217
Goldenberg, Myrna, 260
Goldstein, Katharina (Prevost), 291
Gotfryd, Bernard, 158–59
Gotthold, Helene, 116
Graebe, Hermann, 196
Graf, Willi, 271–72
Grafeneck, 160, 164
Grand Mufti of Jerusalem (Hajj Amin
al-Husseini), 232
Great Depression, 61, 66, 79, 82
Greece, 183, 185–86; murder of Jews
from, 233–34, 276

Greenbaum, Ignac, 267
Grese, Irma, 219
Gross, Jan, 155–56
Grossman, Mendel, 147–48, 153, 246
Grossman, Shmuel, 147
Gross-Rosen, 205, 217, 292
Grynszpan, Herschel, 108–9
Gurs, concentration camp in, 176–77
Gürtner, Franz, 91
Gulag, 133, 134, 191
Gypsies. *See* Roma; Sinti

Habsburg Empire, 40, 63, 185
Hadamar, 160, 164. *See also* "Euthanasia";
T-4 program
Haiti, 124
Hannah, Devorah, 147
Harpuder, Gerda, 122
Hartheim, 164
Harvest Festival, 229–30
Hashomer Hatzair (Young Guard), 211
Hasidism, 20
Heartfield, John (Helmut Herzfeld),
71–72
Heck, Alfons, 95–96, 100–2, 111,
182–83
Heldenbergen, 93–94
Helmbrechts, 292
Herero, 38–39, 58
Herzegovina, 184
Heuaktion (hay action), 214
Heydrich, Reinhard, 60, 90, 142, 241,
249, 272; and deportation and
resettlement schemes, 140–42; and
Einsatzgruppen, 136, 194–95; and
Wannsee Conference, 208–11,
259–60
Heymann, Lida Gustava, 119–20
Hilberg, Raul, 13
Himmler, Heinrich, 83–84, 136, 141,
194–95, 205, 209, 285; as architect
of genocide, 241–42, 252; attacks on
Jehovah's Witnesses, homosexuals and
Roma, 60, 73, 90–91, 222, 257–58; SS

and, 60–61, 89–91, 216–17; at war's
    end, 290, 294. *See also* SS
Hindenburg, Paul von, 41, 64, 89, 91
Hirschfeld, Magnus, 33–34, 74
Hitler, Adolf, 45–58, 88–90, 96,
    135–36, 146, 175, 194; biographical
    information, 18, 47–52; consolidation
    of power, 90–91; inner circle, 58–60;
    murder of disabled and, 126–27,
    159, 161–65; plot to assassinate,
    280–81; pre-war foreign policy,
    85–87; progress of war and, 215,
    224–25, 231–32, 279–80; promise to
    annihilate Jews, 118, 183; response
    to protests, 226; rise to power,
    64–67; second book, 168, 188;
    significance of, 45–46, 69–70, 239;
    Stalin compared to, 181; at war's end,
    293–94; worldview, 49, 52–58
Hitler, Alois, 48
Hitler, Klara, 48
Hitler-Stalin Pact, 117–19, 131–36, 188,
    241
Hitler Youth (Hitler Jugend, HJ), 93, 95,
    100, 110, 183, 249
Hlinka Guard, 243
Hochberger, Isaac, 171–73
Hochberger, Regina, 171–73
Hoche, Alfred, 26, 42
Hoecker, Karl, 287
Hoess, Rudolf, 206, 252, 254
Hoffmann, Heinrich, 47, 206
Holland. *See* Netherlands
Holocaust, 5, 10, 237; legacies of,
    297–309
Home Army, Polish (AK), 144–45. *See
    also* Poland; underground; Warsaw
    uprising
homosexuality/homosexuals: accusations
    used to discredit, 32–33; in
    concentration camps, 95, 114–15, 217,
    219, 222–23; Nazi measures against,
    73–74; prejudices against, 33–34, 73,
    303

Horst Wessel song, 84, 110
Horthy, Miklos, 283
Hossbach Memorandum, 98–99, 106, 168
Huber, Kurt, 271–72
Huberband, Shimon, 146
Hungary, 42–43, 180, 183; Jews in, 228;
    Roma in, 29; war after Stalingrad and,
    228, 283, 293

IG Farben, 252
Iggers, Georg, 93
imperialism, 37–39
incorporated territories, from Poland
    into Germany, 133–34, 155, 247,
    256–57. *See also* Poland
India, 38, 121, 177–78, 232, 257
Indonesia, 38
inflation, 62–66
intentionalists, 46
International Military Tribunal, 307
International Red Cross, 171, 232, 260,
    303
Ioannina, 276
Irish Free State (Eire), 178
Isaacson, Judith Magyar, 286, 288
Isle of Man, 178
Israel, 79, 142–43, 213, 232, 305, 308
Italy, 38, 65, 103, 106–107, 185, 230–35;
    Jews and, 210; military cooperation
    with Germany, 98–99, 117, 180; war
    in, 233–34, 293
Izbica, 242, 264

Jacob, Lili (later Lili Zelmanovic Meier),
    285
Japan, 180, 210
Jarausch, Konrad, 205
Jeckeln, Friedrich, 60, 197, 240
Jedwabne, 9, 155, 192
Jehovah's Witnesses, 34–35, 74–75,
    303–4; in Nazi concentration camps,
    114–17, 217, 219, 222
Jewish Councils (Judenräte), 46, 149–51,
    152–54, 245, 306. *See also* ghettos

Jewish Fighting Organization, Warsaw (ZOB), 269. *See also* resistance
Jewish police, 151–52, 245, 306
Jews, 192, 240–242; in Austria after Anschluss, 104; in concentration and labor camps, 110, 125–26, 217–20; defined and marked, 92, 94; diversity among, 18–24; in ghettos, 145–54; in hiding, 193, 261–63; history of, 16–17, 18–20; Hitler, Nazi ideology and, 3, 52–56; killed by Einsatzgruppen, 195–200, 229–30, 240; Kristallnacht and, 107–14; linked to communism, 41, 134–35, 194, 201, 205, 211; 1933-1935 situation in Germany, 76–80, 91–94, 107–14; as partisans, 212–13; in Poland, 133–40, 141–42, 145–54, 264; post-war, 302–3, 306; as refugees, 188, 191, 304–5; repercussions of war on, 139–40; resistance among, 211–13; World War I and, 20; in Yugoslavia, 185
Judaism, 18–20
justice, post-war, 305–9
Justin, Eva, 114

Kadish, George, 289
Kamenets-Podolsk, 196–98, 240
kapos, 158, 219–20, 286, 288, 298, 306
Kaplan, Chaim, 150–51
Kaplan, Marion, 92
Karski, Jan, 264
Katyn Forest massacre, 225
Kaunas (Kovno), 22–23, 151–52, 211, 261–62, 289–90
Kazakhstan, 2, 191
Kempner, Vitka, 212
Kershaw, Ian, 57
KGB (People's Commisariat for State Security), 181
Kiev, 199–201
killing centers, 151, 268–69, 282–88, 300–2; described, 247–54; knowledge of, 255–57; opened, 206, 247

Kindertransports, 125–26, 178
Klemperer, Victor, 6, 90, 102
Kluger, Ruth, 104
Knappe, Siegfried, 168
Knauer baby, 126–27
Koch, Ilse, 219
Koch, Karl, 219
Kovner, Abba, 211–13, 265–66
Kovno. *See* Kaunas
Krakow, 134, 137, 139, 205
Kristallnacht pogrom, 107–14, 124–25; photography and, 109–11
Kruk, Herman, 288–89
Kulkielko, Renya, 131
Kuperminc, Irka, 153
Kusserow, Wolfgang, 116

labor camps, 217, 258, 288, 290, 303; combined with killing centers, 251–52, 254; Jews in, 240, 260, 267, 269, 285;
Landesberg, Hans, 176–77
Lang, Fritz, 121
Langer, Lawrence, 310
Latter-day Saints, Church of Jesus Christ of, 115
Latvia, 117–18, 141, 191; Soviet takeover, 181
Laval, Pierre, 176
Law for the Prevention of Hereditarily Diseased Offspring (Sterilization Law), 80–82, 115. *See also* eugenics; disabled; sterilization
Law for the Protection of German Blood and Honor. *See* Nuremberg Laws
League of German Girls (Bund deutscher Mädel, BDM), 82–83
League of Nations, 60, 62, 87
Lebensraum, 52, 188, 213–14
Leipelt, Hans, 271–72
Leitner, Isabella, 260
Lendvai, Karoly, 283
Leng, Herta, 112

Lenin, Vladimir Ilyich, 40–41, 63
Leningrad, 119, 282
lesbians, 32–33, 73–74. *See also*
    homosexuals; women
Levi, Elda, 276
Levi, Primo, 220, 234–35
Lewin, Ezekiel, 193
Libya, 231
Lidice, 272
Lieberman, Alex, 253, 255
Lieberman, Rosa, 253, 255
Lifszyc, David, 135
Lindeman, Yehudi (Rudy), 261–62
Linz, 49, 309
Lipton, Sara, 16
Lithuania, 22, 118, 154, 191, 261; Jewish
    partisans in, 23, 211–13, 267–68;
    Soviet takeover, 181
Living Testimonies, Montreal, 262
Liwer, Saloman, 300
Loborgrad (Lobor-Grad), 9–10
Lodz (Łód□), 134, 140, 206, 242; ghetto
    in, 2, 8–9, 148–49, 152–53, 230, 246,
    248
London, 176, 179, 264; governments-in-
    exile in, 138, 184
London, Jack, 84
Longerich, Peter, 60
Lublin, 134, 143, 145, 205, 258; ghettos
    in, 148–49, 151–52, 154; killing
    operations near, 229–30, 257
Ludendorff, Erich, 41, 50, 64
Lueger, Karl, 18, 49
Luftwaffe, 58, 183; use of in the west, 99,
    169–70
Luther, Martin, 17
Luxembourg, 149, 170
Lvov (Lwow, Lemberg, L'viv), 192–94,
    200, 241

Maass, Gerhard, 123–24
Madagascar plan, 146
Majdanek, 22, 158, 205, 229, 238,
    258–59, 301

Malicious Practices Act, 96–97
Mann, Heinrich, 84
Mann, Thomas, 84, 121
Marx, Karl, 19
Marxism, 46
Marzahn, 96, 101, 114–15
Maschmann, Melitta, 82
Masons. *See* Freemasons
Mauthausen, 117, 198, 205, 221–22
May, Karl, 51
Mein Kampf, 47–49, 51, 55, 73, 89, 110;
    and Hitler's antisemitism, 55, 73; and
    Hitler's view of Lebensraum in East,
    188, 194
Mendels, Flora, 243–44
Mengele, Josef, 252, 306
Mennecke, Friedrich, 164
Merin, Moishe, 152
Meseritz-Obrawalde, 164
Meyer, Konrad, 213
Michalowsky, Zvi, 198
Middle East, 180, 306. *See also* Egypt;
    Grand Mufti of Jerusalem; Israel;
    Palestine
Milgram experiment, 298
Milton, Sybil, 2
Minsk, 155
Mischlinge, 92, 209, 242
mixed marriages, Jewish-Christian,
    76–77, 79, 226. *See also* Klemperer;
    Rosenstrasse incident
Mokotow prison, 138, 140
Moltke, Helmuth James von, 280
Molotov-Ribbentrop Pact. *See* Hitler-
    Stalin Pact
Monowitz, 252, 254. *See also* Auschwitz
Montgomery, Bernard L., 231
monuments/ memorials, 29, 158, 199,
    253, 298
Morocco, 176, 231
Moscow, 210, 239, 282
Mosse, George, 79
Münster, 163
Munich, 49, 71, 83, 90, 271–72

Munich Conference, 106–7
Muslims, 16, 18, 185, 266
Mussolini, Benito, 47, 65, 99, 103, 185,
    231; collapse of Fascist regime and,
    233–34

Nama, 38–39, 58
Namibia. *See* Southwest Africa
Naples, 233
Napoleon, 17, 64, 175, 186
National Socialist German Workers'
    Party (NSDAP, Nazi Party), 50; in the
    1920s, 65–66; in the 1930s, 70–79,
    82–85, 88–97
Naval Agreement, German-British, 117
Nazi ideology, 52–58, 159, 169, 226;
    "asocials" in, 32–33; centered on
    antisemitism, 3; homosexuals in,
    222–23; Jewishness considered "race",
    53–54; Roma and Sinti in, 27, 32,
    257; Slavs in, 39–40, 194. *See also*
    Hitler; race and space; war
Nazi revolution, 69–90
Nazi terminology, 5–7, 52–53, 213
Nazism, 3, 52–60, 65–67
Némirovsky, Irène, 173–74
Nero Order, 281–82
Netherlands, 38, 79, 114, 126, 155,
    157, 178, 310; German conquest of,
    169–71; Jews in, 170–71, 243–44,
    261–62
Neuengamme, 29, 297
Neurath, Constantin von, 99
New York, 230, 310
New Zealand, 177
Nietzsche, Friedrich, 49
Night of Long Knives. *See* Röhm Putsch
Nisko, 143
NKGB. *See* KGB
NKVD (People's Commissariat for
    Internal Affairs), 181, 188. *See also*
    Soviet Union
Nomberg-Przytyk, Sara, 220
non-aggression pacts, 87, 117–18

"non-Aryans," 157, 159, 218. *See also*
    Afro-Germans; Jews; Nuremberg
    Laws; Roma
Normandy, 278. *See also* D-Day
North Africa, 137, 176, 210, 230–32,
    265–66
Norway, 157, 159–70, 178
Novgorod, 216
Nuremberg, 95
Nuremberg Laws, 91–95, 115
Nuremberg Trials, 221–22, 307–9

Ober Ramstadt, 109, 112
Odessa, 202
Olympic Games, 1936 in Berlin, 96, 98,
    115
Omdurman, Battle of, 38
Operation Barbarossa, 186
Operation Overlord, 278–79
Operation Reinhard, 242, 247–51. *See
    also* killing centers
Operation Sea Lion, 179
Operation Torch, 231, 266
Order Police, German, 195, 200, 229–30,
    265. *See also* Einsatzgruppen
orchestras, in camps, 218
Oswiecim, 252. *See also* Auschwitz

Pact of Steel, 117
Pale of Settlement, 19
Palestine, 80, 114, 158, 171, 210, 232,
    305
Pan-Germanism, 49
Papen, Franz von, 67
Paragraph 175 (German criminal code),
    73, 95, 222. *See also* homosexuals
Paris, 108–9, 173–74, 181, 244, 279
partisans, 23, 215–17, 249; Jewish, 23,
    265–68; Yugoslavian, 184–85, 293
Pasher, Yaron, 279
Patterson, Orlando, 92
Pauli, Harry, 223
Paulus, Friedrich, 224–25
Pavelic, Ante, 184

Pawiak prison, 138, 140
penal units, 223
Penner Ilona, 125
Penner, Kurt, 125
Pétain, Henri Philippe, 176
"phony war," 168
photography 7–11, 24, 301–2; from killing sites, 197–198, 220–22, 253–55, 284–85; perpetrator photographs, 137–38, 185–87, 215–16, 287; propaganda and intimidation, 76–77, 84–85; and rescue, 172–73; and resistance, 137–38, 221–22, 254, 268; uses and interpretation of, 7–11, 112, 126, 147–48, 174–75, 205, 246, 269–71, 289
pink triangle, 219, 222–23. *See also* homosexuals
Piotrkow Trybunalski, 256–57
Pius XI, 5, 86. *See also* Catholic Church
Pius XII, 143. *See also* Catholic Church
plot of 20 July 1944, 280–81
Plymouth, 179
Podchlebnik, Mordechai, 248
pogroms, 16, 22, 24, 104, 107–14, 193, 202, 195
Poland, 107–8, 114, 118, 171, 191; disabled murdered in, 160–61, 163; effects of war, 62, 131–40; established as state after World War I, 40, 63; German invasion and occupation of, 130–45; German crimes against, 136–40, 249, 282; German plans for, 52, 129, 140–42; German-Soviet arrangement regarding, 117–18, 131; government-in-exile, 133, 138, 140, 145, 178, 282; Jews in, 22, 141–42, 228–30, 241–42; particularities of situation in, 154–59; pre-war relations with Germany, 40, 87; rescue of Jews, 158; underground army in, 138, 144–45, 264, 282
Pomerantz, Jack (Yankel), 22, 131, 134
Ponar forest, 211–12

Portugal, 38, 180
Prague, 176, 259, 293
priests, Roman Catholic, 87, 193, 200–1, 227, 258; attacked and imprisoned, 114–15, 136–38, 143, 217. *See also* Catholic Church
Pripet marshes, 195
prisoners of war, 199, 204, 232, 233, 259, 301; black POWs shot by Germans, 174–75; Soviet POWs, 204–6, 218, 241, 252, 259
Probst, Christoph, 271–72
Professor Mamlock, 119
propaganda, Nazi German, 54–55, 58–59, 81, 228–29; and German war effort, 118, 130–31, 205, 277, 281
protest and non-protest: against killing disabled, 163–64; against killing Jews, 226, 250; against killing Polish civilians, 143–44; against killing Roma, 258. *See also* Germans; international response; resistance
Protestant church in Germany, 75, 78; conflict and cooperation with Nazi regime, 106–7, 163. *See also* Christianity
Protestant Reformation, 17

Quisling, Vidkun, 169–70

race and space, ideology of, 3, 52–53, 56–57; implemented in war, 194
Racial Hygiene and Criminal Biology Institute, 31
Racial Hygiene and Population Research Center, 257–58
racism: anti-black racism, 35–36, 75; and killing of French black soldiers, 174–75. *See also* Afro-Germans; antisemitism; Nazi ideology
Radom, 158–59
Radu, Drina, 203
Radzyn, 22, 131
Rappaport, Herbert, 119

Rassenschande, 92–93, 115
Raubal, Geli, 51–52
Ravensbrück, 101, 114, 217–20, 253,
    292, 297. *See also* concentration
    camps; women
Reck-Malleczewen, Fritz Percy, 51, 67
Red Army, 135–36, 181, 192, 231, 259;
    advancing in 1944-1945, 276–77;
    Battle of Stalingrad and, 223–25;
    Jews and, 266; prisoners of war from,
    204–6; at war's end, 287, 293–94,
    300–1; Warsaw uprising and, 282
refugees, 79, 107, 113–14, 119–26,
    171, 176–80, 211. *See also* displaced
    persons
Reich Citizenship Law. *See* Nuremberg
    Laws
Reich Committee for Scientific
    Registration of Serious Hereditarily-
    and Congenitally-Based Illnesses, 127
Reich Representation of the German
    Jews, 79–80
Reich Security Main Office (RSHA),
    142, 208–9, 213
Reichenau, Walter von, 201
Reichstag, 58, 66–67, 70–73, 98, 118
Reichstag fire, 71–73, 100
Reiprich, Doris, 75–76
Remarque, Erich Maria, 225
reparations, post-World War I, 41–42,
    62–63. *See also* Article 231, Treaty of
    Versailles
reprisals, German use of in World War II,
    185–86, 199, 215, 272
rescue: hiding Jews, 171–73, 193, 261–3;
    of Hungarian Jews, 286; of Jews in
    Poland, 158; of Roma, 258. *See also*
    protest, resistance
resettlement, of ethnic Germans,
    141–42
resistance, 263–72; in camps and killing
    centers, 221–22, 268–69; in Germany,
    270–72, 280–81; Jewish, 264–72;
    obstacles to, 272–73; in Poland,

141–42, 149; among Roma and Sinti,
    268. *See also* partisans; protest
Rhineland, 35–36, 97–98
Rhodes, 210, 234
Ribbentrop, Joachim von, 99, 294
Riefenstahl, Leni, 95
Riga, 152, 240, 259
Righteous among the Nations, 158, 173
Ringelblum, Emanuel, 146
Ritter, Robert, 31, 114
Rivesaltes, 176
Robota, Roza, 288
Röhm, Ernst, 88–89. *See also*
    Stormtroopers
Röhm, Putsch, 88–90
Roma, 5–6, 80, 142, 184–85, 203;
    in concentration camps, 218–20;
    Einsatzgruppen killings and, 195–96,
    200; in ghettos and internment
    camps, 2, 149; history of, 28–29; in
    killing centers, 206, 239, 248–49,
    257–58, 283, 288; post-war problems,
    303–4; prejudices against, 27–32,
    75, 258; pre-war measures against in
    Germany, 75, 94–95; resistance, 288
Roman Catholic Church. *See* Catholic
    Church
Romani language, 257. *See also* Roma
Romania, 43, 180–1, 224; Roma in,
    29; Jews from, 154, 171, 228; after
    Stalingrad, 228, 283
Rome, 86, 99
Rommel, Erwin, 210, 231–2
Roosevelt, Franklin D., 277, 279, 293
Rosenberg, Otto, 96, 101–2, 114–15, 288
Rosenstrasse incident, 226, 258. *See also*
    Germans; mixed marriages; protest;
    resistance
Ross, Henryk, 246
Rotterdam, 170–71
Royal Air Force, 179, 277
Rubinson, Misha, 23, 267
Rumbula massacre, 240
Rumkowski, Chaim, 152–54, 248

Rundstedt, Gerd von, 200
Russia, 19, 38, 40–42, 62–64. *See also*
    Soviet Union
Russian Revolution, 40–41

Sachsenhausen, 101, 114, 222
Salonika, 234
Samarkand, 191
Sartre, Jean-Paul, 154
Schacht, Hjalmar, 98
Schieder, Theodor, 213
Schleicher, Kurt, 89
Schmidt, Georg, 109, 112
Scholl, Hans, 271–72
Scholl, Sophie, 271–72
Schmorell, Alexander, 271–72
Scholtz-Klink, Gertrud, 60
Schrijver, Salomon, 243–44
Schuschnigg, Kurt von, 103
Scientific Registration of Serious
    Hereditarily- and Congenitally-Based
    Illnesses, Reich Committee for, 127
Second World War II. *See* World War II
secrecy, of mass killing operations, 127,
    161–63, 255–57
Security Services (SD), 60, 90, 97, 225
Seelig, Erich, 29
Sephardic Jews, 19, 233–34, 266
Serbia, 183–85. *See also* Yugoslavia
Sevastopol, 212, 227
sexual violence, 55, 137, 141, 144, 215,
    218, 223, 284, 286, 304
Shanghai, 121–23
Sheptytsky, Andrey, 193
Siberia, 119, 134–35, 172, 181, 188, 191,
    286, 300, 303
Sicily, 233
Siegal, Aranka (Piri Dawidowitz), 24,
    283–85
Silesia, 142
Sinti, 5–6, 27–32, 80, 94–96, 101,
    114–15, 257–58, 303. *See also* Roma
Slave labor, 146, 217, 241, 252–53, 278,
    286

Slovakia, 107, 180, 234, 243
Slovenia, 185, 233
Sobibor, 228, 244, 250–51, 256, 268, 310
Social Darwinism, 18, 26, 49, 57, 293. *See*
    also Nazi ideology
Social Democrats, German, 65, 71–74,
    114
Solahütte, 287
soldiers. *See* Allies; Red Army;
    Wehrmacht
Sonderkommandos, Jewish, 247, 251,
    268, 288. *See also* killing centers
Sonnenstein, 164
South Africa, 177, 305
South America, 305–6
Southwest Africa (later Namibia), 38–39,
    58
Soviet Union, 62–63, 99, 117–18, 231;
    Baltic States and, 118, 181; German
    invasion of, 23, 186; German plans
    for, 52, 118; Jews and, 134–35,
    155–56; nature of war in, 186–91,
    216; Poland and, 131–36;
Spain, 16–17, 19, 180; civil war in,
    98–99, 107, 176
Special Operations Executive, 263
Speer, Albert, 277–78, 285
Spitz, Gyula, 197–98
SS (Schutzstaffel), 60, 73–74, 84–85,
    88–89, 208–9, 213–14; concentration
    camps and, 83–84, 218–19, 259;
    ghettos and, 269–70; at killing centers,
    206, 247–54; mass killings and, 140,
    194–200, 216–17, 240–42; in Poland,
    136–43, 144, 160–61, 245–46; at
    war's end, 281, 288, 290–92. *See also*
    Himmler
St Louis (ship), 124–25
stab-in-the-back myth, 42, 56, 64–65,
    73, 109, 204. *See also* World War I
Stabholz, Thaddeus, 238–39
Stalin, Josef, 135, 180–81, 188, 224, 231;
    abuses of regime, 119, 191; pact with
    Hitler, 117–18. *See also* Soviet Union

Stalingrad, 138, 227–30, 266; Battle of Stalingrad, 223–25, 228

Stangl, Franz, 251, 256, 306

Stangl, Teresa, 256

Star of David: to mark Jews, 9, 55, 183, 243–44, 262, 309

starvation: as method of destruction, 39, 146, 149, 204, 215, 241–42, 259, 292, 301

Starzynski, Stefan, 133

Stauffenberg, Claus Schenck von, 5, 280–81. *See also* plot of 20 July 1944

Stein, Edith, 5

sterilization, 75–76, 80–82, 95, 214, 257. *See also* Law for the Prevention of Hereditarily Diseased Offspring

Steyer, Johannes, 74

Stoltzfus, Nathan, 226

Stopes, Marie, 26–27

Stormtroopers (Sturmabteilung, SA), 65–66, 73–74, 84–85; attacks on homosexuals, Jews and Poles, 76, 110, 139–40; Röhm Putsch and, 88–90

Strasser, Gregor, 89

Strength through Joy, 82–83, 147

Stroop, Jürgen, 269

Der Stürmer, 55, 76

Stutthof, 217, 262, 289. *See also* concentration camps

Subcarpathian Rus', 19, 196, 254, 283–85

Sudetenland, 106–7, 113. *See also* Czechoslovakia

Sugihara, Chiune (Sempo), 123

suicide, 51, 59, 150, 153, 221, 235, 248, 257, 294, 308

Sutzkever, Abraham, 253

Swaziland, 94

Sweden, 170, 180; Jews and, 210

Switzerland, 79, 121, 180, 233, 265

Szerynski, Josef, 152

Szwajger, Adina Blady, 133

T-4 Program, 126–27, 159–65, 250, 256. *See also* "Euthanasia," disabled

Tashkent, 191, 300

Tec, Nechama, 145

Theresienstadt (Terezin), 80, 259–60

Thimme, Annelise, 100

Thimme, Friedrich, 100

Third Reich, 62, 69, 73, 84, 90, 144, 273, 293. *See also* Germany; Hitler

Three-Power Pact, 180

Tirailleurs Sénégalais, 175

Tiso, Josef, 107

Tito, Josip Broz, 184, 293

Tokyo, 99

Toll, Nelly, 192–94

Transnistria, 154, 202–3

Transylvania, 283, 286

Trawniki, 123, 218

Treblinka, 122, 228, 251, 256, 268–69

Triumph of the Will, 95

Trollman, Johann (Rukelie), 29

Trujillo, Rafael, 124

tuberculosis, 149, 248

Tucholsky, Kurt, 84

Tunis, 231

Tunisia, 231

Turin, 234

Turkey, 42, 180, 210, 306

twins, experiments on, 252

typhus, 149, 150, 174, 205, 239, 240, 242, 260, 283, 301

Ukraine, 191–92; camp guards from, 218, 247; mass killings in, 154, 195–202, 227; slave laborers from, 305. *See also* Soviet Union

unconditional surrender, 293

underground: Czech, 272; Dutch, 310; Jewish, 133, 265; Polish, 133, 138, 140, 144–45, 221–22, 264. *See also* resistance

United Nations, 305

United Nations Relief and Rehabilitation Administration, 305

United States, 26, 85, 97, 170; destination of refugees, exiles and survivors, 114, 121–22, 124–25, 305; and Jehovah's Witnesses, 34–35; and Jews, 78, 264–65; as occupying power, 308; and World War II, 210
United States, Air Force, 277
United States Holocaust Memorial Museum, 2, 8–9, 125, 246, 267, 287
The Unvanquished (movie), 199
Ural Mountains, 188, 191, 213
Ustasha, 10, 184. *See also* Croatia; Yugoslavia
Uzbekistan, 224, 295, 300

V-weapons, 217, 279
van der Lubbe, Marinus, 71
Vatican, 86–87, 143, 250, 306. *See also* Catholic Church
Vélodrome d'Hiver (Vél d'Hiv), 244
Versailles, Treaty of, 41–42, 86–87, 97–98, 103, 107, 117. *See also* World War I
Vichy, 175; Vichy France, 175–77, 231, 234. *See also* France
Vienna, 49, 50, 99, 111, 293; Jews in, 104, 112, 142
Vilenchiuk, Ida, 268
Vilna (Vilnius), 154, 211–12, 265, 268, 272, 289
Vistula River, 282
vocabulary, problems of, 5–7, 52, 129–30, 245
Volga River, 224
Volksdeutschen. *See* ethnic Germans
Volkssturm, 281–82
Volkswagen, 82–83
Voltaire, 17
Voticky, Anka, 122–23
Voticky, Arnold, 122–23

Wagner, Richard, 49, 293
Wajsman, Romek, 299
Wallenberg, Raoul, 286

Wannsee Conference, 208–10, 259; construction of killing centers and, 209, 247–48, 252
war: cover for killing of disabled, 161–62; German preparations for, 97–99; in Hitler's worldview, 56, 188, 213; outbreak in September 1939, 130. *See also* Hitler; Nazi ideology; race and space; World War II
war criminals, 305–9
Warsaw, 133, 134, 137–38, 251; Warsaw ghetto, 146, 149–51, 153, 238, 257; Warsaw ghetto uprising (1943), 269–71; Warsaw uprising (1944), 282
Wehrmacht (German military), 97–99, 137, 181; bribery of officers, 227; establishment and Nazification of, 87, 91, 99, 103–4; invading, 130–33, 169–70, 183–84; mass killings and, 138, 184–85, 200–2, 204–6; target groups and, 183–86, 223. *See also* Germany; Luftwaffe, World War II
Weilbach, S. (pseudonym), 78, 93, 112
Weimar, 62, 114
Weimar Republic, 33–34, 61–67
Weinberg, Gerhard, 179–80, 194, 210
Werewolf organization, 281
Wessel, Horst, 84
Westerbork, 170, 244, 310
White Rose, 271–72. *See also* resistance
Wiesel, Elie, 286
Wilhelm II, 33
Winter War, 181–82
Wirth, Christian, 250
Wisgardisky, Henia (Heina Lewin), 261–62
Wolf, Friedrich, 119
women: Jewish women, 212, 260–61; Nazi ideas about, 56, 74; Nazi racial laws and, 91; non-Jewish women as victims, 156, 226; as partisans, 266–68; as partners and beneficiaries of Nazism, 60, 136, 218; sexual abuse of, 141, 218. *See also* Germans; Jews; lesbians; resistance; Roma

World War I, 41–43, 185; effects of
German defeat in, 35–36; Hitler's
experience in, 50; impact on Europe,
26, 40, 41–43, 62; Jewish veterans of,
77; as precondition for Nazism, 43.
See also stab-in-the-back myth; Treaty
of Versailles
World War II: final phase, 276–82,
293–95; as global event, 1, 231-32,
295; impact in Germany, 182–83;
in Italy, 233–34; in North Africa,
230–32; in northern and western
Europe, 168–70, 278–80; outbreak
of in Poland, 130–33; relationship
to Holocaust, 1, 3; in Soviet Union,
186–88; in Yugoslavia and Greece,
183–86

Yad Vashem, 158
Yiddish language, 19, 22, 119, 146, 212,
253, 266
Yoors, Jan, 30
Yugoslavia, 183–87, 233; end of war
for, 293; partisans and resistance in,
184–85

Zacharias, Karin (Pardo), 121–22
Zbaszyn, refugee camp in, 108
Zegota, 158
Zelkowicz, Josef, 146–47
Zelma, Georgy, 224
Zionism, Zionists, 80, 115, 146, 152,
211, 305
Zonabend, Nachman, 153
Zyklon B, 206, 238, 241, 250, 252

ABOUT THE AUTHOR

Doris L. Bergen is Chancellor Rose and Ray Wolfe Professor of Holocaust Studies at the University of Toronto, where she teaches in the Department of History. Bergen received her PhD from the University of North Carolina, Chapel Hill, in 1991 and taught from 1991 to 1996 at the University of Vermont and from 1996 to 2007 at the University of Notre Dame. She has also been a visiting instructor at the University of Tuzla in Bosnia, the University of Pristina in Kosovo, and Warsaw University in Poland.

Bergen's research focuses on issues of religion, ethnicity, gender, and violence in Europe in the Nazi era. She is the author of *Twisted Cross: The German Christian Movement in the Third Reich* (1996) and numerous articles and essays on aspects of the Holocaust, comparative genocide, Christian antisemitism, military chaplains, and the Volksdeutschen (ethnic Germans) of eastern Europe during World War II. Bergen has edited three volumes of essays: *The Sword of the Lord: Military Chaplains from the First to the Twenty-First Century* (2003); *Lessons and Legacies VIII: From Generation to Generation* (2008); and *Alltag im Holocaust* (the everyday in the Holocaust), co-edited with Andrea Löw and Anna Hájková (2013). Her book, *War and Genocide,* has been translated into Polish. She is a member of the Academic Committee of the Mandel Center for Advanced Holocaust Studies at the United States Holocaust Memorial Museum in Washington, DC.

CRITICAL ISSUES IN WORLD AND INTERNATIONAL HISTORY

SERIES EDITOR: MORRIS ROSSABI

The Vikings: Wolves of War
by Martin Arnold
Magic and Superstition in Europe: A Concise History from Antiquity to the Present
by Michael D. Bailey
War and Genocide: A Concise History of the Holocaust, Third Edition
by Doris L. Bergen
Peter the Great, Second Edition
by Paul Bushkovitch
A Concise History of Hong Kong
by John M. Carroll
Ming China, 1368–1644: A Concise History of a Resilient Empire
by John W. Dardess
A History of Medieval Heresy and Inquisition
by Jennifer Kolpacoff Deane
Remaking Italy in the Twentieth Century
by Roy Palmer Domenico
A Concise History of Euthanasia: Life, Death, God, and Medicine
by Ian Dowbiggin
The Work of France: Labor and Culture in Early Modern Times, 1350–1800
by James R. Farr
The Idea of Capitalism before the Industrial Revolution
by Richard Grassby
Public Zen, Personal Zen: A Buddhist Introduction
by Peter D. Hershock
Chinese Migrations: The Movement of People, Goods, and Ideas over Four Millennia
by Diana Lary
The Concise History of the Crusades, Third Edition
by Thomas F. Madden

The Great Encounter of China and the West, 1500–1800, Fourth Edition
    by D. E. Mungello
A Concise History of the French Revolution
    by Sylvia Neely
The British Imperial Century, 1815–1914: A World History Perspective
    by Timothy H. Parsons
The Second British Empire: In the Crucible of the Twentieth Century
    by Timothy H. Parsons
The Norman Conquest: England after William the Conqueror
    by Hugh M. Thomas
Europe's Reformations, 1450–1650: Doctrine, Politics, and Community, Second Edition
    by James D. Tracy